SWIMMING POOLS

SECOND EDITION

SWIMMING POOLS

*A Treatise on the Planning, Layout, Design and
Construction, Water Treatment and Other Services,
Maintenance and Repairs*

SECOND EDITION

PHILIP H. PERKINS

C Eng, FASCE, FIMunE, FIArb, FIPHE, MIWES

APPLIED SCIENCE PUBLISHERS LTD
LONDON

APPLIED SCIENCE PUBLISHERS LTD
RIPPLE ROAD, BARKING, ESSEX, ENGLAND

First Edition 1971
Second Edition 1978

British Library Cataloguing in Publication Data

Perkins, Philip Harold
  Swimming pools.—2nd ed.
  1. Swimming pools—Design and construction
  I. Title
  725'.74   TH4763

  ISBN 0 85334-769-7

WITH 118 ILLUSTRATIONS

© APPLIED SCIENCE PUBLISHERS LTD 1978

Printed in Great Britain by Galliard (Printers) Ltd, Great Yarmouth

This book is dedicated to my wife and father-in-law, without whose encouragement and help it would not have been written

Preface

In the period since the first edition of this book was published in May 1971, a number of interesting developments have taken place in the swimming pool field, particularly in the United Kingdom.

In 1976 several years' work on the revision of the Code of Practice for the design and construction of water-retaining structures was completed and the Code was reissued as BS 5337: The Structural Use of Concrete for Retaining Aqueous Liquids. Many experienced engineers were disappointed at the result of the long-drawn-out deliberations of the Code Committee, and some preliminary comments on the new Code are given in Chapter 4.

The 'leisure centre' has arrived, complete with free-formed main pool, artificial waves and subtropical vegetation, the whole structure housing a wide range of leisure activities.

Those responsible for the design and operation of swimming pools have at last realised something known and practised on the Continent for many years—namely, that there are other more pleasant but equally effective materials for sterilising swimming pool water than the malodorous chlorine.

It will seem to some readers that a number of the recommendations in this book are overcautious, as it can be claimed that many swimming pools have been built successfully without so much attention to detail. This is correct as a general statement, but there are sufficient cases where things have gone wrong to prove that there is little margin between success and failure in designing and building swimming pools. When trouble does occur, the client (who has to pay in the long run) is unlikely to adopt a philosophical attitude and be satisfied with an answer referring him to imaginary statistics proving that the rate of failure is within reasonable limits and that he is just unlucky.

The 'package deal' type of contract has been accepted by local authorities as a means of getting public swimming pools built. The author's experience suggests that the results have been disappointing.

The author acknowledges with gratitude the help he has received from many people, organisations and firms, both in the United Kingdom and elsewhere. In particular, he wishes to thank J. F. Malpas and A. Elphick of Wallace and Tiernan; D. Richmond of Barr and Wray; and D. Braham of the Electricity Council, and F. Vaughan of the British Ceramic Tile Council.

PHILIP H. PERKINS

Contents

Introduction

Water is a natural environment for many living creatures and it is believed that life started in the sea. The multicellular millionaire floating in his swimming pool should remember with modesty that he is only doing what his unicellular ancestors did a thousand million years ago. Bathing and swimming for pleasure has been practised by many land animals for unrecorded ages, and human records of the pleasure of immersion in water go back several thousand years.

The earliest well-preserved examples of bathing rooms are to be found in the palaces of the Aegean civilisation. They are notable for their high standard of design and layout as well as their system of water supply and drainage. Some examples are the baths in the Palaces of Knossos and Phaistos about 1700 to 1400 B.C. There are also fine examples on the mainland in the Palaces of Teryns. From these and other archaeological remains it is clear that bathing and swimming played an important part in the life of these ancient peoples.

The Romans developed the planning and construction of baths to a high degree of magnificence. The two oldest Roman baths are at Pompeii, but baths of the same design have been found in many parts of the Roman Empire in such widely separated places as Trier in Germany and Homs in North Africa. In Caracalla there is an enormous open-air swimming pool, built about A.D. 217. The disintegration of the Roman Empire resulted in the destruction of the aqueducts and water supply which served the baths, and so they fell out of use.

From the Renaissance until the nineteenth century there was very little advance in bathing in Europe and the bathing and washing arrangements even for royalty were often very crude. However, in the Middle East bathing and bath architecture flourished under the Islamic rulers, as the baths at Granada in Spain and Constantinople in Turkey still testify.

In Russia steam baths became very popular, but the layout of the baths was generally rather crude and the customary cold plunge following the steam bath often involved a visit to the adjoining lake or river! The principle of the hot steam bath followed by immersion in cold water is followed in the Finnish sauna which has become so popular in Europe and elsewhere in recent years.

Bathing has always been popular in China and Japan, particularly the latter, where many large bathing establishments were built near medicinal springs. One of the best-known is near Matsuyama on the island of Shikoku.

In the United Kingdom the Industrial Revolution led to the building of public baths and wash-houses, as the washing and sanitary arrangements in the vast majority of buildings were virtually non-existent. In Sheffield in 1887 it is reputed that in 68 000 houses there were only 4000 water-closets and considerably fewer baths.

Closely connected with improvements in sanitation and the establishment of public baths and wash-houses was the realisation of the need to sterilise water for drinking, followed by a similar process for the water used in bathing establishments. Chlorine was the first chemical used for this purpose at the end of the nineteenth century.

Little progress in the construction of public swimming pools was made until after the end of World War I, but a considerable number were built in the late 1920s and 1930s. World War II and the economic restrictions imposed afterwards prevented much progress until the middle 1950s. Since then, however, there has been a steady if unspectacular building programme, but the United Kingdom lags far behind the Continent and Scandinavia. The past few years has seen a rapid increase in the number of private swimming pools in many countries of the world; this is due to the general improvement in the standard of living and the difficulty in reaching the seaside at week-ends because of traffic congestion on the road. In Germany it is estimated that there are now 700 000 pools.

The opening up of the private swimming pool market has resulted in large numbers of the general public becoming interested in the layout and construction of swimming pools, whereas in the past this was a subject for local authorities and a few firms of architects.

The present book is intended to bring together under one cover basic information on the planning, design, construction and finishing of swimming pools of all sizes, both open-air and covered. It will be noted that very little has been said in the text about costs; the reason for this is that costs, like fashions, soon become out of date. This applies particularly when the costs relate to a completed job and include labour, materials, overheads and profit. The best method of commissioning the building of a swimming pool will depend on many factors, and a prospective pool owner has a number of ways open to him; these are discussed in some detail in the text.

CHAPTER 1

Part 1: *The Planning and Layout of Swimming Pools*

GENERAL CONSIDERATIONS

In the United Kingdom, the construction of the shell of an open air swimming pool without ancillary buildings (such as plant house, changing rooms, etc.) is unlikely to require a building permit under the Building Regulations 1976, but planning permission may be required. It is therefore advisable for anyone wishing to build a swimming pool to consult their Local Authority (the Planning Officer and the Building Control Officer). Even if application under the Building Regulations is not specifically required for the pool itself, a permit may be needed for any drainage work.

If the water for the pool is to be taken from a public supply or from a river, the water authority concerned should be consulted first.

As to public pools, the Public Health Act 1936, Sect. 233, authorised local authorities to publish by-laws controlling certain matters relating to any swimming pool which is open to the public and for which a charge is made. The matters which can be subject to regulation include:

(a) Maintenance of a proper standard of water purity.
(b) General cleanliness and provision of adequate changing and sanitary accommodation.
(c) Measures for the prevention of accidents.
(d) The conduct of persons using the pool.

Local Authorities are not legally bound to comply with their own by-laws, although they have a clear moral obligation to do so. While the majority of swimming pools under public control in the United Kingdom are maintained at a reasonable standard, some leave a lot to be desired. It is the responsibility of a Local Authority which operates a swimming pool to provide the necessary funds to maintain the whole enterprise at a high standard of cleanliness, hygiene and repair and to ensure that the public's money is properly spent.

1

The experience of the author is that the standards in this country are not as high as those in Germany and Switzerland, where there is a greater appreciation by the public of the need for hygienic habits, and there is certainly far less vandalism. Just two small examples: It is a standard requirement that all bathers should wear bathing-caps, and this is accepted without question. Precleansing showers and foot-baths, including soap, are used conscientiously.

In practice, legal control over water purity and general hygiene in hotel pools, club pools, and private pools in the United Kingdom is minimal. By-laws only apply to such pools if a charge is made for admission, and so control can only be exercised through the 'nuisance clauses' of the Public Health Acts. In other words, a rather unsatisfactory state of affairs. School pools which are maintained wholly or partly by an Education Authority are subject to control at design and construction stages, and to general supervision during operation. However, published reports suggest that in many cases this supervision is more theoretical than real, particularly in respect of the purity of the pool water. The short paper by R. G. Clarke in *Baths Service* (June 1970) highlights this problem.

The author has been unable to find National recommendations for the physical, chemical and bacteriological standards for swimming pool water applicable to all types of pools. The nearest approach to this is the latest edition of the Department of Environment's publication *The Purification of the Water of Swimming Pools*. Section 12 of this booklet contains useful and practical recommendations for the three basic standards referred to above. It would be very useful if the general recommendations for chemical, physical and bacteriological standards were reissued in a form clearly intended to apply to all swimming pools, with perhaps the possible exception of private house pools. For example, the maintenance of a high standard of clarity in the pool water is of great importance from a safety point of view, and this is discussed in Chapter 7.

Regulations in California apply to all pools except private pools maintained by an individual for the use of his family and friends. It is specifically stated that pools belonging to hotels, clubs, schools and health establishments—as well as other categories of pool—do come within the scope of the regulations. All important aspects of design, layout, facilities, construction, equipment, operation and maintenance are detailed, and clear directions given. The bacteriological and chemical quality of the pool water is included. The bacteriological requirement is that not more than 15% of the samples covering any considerable period of time shall: (a) contain more than 200 bacteria per millilitre, as determined by the standard (35°C) plate count; or (b) show positive test for coliform organisms in any of the five 10-millilitre portions of a sample, at times when the pool is in use.

The chemical quality of water in the pool shall not cause irritation to eyes or skin of the bathers, or have other objectionable physiological effects on bathers.

The National Swimming Pool Institute in the United States was formed in 1956. In 1969 the Institute issued a comprehensive publication on suggested minimum standards for residential and public swimming pools. This is an interesting and useful booklet, but it was disappointing to see that there was no guidance given on acceptable standards of purity of the water in the pool. The only reference to the sterilisation of pool water related to minimum residual chlorine contents in residential pools (0·4 ppm) and in public pools (0·6–1·0 ppm). A further valid criticism is that the recommended dimensions for diving areas in residential pools is far below that for public pools. For the latter the Institute recommends the FINA requirements which are considered later in this chapter.

THE BASIC REQUIREMENTS FOR A SWIMMING POOL

The basic requirements for any swimming pool may be summarised as follows:

(1) The pool must be structurally sound.
(2) The pool must be watertight against loss of water when it is full, and, if constructed below ground level, against infiltration of water from the subsoil when it is empty.
(3) It must be finished with an attractive, smooth and impermeable surface.
(4) The water must be maintained at a proper standard of clarity and purity, either by a continuous flow-through system or by means of a correctly designed and operated water treatment plant.
(5) A diving board should only be provided when the minimum depth of water and the dimensions of the diving area comply with the recommendations of the Amateur Swimming Association, as shown in Fig. 1.16.
(6) A walkway, of adequate width and with a non-slip surface, should be provided around the pool.

RECOMMENDED PROCEDURE FOR GETTING A POOL BUILT

The recommendations which follow are intended for private persons and club committees, although the author's experience in dealing with defects in swimming pools suggests that even large hotel groups and local authorities could with advantage take note of some of the points mentioned.

Owing to what is now called the 'unfavourable financial climate', there is an increased tendency for prospective owners to think in terms of building the pool themselves. If this can be done successfully, there is certainly a considerable saving in capital cost, but the 'if' is a large one. Unfortunately, the author cannot recommend this except for small prefabricated pools and those sold in complete kits, or for the very experienced do-it-yourself man who can call on additional labour and specialist contractors when required.

Apart from the do-it-yourself job which is commented on in the previous paragraph, there are two different procedures which can be recommended:

(1) To engage an architect or civil engineer with experience in swimming pool design who will take full responsibility for the preparation of the drawings, specification and other contract documents, recommend to the client on the adjudication of the contract and supervise the work. This procedure is particularly suitable for large covered pools.

(2) To apply to the Swimming Pool and Allied Trades Association (SPATA) for the names of, say, three contractors. General information on the type of pool (open or covered) and the extent to which finance is important in relation to the standard of pool should be given by the client. The reference to finance is realistic because some people can spend a great deal more money than others; some prefer a top-class job while to others functional requirements are more important than finish and sophistication.

When detailed proposals (estimates, sketches and the usual glossy brochures) have been obtained, it is worth while to have these examined by an experienced professional man (architect or engineer). It is particularly desirable that any guarantee offered should be scrutinised; the guarantee, like the pool, should be reasonably watertight. In view of the high cost of swimming pool construction and operation, the fee to the professional adviser is money well spent. Several thousand pools are constructed in the United Kingdom each year, and there seems little doubt that the majority are satisfactory and give good service. However, for the owner who has spent six or seven thousand pounds on an open air pool which he finds unsatisfactory, this philosophical approach has no appeal. In this situation (usually when the pool is completed), he will start to look into the contract to see what the contractor really undertook to do. By dealing through an organisation such as SPATA (mentioned above), definite faults and shortcomings are much more likely to be put right. Also, recent legislation will help to ensure that goods and services are suitable for the purpose for which they were supplied. Firms that claim to be specialists are now required by law to accept responsibility for doing their special work in a proper way, and find it more difficult to 'opt out'.

Irrespective of which procedure is adopted to have the pool built, when trouble arises, the owner may well be faced with a limited choice. Either he can accept what has been done and pay the contractor or he can retain any balance theoretically due and wait for the contractor to take action. As a third choice he may decide to take action against the contractor. The last two options may result in court action, with all that this entails. If the contract contains a suitably worded clause requiring all disputes to be referred to arbitration, then court action can be avoided.

If both parties to the dispute are sensible and do not insist on being represented by solicitors and counsel, arbitration can be impartial, quick and inexpensive. Full details on arbitration, including the names of suitable arbitrators, can be obtained from the Institute of Arbitrators at 75 Cannon St, London EC4N 5BH.

The costs of a court action, even in the County Court (which deals with cases in which up to £1000 is involved), can be unexpectedly high. Actions in the High Court and the Court of Appeal can result in costs which are astronomical. It is normal practice under English law for the successful party to a court action or arbitration to be awarded costs, so that the losing party has to pay his own costs and those of his opponent.

POOLS FOR PRIVATE HOUSES, CLUBS AND HOTELS

GENERAL CONSIDERATIONS—OPEN AIR POOLS
With pools in this category there is generally a limited choice of site since they usually have to be built on the same plot as the main building. However, clubs and hotels are likely to be better off in this respect than private houses, because the plot area is greater: the larger the garden the more scope there is for selecting the most favourable position for the pool. Even with a comparatively small garden there are certain factors which should be taken into account, and these apply to all open air pools in countries with a temperate climate. These factors are:

(1) Select a position which will receive as much sun as possible, preferably in the afternoon.
(2) Avoid the vicinity of large trees, since not only do these cast shadows on the pool—which is usually not welcome—but also leaves fall into the pool and discolour the water and stain the sides. Extra work is thus required to keep the pool clean, particularly in autumn. Another reason for keeping the pool away from large trees is that the roots can damage the drainage and other piping around the pool. If the pool itself is small and light in weight, the roots may disturb the foundations or cause the walls or floor to crack, which

results in leakage. On the other hand, trees on the north side of a pool will not cast undesirable shadows, and if they are neither too close nor too large, they can form a useful wind-break.

(3) If there is an existing wind-break, in the form of an attractive stone, brick or block wall, or thick hedge, it would be advantageous to utilise this if at all possible.

(4) Provision has to be made for emptying the pool and for disposing of the wash-water from filters (when water treatment equipment is provided). The question of levels for drainage of this water is therefore important because pumping is expensive.

(5) The location of existing services—water, electricity, possibly gas, and perhaps access for lorries delivering fuel oil—must be given consideration. If the pool is to have no water treatment plant and no heating, then of course only the water supply is significant. However, it is surprising how soon pool owners realise the importance of water purification and desirability of heating; the latter can increase the period during which the pool can be used with comfort by about 50%.

(6) Following on from the provision of services to the pool is the location of a small building to house the plant and equipment (circulating pump, water treatment and heating installations, and ancillary equipment required for cleaning and maintenance of the pool). The arrangement of the plant house is dealt with in Chapter 7. The erection of such a structure would require a building permit.

(7) There should be reasonable access for plant and materials to build the pool.

With a plot of reasonable size (and swimming pools are seldom found in very small gardens), and keeping in mind the six points mentioned above, there are three basic positions in which the pool can be built:

(a) Adjoining or close to the main building.
(b) More or less in the centre of the garden.
(c) Adjacent to one side, or in a corner of the garden.

Whichever position is decided on, and detailed observations on each are given below, careful thought must be given to general landscaping of the whole garden, with the pool as one of its most attractive features. Figures 1.1 and 1.2 show possible locations.

LOCATION OF POOLS
Pools Adjacent or Close to the Main Building (Fig. 1.1)
An open air pool close to the house, club or hotel can be very attractive. Generally, houses built in a temperate climate in the northern hemisphere

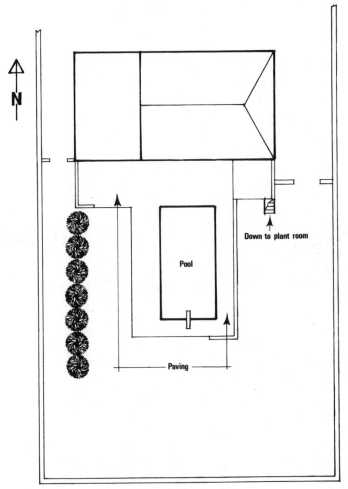

FIG. 1.1.   Pool adjoining house.

are orientated so that the main rooms face south or approximately so; in this case the pool would be on the south side of the building, which would form a natural wind-break to the north.

Advantages of this location are: short distance to walk to and from the pool; service connections (water, electricity, gas and drainage) are likely to be short; saving in cost of paved area around the pool because most of this would be paved anyway as the terrace or patio to the house; such a position does not disturb the layout of the garden, and this may be important if the existing garden is well laid out and a considerable sum of money has been spent on it; greater privacy is achieved at less cost than with other positions; in the case of private house pools, children are under closer supervision from adults who may wish to continue with their other work; and, finally, the pool can be covered in at a later date with considerably less cost than if it is located on its own away from the house. This last factor would only apply if the covering-in were of permanent material and required to fit in with the external elevation of the main building and not detract from a well-landscaped garden.

Disadvantages include: proximity to the main building may result in noise from children using the pool disturbing adults who wish to work or rest in the afternoon; should any leaks develop in the pool shell, or in the water circulation pipework, the resulting percolation of water could damage the foundations of the main building; and, finally, the colour scheme for the pool—often a bright blue or green—may clash with the colour of the outside of the walls of the adjacent building.

Pools In or Near the Centre of the Garden
In this case the pool will form the dominant feature of the garden. Careful landscaping, with special regard to levels, and shape of the pool, are essential for a pleasing result. People often find it difficult to visualise from a two-dimensional drawing what the finished three-dimensional job will really look like. In this case the cost of a simple model and an isometric drawing will be fully justified. The study of photographs of well-laid-out gardens with centrally located pools, supplemented by visits to a few completed jobs, will be well worth while.

The advantages of a central position for the pool include such points as: the pool will form the central feature of a well-laid-out garden; it is independent of the orientation, elevation and colour scheme of the main building; noise and splashing will not disturb non-bathers; and should leaks develop, they will not damage the foundations of the main building.

The disadvantages are: the pool will dominate the garden aesthetically and, unless the garden is a large one, it will severely limit the use to which the remainder can be put; to achieve the best result, greater skill and care is required in the landscaping; the cost is likely to be higher than for a pool adjacent to the main building owing to increase in length of service connections. The paved surround and walkways to and from the house will be exclusively for the pool, and will be in addition to the normal paving around the building; the natural wind-break provided by the house is not available; the pool is more easily overlooked from adjacent buildings and high ground, thus reducing privacy; and, finally, children using the pool are under less control and supervision by adults than with a pool adjacent to the main building.

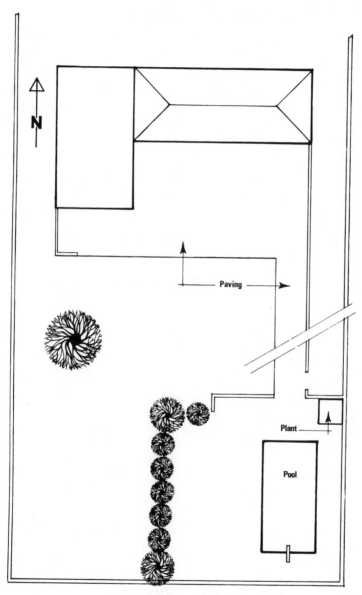

N

Paving

Plant

Pool

FIG. 1.2. Pool at end of garden.

Pools on the Boundary of the Plot (*Fig.* 1.2)
With a pool on the boundary of the plot, the minimum of disturbance is
caused to the layout of the garden, but consideration must be given to the
existing or possible future use of the adjoining land.

The advantages of this position are: as the pool is well away from the
main building, there will be the minimum disturbance to the occupants by
noise; as with the central position, it is independent of the layout,
orientation, elevation and colour scheme of the main building; and if the
water supply is from a stream or river, then the boundary position adjacent
to the water has a number of obvious advantages.

The disadvantages of this position are: the increase in cost due to
considerable lengths of paved walk ways, and the paved area around the
pool; the cost of providing the necessary services (electricity, etc.) is likely to
be higher; the difficulty in supervising children will be greater even than in
the central position; in certain cases the securing of adequate privacy may
be more difficult and expensive to attain. There may also be problems in
providing access for the building materials needed for the construction of
the pool, and this can add appreciably to the cost.

SHAPE AND DIMENSIONS

GENERAL
The shape and dimensions of a swimming pool are mutually
interdependent. The primary use of the pool will largely determine both
shape and dimensions. If the pool is required mostly for swimming,
particularly if there is emphasis on training for competitions, then a
rectangular shape is preferred; also, the length should be some simple
fraction of 100 m, such as 10 m, 12·5 m, 16·67 m, 20 m, which give 10, 8, 6
and 5 lengths for the 100 m. It should also be noted that a simple
rectangular shape in an elegantly laid-out garden can be just as pleasing to
the eye as a more exotic free-formed pool. This is shown in Fig. 1.3. Free-
formed pools are, generally, rather more expensive than rectangular ones;
this applies particularly when the shell is constructed in *in situ* reinforced
concrete owing to the high cost of the formwork. On the other hand, a
reinforced gunite pool can be any shape and size. Chapter 4 deals with the
construction of swimming pools in these two materials. (See Figs. 1.4 and
1.5.) If preformed materials are used, such as aluminium, galvanised steel
and glass-reinforced cement, then it is usually necessary to accept a
rectangular shape; pools of these materials are discussed in Chapter 5.

Whichever shape is chosen, it is advisable for the top of the walls of the
pool and, therefore, the walkway around the pool to be raised slightly above
the level of the surrounding ground, as this helps to keep out dirt and
crawling insects.

FIG. 1.3. View of open-air pool (Courtesy: Sunpools Ltd, Eynsham).

FIG. 1.4. View of open-air free-formed pool (Courtesy: Rutherford Ltd, Battle).

FIG. 1.5. View of open-air free-formed pool (Courtesy: Rutherford Ltd, Battle).

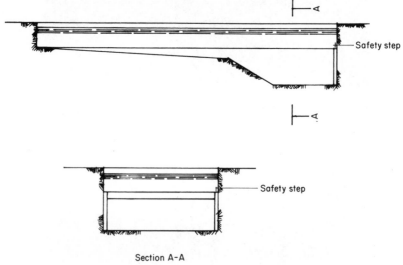

Section A-A

FIG. 1.6. Section through pool showing safety step.

As these pools will be used by non-swimmers of all ages, the author strongly recommends the provision of a safety step around the full perimeter of the pool at a level not exceeding 900 mm (3 ft) below top water level. This is shown in Fig. 1.6. It is interesting to note that safety steps are a standard feature of public and hotel pools in Switzerland.

REQUIREMENTS FOR SWIMMING

It is felt that some general information on the dimensions (length, width and depth) of swimming pools will be useful, because experience suggests that there are many misconceptions on this matter, quite apart from the inevitable differences of opinion. Even the smallest swimming pool must be large enough for a swimmer to take several strokes, and the minimum effective size is likely to be about 5·0 m long by 2·5 m wide with a minimum depth of water of 1·0 m (16 ft 6 in × 8 ft 3 in × 3 ft 3 in). However, a depth of 1·0 m would not be sufficient for even a very flat dive. An experienced swimmer can make a flat dive from 0·30 m (12 in) above water level into 1·20 m (4 ft) of water.

For comfort an allowance should be made of about 3·5 m² (38 ft²) for each person who wishes to swim: in other words, the swimming area of the pool should be based on 3·5 m² per swimmer. Of course, this is to some extent academic, because it is very difficult to control the number of people entering a pool, particularly at hotels and clubs; there are likely to be

TABLE 1.1
Swimming pools for private houses—Dimensions

Item No.	Length, m (ft)	Width, m (ft)	Water depth min., m (ft)	Water depth max., m (ft)	Water area, m² (ft²)	Volume of water m³ (gal)
1	6·00 (19 ft 8 in)	3·00 (9 ft 10 in)	0·90 (3)	1·10 (3 ft 7 in)	18 (194)	18 (3 960)
2	10·00 (33)	5·00 (16 ft 6 in)	0·90 (3)	1·50 (4 ft 10 in)	50 (545)	60 (13 200)
3	12·5 (41)	5·00 (16 ft 6 in)	0·90 (3)	1·50 (4 ft 10 in)	62·5 (675)	75 (16 500)
4	16·67 (55)	6·0 (19 ft 8 in)	1·00 (3 ft 3 in)	1·50 (4 ft 10 in)	100 (1 080)	125 (27 500)
5	16·67 (55)	6·0 (19 ft 8 in)	1·00 (3 ft 3 in)	3·00 (9 ft 10 in)	100 (1 080)	212 (46 640)

NOTE: The pool described in Item 5 is provided with a diving pit having the dimensions shown in Fig. 1.11. Although this pool has the same water area as the pool in Item 4, the volume of water is increased by 70 %, with a significant increase in capital cost and the cost of operation.

periods of peak load when very little, if any, swimming can be accomplished. For proper swimming, a 'lane' at least 2·0 m (6 ft 6 in) wide and 5·0 m (16 ft) long is required. This means that to accommodate four people who really wish to swim (as opposed to just splashing about), a pool 10·0 ft × 4·0 m (33 ft × 13 ft) is required.

The author feels that in pools which are intended only for swimming, and not for diving and water polo, the maximum depth of water need not exceed about 1·5 m (4 ft 10 in). The provision of a depth in excess of this figure really serves little useful purpose, but adds significantly to the capital cost and running expenses of the pool. An exception is where the pool is used for life saving certificates, in which case a depth of 2·0 m (6 ft 6 in) is needed in part of the pool.

Shallow (horizontal) racing dives can be made by experienced swimmers in as little as 1·20 m (4 ft) of water.

If the pool in Item 3 of Table 1.1 had a maximum water depth of 2·0 m instead of 1·5 m, then the volume of water would be increased by 20 %, with a somewhat similar increase in the capital cost of the pool, water treatment equipment and operation (power, chemicals and heating).

REQUIREMENTS FOR DIVING
The depth of water for competitive diving is covered by the regulations of the Amateur Swimming Association and similar international organisations. The requirements in force when this book was revised are shown in Tables 1.6 and 1.7 and Fig. 1.16. The natural question is whether these are basically designed for the safety of the divers or for some other reasons. There is no doubt that the requirements are intended to ensure maximum safety for the persons diving into the pool. It therefore follows that the recommendations should apply to all pools where diving boards are provided, irrespective of whether the pool belongs to a private house, hotel, club, school or public authority, and irrespective of whether the diving is for pleasure or competition. This may sound a counsel of perfection and unnecessarily restrictive. Pools for private houses, schools, clubs and hotels often have 1 m spring boards, and in such cases the diving pit should conform with the appropriate sections of Table 1.6 and Fig. 1.16. Should an accident occur to a person diving into a pool with a diving pit which does not conform with the appropriate recommendations, the owner may be faced with a claim for damages.

COVERED POOLS FOR PRIVATE HOUSES, CLUBS AND HOTELS

There are obviously many advantages in having a covered swimming pool instead of an open-air one. The disadvantage is the additional cost, which can be considerable. An important point is the location of the swimming pool in relation to the rest of the building and, in particular, the use to which the adjacent rooms are put. One point is quite clear: that by having a covered pool, i.e. a pool inside a building, it can be used in comfort 365 days of the year, compared with a maximum of about 150 days for an open-air pool. The initial capital investment and the annual operating costs of a covered (indoor) swimming pool are much greater than those of a pool in the garden. It is relevant to mention that swimming is a recognised

FIG. 1.7.   View of private pool with anodised aluminium enclosure with roof in the open position (Courtesy: Clear Span Ltd, Oldham).

therapeutic exercise and is often recommended for persons suffering from back ailments and muscular strains of the legs and arms. In these circumstances an indoor pool is not just a luxury. Figures 1.7–1.10 show some well-designed indoor pools in this country and abroad.

Unfortunately a problem arises with covered pools—namely, condensation on ceiling and walls. Condensation occurs when the interior surfaces of the pool hall fall below the dew point. Technical solutions to this problem are readily available, but it must be dealt with at the design stage. The author feels strongly about this, because he has been involved in a

number of cases where the owner was not clearly informed of the effect of
the omission of the necessary precautions when the estimates of cost were
discussed. In all cases the owners were very disappointed and severely
critical of their professional advisers.

Condensation can be virtually eliminated by a balanced combination of
thermal insulation together with well-designed ventilation and heating of
the pool hall. This will require an appreciable amount of thermal energy

Fig. 1.8.   View of private pool in Hampstead (Courtesy: James Cowan, Architect).

with consequent high operating costs; there are now available proven
methods of energy conservation in swimming pools and pool halls, and this
subject is discussed briefly in Chapter 7.

It should be remembered that if work to reduce or remedy condensation
is carried out after the completion of the building, it will cost a great deal
more than if it were done in the first place.

It is recommended that the swimming pool hall should be separated from
the main building by an enclosed heated and ventilated area. This will
prevent warm humid air from the pool hall entering the main structure.
Such a layout is particularly important if chlorine is used as the principal
sterilising agent for the pool water; the threshold of smell for chlorine

compounds arising from chlorine in the pool water is about 1 part per million or less.

On the Continent most houses have basements in which the central heating plant is located. The area required for the plant is comparatively small and so, by extending the basement area (a simple operation when the building is being designed), a suitable area can be provided for a small

FIG. 1.9.   Interior view of pool in Fig. 1.8 (Courtesy: James Cowan, Architect).

swimming pool. This arrangement is frequently adopted in Germany, Switzerland and Austria.

For those owners who feel that the capital investment and annual operating costs for a completely covered-in swimming pool are too high, a 'Russian Shelter' type of structure can provide the next best answer. This consists of four walls and a roof which has a narrow longitudinal opening running practically the full length of the building. This narrow opening acts as permanent ventilation and helps to reduce condensation, while the walls

FIG. 1.10.   View of indoor–outdoor pool at Park Hotel, Flims Flims Waldhaus, Switzerland
(Courtesy: H. Nussli, Manager).

and the roof provide good protection against the wind. Construction can be
quite simple; precast concrete portal frames, concrete block or brick, or
clay brick walls, with asbestos-cement or aluminium sheets for the roof.
With this type of construction it is not usual to provide heating and
mechanical ventilation to the pool hall.

It has been mentioned that the capital investment and annual
operating expenses of a covered swimming pool prevent many people from
going in for this type of project. A covered pool provides excellent
swimming all year round, and other recreational facilities such as table
tennis, sauna, solarium, etc., can be readily incorporated into the building.
A heated open-air pool only provides swimming in comfort for about 150
days in the year. The author has read about an interesting project in which
the provision of a covered pool with many facilities, such as showers, toilets,
games room and sauna, became a practical financial proposition for a
group of people who would otherwise not have been able to afford the cost.

The following is the actual 'case history' which was described a few years
ago in the journal *Schöner Wohnen* and which shows how the problem was
successfully solved in Germany. A group of about 20–25 families, living
close together, formed a small committee and worked out the basic
principles. The group then formed a club and a carefully drawn-up contract
and rules were prepared and explained in detail to all participants. The

necessary area of land had to be found close to where the families lived. It is essential that the families who enter this type of scheme should be compatible in financial resources and age, with particular reference tc families with children, and with similar ideas of behaviour. If the group includes an architect or engineer and a solicitor, so much the better. The working out of the 'user rules' and the clear willingness of the club members to keep to them is of fundamental importance. The rules for the reported case included the following:

(1) All visitors (i.e. anyone who is not a member or a child of a member) are recorded in a book and required to pay an entrance fee, which can be varied according to the anticipated intensity of use by the members.

(2) All persons using the sauna have to pay.

(3) All bathers are required to take proper pre-cleansing showers, with particular reference to disinfection of the feet. Bathing caps must be worn by both sexes.

(4) Diving from the side, pushing, ducking and general 'horse play' are forbidden.

(5) Smoking and use of radios, transistors and other 'musical' instruments are forbidden.

(6) Children under the age of 12 years are not admitted to the pool unless accompanied by an adult.

(7) People are discouraged from bathing alone, but this is left to personal discretion.

(8) All members should know where the cleaning materials are and be encouraged to use them.

(9) An executive committee must be appointed and daily inspection and checking of the water and installation undertaken by the members in rotation.

(10) Cleaning, servicing and maintenance is given to a firm on an annual contract basis.

The project was carefully designed and high-quality materials specified, and the work was carried out by an experienced contractor. With an original number of 20 families, the cost worked out at a little more than 50% of the cost of providing a separate open-air pool for each family. The whole scheme was a great success. The author realises that the idea is not universally applicable, but he is sure that it is worth investigating, particularly on new private estates.

OTHER NEW IDEAS
Regarding new ideas, a novel method of constructing walls and roof using a pneumatic former was introduced by Holst Specialised Structures

Ltd. The use of 'thin' shells, i.e. structures curved in two directions, is not new, but the patented method of forming the shell (the 'Parashell') is of considerable interest. The cost of formwork for *in situ* concrete shell roofs is very high and in some cases can make this form of construction uneconomic compared with other designs. The 'Parashell' uses a nylon-reinforced Neoprene membrane which is laid out on a floor slab (which has to be circular on plan) and is anchored to the periphery of the slab, which is designed as a foundation beam. Steel reinforcement is laid out on the membrane and concrete of specially selected mix proportions is spread uniformly over the membrane to a predetermined thickness. A top cover of PVC sheeting is then placed over the plastic concrete and secured to the foundation beam. Air is pumped in under the Neoprene membrane, which is raised slowly to its design shape. In the elevated position the concrete is compacted by special equipment which travels in a circular direction over the whole surface.

At the time of writing, the author knows of only two such domes in the UK: those at a school at Mildenhall, Suffolk, and a Girls College at Malvern. It is claimed that about 600 similar domes have been built in other countries during the past 11 years. It appears that there are special problems associated with this method: these include design of the concrete mix; assembly of the reinforcement; occurrence of honeycombing in the

TABLE 1.2
Swimming pools for clubs and hotels—Dimensions

Item No.	Length, m (ft)	Width, m (ft)	Water depth min., m (ft)	Water depth max., m (ft)	Water area, m² (ft²)	Volume of water m³ (gal)
1	12·50 (41)	6·00 (19 ft 8 in)	0·90 (3)	1·10 (3 ft 7 in)	75 (810)	75 (16 500)
2	16·67 (55)	8·00 (26 ft 3 in)	0·90 (3)	1·50 (4 ft 10 in)	133 (1 436)	160 (35 200)
3	20·00 (65 ft 5 in)	8·00 (26 ft 3 in)	0·90 (3)	3·00 (9 ft 10 in)	160 (1 728)	312 (68 640)
4	25·00 (82)	12·50 (41)	0·90 (3)	3·00 (9 ft 10 in)	312 (3 370)	562 (123 640)

NOTES: In the pools described in Items 3 and 4 the floor gradients for the shallow part of the pool are 1 in 18 and 1 in 26, respectively. The former is rather too steep for small children who cannot swim and therefore special notices to this effect should be clearly displayed. Floor gradients are discussed later in this chapter.

Figure 1.10 shows a hotel pool in Switzerland.

concrete; measures required to ensure stability of the structure before the concrete is mature; and water proofing of the whole structure.

A number of firms market flexible 'shells' or covering to pools. These enable the pool to be used irrespective of the weather, but they are not exactly beautiful, and severe condensation often occurs. The cost is a small fraction of that of a permanent structure.

Table 1.2 gives typical dimensions, etc., for pools for clubs and hotels.

SCHOOL POOLS

With school pools there is generally a much wider choice of site since the pool forms part of the recreational facilities of the school. It may therefore be constructed as part of the sports ground buildings, or it may form part of the main school building and is then often next to the gymnasium.

It is now accepted that, ideally, all schools should have at least a teaching or learner pool. It is better if this can be a separate unit on its own, but if space or finance will not allow this, then it has to form part of a larger pool used by the more experienced swimmers. In the United Kingdom it is the general wish of the Department of Education and Science that all schools should, as far as possible, have swimming pools. Almost all school authorities accept this point of view, and a large number of parents'

TABLE 1.3
Swimming pools for schools

Item No.	Length, m (ft)	Width, m (ft)	Water depth min., m (ft)	Water depth max., m (ft)	Water area m² (ft²)	Volume of water m³ (gal)
1	10·00 (33)	5·00 (16 ft 6 in)	0·90 (3)	1·10 (3 ft 7 in)	50 (545)	50 (11 000)
2	16·67 (55)	8·00 (26 ft 3 in)	0·90 (3)	1·50 (4 ft 10 in)	133 (1 436)	160 (35 200)
3	20·00 (65 ft 5 in)	10·00 (32 ft 9 in)	0·90 (3)	1·50 (4 ft 10 in)	200 (2 160)	240 (52 800)
4	25·00 (82)	12·50 (41)	0·90 (3)	1·50 (4 ft 10 in)	312 (3 370)	314 (82 280)
5	25·00 (82)	12·50 (41)	0·90 (3)	3·00 (9 ft 10 in)	312 (3 370)	562 (123 640)

NOTE: The pool described in item 5 is provided with a diving pit having the dimensions shown in Fig. 1.11. Although this pool has the same water area as the pool described in item 4, the volume of water is increased by 50 %, resulting in a significant increase in capital cost and the cost of operation.

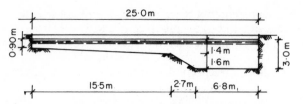

FIG. 1.11.   25 m pool with diving pit for 1·00 m spring board.

organisations have been set up to help finance the building of school pools. While this is very commendable, there is no doubt that many of the pools which have been constructed by such organisations are lamentably sub-standard in both design and construction. In the United Kingdom some County Education Authorities have in the past found themselves in the position where they do not have the legal power to intervene and prescribe

FIG. 1.12.   View of 25 m school pool used for competitions (Courtesy: Rutherford Ltd, Battle).

minimum standards for school pools constructed by voluntary sub-
scriptions. However, in recent years the situation seems to have improved
somewhat, and Education Authorities are making it clear to parent
organisations that pools must be built and equipped to a reasonable
standard, otherwise the Authority will not take the pool over and maintain
it.

On the other hand, Education Authorities themselves are not blameless
when it comes to maintaining school pools, however built, at a satisfactory
standard. Details of these shortcomings are given in an article by R. G.
Clarke in *Baths Service* (June 1970). A school swimming pool must be
provided with efficient water treatment equipment. Once installed, the plant
must be properly operated and this requires a trained operator. The author
considers it most irresponsible to entrust such duties to an untrained,
inexperienced caretaker. Such a proceeding is unfair to the caretaker and
potentially dangerous to the pupils who use the pool.

The bathing load for school pools is easier to determine than for public,
hotel and club pools. The standard of control of the users is (or should be)
much higher. For a school having 400 or more pupils, a pool 25 m × 12·5 m

Fig. 1.13.   View of covered school pool showing laminated timber roof trusses (Courtesy:
Rainham Timber Engineering Co. Ltd, Rainham).

(82 ft × 41 ft) is desirable. Suggested dimensions for school pools are given in Table 1.3, and Fig. 1.11 shows the pool described in item 5 of this Table. Figures 1.12 and 1.13 show two well-designed school pools.

TEACHING OR LEARNER POOLS

This section deals with the general matters relating to layout and dimensions of teaching pools irrespective of whether they belong to a school or form part of a large swimming pool complex run by a public authority. The principal feature of this type of pool is that it must be absolutely safe for non-swimmers. It is rectangular on plan, with an almost flat bottom; the depth generally varies from 0·80 m (2 ft 7 in) to 1·0 m (3 ft 3 in). The maximum depth should not exceed 1·20 m (4 ft). The Amateur Swimming Association recommends a minimum length of 12·0 m (39 ft 6 in) and a minimum width of 7·0 m (23 ft). A useful feature for teaching pools is for the walkway around the pool to be lower than the deck level, so that the instructor can carry out his duties without having to bend down.

With local authority pools, in the United Kingdom, it is customary for the teaching pool to be in a separate part of the building and for the temperature in that part to be a few degrees higher than in the main pool hall. Table 1.4 shows suitable dimensions and water volumes for teaching pools.

Some of the special problems of learner pools which form part of a swimming pool group constructed by a public authority are discussed later in this chapter. While the actual dimensions of learner pools are not critical

TABLE 1.4
Teaching pools

Length, m (ft)	Width, m (ft)	Depth, m (ft)	Capacity, m^3 (gal)
12·5	7·0	0·75–0·90	72
(41 ft)	(23 ft)	(2 ft 6 in–3 ft 0 in)	(16 000)
16·67	8·0	0·75–0·90	108
(55 ft)	(26 ft)	(2 ft 6 in–3 ft 0 in)	(24 000)
20·0	10·0	0·75–0·90	165
(66 ft)	(33 ft)	(2 ft 6 in–3 ft 0 in)	(36 000)
20·0	12·0	0·75–0·90	210
(66 ft)	(39 ft)	(2 ft 6 in–3 ft 0 in)	(44 000)
25·0	16·67	0·75–0·90	340
(82 ft)	(55 ft)	(2 ft 6 in–3 ft 0 in)	(74 000)

FIG. 1.14. View of teaching pool, free-formed in reinforced gunite, with sloping beach, at Rushcliffe Leisure Centre, Nottingham (Courtesy: Cement and Concrete Association, photographer Trevor Jones).

in the same way as for pools used for competitions, the author considers there is an advantage for practising if the length or width is a simple fraction of 100 m. Another feature which is useful in a wide pool is the provision of wide shallow steps for the full length or width of the pool because this enables mothers to take even very small children into the pool with them.

Figure 1.14 shows a well-designed and well-equipped teaching pool.

PUBLIC SWIMMING POOLS UNDER THE CONTROL OF LOCAL AUTHORITIES

GENERAL CONSIDERATIONS

In the United Kingdom most large pools are covered, since this enables them to be used throughout the year. There are, of course, a number of large open-air pools, some owned by local authorities and some by private companies, but these operate for only about four to five months out of twelve—generally from May to September; and only a few of these are heated. The shape of most of these pools is rectangular, and the dimensions vary according to estimated use at the time the pool was designed.

Open-air unheated pools tend to be rather larger than the closed pools, and there are many reasons for this. During periods of hot weather many people, including children, go to open-air pools, although they may not go to the closed ones in the winter. The above-ground building work consists only of plant room, changing accommodation, showers and sanitary blocks and a small covered café with kitchen which can be constructed at comparatively low cost. In the case of closed pools, a high proportion of the total capital cost is in the superstructure.

During the past few years the idea of an outdoor/indoor pool combination has gained ground. At the 39th Annual Conference of the Institute of Baths Management, held in September 1969 at Torquay, a paper on this subject was presented by T. Lindley, General Manager of the Baths Department, London Borough of Richmond-upon-Thames. The basic theme of Lindley's paper was that by providing an attractive and comfortable (heated) open-air swimming pool for use during the summer the public are encouraged to continue their swimming during the winter in the adjacent indoor pool. In other words, the provision of the open-air pool increases the attendance at the indoor pool in winter.

PUBLIC SWIMMING POOLS—LOCATION

It is obviously impossible to lay down hard and fast rules as to exactly where a public swimming pool should be built, but the following are the principal factors which should be given careful consideration in the selection of a site.

Pools in Built-up Areas

(1) The type of district (residential, commercial, industrial or mixed) and any changes in character which may be expected during the following twenty or so years.

(2) The number of ratepayers in the district who may be reasonably expected to use the pool, including estimated increase or decrease.

(3) Traffic conditions around the site as existing, and any changes which may occur through development of the adjoining areas and provision of through traffic routes.

(4) Availability of public transport; car parking areas, existing or which can be provided; circulation arrangements through existing streets for school buses, including put-down and pick-up points (it must be remembered that the construction of a large swimming pool and recreation building will draw traffic to the site).

(5) Location and suitability of existing services, such as sewers, water supply, electricity, gas and telephone.

(6) Subsoil conditions from a load-bearing point of view, and possible aggressive action on the concrete of the foundations of the

superstructure and the pool shell; areas subject to mining subsidence.

(7) Any special requirements regarding external elevation or height of the building which may be imposed because of the architecture of adjacent buildings;

(8) Careful investigation for existence of old sewers, culverts, etc., crossing the site, for which there may be no records.

The provision of adequate parking facilities is of great importance. There is however, a difficult problem to solve—namely, that the number of persons using the pool and other recreation facilities at any one time varies enormously. A car park which is filled to capacity about once a week in winter and a few times a week in summer may be almost empty the rest of the time.

Pools in Outer Suburbs or in Large Open Spaces
While some of the factors already enumerated for pools in built-up areas are applicable, many of the problems of siting are different, or the relative importance of the factor is changed. Therefore, although there will be some repetition, all the various matters requiring consideration will be enumerated.

(1) The type of surrounding district and any changes which are anticipated during the following two decades. This applies particularly to increases in population due to new development.

(2) Traffic conditions around the site are likely to be of less importance than with a location in a densely built-up area. Problems of parking, both present and future, would be more easily solved; this also applies to circulation.

(3) The present and future availability of public transport may present more serious problems than in a city.

The previous remarks on the need for adequate parking facilities for pools in built-up areas are of even greater importance here because a much higher percentage of the users will come from a greater distance away and public transport is likely to be less frequent. The problem of the provision of over-capacity mentioned for town pools is of less significance. It is an unfortunate fact that once a car park has been provided it is very difficult to find the land to enlarge it at a later date.

(4) The existing services, such as sewerage, water supply, electricity, gas and telephone, may have to be substantially increased, and this can involve considerable expenditure.

(5) Investigation of subsoil conditions may be even more important, as

there is likely to be less information available owing to absence of buildings in the vicinity.

(6) There may be greater freedom in the choice of building materials for the external shell of the superstructure and generally in the treatment of the elevations.

(7) The type of use may differ from that experienced in a pool in a densely built-up area because younger children will have to come with their parents; this will affect the proportion of men to women and of adults to children.

TYPES AND SHAPES OF PUBLIC SWIMMING POOLS

When the first edition of this book was published in 1971, the standard shape of public swimming pools in the United Kingdom was rectangular or L-shaped. Since then, however, the leisure centre has appeared, and with this new concept the shape, type and use of the pool itself have changed considerably. In leisure centres the pools are now usually 'free-formed', and incorporate artificial waves, a sloping 'beach' and sometimes islands with palm trees. In the smaller sports centres which comprise one or more pools, the rectangular and L-shape are still maintained.

In the past a number of public authorities have favoured large rectangular pools with two shallow ends, apparently with the idea that this provides a larger area of shallow water. It will be seen in the section dealing with gradients in pool floors (p. 31) that a minimum gradient of 1 in 70 is needed for efficient emptying. In a pool 33·33 m (110 ft) long the increase in depth from end to end need only be 0·50 m (1 ft 8 in). A serious disadvantage

FIG. 1.15.   Section through pool with two shallow ends.

with a pool that has only shallow water is that it can only be used for teaching and non-competitive swimming. For competitions a minimum depth of 1·80 m (5 ft 10 in) is required in front of the starting blocks; for life-saving certificates part of the pool must be 2 m (6 ft 6 in) deep.

Figure 1.15 shows a section through a pool with two shallow ends.

DIMENSIONS OF PUBLIC SWIMMING POOLS

One of the basic requirements for the majority of public swimming pools is that they can be used for competitive swimming, and sometimes for diving and water polo.

The pool sizes likely to be required are shown in Table 1.5. Swimming

TABLE 1.5

Length, m (ft)	Width, m (ft)	Min depth at starting blocks, m (ft)
25 (82 ft)	12·6 (41 ft 6 in)	1·8 (5 ft 10 in) over a length of 6 (20 ft)
33·33 (110 ft)	12·6 (41 ft 6 in) or 14·7 (48 ft 3 in) or 16·8 (55 ft 2 in)	
50 (165 ft)	20 (66 ft)	

lanes should be 2·1 m (7 ft) wide; sometimes the lanes adjacent to the pool sides are made slightly wider to help dampen the effect of back-wash. Requirements for diving are shown in Tables 1.6 and 1.7, and in Figs. 1.16 and 6.15. For water polo a minimum water depth of 1·8 m (5 ft 10 in) is required, and the playing area must not exceed 30 m × 20 m (98 ft × 66 ft), and must not be smaller than 20 m × 8 m (66 ft × 26 ft). In addition, there should be a distance of 1·0 m (3 ft 3 in) between the goal line and the back of the goal net.

For competitive swimming the FINA regulations require a minimum

TABLE 1.6 (see Fig. 1.16)

Description	Spring boards, m		Fixed boards, m		
A Board height above water	1·0	3·0	5·0	7·5	10·0
B Clearance forward	7·5	9·0	10·25	11·00	13·5
C Clearance to sides	2·5	3·5	3·8	4·5	4·5
D Clearance behind	1·5	1·5	1·5	1·5	1·5
E Depth maintained at sides	2·2	2·7	3·0	3·0	3·0
F Depth maintained forward	5·3	6·0	6·0	8·0	10·5
G Depth of water	3·0	3·5	3·8	4·1	4·5
H Clearance overhead	4·6	4·6	3·0	3·2	3·4
I Distance centre to centre of adjoining boards	2·0	2·5	2·5	2·5	2·5
J Board length	4·8	4·8	5·0	6·0	6·0
K Board width	0·5	0·5	2·0	2·0	2·0
L Distance in front of plummet over which the height H is to be maintained	2·75	2·75	2·75	2·75	2·75

TABLE 1.7

Length (in direction of dive), m (ft)	Width, m (ft)	Water depth, m (ft)
16·5 (54 ft)	12·5 (41 ft)	4·5 (14 ft 8 in)
18·0 (59 ft)	15·5 (51 ft)	4·5 (14 ft 8 in)
10·0 (32 ft 10 in)	10·5 (34 ft 5 in)	3·0 (9 ft 11 in)

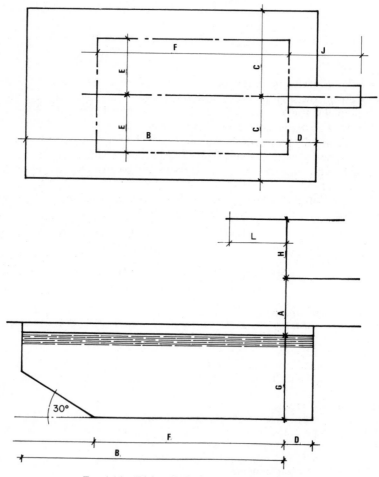

FIG. 1.16.   Diving pit for competitive diving.

water depth in front of the starting blocks of 1·80 m (5 ft 10 in), which must extend forward over a length of 6 m (20 ft) measured from the starting point.

Stairs and steps must be accommodated outside the pool dimensions, and more details of these are given in Chapter 6.

For life-saving certificates, a water depth of 2·0 m (6 ft 6 in) is required and this should extend for a length of 6·0 m (20 ft), over the full width of the pool.

GRADIENTS FOR THE FLOORS AND FOR WALKWAYS AND FLOORS OF SHOWER ROOMS AND WET AREAS

While this section deals with public swimming pools, the information given should be of interest to the designers of hotel, club and school pools.

The Pool Floor

The floor of the pool must be laid to fall towards the outlet with such a gradient that the pool can be effectively emptied. At the same time the gradient should not be so steep that learners and non-swimmers can overbalance; this does not apply to the short steep section leading down to a diving pit. A detailed discussion on this subject is given in an article by H. P. Hyde in *Baths Service* (April 1970).

Hydraulic considerations for efficient emptying require a gradient of about 1 in 70, which is well below that required for safety—namely, about 1 in 30. It is generally recommended that if the main pool floor has a gradient steeper than 1 in 25, notices to this effect should be clearly displayed. In shallow water where the gradient exceeds 1 in 30 non-slip tiles should be used. The gradient should be uniform between clearly marked positions; depth markers on the side walls are most desirable.

The Floors of Walkways and Other Wet Areas

Walkways and the floors of all 'wet' areas should always be provided with a non-slip surface. In addition, they must be laid to adequate falls to outlet points. The requirements for a non-slip surface and a self-cleansing surface (which means maximum ease of cleaning) are to some extent in conflict, and therefore a practical compromise has to be reached. There are certain problems associated with the surfacing of walkways and the floors of shower rooms, changing rooms and similar 'wet' areas, and these are discussed in detail in Chapter 6. A gradient of 1 in 40 (25 mm in 1 m) is recommended, although the author has heard a figure of 1 in 24 recommended.

Facilities for Diving

There are many advantages in having the diving area clearly separated from the main swimming area. This can be arranged by producing either a separate diving pit, or a diving pit in an adjacent and connected part of the pool, such as an L-shaped pool with the diving pit in the short leg.

In the past it has been the practice to provide for diving in a deep section at one end of the main pool, but the author is pleased to note that there has been a change in recent years and that most modern swimming pool complexes contain a separate diving pool. The advantages of this include the following:

(a) Swimming and diving can take place simultaneously without any risk of one interfering with the other.
(b) The dangers inherent in diving into a pool crowded with swimmers is eliminated.
(c) While at first sight it may appear that the provision of a separate diving pit will increase the capital cost of the project, this is not necessarily so.

Irrespective of whether the diving pool forms part of the main swimming area or is separate, it must be constructed to certain specified dimensions laid down by the Amateur Swimming Association which are shown in Table 1.6; Table 1.7 gives some typical dimensions for separate diving pits. In some cases the depth of water for 10·0 m boards is now 5·0 m (16 ft 6 in).

PUBLIC SWIMMING POOLS—INDOOR POOLS: OVERALL USE AND LAYOUT OF THE BUILDING

GENERAL CONSIDERATIONS

The question as to whether the building should accommodate only the swimming pool(s) together with the necessary ancillary facilities, or whether other sports and cultural uses should be incorporated, either into the same building or as a group of connected buildings, can be discussed only in very general terms. The decision will depend on a large number of factors, the relative importance of which is likely to be different in each case. Assuming that there is a need for such a sports centre, then the question of finance and the size of the plot(s) available and the maximum height of building allowed on the site must be considered; in addition, there are also all the factors previously mentioned in this chapter.

There are obvious advantages in bringing a number of recreational facilities together under one roof, and the overall cost of the combined centre is likely to be less than providing them separately. On the other hand, there is continuous pressure to provide new swimming pools and the necessary finance is not always available to build large leisure centres, which can cost anything from £1 million to £3 million.

It is rather fruitless to compare the overall cost of two swimming pool projects, because a close examination of the breakdown of costs will show how different the two projects are.

The detailed arrangements and layout of the access, entrances, exits, changing accommodation, pre-cleansing areas and spectator accommodation, as well as the many additional recreation facilities which are now included in large sport and leisure centres, depend on very many factors. Many of these are outside the scope of this book, and the notes which follow are intended to emphasise basic principles relevant to swimming pools.

ENTRANCES AND EXITS AND CIRCULATION ARRANGEMENTS FOR THE PUBLIC
The entrance for swimmers and non-swimmers, including spectators for competitions, should be through the main entrance hall, passing the pay desk on the way. Coin-operated ticket machines have been tried in a number of public pools, but generally these are not favoured by baths managers. The reason for this is that many people come to the pool without the necessary small change, which means that either they cannot get in or a member of staff has to be on duty to provide the change; in the latter case there is no saving over a cash desk. In large pools with heavy peak loads there may be a case for a cash desk and ticket machine, but this would necessitate the use of a turnstile or similar entry control. Once past that, however, the swimmers and non-swimmers must be separated—in this context 'non-swimmers' means people who are not going to change into their bathing costumes.

The only access to the swimming pools must be through the changing rooms, pre-cleansing footbaths and/or showers, while the spectators must go to their places another way. It is recommended that changing and sanitary accommodation for the bathers should be on the same level as the walkways around the pool; stairs and steps should be avoided.

While a spacious entrance hall is very impressive and an attractive architectural feature, it is seldom really necessary from a functional point of view. By keeping the dimensions to those required for comfort and easy circulation, money can be saved. The provision of covered ways around the building for queueing for entrance to galas and competitions should be considered. Some layouts are shown in Fig. 1.17.

Where teaching pools are provided, these are often used exclusively on certain days by schools and clubs and not by individual members of the public, and a separate entrance (which is also the exit) can be very useful. In this way school buses can discharge their occupants near the entrance, and an appreciable amount of dirt is avoided in the main entrance hall.

In the United Kingdom there is a tendency to locate the learner pool in a

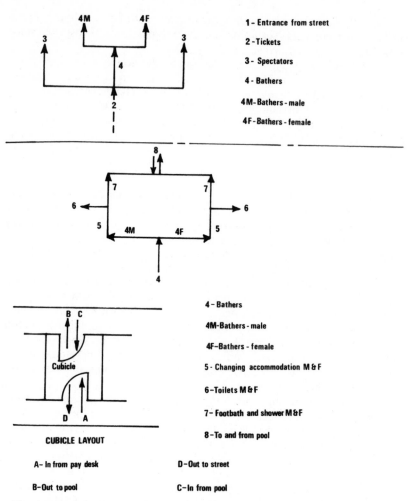

1 - Entrance from street

2 - Tickets

3 - Spectators

4 - Bathers

4M - Bathers - male

4F - Bathers - female

4 - Bathers

4M - Bathers - male

4F - Bathers - female

5 - Changing accommodation M & F

6 - Toilets M & F

7 - Footbath and shower M & F

8 - To and from pool

CUBICLE LAYOUT

A - In from pay desk   D - Out to street

B - Out to pool   C - In from pool

FIG. 1.17.   Circulation arrangements and cubicle layout for a large swimming pool.

separate hall. While this has undoubted advantages, there are also some disadvantages, particularly from the point of view of the supervision of children by their parents, who may also want to swim and have older children who can safely bathe in a large pool. It is always difficult, and sometimes quite impossible, to find a solution which satisfies everyone under all circumstances, but it must always be remembered that the pool facilities are provided for the benefit and enjoyment of the public, and not

to satisfy academic theories of the designers. It should be p
arrange the layout so that the learner pool hall is next to the maii
(for easy access by parents). At the same time provision must b
close off this access when the learner pool is reserved for schools oɩ ciubs. It
is the author's view that all learner pools which are open to the public should
be designed and made available for use by parents who wish to teach their
children to swim, and not be reserved exclusively for professional teachers
and classes.

PRE-CLEANSING AREAS—SHOWERS AND FOOTBATHS

One of the most striking features of public swimming pools in Switzerland
and Germany is the emphasis placed on personal hygiene by the public
using the pool. Another is the high standard of cleanliness and maintenance
of the changing rooms, pre-cleansing areas and toilets, and in fact all parts
of the building. It is obvious that the public and baths personnel work
together to achieve these results. Unfortunately, standards in the United
Kingdom are, on the average, appreciably lower, even when the older, pre-
World War II pools are excluded.

Unless the public are prepared to use showers, footbaths, and wash-hand
basins in a civilised way, then it is extremely difficult to maintain a proper
standard. There are some advantages in having the showers pre-set at about
32 °C (90 °F). Push-button, time-controlled valves for the showers (about
$1\frac{1}{2}$–2 min) are also useful in helping to reduce waste of water. Soap should be
provided, at least for foot cleansing. It is axiomatic that the layout should
be such that all bathers have to pass through the pre-cleansing area before
entering the pool. On the Continent bathing caps for both sexes are
compulsory in public pools and hotel pools. The caps can be hired at the
same time as the entrance ticket is issued. Waste water from showers and
footbaths should be taken to the foul drainage system of the building.

There should be an adequate number of showers, with a water supply
pipework of sufficient size to allow all showers to be operated
simultaneously. The Technical Unit for Sport (TUS), in their *Design
Bulletin No. 1*, recommend one shower for every eight changing places
provided; this appears adequate.

One further point is that some bathers like to take a shower after
swimming, particularly if the pool water is chlorinated.

CHANGING ACCOMMODATION

The changing accommodation can be arranged in many ways; one layout is
that the bathers returning to the cubicles from the pool enter them by the
same route as they left them; they then change into their street clothes and
leave the cubicle by the door through which they entered originally. This
arrangement, which is rather expensive, is shown diagramatically in Fig.

1.17. The size of the cubicles varies, but dimensions of 1·0 m long by 0·90 m wide (3 ft 3 in × 3 ft 0 in) is about the minimum; a size of 1·0 m × 1·0 m is rather better.

The various systems of changing and keeping clothes may be summarised as follows.

Method 1: One cubicle per bather, who has a key and keeps his clothes in the cubicle.

Method 2: Cubicles for dressing and undressing to which the user does not have a key; one locker for each bather, who has a key, and keeps his or her clothes there.

Method 3: Cubicles and wire baskets with or without hangers. The bather collects the hanger, etc., on his way in, enters a free cubicle, undresses, places his clothes on the hanger and in the basket, and hands these in to an attendant against a numbered disc or similar. On returning from the pool, he hands in the disc and collects the hanger with his clothes.

Method 4: A combination of one of the above with a communal changing area. In other words, people who want privacy can pay extra for a cubicle, and those who do not mind sharing use the communal area at a lower price. The wire baskets should preferably be covered with nylon rather than PVC because the former is much more durable.

The design of the cubicles is important from the point of view of the users. The author definitely favours a timber door and a hinged seat, so that with the seat in the lowered (sitting) position the door is securely closed. It is appreciated that this results in a considerable increase in cost compared with a plastic curtain, but the charge for using this can be higher than for the more simple type which provide less privacy. In other words, both types of cubicle can be provided and those who wish for greater privacy can have it if they pay extra.

The changing accommodation recommended by the TUS in their *Bulletin No.* 1 is reasonable. This in effect amounts to:

(a) One changing place for each 8·4 m² (91 ft²) of pool area for normal swimming pools. This is increased to one place for each 6·5 m² (70 ft²) in leisure centre pools.

(b) For learner pools one place for each 4·2 m² (45 ft²) of water area.

(c) When there is a separate diving pool, an extra two places should be provided.

The author feels that in those centres which cater specially for family activities provision should be made for a limited number of family changing cubicles, so that very young children can change with their parents.

SANITARY ACCOMMODATION FOR POOL USERS

The amount of sanitary accommodation (WCs, urinals and wash basins) required will depend on the estimated peak load and the proportion of men to women. The Institute of Baths Management, in their *Swimming Pool Design Guide No.* 1, state that the ratio of men to women encountered in public swimming pools in the United Kingdom varies between 3:1 and 4:1.

The accommodation recommended in this book is:

Women: 1 WC for each 30 up to the first 100, and then 1 for each additional 40. A minimum of 3 WCs should be provided. 1 wash-hand basin for each WC.

Men: 1 WC for each 50 up to the first 100, and then 1 for each additional 75, with a minimum of 2 WCs. 1 urinal stall for each 40, with a minimum of 3 stalls. 1 WHB for each WC.

Methods for calculating the total number of bathers which can be reasonably accommodated at any one time are given later in this chapter. On the basis of these figures, for a pool 33·33 m (110 ft) long and 13 m (42 ft) wide, without diving pit, and having a surface area of 433 m^2 (4676 ft^2), the number of users accommodated would be about 300. Assuming 3 males to 1 female, this would give 225 males and 75 females. The accommodation thus required:

Women: 3 WCs and 3 WHBs.
Men: 4 WCs, a 6-stall urinal and 4 WHBs.

It may be of interest to compare the above accommodation with that which would be provided for an ordinary swimming pool under para. 126 of the TUS *Bulletin No.* 1, which is: for 433 m^2 (4676 ft^2), the number of changing places would be 433 ÷ 8·4 = 52. With a ratio of 3 male to 1 female, there would be 39 male places and 13 female; the sanitary accommodation would be:

Men: 3 WCs, 3 urinal stalls and 3WHBs.
Women: 2 WCs and 3 WHBs.

The author feels that the additional accommodation which he recommends is worthwhile, the extra cost being insignificant in relation to the overall cost of the whole project. The need for a high standard of maintenance is emphasised.

USER CAPACITY OF SWIMMING POOLS—POOL LOADING

Having settled the general principles of layout and circulation, showers and toilets, consideration will be given to the question of estimated ca

the pool. This is not easy to do, and again there are considerable differences
of opinion on this matter among baths managers. There appears to be no
mention of this subject in the TUS *Design Bulletin No. 1*. However, the
report of the Sports Council's Working Party on swimming pool capacities,
if read together with the comments of the Institute of Baths Management,
is interesting and practical. It is hoped that information and suggestions
given here will alert designers to the problems involved and thus ensure that
they are given careful consideration.

Table 1.8 gives some American recommendations published in
Swimming Pools, by the Council for National Co-operation in Aquatics, in
1972.

TABLE 1.8

*Area required in swimming pools per person according to depth of
water and use*

Description	Indoor ft² (m²)	Outdoor ft² (m²)
Water not exceeding 5 ft deep (1·52 m)	14 (1·3)	15 (1·40)
Advanced swimming	20 (1·86)	25 (2·32)
Learner pools	40 (3·72)	45 (4·18)
Recreational swimming	20 (1·86)	25 (2·32)

In the United Kingdom *Design Bulletin No. 4*, issued by the Ministry of
Housing and Local Government, suggests the following figures:

Non-swimmers: 10 ft² (0·93 m²) per person assumed to be in the water
at one time, plus $\frac{1}{3}$ of this number out of the water—
probably at the side of the pool.

Swimmers: 36 ft² per person in the water, plus $\frac{1}{3}$ of this number at
the side of the pool.

Diving: Assuming there is a diving area in the main pool, three
divers in the water and nine waiting at the pool side.

The author accepts the figures for the diving pit and the swimming zone as
reasonable from the point of view of comfort for those in the water, but
considers the figure of 10 ft² (0·93 m²) per person in the bathing (non-
swimming) area to be too crowded. This figure of 10 ft² only allows each
non-swimmer a space of 3 ft 2 in (0·96 m) by 3 ft 2 in to move around in. An
absolute minimum of 1·25 m² (13·5 ft²) should be allowed.

For a pool with an area of 13·33 m × 13·0 m not exceeding 1·50 m (5 ft)
deep having a total water area of 433 m² (4660 ft²), which was used in the

calculation of the sanitary accommodation, the pool loading would be calculated as follows:

Non-swimmers: $13 \cdot 0 \times 13 \cdot 33$—in the area of the pool not exceeding $1 \cdot 50$ m deep;
$= 173$ m^2 at $1 \cdot 25$ m^2 per person in the water
gives 140 bathers
plus 50 waiting at the side.

Swimmers: $13 \cdot 0 \times 20 \cdot 0$—in the area of the pool reserved for water polo;
$= 260$ m^2 at $3 \cdot 5$ m^2 per swimmer in the water
gives 75 swimmers
plus 25 waiting at the side.

Totals: 290 (215 people in the water and 75 people waiting at the side).

On the Ministry basis of calculation, there would be 185 non-swimmers in the shallow end of the pool instead of the 140 calculated by the author's basic figures, i.e. an additional 45 persons, or 32%. When visiting public swimming pools it has always seemed to the author that the number of persons in bathing suits who are not actually in the water, i.e. sitting and walking about and talking, etc., number at least 50% and may be as much as 100% of the number in the pool itself. Taking 80% as a compromise, the number of people who could be accommodated in reasonable comfort at any one time would, on this basis, be:

in the water (as previously calculated)	215
outside the water, 80% of 215	172
total:	387
say:	400

The figure given above is relevant to covered pools, and brings out the necessity for adequate width of the walkways around the pool and provision of warmed benches, which are mentioned later in this chapter. For pools with an open or partially open sun terrace for use by bathers, the number of people using the terrace on a warm sunny day is likely to be appreciably higher than those actually in the pool. Circumstances such as this are very relevant when designing the changing rooms and other facilities. In West Germany a number of designers work on the basis of $A/3$ as the number of persons actually in the water at any one time, where A is the water area in square metres.

SPECTATOR ACCOMMODATION

Accommodation for spectators can be divided into two categories:

(1) Standing and/or seating for friends and relatives of bathers.
(2) Permanent seating for galas and competitions.

It is desirable that part of the accommodation under (1) should be located as near as possible to the learner pool, as many parents like to watch their children under instruction. If a separate diving pit is provided, this will attract spectators and a limited amount of seating for this is justified. Part of the accommodation for casual spectators (category 1), can be included as a section of the refreshment facilities.

Fixed seating for spectators watching competitions requires special planning and the capital cost can be considerable. A valid question is therefore the extent to which this seating is really needed—that is, the use which will be made of it. This can be expressed in the number of times a year that the accommodation will be utilised on a percentage basis, i.e. 100 % (a 'full house'), 75 %, 60 %, 50 %, 40 %, etc., of maximum capacity. The result of such an investigation can be surprising and may cause a more realistic approach to the problem. The Sports Council, in *TUS Bulletin No.* 1, para. 133, say '... It is doubtful whether permanent spectator accommodation (seating) for galas and competitions is really necessary in pools of a local—as opposed to regional—nature. Many postwar pools have been equipped with spectator seating which is rarely used to its capacity. ...' It is appropriate to remember that the public will have to pay for the capital investment, even though some part of the operating costs of the centre is covered by income.

It is essential that the spectators should have no means of access to the pool, or any parts of the pool hall used by the bathers. Separate sanitary accommodation for the spectators must be provided; recommendations for this are given in **MOHLG** *Design Bulletin No.* 4, p. 11, as follows:

Men: 1 WC for the first 200, 2 WCs for 200–500,
         3 WCs for 500–1000:
         1 urinal stall for every 50:
         1 WHB for every 60.

Women: 1 WC for the first 100, 2 for 100–250,
         3 for 250–500, 4 for 500–900:
         1 WHB for every 60.

In the opinion of the author, even though accommodation to the above standard has been provided in the past, this is inadequate. Assuming that the seating accommodation will be filled, then the following toilet facilities should be provided:

Men: WCs, minimum 2; 1 for each 100–500, then 1 for each 200: Urinals, minimum 3 stalls; 1 stall for each 40–300, then 1 stall for each 50: WHBs, 1 for each WC.

Women: WCs, minimum 3; 1 for each 50–300, then 1 for each 75: WHBs, 1 for each WC.

OTHER SWIMMING POOL SERVICES AND INSTALLATIONS

There are a number of other arrangements, and services which have to be included in a large swimming pool:

(1) Ticket office off the main entrance hall.
(2) Office for baths supervisor, staff rooms, canteen, showers and sanitary accommodation for staff of both sexes.
(3) First aid room with all necessary life-saving appliances.
(4) Adequate storage space for all sports equipment and other equipment and materials needed for the maintenance of the pool and building. In many pools, which in all other respects are excellent, completely inadequate areas have been allocated for storage of all the many items of stores and equipment which are in constant use.
(5) Provision for the partaking of light refreshment by the public. The minimum needed would be an area with seats and fixed tables and coin-operated vending machines. Vending machines are very profitable and take up little space. The important points when installing these are that they must supply food and drink of high quality, be kept fully stocked, be properly serviced and promptly repaired.
(6) Plant room(s) for water treatment and heating and air conditioning plant. A small but separate room for the chlorinator(s) and cylinders. Another small room for the chemical feed equipment.
(7) Battery room for the electric batteries used for emergency lighting for the whole building.
(8) Room for main switchgear and fuses.
(9) Public address system; a number of small loudspeakers is likely to be more effective than a single one.
(10) An adequate number of electric clocks.
(11) Electrically operated hair driers.
(12) An events indicator board for competitions.
(13) Spotlights for use with competitions.
(14) Judges' box for competitions.
(15) Bicycle sheds.
(16) Large car park (see previous comments on area required).

(17) Provision for the storage of refuse, bearing in mind the need for ease of collection.
(18) Adequate number of receptacles for rubbish in and around the building.
(19) Public telephones.
(20) Fire alarms and fire-fighting appliances.
(21) Burglar alarms.

Certain additional facilities which are often provided on the continent, but are not so common in the United Kingdom, include the following:

(1) Special quick drying rooms which can be used by persons who have been in the water, but want to sit around in their bathing costumes (perhaps to watch diving), with the intention of bathing again later. The air temperature in the pool hall is usually maintained slightly above the temperature of the water in the pool: assuming a water temperature of 24 °C (76 °F), the air temperature would be about 25–26 °C. Even so, some people would feel distinctly chilly sitting or standing around in a wet bathing suit. This situation can be greatly improved by the provision of an adequate number of warmed benches and radiant heating panels in the walls. These special rooms are kept at a temperature of 50–55 °C (122–131 °F) and are generally quite small.
(2) Powder rooms for women, provided with chairs or stools, mirrors and coin-operated hair dryers.
(3) With the advent of long hair for the male sex, coin-operated hair driers are likely to be used as much in the men's changing rooms as in the women's.
(4) Spin dryers and/or hot-air dryers for bathing costumes, so that these can be taken home in reasonable comfort; this is particularly useful for those using public transport.
(5) Facilities for hiring towels and for washing and sterilising them afterwards on the premises; also hire of bathing caps.

FACILITIES IN PUBLIC SWIMMING POOL ESTABLISHMENTS
Many facilities in addition to swimming and diving are now included in sports and leisure centres:

(1) Multi-purpose sports hall.
(2) Squash courts.
(3) Indoor bowling green(s).
(4) Bowling alley.
(5) Gymnasium.
(6) Weight-lifting room.

(7) Physical fitness room.
(8) Shooting gallery.
(9) Rooms for whist drives and small functions.
(10) Sauna and/or Turkish baths and massage.
(11) Solarium and massage.
(12) Hydrotherapy pool.
(13) Facilities for the disabled.
(14) Movable swimming pool floors.
(15) Wave-making machines.

Facilities under (1)–(10) and (12)–(15) are now known and provided in the new leisure centres in the United Kingdom, but solaria are rather new. They are often provided with swimming pools in private houses and high class hotels on the continent.

It seems that the majority of people who live north of the Alps are sun lovers and consider that the possession of a tan is both attractive and healthy. Doctors who have studied the effects of sunbathing on the human body have reservations on the benefits claimed. Nevertheless the provision of a solarium will be popular and should produce a good revenue. Natural sunlight occurs within a comparatively narrow band of electromagnetic radiation which includes visible light and an invisible part lying on either side of it—namely the infra-red and the ultra-violet. The infra-red is heat rays and the ultra-violet imparts the much desired tan. It is important that the amount of rays in different parts of the ultra-violet spectrum should be correctly balanced, and the whole installation must be under proper control, and the sessions must be accurately programmed. The sessions are usually timed for 10, 15, 20 or 30 min, and audible signals inform the user when half the session is over; on completion there is usually a cooling-off period of about 5 min.

Saunas have grown considerably in popularity in recent years and are now considered a profitable proposition by baths managers. They are also often found in hotels and private houses.

HYDROTHERAPY POOLS

The advantages of carrying out special exercises under water have been known to the medical profession for many years. While spas in the United Kingdom have declined in popularity to almost vanishing point, this has not been the case on the Continent. These special health resorts, with names starting with 'Bad' in Germany, Austria and Switzerland, continue to flourish and attract large numbers of visitors. The author has visited a number of these towns and found them very pleasant and attractive (Figs. 1.18 and 1.19). The special swimming pools contain mineralised ('spa')

Fig. 1.18.   View in summer of open-air thermal swimming pool at Leukerbad, Switzerland
(Courtesy: *Swiss Hotel Journal*).

Fig. 1.19.   View in winter of open-air thermal swimming pool at Leukerbad, Switzerland
(Courtesy: *Swiss Hotel Journal*).

water, which in some places is slightly radioactive. There are usually a number of pools which are claimed to be particularly suitable for different ailments. Under-water massage by a powerful jet is more or less a standard fitting in these public pools and in the hotel pools.

In the United Kingdom there are many therapeutic pools, but these are attached to hospitals, recuperation homes and similar institutions. This means that they are only used by people who are definitely in need of the treatment which has been prescribed by a physician. They are not part of a

FIG. 1.20. A patient being lowered into a hydrotherapy pool (Courtesy: Felix Walter, Architect).

holiday resort. Three examples are the pools at the Stoke Mandeville Hospital; at Cowbridge, South Wales; and at Edgware, London (built for the John Grooms Association for the Disabled). Figure 1.20 shows a patient being lowered into a hydrotherapy pool.

Important features in the design and layout of such pools include the following:

(1) The floor should be almost level, with just sufficient slope to enable the pool to be emptied. A gradient of about 1 in 100 should be just about sufficient.

(2) The floor of the pool must be non-slip, also all areas which are likely to become wet.

(3) In the design stage careful thought should be given to the special equipment and fittings required so that these can be fixed as the work proceeds.

(4) If the pool is not a deck-level one (the latter has many advantages, but these may not be applicable in all cases), then glazed ceramic scum channels should be provided.
These are more efficient in removing surface contamination and ensuring proper water circulation than skimmer outlets.

(5) All fittings should be stainless steel, austenitic type 316 S16.

(6) The turn-over period (the time required to completely circulate all the water contained in the pool), should not exceed 3 h; some pools operate on as short a period as $1\frac{1}{2}$ h.

(7) The water and air temperature should be maintained at a higher level than in normal swimming pools. A minimum water temperature of 30 °C (86 °F) with the air temperature at about 33 °C (91 °F) has been adopted in many pools.

(8) If highly saline or spa water is used in the pool, then it is necessary to consider carefully the possible corrosive effect on the structure and finishes of the pool and all fittings in contact with the water. Even stainless steel type 316 S16 can be attacked by some saline waters, depending on the chemical composition of the dissolved salts.

An interesting therapeutic pool is the one in the Blythedale Children's Hospital at Valhalla, New York. It is built entirely in high-quality austenitic stainless steel. Fabrication was by welding, and the joints were then ground and buffed. The sheets were provided with a special non-slip finish. While this method of construction provided a first-class finish from a hygiene point of view, the author was surprised that the turn-over period for the pool water was as long as 6 h.

FACILITIES FOR THE DISABLED IN PUBLIC SWIMMING POOLS

The first question which arises when considering the use of a public pool by seriously disabled persons is how these two uses can be satisfactorily reconciled. Obviously the dual use will place certain restrictions on the type of disability which can be accommodated in a public pool as compared with the special hydrotherapy pools discussed in the previous section. The specification and design of the necessary arrangements require detailed study. All that can be done here is to emphasise the need to provide the facilities and to consider the more important factors involved. For additional information readers should refer to the Bibliography at the end of this chapter.

The fact is that in public swimming pools facilities can be reasonably easily provided which will enable disabled persons to use the pool at the same time as the general public. Work in this field has been done by a number of organisations, of which the best-known is probably the Thistle Foundation. The Foundation sponsored a special study of the design of sports centres and swimming pools with particular reference to the needs of the physically disabled. This was written by Felix Walter, FRIBA, and published in June 1971. Thanks to the efforts of these organisations and many private persons, a number of the public pools built in the United Kingdom during the past ten years are provided with special facilities which enable them to be used and enjoyed by the disabled. These include the Carn Brea Centre in Cornwall; the Sports Centre at Guildford, Surrey; the Royal Commonwealth Pool at Edinburgh; the Bellahouston Sports Centre, Glasgow; and the Morden Park Pool at Morden, Surrey.

With existing pools it is often easier to adapt a learner pool for use by disabled persons than to provide the necessary facilities in the main pool. This is because of the shallow depth, the flat floor gradient and the higher water temperature (and air temperature when the learner pool is separated from the main hall). However, Felix Walter in his booklet gives a number of sound reasons why learner pools are not necessarily suitable for this dual use. The important requirements may be divided into two classes, external and internal. External requirements include the following:

(1) Access should be provided for ambulances to a special side entrance.

(2) Ramps are required irrespective of the provision of steps. The gradient of the ramp needs careful consideration, taking into account such factors as how the disabled will negotiate it and its length. An absolute maximum gradient of 1 in 10 is considered desirable even for very short ramps not exceeding 3 m (10 ft) in length.

(3) External paving used for access should have a durable, non-slip, but not loose, surface. *In situ* concrete with a ribbed surface and precast non-slip slabs, as well as the recently introduced concrete paving blocks, are entirely suitable.

(4) Reference should be made to British Standard Code of Practice CP96: Access for the Disabled to Buildings.

Internal requirements include the following:

(1) As far as is practical the special access arrangements should be extended inside the building so that the disabled can reach all the facilities offered by the Centre, particularly those associated with swimming, such as the viewing area, and refreshments.

(2) Special sanitary accommodation should be provided and located in a readily accessible position. It can often form part of the spectator accommodation mentioned earlier in this chapter.

(3) The widths of corridors and doors must be adequate for wheelchairs, and the same applies to lifts.

(4) Special changing facilities must be available with direct access to the pool, preferably the shallow end. The pre-cleanse area must incorporate arrangements so that the disabled can use both showers and footbaths.

(5) The overall design of the main swimming pool, including water and air temperature, must be based on the needs of the majority of users—namely, able-bodied persons. However, deck-level pools have advantages which outweigh their shortcomings.

(6) Heating beneath the walkway slabs and warm benches around the pool are desirable, and certainly attractive for all categories of user. They are found more frequently on the Continent than in the United Kingdom.

(7) Access into the pool can be designed with very little extra cost so as to help disabled persons, and certainly with no inconvenience to normal users.

(8) In addition to normal access by steps, special equipment may be provided to enable severely handicapped persons to enter the pool provided this does not interfere with normal use by the general public.

SWIMMING POOLS WITH MOVABLE FLOORS

The desirability of separate pools for swimming, diving and teaching has been emphasised earlier in this chapter. Such separation does cost a great deal of money, and this led to the development on the Continent of hydraulically operated floors so that the depth of water could be reduced over part of the pool by raising a section of the floor. The shallow area thus formed can be used for teaching. Several hundred pools with this equipment have been constructed in West Germany and Holland. In many pools complete segregation of the shallow and deep water is ensured by a hydraulically operated separating wall. Some details of the equipment are given in Part 2 of Chapter 6.

WAVE-MAKING MACHINES

A very popular feature of many pools on the Continent is artificial waves. When the first edition of this book was published in 1971, there was only one pool with wave-making equipment in operation in the United Kingdom—namely, the Porto Bello open-air pool at Edinburgh. Since 1971, wave-making machines have been installed in a number of new pools, including the leisure centres at Whitley Bay, Rotherham, Swansea and Swindon. Several pools now under construction will have this equipment. Judging from attendance records at these pools, the public likes the new feature very much. The wave-making machines are usually operated for about 15–20 min once or twice an hour. Further information on wave-making machines is given in Part 2 of Chapter 6; a view of waves in the main pool at Swansea Leisure Centre is shown in Figure 6.11.

POOLS USED FOR SUB-AQUA ACTIVITIES

Sub-aqua activities are becoming increasingly popular in all parts of the world. The British Sub-Aqua Club (BSAC) claims to be the largest single diving club in the world with over 29 000 members.

Training in the sea, lakes and rivers in the United Kingdom is often difficult owing to low visibility, currents, low temperature, etc. There are clear advantages if training can be carried out in a swimming pool. The BSAC requires that every novice of the Club should receive basic training in

FIG. 1.21.   View of sub-aqua training in public swimming pool (Courtesy: British Sub-Aqua Club, photographer Trevor Jones).

a swimming pool. This means that the future expansion of the sport is dependent on swimming pool facilities being readily available. The use of public pools for sub-aqua activities is not always permitted by baths managers owing to their apprehension about damage to the pool by the divers' equipment. The equipment used by the Club members should not cause damage to a swimming pool which has been finished with high-quality tiles or mosaic. Glass-fibre polyester laminates of adequate thickness and correctly applied should also stand up to sub-aqua activities. In any pool, repairs to tiling and mosaic will become necessary in the course of time; as mentioned in Chapter 8, damaged tiles and small areas of mosaic can be repaired under water without the necessity of emptying the pool.

The 39 page booklet *Pools for Sub-aqua Use*, issued by the BSAC, gives detailed information on all matters relating to aqualung diving, and all interested readers should obtain a copy.

As far as the pool itself is concerned, the requirements for sub-aqua activities are very modest. The absolute minimum dimensions are

FIG. 1.22.   View of diving pit 6·8 m deep at Swansea Leisure Centre, used for sub-aqua activities (Courtesy: Cement and Concrete Association).

5·00 m × 3·60 m with a minimum water depth of 1·50 m (16 ft 5 in × 11 ft 10 in × 4 ft 10 in). If it is decided to provide a special pool for aqualung divers, then a pool with a stepped floor and a free-formed shape and a depth of at least 3·50 m (11 ft 6 in) would be satisfactory. From this it can be seen that all public pools and many club, hotel and school pools are suitable for a limited amount of sub-aqua activities (see Fig. 1.21). The new leisure centre at Swansea contains a diving pit with a water depth of 6·8 m (23 ft) for sub-aqua use (Fig. 1.22).

VANDALISM

One of the most vexing and difficult problems facing baths managers at the present time is vandalism. This does not seem to follow any set pattern or occur in a particular type of area or district. The possibility of vandalism must be kept in mind when the designer is considering his 'details' and finishings. It has already been emphasised that close liaison and exchange of views between the designer and the baths manager during the preliminary design stage is of the utmost importance, but the problem of vandalism makes this contact essential when final details are being worked out.

The use of closed-circuit television has been suggested, but the author has not come across its actual use in the United Kingdom in a public swimming establishment. It is not possible to list all the items which can usefully be given special consideration to prevent or reduce damage by vandals, but detailed discussions with the baths manager will yield extremely useful results. The following are some of the many items involved:

Theft-proof plugs to wash-hand basins.
Spring-loaded taps.
Press-button showers, or foot-operated showers, at preselected temperature, operating for a fixed time.
All pipework to fittings to be either behind a removable grill (but no wing-nuts); or securely fixed to battens so that the pipes cannot be pulled off the wall.
Soap containers to be of the recessed type.
Toilet paper to be the folded type in cheap plastic holders.
Towels in toilets should be omitted and hot-air hand driers installed. These should be either recessed into the wall or fixed to both wall and floor.
Items like hair driers must be similarly fixed.
The most simple type of fastening on the toilet doors should be provided, but it must be robust and metal should always be in contact with metal.

In the changing cubicles the provision of plain seats and a simple hook with the top section sufficiently short for it not to provide a hand-hold for swinging or pulling. Duck-boards are not recommended. Cubicle doors must be of the most simple and robust type; an alternative is a strong curtain with the overhead rail sufficiently strong to resist swinging on.

It is advisable for all parts of the changing area, including the showers, and toilets (except the WCs) to be open to the general view of the people using the accommodation. Vandals are only likely to operate when they are out of sight of the general adult public.

Part 2: *External Works—Paving and Landscaping*

GENERAL CONSIDERATIONS

External works on a large scale are only likely to be required for major projects such as leisure and sports centres. Nevertheless some external works are needed for even a small private pool, and it is important to remember that good landscaping can transform a rather dull uninteresting site into an area of great beauty. The advice of an experienced landscape architect is always worth having.

As most open-air pools are either wholly or partly below ground level, the excavated material can be used to adjust levels and to form terraces and banks. On a sloping site the pool may be constructed into the side of the 'hill', but in such a case care must be taken to ensure that the whole of the pool is supported on solid undisturbed ground. The construction of a pool with the floor designed as a suspended slab, supported on columns or load-bearing walls, can be very expensive and for this reason is seldom adopted. Exceptions are large covered pools with plant rooms below, and this is discussed in Chapter 4.

Another important point to be considered when forming embankments is that the pool and surrounding area should receive the maximum amount of sun and be sheltered from the wind, particularly from the north and east. Natural depressions in the ground or previously excavated areas can be very useful in saving excavation for the pool. When the site is sloping or is in any way unsymmetrical, the construction of a free-formed pool instead of a rectangular one can be advantageous and may assist in producing an attractive layout. Consideration can be given to a circular pool for private houses, clubs and hotels.

It is always advisable for the edge of the pool and perimeter paving to be raised slightly—say 150 mm (6 in) above the level of the adjoining ground—because this helps to prevent insects crawling into the pool and will generally result in improved cleanliness of the pool. The paved walkways

53

and other areas around the pool should be laid to an adequate cross-fall; a minimum of 20 mm in 1 m, away from the pool, is recommended. This is to prevent rain water, and water used for washing down the paving, draining back into the pool. The use of precast concrete slabs or natural stone flags is preferable to *in situ* concrete when the paving is laid on filled areas. The precast or stone slabs can be laid on a sand bed or a layer of weak lime mortar and left with open (ungrouted) joints. In this way they can be easily taken up, the levels of the bed adjusted, and the slabs relaid should the surface become uneven owing to settlement of the filling below. The problems of settlement of any made-up areas which have to be paved are very real ones. Many owners are bitterly disappointed when they find their beautifully laid-out terraces have developed a surface rather like a choppy sea with a considerable amount of cracking. This trouble can be avoided by following the procedure outlined above and by those responsible for the job giving a clear explanation to the client. Some detailed recommendations for paving and walling will now be given.

EXTERNAL PAVING

External paving really consists of two types, the paving immediately next to the pool on which the bathers will walk and that further away, which may form part of a terrace to a cafe, and also includes car-parking areas. Paving around the perimeter of the pool and any area on which bathers will walk with wet feet should have a non-slip surface. There is a wide choice of materials on the market, which include precast concrete, reconstructed stone, natural stone, *in situ* and precast terrazzo, ceramic tiles, clay bricks, synthetic rubber tiles and man-made fibre coverings of various types. It should be noted that terazzo becomes very slippery when it is wet and to give a non-slip surface to terrazzo will completely alter its appearance. For edging of paved areas, stone setts, precast concrete and clay bricks can all be used.

The method of laying slabs, tiles and bricks to carry foot traffic is basically the same, namely:

(a) The top soil should be removed down to the correct level.
(b) A layer of sand or granular material should be evenly spread on the levelled surface of the natural ground. This is compacted by rolling or other means to a thickness of 50–75 mm (2–3 in). If granular material is used, this should be 'blinded' with about 25 mm (1 in) of sand.
(c) The paving slabs or tiles should be laid either direct on the compacted bed or on 25–40 mm ($1-1\frac{1}{2}$ in) of a weak cement–lime

mortar, with mix proportions of about 1 part cement, 1 part lime and 5 parts sand. A masonry cement can also be used instead of the cement–lime, in the proportions of 1 part masonry cement to 6 parts sand. Full bedding is recommended rather than the 'five-point' or mortar pat method (this latter consists of supporting the slab on 4 or 5 pats of mortar). If the slabs are fully bedded, there is much less chance of them cracking owing to a sudden load coming on an unsupported part of the slab. The slabs or tiles can be laid with close joints, say 3–6 mm ($\frac{1}{8}$–$\frac{1}{4}$ in). The joints can be filled with mortar or slurried over with a very thin mortar, or just left open, when laid on compacted fill. Coloured mortar can be used for the joining mortar if required.

When laying and jointing coloured flags and tiles, great care must be exercised to prevent grout or mortar getting on the coloured surfaces of the paving. If the paving is stone or concrete, the mortar or grout will be absorbed to some extent into the surface and it may be impossible to completely remove the stains. With quarry or other glazed clay tiles, the mortar can be removed by gentle chipping followed by a dilute acid wash, but this must be done in small areas at a time.

Terrazzo, *in situ* and in the form of tiles, is very attractive but, used as paving around and in the close vicinity of swimming pools, it is liable to become slippery after a short time and is therefore not very practical for use around the pool. Methods for dealing with slippery paving are discussed in Chapter 8.

If the terrazzo is used away from the pool where it will not be walked on by bare feet, it can be considered an excellent and durable floor surfacing and most attractive in appearance. Terrazzo tiles are laid in the same way as any other precast tiles, but a few notes on *in situ* terrazzo will be given.

The laying of *in situ* terrazzo is highly specialised work and should be entrusted only to experienced contractors. It consists of white Portland cement and marble chippings. Sometimes pigments are added to the white cement, and marble of different colours can be used. Specialist firms seldom use coloured cements. The size of the marble chippings varies from 3 to 5 mm ($\frac{1}{8}$ to $\frac{3}{16}$ in). The terrazzo is laid on a cement/sand screed to a thickness of about 20 mm ($\frac{3}{4}$ in), in bays which can vary in size from 1·0 to 7·0 m² (10 to 70 ft²); the bays should be as square as possible and separated by strips of ebonite, brass or aluminium. The mix proportions are 1 part cement to 2 or 3 parts of marble chippings. Natural sand is never used. The mix is spread and compacted in the bays by a screeding board and then a few hours later it is compacted further by rolling. It appears to be the accepted practice among terrazzo layers not to cure the freshly laid terrazzo, and this may account to some extent for the number of floors which exhibit serious cracking and crazing. About three days after laying, the first coarse grinding is carried out and this is followed a few days later by a second finer grinding and polishing. Final treatment consists of the application of a special sealant and polish.

ACCESS-WAYS FOR VEHICLES AND CAR-PARKING AREAS

These areas can be surfaced with *in situ* concrete (plain or reinforced), concrete block paving, clay brick paving or 'black-top' (cold rolled asphalt). If *in situ* concrete is used, it should be air-entrained to resist the effects of frost and de-icing salts; and the bay layout, thickness, weight of reinforcement and mix proportions should all be clearly specified. Detailed advice can be obtained from the Cement and Concrete Association (see Appendix 3).

The use of high-quality and high-strength concrete paving blocks for roads, car parks and pedestrian ways has been popular on the Continent for

FIG. 1.23.   View of external block paving (Courtesy: Cement and Concrete Association).

many years and has now been introduced into the United Kingdom by the Cement and Concrete Association. Complete details, including specification for the blocks and information on layout and construction, are given in the publications of the Association (see the Bibliography at the end of this chapter). The blocks can be rectangular or 'shaped' and can be obtained in a limited range of colours. The paving blocks are laid by hand on a bed of sand compacted to a depth of 50 mm (2 in), and then vibrated to their final level by a plate vibrator. After initial vibration, sand is brushed over the surface and vibrated into the joints. Edge restraint is required in the form of a kerb. Figure 1.23 shows an area of block paving.

GARDEN WALLS

GENERAL

Garden walls are of two basic types, earth-retaining walls and free-standing walls. Both types of wall should have a proper foundation resting on solid undisturbed ground. If the depth of 'made-up' ground is considerable, then the wall can be supported on a ground beam which in turn is carried on piers, as shown in Fig. 1.24. When excavating foundations, care should be taken to prevent soil getting mixed into the concrete when the latter is being placed in the trench.

The concrete mix proportions for ground beams are:

1 part ordinary Portland cement, 2 parts damp concreting sand and 3 parts coarse aggregate (20 mm = 3/4 in).

For strip foundations and piers to carry ground beams a rather leaner mix can be used:

1 part ordinary Portland cement, $2\frac{1}{2}$ parts damp concreting sand and 4 parts coarse aggregate (20 mm). A 1:6 all-in aggregate can also be used.

EARTH-RETAINING WALLS

These walls can be vertical or sloped back at an angle. Vertical walls generally have to be thicker than battered walls as they have to resist a greater overturning force. An approximate rule for vertical walls is that the thickness should not be less than about 35 % of the height measured from the top of the foundation to the top of the wall. This type of wall resists the forces exerted by the soil at the back, by its mass (weight); that is why it has to be comparatively thick. It is advisable for 'weep' holes to be provided in the bottom of the wall to help drain the ground. This is shown in Fig. 1.24(b). The dimensions of the foundation concrete can be taken as:

Width: thickness of wall + 300 mm (12 in).
Depth: 200 mm(8 in).

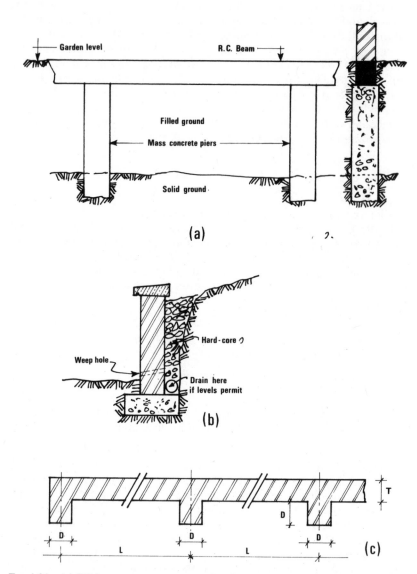

Fig. 1.24. (a) RC beam on mass concrete piers for support of garden wall. (b) Garden retaining wall. (c) Plan of free-standing wall with piers.

Solid dense aggregate concrete blocks can be used for garden retaining walls up to about 750 mm (2 ft 6 in) high, provided the blocks are 200 mm (8 in) thick. Hollow concrete blocks 200 mm (8 in) thick, with the hollows filled with *in situ* fine concrete, can be used for walls up to about 1·10 m (3 ft 6 in) high. Special split blocks can be obtained which can hardly be distinguished from natural stone, and these make very attractive walls.

Higher walls can be built using hollow concrete blocks which are reinforced vertically and horizontally with the voids filled with fine *in situ* concrete. The vertical reinforcement must be securely anchored into the concrete foundation. There are empirical methods for design for this type of wall, and advice can be obtained from the Cement and Concrete Association.

Walls constructed of bricks and blocks and natural stone should be provided with an adequate throated coping. This can be in precast or *in situ* concrete or natural stone. Apart from giving a finished appearance to the wall, a coping serves the important purpose of protecting the wall from water penetration from above, which can eventually lead to deterioration of the wall. Also, by directing the water away from the face of the wall, it helps to prevent unsightly staining.

EMBANKMENTS

The sides of embankments can be supported or secured from erosion by retaining walls, soil stabilisation techniques, correct drainage or simple planting.

During the past few years, man-made fibre fabrics have come onto the market which have proved very useful in stabilising slopes, either on a permanent basis or temporarily until vegetation has had time to take root and grow over the slope. These fibre mats are proprietary materials: some of the best-known are 'Terram' and 'Paraweb', manufactured by ICI; 'Typar', by Dupont; the Celanese 'Mirafi'; and 'Soda-spun', by Revertex.

A relatively new method of supporting embankments is 'reinforced earth'. This technique seems to have been originally developed by Henri Vidal and certain features of the process have been patented by Vidal and other engineers. The Department of the Environment in the United Kingdom have produced their own system and this is being used on a number of motorway projects. At the time of writing there is a court action between Henri Vidal's Reinforced Earth Company and the British Government.

The basic concept of the DoE design is that if reinforcing elements capable of withstanding tension are inserted into a soil, the soil is then able to withstand both compressive and tensile forces. The soil used is generally granular and the horizontal reinforcement can be heavily galvanised steel strips or stainless steel flats. A number of plastics are also under trial to

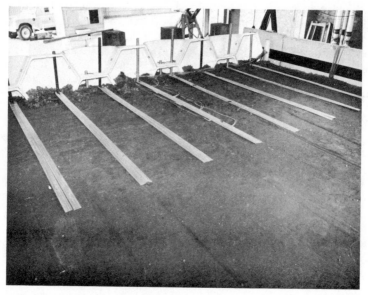

FIG. 1.25. View of an experimental assembly of facing units and ties for reinforced earth (Courtesy: DoE Transport and Road Research Laboratory).

replace steel for this horizontal reinforcement. To contain and stabilise the face of the embankment, the following types of thin facing can be used; glass-reinforced cement, glass-reinforced plastic and precast concrete panels. Figure 1.25 shows the DoE method of construction.

FREE-STANDING WALLS
General Considerations
Boundary walls, walls to act as wind-breaks, screen walls (Fig. 1.26) and walls to divide one part of a garden from another are usually known as 'free-standing' walls. Although these walls do not carry any external loads (as do the walls of a building or an earth-retaining wall), they have to resist wind pressure, and must therefore be properly built on a sound foundation. It is not uncommon for poorly built walls to be blown down by gale-force winds.

Walls can be built in concrete blocks, clay bricks and natural stone. The most commonly used materials are the first two, and the notes which follow apply to these.

The most important quality which the wall must possess is stiffness. Also, it must be built in such a way that expansion and contraction (whether caused by temperature or by moisture changes in the walling material) will

FIG. 1.26.   View of private pool showing pierced concrete blockwork for screen walls
(Courtesy: Cement and Concrete Association).

not result in cracks. Stiffness can be achieved by adequate thickness, piers
and cross-walls. The relationship of thickness, length and height is
important, and there are a large number of possible combinations of these
three factors.

Concrete Block Walls
A few combinations of thickness, length and height, are set out in Table 1.9,
which should be read in conjunction with Fig. 1.24(c). The height of the wall
is the height from the top of the foundation concrete to the top of the wall.

When building in concrete blocks, it must be remembered that they are a
different material from clay bricks, and should not be looked upon as just

TABLE 1.9   (see Fig. 1.24c)
Concrete block walls

Thickness of wall, T	Width of pier, D	Length of wall panel (max.), L	Height of wall (max.), H
100 mm (4 in)	100 mm (4 in)	1·80 m (6 ft)	900 mm (3 ft)
150 mm (6 in)	150 mm (6 in)	2·50 m (8 ft)	1·50 m (4 ft 10 in)

clay bricks of a different size. For this reason rather different building methods should be used if cracking is to be avoided. The moisture and thermal movements of the two materials (clay and concrete) are quite different, and with concrete block walls straight vertical joints should be provided for the full height of the wall at intervals along its length. The distance apart of these vertical movement joints can be taken as twice the height of the wall measured from the top of the foundation concrete. However, for low walls not exceeding about 1·25 m in height a distance of 3·0 m (10 ft) between movement joints would be satisfactory.

To improve stability at the movement joints it is advisable to provide dowels in the bed joints. The dowels can be galvanised mild steel flats, about 300 mm (1 ft) long and 50 mm (2 in) wide. Before being laid, each dowel should be coated with grease over half its length to debond it from the mortar. Care must be taken to ensure that all debonded halves are on the same side of the joint.

Very attractive screen walls of 'pierced' concrete blocks are often used in landscaped gardens. The wind resistance of such walls is greatly reduced compared with solid walls, as about 50 % of the wall area is 'open'.

Clay Brick Walls
Table 1.10 illustrates two possible combinations of thickness, length and height for free-standing clay brick walls. A reader who wishes to construct any appreciable length of this type of wall in clay bricks should obtain a copy of the Brick Development Association's Technical Note, details of which are given in the Bibliography.

TABLE 1.10 (see Fig. 1.24c)
Clay brick walls

Thickness of wall (nominal), T	Width of pier (nominal), D	Length of wall panel (max.), L	Height of wall (max.), H
100 mm (4 in)	100 mm (4 in)	1·80 m (6 ft)	900 mm (3 ft)
100 mm (4 in)	225 mm (9 in)	1·80 m (6 ft)	1·80 m (6 ft)

When laying and jointing coloured concrete and natural or artificial stone paving or blocks, and clay bricks, care should be exercised to prevent mortar or grout getting onto the surface. If this does occur, it should be wiped off immediately, because unless this is done, it may be impossible to remove the stain at a later date. This is because the surface is absorbent. Mortar and grout droppings may be easier to remove from clay bricks than from concrete or stone, as a blow-lamp can often be used. This dries out the mortar/grout completely, which can then be brushed off; with care, no harm is done to the bricks. For advice on removing stains from concrete, reference should be made to the booklet issued by the Cement and Concrete Association; however, it is always advisable to try out the proposed method on a small area first.

The quantity of mortar required for building walls of concrete blocks and clay bricks is given below. The figures are approximate and include an allowance for waste.

Concrete blocks, 400 mm × 200 mm × 100 mm (16 in × 8 in × 4 in) with joints 10 mm ($\frac{3}{8}$ in) wide require about 9 litres of mortar per m^2 (about 0·25 ft^3/yd^2).
On the other hand, clay brick walls with 10 mm ($\frac{3}{8}$ in) wide joints require about 25 litres of mortar per m^2 (about 0·75 ft^3/yd^2).

From the above it can be seen that concrete blocks require far less mortar per unit of area than do clay bricks; because of their large size, they are also much quicker to lay.

Walls Without Mortar Joints
It is now possible to build concrete block walls without using mortar in the joints. This technique was developed in the United States and was introduced into the United Kingdom recently. The blocks should be good-quality Class A blocks to BS 2028; they are laid dry, and then rendered on both sides with a single coat of glass-fibre-reinforced cement–sand mortar, prepared and sold under the name of 'Fibrocem Blockmix'. The rendering ensures that the wall is stable; full details can be obtained from the Blue Circle Industries. The use of this material in a parapet wall is shown in Fig. 1.27.

Coloured Concrete and Mortar
Many clients and architects specify coloured concrete and/or mortar. Until a few years ago pigmented cements could be obtained on the retail market in the United Kingdom, but this is no longer the case. Therefore, for the majority of work, pigments have to be mixed with the cement on site, and then the pigmented cement is batched with the aggregate and water in the usual way. This procedure is unlikely to give as good results as when the pigment was ground in with the cement at the works. Pigments for cement can be obtained in a limited range of colours; greens and blues are more expensive and also more likely to 'fade' when used externally.

When using coloured concrete and mortar, it is important to realise that complete uniformity of colour cannot be obtained. This is due to small variations in mix proportions, compaction and finishing, which all affect

FIG. 1.27.   View of parapet wall and fascia finished in Fibrocem Blockmix (Courtesy:
Cement Marketing Co.).

the light-reflecting qualities of the hardened concrete/mortar. It is by
reflected light that all normal objects are seen.

If it is intended to specify black concrete or mortar, then it is most
desirable to seek expert advice from such an organisation as the Cement
and Concrete Association. Even though the pigmented cement may look
quite black, when it is mixed with water and aggregate, it is unlikely that
resulting material will have a colour other than a dark grey. Careful
selection of coarse and fine aggregate is essential and for important work
samples should be made. Portland cement products when damp sometimes
leach lime onto the surface, and on 'black' concrete this can appear as
unsightly greyish stains.

BIBLIOGRAPHY

AMATEUR SWIMMING ASSOCIATION, *Notes for the Guidance of Designers*, London,
    1967, p. 25.

Anon., Reinforced earth walling. *DoE Construction*, **12** (Dec. 1974) 7, 8.

Anon., *Handbook of sport and recreational buildings*, Section 1, Technical Study 1, *Architects J.*, 27 July 1977.

Anon., *Briefing Guide–Swimming Pools*. AJ Information Library, *Architects J.*, Aug., Sept., Oct. and Nov. 1977.

Brick Development Association, Free-standing brick walls. *Technical Note*, Vol. 1, No. 5, July 1972, p. 8.

British Standards Institution, Code of Practice CP 96: *Access for the Disabled to Buildings*.

British Standards Institution, Code of Practice CP 121: *Walling*, 1973; 121–201: *Masonry Walls;* and 121–202 *Masonry Rubble Walls.*

British Sub-aqua Club, *Pools for Sub-aqua Use*, 1974.

Cement and Concrete Association, Chemical methods of removing stains from concrete, 45.015, 1968, 7 pp.

Clarke, R. G., Problems experienced with school swimming pools in the Easthampstead Rural District. *Baths Service* (June 1970) 144–146.

Council for National Co-operation in Aquatics, *Swimming Pools—A Guide to Their Planning, Design and Operation*, Hoffman Publications Inc., Florida, 1972.

Department of the Environment, *The Building Regulations* 1976, HMSO, London.

Enoch, M. D., *Concrete for Sports and Play Areas*, Cement and Concrete Association, London, 48.042, 1976, p. 46.

Fabien Dietrich, *Bader Handbuch fur Baderbau und Badewesen*, Georg D. W. Callwey, München, 1960, p. 440.

Garden, G. K., *Indoor Swimming Pools*, Canadian Building Digest Division of Building Research, National Research Council, November 1966, CBD 83, pp. 83-1–83-4.

Herraman, T. A., Australian pool design. *Baths Service* (July 1975) 147.

Jeffery, J. A., Design and management of aquatic facilities, Paper presented at Institute of Baths Management Conference, Brighton Sept. 1973.

Laws and Regulations Relating to Swimming Pools, Excerpts from the Californian Health and Safety Code and Californian Administration Code.

Lilley, A. and Collins, J., *Laying Concrete Block Paving*, Cement and Concrete Association, 46.022, Jan. 1976, p. 15.

Lusher, P. E., Indoor swimming pools—recommended safe loading capacities. *J. Inst. Baths Management*, **27**(3) (March 1968) 56–8.

Mildenhall, H. S., *Laying Precast Concrete Paving Slabs*, Cement and Concrete Association, London, 48.033, 1974, p. 11.

National Swimming Liaison Council, Swimming pool floor gradients, Hyde H. P. *Baths Service* (April 1970) 83–5.

National Swimming Pool Institute, *Suggested Minimum Standards for Residential and Public Swimming Pools*, Washington, D.C., 1969.

Perkins, P. H., *Floors—Construction and Finishes*, Cement and Concrete Association, London, 1973, p. 132.

Sports Council, *TUS Bulletin No. 1: Public Indoor Swimming Pools*, HMSO, London, 1973.

Swimming Pool Institute of South Africa, The, *Planning a Domestic Swimming Pool*, Chs. 1–8.

Van Wieringen, D. M. Swimming pools in Amsterdam. Paper presented at Institute of Baths Management Conference, Blackpool, Sept. 1976.

Walter, F., *Sports Centres and Swimming Pools*, The Thistle Foundation, 1971.

CHAPTER 2

Materials Used in the Construction of Swimming Pools and Ancillary Structures

GENERAL CONSIDERATIONS

There is a wide range of materials which can be used in the construction of swimming pools, and this range is constantly increasing as new products come on to the market. Many of the materials are well-known and are in everyday use for the construction of all types of buildings. In the United Kingdom a large number of these materials are covered by British Standard Specifications, and their method of use by Codes of Practice.

Generally, British Standard Specifications lay down basic requirements and tests for specific materials and the tests are often of an 'end product' performance type so as to leave the manufacturer as free as possible in the manufacturing process, provided he uses raw materials of an accepted quality. On the other hand, Codes of Practice tend to concentrate on principles of design and recommended methods of construction for the particular type of work to which they refer. Appendix 1 shows the titles and numbers of the more important Standard Specifications and Codes of Practice. The author considers that notes on the basic properties and appropriate uses of some of these materials will be helpful and these are given in the following pages. Information on methods of manufacture and details of requirements of the relevant British Standard are not included, but may be touched upon in special cases.

CEMENTS

These may be classified as 'Portland' cements and 'non-Portland' cements. As the quantity of non-Portland cements likely to be used in a swimming pool project is very small, this type will only be mentioned very briefly here.

PORTLAND CEMENT (PC): ORDINARY (OPC) AND RAPID-HARDENING (RHPC)

Many 'ordinary' Portland cements manufactured in the United Kingdom comply with the strength requirements of the British Standard (BS 12) for rapid-hardening PC. This fact is important in the construction of water-containing structures because it means that the rate of evolution of heat of hydration is somewhat higher, resulting in slightly higher temperatures in the concrete. This is referred to again in Chapters 3 and 4.

Rapid-hardening Portland cement is similar to ordinary Portland, but it is ground rather finer (the specific surface is usually between 3500 and 4000 cm^2) and sometimes slight adjustments are made to the chemical composition to increase the rate of hardening. It should be noted that the rate of hardening does not depend on the fineness alone and that chemical composition is also important.

SULPHATE-RESISTING PORTLAND CEMENT

This cement is similar in its strength and other physical properties to ordinary Portland cement, but the tricalcium aluminate content (C_3A) must not exceed 3 % in order to comply with the relevant British Standard, BS 4027. It is the tricalcium aluminate in Portland cement which is attacked by sulphates in solution; the chemical compound ettringite is formed and, as the crystals of ettringite are larger than the crystals of C_3A, this expansion has a disruptive and weakening effect on the concrete.

Some types of sulphate-resisting Portland cement have a lower heat of hydration than ordinary Portland cement, and may therefore be considered as a type of low-heat cement. However, this must not be assumed without confirmation by the manufacturers. Calcium chloride must not be used with sulphate-resisting Portland cement; in fact, it is generally advisable to consult the manufacturer before using any admixture with this cement.

ULTRA HIGH EARLY STRENGTH PORTLAND CEMENT

This is a Portland cement which was first marketed in the United Kingdom a few years ago under the trade name of 'Swiftcrete'. An Agrément Certificate No. 73/170 has been issued, but there is no British Standard for this cement. It is described by the manufacturers as an extremely finely ground Portland cement which contains a higher proportion of gypsum than ordinary Portland, but otherwise it complies with BS 12; it contains no other additives. The specific surface of the cement is between 7000 and 9000 cm^2/g, compared with an average of 3400 cm^2/g for OPC and 4300 cm^2/g for an average RHPC. The Agrément Certificate confirms that tests have shown that the strength at 24 h is not less than that of an RHPC at seven days. The cement is appreciably more expensive than OPC, but this is unlikely to be important in those special cases where very high early strength is required.

PORTLAND MASONRY CEMENT

This cement is used for jointing mortar for building blocks, bricks and masonry; it can also be used for the second and subsequent coats of external rendering. The use of this cement for these purposes obviates the addition of lime to a cement–sand mortar; for example, a mortar may be either $1:1:5$ (cement:lime:sand) or $1:4\frac{1}{2}$ (masonry cement:sand). Masonry cement contains additives to impart workability and improve water retention, and is particularly useful in cases where lime is not required on the site for other purposes than the mortar. The British Standard is BS 5224.

WHITE AND COLOURED PORTLAND CEMENTS

White Portland cement is a true Portland cement and complies with the relevant British Standard for ordinary Portland cement. The basic materials used in the manufacture of these white cements are carefully selected (the clay is a white china clay), and they contain negligible amounts of manganese and iron; the manufacturing process is controlled so that the resulting colour is white instead of grey.

Coloured Portland cements (other than white and pastel shades) consist of ordinary Portland with a pigment ground in at the works. The pigments used are covered by the requirements of BS 1014: Pigments for Cement and Concrete. Coloured Portland cements are now covered by BS 12. Coloured Portland cements are not at present available on the retail market in the United Kingdom.

NON-PORTLAND-TYPE CEMENTS

High-alumina Cement (HAC)

In the past four years or so there has been controversy in the United Kingdom on the structural use of HAC, and a considerable amount of ill-informed comment appeared in the national press and in some technical journals.

High-alumina cement differs fundamentally from Portland cement, as it consists predominantly of calcium aluminates. It is a much darker colour than OPC and RHPC, but the lighter shades of HAC may approach the colour of the darker shades of sulphate-resisting Portland cement.

The setting time is similar to that of OPC, but the rate of gain of strength is very rapid: it reaches about 80% of its 'ultimate' strength in 24 h, compared with Portland, which reaches about 80–85% of its practical ultimate strength in 28 days. The rapid increase in strength is accompanied by a rapid evolution of heat of hydration. This has advantages and disadvantages. It is extremely useful when working in low temperatures, and it enables emergency repairs to be carried out within a short period, e.g. over a weekend. Wet curing is essential and the concrete must be placed in relatively thin layers so that the heat generated can be dissipated quickly.

Probably the most controversial matter relating to HAC is 'conversion'. Published work on the subject shows that the effect of conversion on the strength and durability of the concrete depends largely on the rate at which it takes place; this in turn is determined mainly by the water/cement (w/c) ratio, the temperature during the maturing period and the environment in which the concrete exists during its working life. The original water/cement ratio will largely determine the strength of the concrete after conversion. Unpublished work by D. E. Shirley, a report by French and others in the journal *Concrete* (August 1971) and a report by C. M. George in 1975 all suggest that the phenomenon of conversion can be allowed for in the mix design procedure. A further point in connection with conversion is that after the minimum point has been reached, a high-quality concrete with a low w/c ratio will start to increase in strength. It should be noted that about 80 % or more of HAC is used for refractory concrete where structural strength may be of little significance.

For high strength and long-term durability, including chemical resistance, it is generally considered that a minimum cement content of $400 \, kg/m^3$ ($670 \, lb/yd^3$) and a maximum w/c ratio of 0.4 is required. High-quality HAC concrete exhibits improved resistance to sulphates and certain dilute acids, compared with Portland cement concrete. Such concrete is very durable in sea-water.

For further information on this cement and concrete made from it, the reader should refer to the Bibliography at the end of this chapter.

It is most unlikely that this cement would be used in the construction of swimming pools and ancillary buildings. However, it could be useful for mortar for bedding and jointing tiles, and for screeds and rendering in sea-water pools and possibly for pools containing spa waters, but before deciding on its use the advice of the manufacturers should be sought.

Supersulphated Cement
The first British standard for this cement was issued in 1968 and is BS 4248. The cement is made from blast furnace slag and contains calcium carbonate and calcium sulphate. It offers greater resistance than Portland cement to attack by sulphates in solution and many dilute acids. However, it has a low heat of hydration and is sensitive to the effect of low temperature. Special care is needed in mixing and curing. At the time of writing, this cement is no longer made in the United Kingdom but it can be imported from the Continent.

COMPARISON BETWEEN PORTLAND CEMENT STANDARDS IN THE UNITED KINGDOM AND THE UNITED STATES

International tendering is now much more common than it used to be; contract documents are prepared in one country for projects to be executed in another, by contractors from a third country. All major construction projects use large quantities of Portland cement and therefore the author felt that some information on United Kingdom and the United States cements would be useful. It must be realised that detailed comparison is very difficult owing to differences in the requirements of the National

TABLE 2.1

Type of Cement	ASTM No. and Type (USA)	BS No. (UK)
Ordinary Portland	C.150–67 Type I	BS 12
Rapid-hardening Portland	C.150–67 Type III	BS 12
Sulphate-resisting Portland	C.150–67 Type V	BS 4027
Sulphate-resisting/low-heat Portland	C.150–67 Type II	No equivalent
Low-heat Portland	C.150–67 Type IV	BS 1370
Air-entraining and various	C.175–67 Types IA, IIA & IIIA	No equivalent cements

Standards, in the raw materials and in the methods of test. However, approximate equivalence is shown in Table 2.1. It should be clearly understood that, for example a sulphate-resisting Portland cement to BS 4027 is not the exact equivalent of a cement to US standard ASTM C 150–67, Type V, but, in use in good-quality concrete, they would perform the same functions equally well.

AGGREGATES FOR CONCRETE

There are two basic types of aggregate for structural concrete:

(a) Aggregates from natural sources, which include crushed quarried rock, pit and river gravels, and sea-dredged shingle.
(b) Artificial lightweight aggregates such as expanded and sintered clays and shales and PFA (pulverised fuel ash).

The author does not know of any water-retaining structures in the United Kingdom constructed with lightweight aggregates, but this material is being used to an increasing extent for medium-strength structural concrete for buildings; it is therefore useful for pool-halls and ancillary buildings.

AGGREGATES FROM NATURAL SOURCES
The characteristics of crushed rocks, pit and river gravels are so well known that they will not be discussed here, except to say that the relevant British Standard is BS 882/1201. However, the increasing use of sea-dredged aggregates in the United Kingdom has caused some controversy, and so detailed comments will be given. The two important factors in sea-dredged aggregates are the chloride content and the shell content, and there is a divergence of views among architects and engineers on the significance of both.

Sea-water in temperate climates contains about 35 000 ppm (mg/litre) of total dissolved solids, of which about 60% is sodium chloride. It is the chloride content which is important in reinforced concrete, as the chloride ions are aggressive to the steel reinforcement. Chloride can be calculated from sodium chloride:

$NaCl = 23 + 35 \cdot 5 = 58 \cdot 5$
Therefore % of $Cl = 35 \cdot 5 \div 58 \cdot 5 \times 100 = 60\%$

Information on the limitation of chloride content of aggregates and concrete is given in the section on Admixtures.

Regarding the shell content, this can be important if the shells are large (in the coarse aggregate) or flat and elongated, or very fine (in the fine aggregate). The large shell can adversely affect durability and appearance for fair-faced work, while the poorly shaped fine shell can increase the water demand of the mix, resulting in lower strength for the same workability. The requirements for limiting the shell content vary, but in the United Kingdom the following figures would be generally considered reasonable:

	Max. shell content
Coarse aggregate	
38 mm ($1\frac{1}{2}$ in)	2%
20 mm ($\frac{3}{4}$ in)	5%
10 mm ($\frac{3}{8}$ in)	15%
Fine aggregate	30%

It is, of course, better if the aggregates are washed in fresh water, but this is not essential provided the chloride content limit mentioned above is not exceeded.

ARTIFICIAL LIGHTWEIGHT AGGREGATES
These are usually expanded sintered clays and shales and pulverised fuel ash (PFA). For use in the United Kingdom they should comply with BS 3797;

methods of sampling and testing are covered by BS 3681. These aggregates will make perfectly satisfactory structural concrete having a minimum compressive strength at 28 days of up to $28\,N/mm^2$ ($4000\,lbf/in^2$). The special features of these aggregates, namely light weight and good thermal insulating properties, are useful in the superstructure but are generally not important in the structural shell of a swimming pool.

STAINLESS STEEL

Stainless steel is used for many fixtures in and around swimming pools. There are three basic groups of stainless steel, martensitic, ferritic, and austenitic. Of these the austenitic is the most widely used for swimming pool work. Austenitic steel is an alloy of iron, chromium and nickel, and two types in this group contain a small percentage of molybdenum. The British Steel Corporation recommend the use of austenitic type 316 S16 in the pool itself and its surroundings. Stainless steel of the correct type is very resistant to corrosion, but if it is intended to be used in highly saline water, the advice of the BSC, Stainless Steel Division, should be sought. Mild steel in contact with stainless steel may suffer accelerated corrosion, as it may be anodic to the stainless steel. Therefore special care should be taken when fixing stainless steel fittings into reinforced concrete. References can be made to the Corrosion Advice Bureau of the British Steel Corporation, or the Building Research Station.

NON-FERROUS METALS

A limited number of non-ferrous metals are used in fixtures and fittings in swimming pools and ancillary structures.

PHOSPHOR-BRONZE AND GUNMETAL

Bronze is a copper–tin alloy, and phosphor-bronze contains phosphorus in the form of copper phosphide. It is resistant to conditions which are corrosive to ferrous metals. Gunmetal is bronze with about 9 % tin, and the same general remarks apply.

COPPER

Copper is resistant to most conditions met with in construction of buildings. It is not corroded by Portland cement concrete unless chlorides are present in the concrete. Copper is cathodic to steel and therefore, if the two metals are in contact in the presence of moisture, the steel is likely to corrode while the copper will be protected. Owing to the unauthorised use of calcium chloride as an accelerator in concrete and mortar, the Copper

Development Association recommend that piping buried in the floor slab or screed should be sheathed with PVC. Copper has a high coefficient of expansion, about double that of concrete, and for heating and hot-water pipes this must be allowed for in the pipework design. Ordinary moist air produces a thin coating of green basic sulphate on the surface. This is sometimes called verdigris, but the latter is more correctly the basic acetate formed by action of acetic acid on copper.

ALUMINIUM

If unanodised aluminium is fixed in direct contact with damp concrete, it is likely to be attacked by the caustic alkalis in the cement. A thick coating of bituminous paint or other suitable protective layer should be used. Anodising improves the durability, resistance to corrosion and aesthetic appearance of aluminium. Anodising consists of the imposition on the metal of a thick coating of the metallic oxide, which is built up in layers by a special process. The oxide film can be pigmented and the surface is normally sealed by immersion in hot water containing chromates. Generally aluminium is anodic to steel but certain alloys of aluminium may be cathodic; therefore care must be exercised if the two metals are likely to be in direct contact.

ADMIXTURES

An admixture is a chemical compound which is added to concrete, mortar or grout, while it is being mixed, in order to change some property of the mix. Admixtures can be very useful when properly used, but they should only be specified when really required to fulfil a particular purpose and should not be added to any cement, except ordinary and rapid-hardening Portland cement, without the approval of the manufacturer of the cement. The five main purposes for which admixtures are used are:

(a) To accelerate the setting of the concrete, mortar or grout.
(b) To accelerate the hardening.
(c) To increase the workability.
(d) To retard the setting.
(e) To entrain air in the mix.

Reference can be made to BS 5075: Concrete Admixtures.

ACCELERATORS

(a) It is sometimes necessary to speed up considerably the rate of setting of grout or mortar (and less frequently concrete), generally for repair work and stopping leaks in concrete walls and floors.

Silicates, carbonates and chlorides are used for this purpose, and with some compounds the setting times can be reduced to a few seconds. The durability and strength of some formulations is poor, and this aspect should be looked into in important jobs.

(b) Admixtures to accelerate the rate of hardening are becoming increasingly popular for use in cold weather. The subject of cold weather concreting is dealt with in some detail in Chapter 3. These accelerators as they are called, are mostly based on calcium chloride as the active ingredient, and when they are used two important facts must be kept in mind; the first is that calcium chloride is aggressive to steel reinforcement (i.e. the chlorine ions are), and the second is that this compound tends to increase drying shrinkage in concrete, mortar and grout.

Because of the dangers inherent in the use of calcium chloride, there has been intensive research to find substitutes which are technically and economically satisfactory. Calcium formate and sodium carbonate are two such compounds, but apart from their higher cost (compared with $CaCl_2$), there are indications that they are rather less reliable in use. If sodium carbonate is used, a dose of 1 % by weight of cement is likely to be adequate for obtaining both a rapid set and an increase in the rate of gain of strength.

In May 1977 the British Standards Institution issued Amendment No. 3 to Code of Practice CP 110: The Structural Use of Concrete. This amendment virtually forbids the use of chloride-containing admixtures in reinforced and prestressed concrete, and strictly limits the total chloride concentration in marine-dredged aggregates. The Amendment is a very important document and one with which many specifiers, users and manufacturers of accelerating admixtures based on calcium chloride do not agree. The Amendment recommends that admixtures containing chlorides should not be used in prestressed concrete, or in concrete containing embedded metal, unless the chloride content does not exceed 0·03 % by weight of the cement or 2 % by weight of the admixture used, whichever is the greater.

As far as marine aggregates are concerned, the limits imposed on total chloride content of the concrete or mortar arising from the aggregates and all other sources, are:

(a) 0·06 % by weight of the cement in prestressed concrete, structural concrete which is steam-cured, and any concrete made with sulphate-resisting Portland cement or supersulphated cement.

(b) 0·35 % for 95 % of the test results with no result greater than 0·50 % by weight of the cement, in reinforced concrete made with OPC and RHPC, and in plain concrete which contains embedded metal and is made with OPC and RHPC.

PLASTICISERS

Admixtures which are used to improve the workability and cohesion of concrete, mortar and grout can be divided into two main groups:

(1) Lignosulphonates, also known as lignins or soaps. These have the property of reducing the water demand of the mix so that for the same workability less water is required. Alternatively, they give increased workability with a fixed w/c ratio. Generally, the maximum reduction in w/c ratio with constant workability is about 10%.

(2) Finely divided powders, such as PFA, powdered hydrated lime, powdered limestone and bentonite, and Portland cement itself. With a fixed w/c an increase in cement content will improve workability.

SUPERPLASTICISING ADMIXTURES

The use of 'superplasticisers' is comparatively new in the United Kingdom, but these compounds have been used successfully in Japan since about 1967 and in Germany since about 1972. Superplasticisers are chemically distinct and work in a quite different manner compared with normal workability aids as described in the preceding section. The new materials can be used for two purposes:

(a) To produce a concrete which has a 'normal' w/c ratio, i.e. about 0·5, but which possesses extreme workability; in other words, a flowable concrete with a virtually collapse slump.

or

(b) To produce concrete with normal workability, but with a very low w/c ratio, thus imparting high strength.

Research in Japan, Germany and the United Kingdom, including extensive site tests, have shown that the use of these compounds has no injurious effects on the concrete, from the point of view of durability, strength, impermeability and protection of steel reinforcement. For site use there is a distinct danger of segregation, and therefore it is essential for trial mixes to be carried out. In the finally adopted mix the type and source of cement, the type, grading and source of fine and coarse aggregates, and the w/c ratio must exactly follow the accepted trial mix. The maximum workability is only retained for about 30–60 min and then the concrete quickly reverts to normal conditions of slump.

RETARDERS

Retarders, when used in the concrete mix (as opposed to application on the surface of formwork), are intended to slow down the rate of evolution of heat of hydration of the cement. This can be very useful when placing large volumes of concrete, particularly if the mix has to be rich for strength or durability reasons, in hot weather. The reason for this is that high temperatures speed up the chemical action between the water and the cement, thus increasing the rate of evolution of heat of hydration, resulting in a higher temperature in the hardening concrete.

Another occasion when retarders are useful is when there is a delay between the initial mixing (addition of the water) and the final placing and compaction of the concrete. This can happen, for example, when ready-mixed concrete has to be transported a long distance. When this delay is accompanied by a high ambient temperature, the use of a retarder may be essential.

Retarders are usually sugars and similar compounds; borax is also used. The dosage must be strictly controlled, because an overdose may result in the concrete never reaching the required strength. It is generally impractical to estimate in advance the actual period of retardation which will be achieved, and trial mixes under controlled conditions are essential on any important job.

AIR-ENTRAINING AGENTS

These should not be confused with aerating compounds which are used in the production of aerated lightweight concrete. The effect of an entraining agent in a concrete mix is to produce minute bubbles of air, and the dosage should be such that the total air content of the compacted concrete is within the range $4\% \pm 1\frac{1}{2}\%$. The minute bubbles of air alter the pore structure of the concrete, and this has been found to give protection against the effect of frost and temperatures below $0\,°C\,(32\,°F)$. The entrainment of air, however, lowers the compressive strength of the concrete, although this is partly compensated by the fact that most air-entraining agents also act as plasticisers, so that with the same workability the w/c ratio can be reduced. It is recommended that all external paving, especially paving likely to come into contact with de-icing salts or to be subject to frost action, should be air-entrained. This should effectively prevent scaling of the surface.

GENERAL

At the time of going to press there is no British Standard for admixtures for concrete. In the United Kingdom concrete admixtures are seldom added to the cement by the cement makers (Portland masonry cement and extra-rapid-hardening Portland cement are exceptions). However, in the United States it is quite usual for cement manufacturers to include more than one admixture in their cements. It is worth while noticing that when the compound is added to the cement in the factory, it is called an 'additive'; but when it is added at the site, it is known as an 'admixture'.

PULVERISED FUEL ASH (PFA OR FLY-ASH)

Pulverised fuel ash is the residue from the burning of pulverised coal in electricity generating stations. It is a very fine powder—the fineness is similar to that of Portland cement. The main chemical constituents are the oxides of silicon, aluminium and iron, with some carbon. With high-grade PFA the residue of combustible material should not exceed 10 % and may be as low as 2 %. The actual composition, and particularly its pozzolanic characteristics, vary from one power station to another. The effect of the addition of moderate quantities (up to a maximum of 20 % by weight of the cement) to a concrete mix is slightly to increase the workability and reduce the early (28 day) strength. However, the strength at one year may have substantially recovered its original (100 % cement proportion) value. The relevant British Standard is BS 3892.

PFA is marketed by the Electricity Generating Board under an intensive sales campaign. Very large quantities are produced annually in the coal-burning power stations. It is used extensively as filling for embankments and similar work.

CONCRETE BLOCKS FOR WALLS

Concrete blocks are not generally recommended as the structural material for the walls of swimming pools, and there is a detailed discussion on this particular point in Chapter 5. They can, however, be used with confidence in the superstructure and ancillary buildings, as both panel and load-bearing walls.

The British Standard for concrete blocks is BS 2028:1364, and this was completely revised in 1968. Among the many important changes made was the revision of the categories of blocks to provide a considerable increase in the crushing strength; the standard now includes blocks with a minimum crushing strength of 28 N/mm^2 (4000 lb/in^2). Concrete blocks are now established in the United Kingdom as a first-class building material—a position they have held in the United States for many years.

The important thing to remember about concrete blocks is that they are a quite different material from clay blocks, and therefore different design and construction techniques have to be adopted to obtain the best results. Probably the most important of these relates to moisture movements on the dimensional stability of the blocks. This makes it essential for movement joints to be provided in the correct places: unless these joints are properly designed and located, cracking may occur with consequent disappointment on the part of the user. A further point is that concrete blocks are made purposely less dense than *in situ* concrete; otherwise they would be too heavy for handling. Even so, blocks of the highest strength class are quite heavy, and this must be kept in mind.

MORTARS

Until fairly recently mortars were composed of cement, lime and sand, in varying proportions according to the job on which they were used. However, during the past eighteen years or so, new materials have come on to the market; these are masonry cements and admixtures, which modify and improve the quality of the mortar. In the past, little interest was shown in the strength and other properties of building mortars but, owing to the Code of Practice requirements in the United Kingdom for load-bearing brickwork and blockwork (CP 111), and the increased use of this type of construction for high buildings, much greater attention is now paid to the properties of bedding and jointing mortars. Ready-mixed mortars are now available and are used on many jobs, thus eliminating the storage and slaking of lime on the site.

Bedding and jointing mortars must be proportioned to suit the type of blocks and bricks with which they are used. High-strength, rigid mortars are suitable for use only with clay engineering bricks, such as Staffordshire Blues and Southwaters. Ordinary building bricks and concrete blocks should be bedded and jointed in a comparatively weak mortar; a typical mix would be 1 part ordinary Portland cement, 1 part slaked lime and 5 or 6 parts sand. If masonry cement is used, then the mix should be 1 part masonry cement and $4\frac{1}{2}$ or 5 parts sand. Relevant British Standards are BS 4551, BS 4887 and PD 6472.

OTHER MATERIALS

EPOXIDE RESINS

Epoxide resins are one of the most versatile of the 'new' synthetic materials which have entered the building and construction industry in recent years. It is therefore felt that some general information on the materials themselves and their range of uses would be of interest.

Epoxides are synthetic resins produced as a by-product of the petrochemical industry; they are sometimes called 'epoxy' resins. The basic compounds are produced by such firms as Shell Chemicals, the Borden Chemical Company, Bakelite Ltd, Dow Chemicals and CIBA Ltd. These basic compounds are then formulated into the commercial range of epoxide resins, each of which has its own special characteristics. The formulating is carried out by a large number of firms who set out to produce resins with special characteristics to meet the user requirements. Great ingenuity is displayed for the formulators and the range of use of these resins is being continually extended. The resins are still comparatively expensive.

In order to obtain the most suitable resin for a particular job, the user should provide the formulator with as much information as possible. This should include the details of the service conditions and the conditions of temperature and humidity which will exist on site during the application of the resin.

Generally, epoxide resins possess the following characteristics:

(a) Excellent bond to concrete, metals and many other materials.
(b) High compressive, tensile and shear strength.
(c) Toughness.
(d) Good chemical resistance to a wide range of acids and a rather narrower range of alkalis.
(e) Low drying shrinkage.
(f) High rate of gain of strength.
(g) Excellent durability in almost all weather conditions likely to be met in practice.
(h) High coefficient of thermal expansion compared with concrete and steel.
(i) Rather poor fire resistance, compared with concrete and brick.
(j) Unless specially formulated, they must be applied to dry surfaces, and ambient air temperature and relative humidity during application must be kept within quite narrow limits.

The resins are usually two-pack materials, consisting of the basic resin and an accelerator (or activator, as it is sometimes called); the two materials are then thoroughly mixed together before use. Certain special features relating to the mixing and application of these resins may be of interest.

Pot-life
This is the period which can be allowed to elapse after the mixing of the resin and accelerator and the completion of the application of that particular batch. This period can vary from about 30 min to 48 h; it is therefore essential for the user to know beforehand what the pot-life of the resin is.

Hardening
This is the physical setting of the plastic resin and generally takes up to 8 h. As each coat must harden before the next one is applied, knowledge of the hardening characteristics of the resin is of great importance.

Curing
Curing is the joining together (linkage) of the molecules; it is the process which gives the strength and durability characteristics to the resin, and usually takes seven days.

VINYL RESIN PAINTS
These paints consist of polyvinylchloride acetate resins, organic solvents and pigments. They possess considerable resistance to dilute acids and

alkalis and saline water. However, these types of paint must be applied in very thin coats by spray or roller. They are not suitable for application to rough surfaces such as concrete because 6–8 coats may be required to obtain adequate coverage with a smooth finish. The advantage is that the hardened paint films are slightly flexible. Adhesion to bare steel is rather poor, but this can be overcome by the use of a special primer.

POLYURETHANE PAINTS

These paints are a pigmented solution of selected polyesters which are mixed with a curing agent (sometimes called a hardening component) just before use; in other words, the paint is a two-pack material. Polyurethane paints are very resistant to acids and the colours may be rather more resistant to chalking than epoxide resin paints. To improve the bond to bare steel, a special primer is required. Although these paints are very resistant to the penetration of moisture in the hardened (cured) state, they are sensitive to air temperature and humidity during application.

BUTYL RUBBER SHEETING

This material has been described as a copolymer of polyisobutylene with a small percentage of isoprene. It is a tough black flexible sheeting with considerable abrasive resistance. It is used as a watertight membrane in some types of swimming pool construction; these are described in detail in Chapter 5, and in Chapter 8.

The sheets can be joined together by hot vulcanising in the factory (which gives a very strong joint), or by surface adhesives on the site (which results in an appreciably weaker joint). The thickness of the sheets varies from about 0·50 mm to 2·0 mm (1/50 in to 1/12 in). Butyl rubber can be painted by a special paint, but the paint does not bond well to the rubber, and so if the paint film is damaged, large areas are liable to be stripped off.

POLYISOBUTYLENE SHEETING

Polyisobutylene, like butyl rubber, is derived from the petrochemical industry. It appears to have originated in Germany and was first sold in the United Kingdom under the trade names of 'Opanol' and 'Rhepanol'. It is now made under licence in this country and sold as PIB. Although it is closely allied to butyl rubber, many of its physical properties are different. One of these properties is low restitution compared with butyl rubber; this means that, when polyisobutylene is stretched, there is less tendency to regain its original dimensions and so stress is reduced. The abrasive resistance is less than that of butyl rubber. The usual thicknesses are 1 mm, $1\frac{1}{2}$ mm and 2 mm (1/25, 1/16 and 1/12 in).

The material is used as complete watertight lining to swimming pools and is always fully bonded to the base concrete. The joints are made by cold solvent welding in which there is molecular transfer between one sheet and another. This gives a much stronger joint than surface adhesives. It can be painted, but the same remarks apply as to butyl rubber. Details of its use are given in Chapter 5 and in Chapter 8.

JOINT FILLERS AND SEALANTS

These materials are very important in swimming pool shells, in the tiling and mosaic, and in certain parts of the superstructure.

JOINT FILLERS
These are sometimes termed 'back-up' materials. They are used in full movement joints to provide a base for the sealant, and to help prevent the ingress of stones and debris during the construction period. The fillers are normally in sheet form and are made from prepared fibres, cellular rubber and granulated cork bonded with resin. Desirable characteristics include: durability, resilience, the ability to be cut to shape and ease of insertion into the joint. They should also not extrude so as to interfere with the sealing compound when the joint closes.

JOINT SEALANTS
The materials used to seal joints in structures can be divided into two basic groups:

(1) Preformed materials.
(2) *In situ* compounds.

To be satisfactory both groups should possess the following characteristics:

(a) For external use, and in water-retaining structures, the sealant itself must be impermeable.
(b) It must be very durable under the anticipated conditions of use.
(c) It must bond well to the sides of the groove in which it is inserted.
(d) It should preferably be non-toxic and non-tainting when used in contact with swimming pool water, and should not support the growth of fungi and bacteria.
(e) As movement takes place across the joint, the sealant must deform in response to that movement without deterioration.

The sealant is accommodated in a groove, and research in both the United Kingdom and the United States has shown that the shape and dimensions of this 'space' are important in ensuring a satisfactory and durable seal. In general terms, the depth or thickness of the sealant should be about half its width. It is important that the sealant should not bond to the inert filler in the joint. If there is no filler, as in the case of a sealing groove for a contraction joint or stress-relief joint, then the sealant should bond only to the sides of the groove.

Preformed Materials

The majority of these high-grade materials are based on Neoprene and are imported from the United States and the Continent. A preformed sealing strip or gasket requires a very accurately formed joint. When correctly installed, cellular Neoprene strips will remain watertight against pressures up to 1 atm (10 m head; 33 ft). A channel-shaped Neoprene gasket has recently come onto the United Kingdom market; this spans the joint and is fixed with an adhesive primer into grooves cut (or formed) parallel to the sides of the joint. This is shown in Chapters 4 and 8 (Figs. 4.9 and 8.4). One of the great advantages of Neoprene is that it is very durable under a wide range of aggressive conditions. Neoprene is now being replaced by a newer material, EPDM.

In situ Compounds

These sealants can be divided into four types:

(a) Mastics.
(b) Thermoplastics (hot- and cold-applied).
(c) Thermosetting compounds (solvent release).
(d) Thermosetting compounds (chemically curing).

The compounds likely to give satisfactory results in swimming pools and ancillary structures are (b) and (d) above.

Of hot- and cold-applied thermoplastics, the hot-applied are in more general use for external paving and are covered by BS 2499: Hot Applied Sealing Compounds for Concrete Pavements. The movement range which this type can accommodate is small compared with thermosetting chemically curing elastomers. A typical example is a rubber-bitumen. Of the cold-applied, the most popular type for water-retaining structures is a rubber-asphalt.

Thermosetting chemically curing compounds are one- or two-component compounds which cure (mature or harden) by chemical reaction to a solid state from a liquid or semi-liquid. In this group are polysulphides, silicone rubbers, polyurethanes and epoxies. They are resilient and flexible, and the high-grade materials possess good weathering properties. Some, particularly the epoxies and polyurethanes, are inert to a wide range of chemical compounds. The sealants most used in swimming pools are polysulphides and silicone rubbers. As will be discussed in Chapters 6 and 8, the results of using both these sealants (polysulphides and silicone rubbers) under continuous immersion in warm chlorinated water have sometimes been unreliable and disappointing.

BIBLIOGRAPHY

AMERICAN CONCRETE INSTITUTE, Admixtures for concrete, Committee 212. *J. ACI*, **60**(11) (1963) 1481–1526.

AMERICAN CONCRETE INSTITUTE, Guide to joint sealants to concrete structures (Title 67-31). *J. ACI* (July 1970) 489–536.

BRITISH STEEL CORPORATION, *The Corrosion Resistance of Stainless Steels* Booklet No. 2, 1965, p. 16.

BUILDING RESEARCH STATION, *Applications and Durability of Plastics*, Digest No. 69 (2nd Series), April 1966, p. 8.

BUILDING RESEARCH STATION, *Concrete in Sulphate Bearing Soils and Ground Waters*, Digest No. 174, HMSO, London, 1975, p. 4.

CEMENT AND CONCRETE ASSOCIATION, THE, AND CEMENT ADMIXTURES ASSOCIATION, THE, *Superplasticizing Admixtures for Concrete*, London, 1976.

CONCRETE SOCIETY, THE, Admixtures for concrete. *Concrete* (Jan. 1968) 39–46.

CROWDER, J. R., Plastics in domestic and industrial plumbing. Paper presented at the Pipes and Pipelines Engineering Convention, London, 1968, p. 7.

EVERETT, L. H. and TREADAWAY, K. W. J., *The Use of Galvanized Steel Reinforcement in Buildings*, Building Research Station Current Papers CP3/67, London, 1967, p. 10.

FRENCH, P. J. *et al.*, High concrete strengths within the hour. *Concrete* (August 1971) 253, 258.

LEA, F. M., *The Chemistry of Cement and Concrete*, 3rd edn, Edward Arnold Ltd, London, 1970, p. 725.

MIDGLEY, H. G. and MIDGLEY, A., *The conversion of high alumina cement. Mag. Conc. Res.*, **27**(91) (June 1975) 59–77.

PERKINS, P. H., *The Use of Portland Cement Concrete in Sulphate-bearing Ground and Ground Water of Low pH*, Cement and Concrete Association, ADS/30, April 1976, p. 16.

SHIRLEY, D. E., Principles and practice in the use of high alumina cements. *Municipal Engineering*, **145**(4 and 5) 1968.

CHAPTER 3

General Requirements for Concrete Used in Swimming Pool Shells, Superstructures and Ancillary Buildings

GENERAL CONSIDERATIONS

Concrete is the principal material used in the construction of swimming pool shells, and is widely used in the superstructure and associated buildings. All structural concrete has to possess certain essential properties, namely:

Impermeability.
Durability.
Strength.

If the concrete has to form the final finish to the building or part of the building, then additional requirements must be written into the specification.

All these properties can be obtained by correct design of the mix (i.e. by finding the most suitable proportions of cement, aggregates and water, including type and grading of the aggregates), proper mixing, correct placing, compacting and curing.

For the type of structure being considered here, if the mix gives impermeability and durability, then strength should follow automatically, but it should be noted that the opposite is not necessarily so. In other words, the fundamental requirements are the first two items. In the case of the pool shell, owing to the low design stresses normally adopted, the actual strength achieved by the required mix proportions is likely to be appreciably higher than that required by design considerations alone. The term 'strength' is taken to mean the compressive strength as measured on standard test cubes crushed at 7 and 28 days after casting, the 28 day strength being the essential factor. For the pool shell, reference should be made to Section 6 of BS. 5337: The Structural Use of Concrete for Retaining Aqueous Liquids. This in turn refers to Section 6 of CP 110: The Structural Use of Concrete, and to

85

Sections 2, 5 and 6 of CP 114 for reinforced concrete and Sections 2, 4 and 5 of CP 115 for prestressed concrete.

The author does not propose to quote from these Codes, as the requirements should be read as printed in the Codes themselves. It is important to remember that the 'minimum' strength (called the 'characteristic' strength in CP 110) is a statistical minimum and not an absolute one. It is unfortunate that many disputes arise on site due to confusion over this expression. Another fruitful source of dispute is the relationship between the strength of test cubes made in accordance with BS 1881: Methods of Testing Concrete and the strength of cores taken and tested in accordance with the same Standard. This is discussed in Appendix 6 of this book. A further factor in testing concrete is that the strength of cubes can vary by as much as $15 \, N/mm^2$ ($2000 \, lbf/in^2$) owing to variation in the source of the aggregate.

The three essential properties of impermeability, durability and strength mentioned at the beginning of this section are what may be termed 'engineering' requirements; in other words, the appearance of the concrete surface is of secondary importance. This is valid as far as the shell of the swimming pool is concerned, but surface finish can be of great importance in other parts of the structure, and this is discussed briefly in the next section.

CONCRETE FOR SUPERSTRUCTURES AND ANCILLARY BUILDINGS

For building structures, the design and specification of the concrete should in general follow the recommendations in CP 110: The Structural Use of Concrete, particularly Section 6: Specification and workmanship: concrete.

While the author, in common with many engineers, has reservations about the advantages claimed for limit state design compared with the older eleastic theory based on CP 114, there are many excellent recommendations in CP 110 relating to the quality of concrete and protection of reinforcement.

In view of the fact that there are four Codes (CP 110, 114, 115 and 116) all dealing with concrete structures and running in parallel, it seemed completely unnecessary to produce a further Standard—namely, BS 5328: Methods for Specifying Concrete.

As with the pool shell, the author recommends that the specification for the concrete should be based on a minimum cement content and maximum w/c ratio, with a characteristic strength as a subsidiary requirement. The minimum cement content set by the designer should not be reduced by the substitution of PFA or similar pozzolanic materials. If it is considered that

PFA is needed to give some desirable characteristic to the concrete mix which would otherwise be missing, then the PFA admixture should be added to the mix in the same way as any other admixture. The long-term effect on durability of the substitution of part of the minimum cement content by some other material is, in fact, completely unknown, and until this can be accurately assessed, this substitution should not be permitted.

In many projects nowadays, the contractor wishes to pump the concrete and to cast suspended slabs in large areas, thus saving time and money. This can raise important problems which can, however, be resolved by common-sense and reference to basic principles of concrete technology. With regard to pumping, the basic requirement for the mix must be met. This is discussed in Chapter 4, in the section dealing with Medium to Large Pools. The casting of large areas of concrete in one continuous operation is dealt with in the same chapter.

In many projects the specification requires that certain parts of the

FIG. 3.1. View of a sports centre renovated with Sandtex-Matt (Courtesy: Cement Marketing Co. Ltd).

FIG. 3.2.   View of sports centre at Bath showing exposed aggregate concrete columns and facing blockwork panels (Courtesy: Cement and Concrete Association).

concrete structure must be provided with an acceptable finish without the application of additional layers or coatings. In other words, the concrete itself will form the final finish. This will require special consideration from the point of view of mix design and selection of aggregates, involving the preparation of trial panels. Plain smooth surfaces are not recommended, as it has been found to be impracticable to produce such surfaces free from any visible defects, such as staining, differences in colour, blow-holes, etc. To overcome this problem, exposed aggregate (achieved by various techniques) and deeply moulded surfaces should be specified. Large areas of concrete can with advantage be broken up into smaller areas each having a different finish. The judicious use of decorative panels having a durable coloured finish can be very attractive. The application of decorative finishes in the form of special rendering and paint systems does introduce a maintenance problem, but the author feels that this should not be allowed to interfere unduly with architectural treatment (see Fig. 3.1). Figure 3.2, shows a good example of high-quality concrete finish to a new sports centre.

The above is only the briefest outline of this important subject, and readers should refer to the Bibliography at the end of this chapter for detailed information.

THE DESIGN OF CONCRETE MIXES

Mix design is defined in BS 2787: Glossary of Terms for Concrete and Reinforced Concrete as: 'The calculation of the correct proportions of the constituents of concrete, taking into account such matters as the shape and grading of aggregates and the workability and strength required in the concrete.'

In this section it is proposed to give some information on the various factors involved in obtaining the required strength, impermeability and durability in the hardened concrete. This is, in fact, a subject on which a number of complete books and papers have been written, and a few of these are included in the short bibliography at the end of this chapter. Assuming that the correct type and quality of cement and aggregates are to be used (some basic information on these materials and their characteristics has been given in Chapter 2), the following are the most important of the many factors which influence the quality of the hardened concrete:

The water/cement ratio (w/c).

The aggregate/cement ratio (a/c) which also determines the cement content of the mix.

The grading, maximum size, shape and surface texture of the fine and coarse aggregates.

These three factors are all inter-related, but even when they have been carefully and correctly determined, high-quality concrete will result only if the ingredients are properly mixed, and this must be followed by correct placing, thorough compaction and curing. The mixing, placing and compaction are, however, considered separately to the design of the mix.

It has already been pointed out that the requirements of impermeability and durability in water-retaining structures have priority over compressive strength. The first two are usually obtained in the design stage by fixing a maximum a/c ratio or a minimum cement content (which comes to the same thing); this is coupled with either a maximum w/c ratio or a requirement on workability—measured by a slump test or a compacting factor test—or both these requirements. As the strength requirement is comparatively low, the author favours a restriction on the w/c ratio; a maximum 'free' w/c ratio of 0·50 is reasonable. The necessary workability can frequently be obtained with a free w/c ratio of 0·45–0·50.

The 'free' w/c ratio is the total water in the mix which is available for hydrating the cement; it is the water held on the surface of the aggregates plus the water added at the mixer, but does not include the water absorbed by the aggregates. When deciding how much water to add at the mixer, an allowance must be made for the water held on the surface of the fine aggregate. A workable mix is needed in order that the concrete can be fully compacted, because without proper compaction the best mix will result in a porous concrete.

CEMENT CONTENT

An adequate, but not excessive, cement content is necessary for durability and impermeability, and this is likely to be in the range of 330–400 kg/m³ (550–670 lb/yd³) of compacted concrete. Requests to replace a certain percentage of the minimum cement content by pozzolanic material such as PFA should not be agreed to unless the designer is satisfied that both durability and impermeability will not be reduced. For swimming pool shells a minimum cement content of 360 kg/m³ (600 lb/yd³) is recommended.

The author does not agree with the Code recommendation, in Table 8 and Clause 4.9 of BS 5337, that a minimum cement content of 290 kg/m³ (480 lb/yd³) is satisfactory for Class B exposure conditions (exposed to continuous or almost continuous contact with liquid).

The two main reasons for setting an upper limit to the cement content is that the more cement there is in the mix, the higher will be heat of hydration and the more rapid its evolution, thus increasing the risk of thermal contraction cracking. The second is that, with a constant w/c ratio, the higher the cement content, the more water there will be in the mix, thus increasing drying shrinkage. Problems arising from heat of hydration are discussed in Chapter 4. It should also be remembered that cement itself is a good workability aid.

After deciding on a minimum cement content, the next step is to consider the degree of workability required for the expected conditions of placing. With the cement contents mentioned above, the strength requirements should be easily met; in fact, they are likely to be well in excess of those required for design purposes.

WORKABILITY

The chief factor influencing workability is the w/c ratio, which should be measured by weight. With other factors constant, the more water there is in the mix, the more workable the concrete will be. When very workable concrete is required, as with placing concrete under water by means of a tremie pipe, a high cement content is needed. In this context, w/c ratio means the 'free w/c ratio' as previously defined. It is essential to realise that, when calculating the w/c ratio, the water on the surface of the aggregates has to be included.

The two tests used on site to measure workability are the slump test and the compacting factor test; the latter is the more reliable and gives a better measure of the workability, particularly when poker-type vibrators are used for compaction, but the slump test is easier and quicker to carry out and is adequate for most purposes; it is the one generally adopted. There is a third method of measuring workability, and this is by the Vee Bee Consistometer, but this is seldom found on construction sites.

Assuming that the w/c ratio and the aggregate grading and other characteristics are constant, then the workability will increase with increase in cement content.

With the other factors constant, the workability is directly related to the w/c. As the water content increases, the workability increases and strength decreases at an even higher rate.

CHARACTERISTICS OF THE AGGREGATES

The three most important characteristics are maximum size of the coarse aggregate, the grading of the fine and coarse aggregates, and the shape and surface texture of the aggregate particles.

Maximum Size of Aggregate

As the maximum size of the coarse aggregate increases up to about 50 mm (2 in), the workability will also increase (other factors remaining unchanged). Thus, of two mixes having the same cement content, w/c ratio and aggregate type, the mix with 40 mm ($1\frac{1}{2}$ in) aggregate would be more workable than the one with 20 mm ($\frac{3}{4}$ in) size. It should be noted that when using a concrete with a small-size aggregate, such as 10 mm ($\frac{3}{8}$ in), more cement is needed in order to obtain the required workability.

Shape of Aggregate Particles

The more rounded the shape and the smoother the surface of the aggregate particles, the more workable the mix will be. From this it can be seen that rounded shingle would give better workability than a crushed rock.

Grading of Aggregates

Of the three characteristics of aggregates mentioned, the grading has the greatest affect upon workability. Most concretes are made with aggregates having a continuous grading, although for certain purposes, generally architectural, gap-graded aggregates are specified. The meaning of a gap-graded aggregate is simply that one part of the curve which is obtained when the aggregate is sieved through a set of standard sieves is horizontal. For example, there may be virtually nothing retained on a No. 14 sieve, i.e. the percentage passing the No. 7 sieve is the same as that passing the No. 14, so that the grading curve at that section is horizontal.

A gap-graded aggregate may make a perfectly satisfactory concrete (the author has experienced this with sands in the Middle East), but to obtain consistent results, closer supervision is needed, and compaction by vibration is more or less essential. With grading generally, the following points apply: with a low workability, say 25–40 mm slump, and coarser grading, in either fine or coarse aggregate, it is necessary to use a lower w/c ratio: however, with increase in workability produced by a higher w/c ratio, these coarser gradings tend to segregate, and so one needs a higher proportion of fine material, which in practical terms means more sand in the mix.

From this, it can be seen that on construction sites where vibration is used to compact the concrete (and, consequently, a low-slump concrete is used) a coarser grading can be used, but if hand compaction has to be adopted, then more sand is needed in the mix and a higher w/c ratio to increase the workability. Concrete with a slump of 25 mm (1 in) and less cannot be compacted by hand.

Another important point is the percentage of sand (in relation to the total aggregate content). The larger the maximum size of the coarse aggregate the lower the percentage of sand required for a given workability. The three usual maximum sizes of coarse aggregate for reinforced concrete are: 10 mm ($\frac{3}{8}$ in); 20 mm ($\frac{3}{4}$ in); and 40 mm ($1\frac{1}{2}$ in).

The usual percentages of sand required with the above sizes vary within the following limits:

10 mm ($\frac{3}{8}$ in)	50–55 % sand.
20 mm ($\frac{3}{4}$ in)	30–45 % sand.
40 mm ($1\frac{1}{2}$ in)	25–40 % sand.

All-in aggregates often contain a high percentage of sand.

The workability required to obtain full compaction of the concrete will depend on the method of placing, the method of compaction and the amount and distribution of the reinforcement. The more congested the reinforcing steel the more difficult it will be to ensure full compaction of the concrete, and the workability may have to be increased to meet this condition. Reinforced-concrete designers should always keep this fact in mind.

THE USE OF ADMIXTURES IN CONCRETE MIXES

The main types of admixtures used in concrete mixes have been described in Chapter 2. Some general advice on the use of these compounds will be given here. The first point to note is that an admixture should not be used unless the person responsible for the mix design is satisfied that it is really needed to produce concrete of the required quality. It is generally better, and cheaper, to make some adjustments to the mix design rather than to use an admixture, provided, of course, that this will give the desired result.

Plasticisers are probably the type most likely to be used in water-retaining structures, since they will increase the workability while the w/c ratio is kept constant. The so-called 'water proofers' will never make an otherwise porous concrete watertight; they will improve workability and thus allow the w/c ratio to be reduced with the workability kept constant. Some have the effect of altering the surface tension characteristics of the concrete so that water falling on to the surface will form small globules and flow off rather than soak in. However, this change in surface tension is broken down as soon as the concrete surface is completely covered with water under pressure. This type of admixture can have an adverse effect on the bond between rendering and the base concrete.

Reference has been made in Chapter 2 to the virtual prohibition of the use of accelerators in reinforced and prestressed concrete and mortar contained in Amendment No. 3 to CP 110. The effect of this will be to encourage the use of accelerators which do not contain chlorides. Such compounds as sodium carbonate and calcium formate have been used on a very small scale, as their action has not proved very reliable. If it is necessary to increase the rate of evolution of heat of hydration of the cement, thus reducing its setting time and increasing rate of gain of strength, then other methods can be used; these include:

(a) The use of heated concrete.
(b) An increase in the cement content of the mix.
(c) Insulated and heated formwork, and the use of heated blankets.

CONCRETING AND BUILDING IN COLD WEATHER

GENERAL
There are a number of problems to be overcome when carrying out building and other construction work in cold weather. The principal one relates to the use of *in situ* Portland cement, concrete and mortars. One thing must be made clear, and this is that on a small job concrete and mortar are just as vulnerable to the effect of low temperatures as the same materials on a large contract: in fact, they may be more vulnerable, as the surface area-to-volume ratio is likely to be high on the small construction site. The term mortar includes any cement–sand mix such as bedding mortar for bricks and blocks, rendering and floor screeds.

CONCRETING (PORTLAND CEMENT CONCRETE)
There are a number of factors involved. These include:

(a) when the temperature of plastic concrete is lowered, the rate of hardening decreases; and as freezing point is approached, the hardening process practically ceases altogether.

(*b*) If the concrete is not saturated with water, has reached a compressive strength of about $3 \cdot 0$ N/mm^2 (450 lb/in^2) and is a reasonably rich mix (minimum 300 kg/m^3: 500 lb cement in a yd^3) then, even if the concrete does freeze, no permanent damage will result. When the temperature rises again, the concrete will thaw out and the hardening process will start again and continue at a rate proportional to the temperature of the concrete.

(*c*) Although most publications on the subject say a great deal about ambient air temperatures, these are relevant only because of their direct effect on the temperature of the concrete—it is the concrete temperature which is important.

(*d*) Whatever precautions are taken to prevent damage to the concrete by low air temperatures, they must all be directed towards keeping the temperature of the concrete as high as possible within certain limits, i.e. the temperature of the concrete at the time of casting should not exceed about 30 °C (86 °F) and should not be lower than about 10 °C (50 °F).

The above are the basic principles: it is hoped that the following recommendations will enable these to be applied on site:

(1) Frozen aggregates or icy water must not be used for mixing the concrete.

(2) Concrete must not be placed on frozen ground or in frozen forms.

(3) An 'anti-freeze' such as is used in the radiators of cars must not be used in the mixing water, since many of these liquids contain chemicals which may permanently damage the concrete.

(4) It is not advisable to use a mix leaner than $6 \cdot 0$ a/c ratio, even though the specified compressive strength can be obtained with a leaner mix.

(5) Wet curing techniques, such as water spray, etc., which are used in warm weather, should not be adopted in cold weather.

(6) The necessary steps should be taken to ensure that the concrete temperature *at the time of placing* is not lower than about 10 °C (50 °F). This can be done in two ways:

   (*a*) By ordering ready-mixed concrete: many large suppliers will supply heated concrete in the winter and this will save a great deal of trouble and expense on the site.

   (*b*) By covering the aggregate stock-piles with tarpaulins and by heating the mixing water (but only to a maximum temperature of 60 °C, or 140 °F). A higher temperature may cause a flash set in the cement. If the concrete has to be transported any distance from the mixer to the site of placing, it should be covered with tarpaulins.

(7) The aim should be to induce a rapid gain of strength. There are various ways in which this can be achieved, and these may be listed as follows:

    (*a*) By using a richer mix than the minimum previously mentioned. An extra $1\frac{1}{2}$ bags of cement in a cubic metre (1 bag per yd^3) of concrete will help appreciably.

    (*b*) By changing from ordinary Portland cement to rapid-hardening for the superstructure and ancillary buildings. It is recommended that calcium chloride should not be used in a concrete containing steel reinforcement.

    (*c*) Subject to (*b*) above, a chloride-free accelerator can be added to the mixing water when using OPC or RHPC (but not to sulphate-resisting Portland Cement). The addition of the accelerator on site is mentioned because it is a method widely adopted, but it is absolutely essential that the correct dosage and thorough dispensing into the mixing water be ensured.

    (*d*) The concrete should be well insulated immediately compaction and finishing is complete. The method of insulation will depend on the type of member(s) concreted.

Foundations
These should be covered with straw or mineral wool blankets and/or tarpaulins. The insulation must be kept dry, as many insulating materials lose most of their insulating properties when saturated.

Walls, Columns, Beams
Timber formwork provides good insulation and, unless the site is very exposed or heavy rain is expected, only the top of the concrete need be covered. Steel forms have about 20–30 times the thermal conductivity of 20 mm ($\frac{3}{4}$ in) plywood, i.e., the heat loss through steel forms may be 20–30 times greater than through 20 mm ($\frac{3}{4}$ in) timber, provided the latter is not saturated. Tarpaulins may therefore be needed to prevent the timber forms getting saturated by rain and then freezing.

Floors
Irrespective of whether these are supported on the ground or suspended (and the latter, of course, includes roof slabs), such slabs are particularly vulnerable to low air temperatures because the surface area-to-volume ratio is high. For this reason, external paving should not be carried out in very cold weather; the cost of providing the necessary protection is very high.

Screeds
As mentioned above, floor and roof slabs are particularly vulnerable to the

effect of freezing or near-freezing temperatures, and screeds are much more vulnerable than the base slabs. However, floor screeds are usually laid towards the end of the building operation, when roof, walls and windows are fixed. This means that the screed will be laid under cover; and provided the floor slab is not frozen, door and window openings are kept closed and the screed is covered with some insulating mats or tarpaulins, no harm should result. The rate of gain of strength will, however, be slowed down, and this must be allowed for. Wet curing should not be adopted: covering with polythene sheets and straw mats or thick building paper will serve the combined purpose of insulation and curing.

Blockwork and Brickwork
It is the mortar in the joints which is vulnerable to freezing. The jointing mortar is always appreciably weaker than the blocks or bricks. It must be remembered that low temperatures reduce the rate of gain of strength of mortars just as in the case of concrete. Therefore, when laying blocks or bricks in very cold weather, heavy loads should not be imposed on the walls or floors until a longer period has elapsed. 'Free-standing' walls are particularly vulnerable to gale-force winds under these circumstances.

Non-load-bearing Walls
The mortar mix is usually 1 part ordinary Portland cement to 1 part slaked lime and 6 parts sand (by volume), or 1 part masonry cement and 5 parts sand. Care should be taken to prevent the bricks or blocks becoming saturated by covering with tarpaulins; a tarpaulin over the sand used for mortar is also desirable. Frozen sand and icy water must not be used. Work should be covered up at night; if day temperatures are close to freezing, then the work should be kept covered for about 3–4 days.

An air-entraining admixture can be used with advantage in the mortar mix. This type of admixture acts as a plasticiser and is particularly useful when using a lean cement–sand mix without lime. The bricks should not be immersed in water before laying.

Walls Below Damp-proof Courses
Stronger blocks are used and a stronger mortar is needed; a suitable mix for the mortar would be 1:1:3 (cement:lime:sand) or 1:3 masonry cement and sand. The same precautions as previously described are required.

Walls of Engineering Bricks
These are denser and much stronger than ordinary building bricks, and a richer, stronger mortar is required. A mix of 1:3 cement:sand is recommended.

Load-bearing Walls
For general load-bearing walls, the mortar should not be leaner than 1:1:5 (cement:lime:sand) or 1:4 masonry cement:sand. The same precautions as before are required.

The Use of Accelerators in Mortars
There is a wide divergence of views on the usefulness or otherwise of calcium chloride in a mortar mix and there is conflicting evidence from research on this problem. However, if an entraining type of plasticiser is used, there is no need to use calcium chloride. The entrained air will effectively prevent damage to the mortar should it actually freeze, but, of course, at and near freezing point the rate of gain of strength is for all practical purposes zero.

POINTING AND RENDERING
Pointing and rendering of brickwork, blockwork and masonry should not be carried out in very cold weather. All fair-faced work requiring pointing should be built with the joints recessed ready for pointing in warmer weather. As with pointing, rendering is best left for warmer weather. Owing to the very high surface-to-volume ratio, rendering is particularly vulnerable to freezing temperatures. It is most important to realise that rendering should not be applied to frozen, partly frozen or saturated backgrounds; this means that even though the air temperature may be above freezing, the condition of the wall itself must be taken into consideration.

CONCRETING IN HOT WEATHER

The information and recommendations given here apply to work in temperate climates such as that of the United Kingdom. In the summer construction work proceeds at full speed, but on a hot sunny day trouble can be experienced with the premature stiffening of concrete, which makes compaction difficult: also, there is increased risk of plastic, thermal and shrinkage cracking. The whole subject is very complicated, and some aspects of it are not yet fully understood, so that only the outline of the problem and some general recommendations will be given.

The addition of heat to concrete to speed up the chemical action of the hydrating cement, and thus the rate of increase of hardening, has been discussed earlier in this chapter under the heading of Concreting and Building in Cold Weather. The same principles apply irrespective of the source of heat; in the summer it is the sun, and the formwork, mixing water and the aggregates are all warm or hot, depending on the circumstances of the work on site. The first thing to remember is that the higher the initial temperature of the concrete at the time of mixing, the more rapid will be the evolution of heat of hydration of the cement, and the higher the maximum temperature reached by the maturing concrete once it has been placed in the forms. It is therefore important to take all practical steps to reduce the initial temperature of the concrete. This can be done by:

(a) Keeping the mixing water cool; using an insulated storage tank or painting the outside of the tank white. A few coats of whitewash can be very effective.

(b) Spraying the aggregate stock piles with water. The latent heat of converting water to vapour is 540 cal/g, or 540 000 cal/litre; (2·28 kJ and 2280 kJ, respectively).

It is worth while remembering that the temperature of the cement has only a marginal effect on the temperature of the concrete. The rate of evolution of heat of hydration of ordinary Portland cement during the first 7 days is usually taken as 80–85 cal/g. Normal concrete mixes made with ordinary Portland cement placed in 20 mm ($\frac{3}{4}$ in) plywood forms, during average summer weather in the United Kingdom, with a concrete thickness of about 300 mm (12 in), is likely to rise in temperature about 25–30 °C in the first 20–30 h after casting.

The next thing to consider is the effect of a comparatively high initial concrete temperature, say 20 °C, combined with high ambient air temperature. These together will speed up the chemical action between the water and the cement, and increase the rate of evaporation of moisture from the surface of the concrete. The high concrete temperature will tend to increase temperature stresses in the hardening concrete, particularly as it falls after about 20–30 h. It will also induce early stiffening of the concrete, thus making it more difficult to compact it; concrete which is not fully compacted tends to be weak and porous. The rapid evaporation of water from the fresh concrete can result in plastic shrinkage cracking. The evaporation of moisture is increased if the fresh concrete is exposed to strong drying winds or hot sun. Plastic shrinkage cracking consists of fine cracks on the surface of the concrete slab, but usually extending downwards only 25 mm (1 in) or so.

The stresses induced in concrete by high temperatures are difficult to deal with on most jobs because they call for expensive and elaborate precautions which are justified only on special projects such as dams. The incidence of plastic cracking, however, can be very much reduced by immediately covering the concrete, after it has been compacted and finished, with tentage including side flaps so that the surface of the concrete slab is sheltered from the direct rays of the sun and from wind. The use of a curing membrane which is sprayed on to the slab is unlikely to give sufficient protection on hot summer days. Polythene sheets or reinforced waterproof building paper, well lapped and held down around the edges is satisfactory.

THE PROTECTION OF STRUCTURAL MATERIALS IN AN AGGRESSIVE ENVIRONMENT

GENERAL CONSIDERATIONS

At the present time there is no material known which is completely inert to chemical action. The materials used in the construction industry are no exception to this, and therefore all of these, whether used for structural purposes or decoration, are liable to deteriorate owing to chemical attack. Ferrous metals rust, timber decays, and concrete is attacked by acids and sulphates in solution. Fortunately, either the protection of most materials is not necessary because they have a very long life without it or the provision of protective coatings is comparatively easy and cheap.

The material which is most used in the construction of swimming pools and related structures is Portland cement concrete, and, under what may be termed normal conditions, this has an almost unlimited life. Concrete made with 'naturally occurring' cements (pozzolanic materials such as trass) has been found in excellent condition after more than 2000 years, and there is no reason to believe that, under similar conditions, modern Portland cement concrete has a shorter life. For the sake of brevity and simplicity, only one material will be considered in this chapter, and this is concrete. Information on metals and their protection is given in Chapters 2 and 6.

CONCRETE

Concrete is used for the pool shell and the foundations and structural members of the pool hall and ancillary buildings. It has, therefore, to withstand attack from atmospheric pollution, aggressive groundwater and the water in the pool unless this is maintained at the correct pH. This latter problem—water treatment—is dealt with in some detail in Chapter 7.

Generally, to resist attack from aggressive chemicals in the atmosphere, high-quality well-compacted Portland cement concrete does not need any protective treatment. However, almost all structural concrete contains steel reinforcement, and this does require protection. The protection is provided by an adequate depth of cover of high-quality concrete, which ensures an intense alkali environment around the reinforcement. If, during the lifetime of the structure, the alkalinity is reduced, owing for example, to continued ingress of moisture or the presence of chloride ions above a certain concentration (about 0.35% by weight of cement), then corrosion will start. It has been estimated that the corrosion products (rust) occupy a volume 3–8 times the original volume of steel. The expansion resulting from this increase in volume will crack and spall the concrete, thus exposing more steel to attack. The prevention of corrosion of the concrete itself is therefore of prime importance.

In the case of swimming pools and ancillary structures, aggression to the concrete is only likely to arise from chemicals in the subsoil and/or groundwater. It is emphasised that the water in the pool itself will not attack good-quality concrete and cement mortar, provided the treatment plant is properly operated. Information on water treatment is given in Chapter 7.

The very small amount of chlorine compounds in the air in swimming pool halls will not be aggressive to Portland cement products of reasonable quality. However, this atmosphere is very aggressive to unprotected ferrous metals, such as mild and high-tensile steel.

The first line of defence when subsoil conditions are likely to be aggressive to concrete is to ensure that concrete is dense and impermeable. In practical terms this means a minimum cement content of $360\,\text{kg/m}^3$ $(600\,\text{lb/yd}^3)$, a maximum w/c of 0·50, combined with full compaction and adequate curing. These basic requirements are also essential when sulphate-resisting Portland cement is used. Soil and groundwater in industrial tips can be very aggressive to concrete. Probably the most aggressive chemical found in industrial tips is sulphuric acid, but other acids, such as nitric and hydrochloric, as well as phenols and nitrates and high concentrations of sulphates, are also found. Where the presence of such tip drainage is suspected, careful groundwater sampling must be carried out and expert advice obtained on the protective measures required, from such organisations as the Cement and Concrete Association and the Building Research Station.

Most naturally occurring groundwaters are harmless to good-quality well-compacted concrete, but there are occasions when the subsoil water is potentially aggressive. For structures of any importance, and swimming pools are among these, trial bore-holes should be put down and the testing should include chemical analysis of both the soil and ground water.

Interpretation of Trial Boring Reports

When considering ground and groundwater analysis reports, with a view to deciding on whether or not protective measures are needed, and if so, what these measures should be, the following points have to be kept in mind:

(a) There are many practical difficulties in obtaining truly representative samples of soil and groundwater for analysis and in carrying out the analysis itself. The figures obtained may therefore represent maxima, minima or average conditions.

(b) Aggressive chemicals in a dry condition are unlikely to attack concrete.

(c) Seasonal fluctuations, as well as the direction and velocity of flow of the groundwater, may have an important bearing on the severity of the attack.

(d) Consideration should be given to any possible changes which may occur in subsoil conditions during the lifetime of the structure. For example, the construction of subsoil drainage at a higher level may effectively cut off the flow of groundwater and thus reduce or completely eliminate aggressive conditions.

(e) The pH of groundwater is a useful figure to have, but it does not indicate the amount and type of acid, or alkali present; in the case of acids, both these figures are important.

(f) In cases where the ground or groundwater is aggressive the estimated risk of attack on the concrete has to be assessed; the following conditions are listed in order of increasing severity of attack:

> Dry ground conditions.
> Stagnant groundwater.
> Flowing groundwater.

It is unlikely that good-quality concrete will be attacked in well-drained soils above the water table, under climatic conditions existing in a temperate climate. In a hot climate the evaporation from a water table can be so great that attack may occur even though the concrete is well above top water level.

(g) The thickness of the concrete is important, because thin sections are obviously more liable to serious damage than thick ones under the same aggressive conditions. The provision of an extra 'sacrificial' thickness of concrete is often worth consideration.

(h) The density, cement content and w/c ratio of the concrete have a very important influence on its resistance to attack. The higher the density and cement content, and the lower the w/c ratio, the more resistant the concrete will be.

Having considered the basic principles, the next point for examination is what are the likely forms of attack from the soil and groundwater. This attack is usually due to two main conditions, or a combination of both:

> Acids in the soil or groundwater.
> Sulphates in the soil or groundwater.

ATTACK BY ACIDIC GROUNDWATER

All Portland cement concrete is vulnerable to acid attack. The two questions to be decided are how severe is the attack likely to be and what precautions should be taken. The alkalinity or acidity of a water is usually determined by measuring the pH (hydrogen ion concentration). Waters with a pH above 7·0 are alkaline and with a pH below 7·0 are acid; 7·0 is known as the neutral point. It should be noted that the pH scale is logarithmic, so that a pH of 5·0 indicates an increase of acidity of 10 times compared with a pH of 6·0. This is not necessarily as serious as it sounds, because the pH by itself does not indicate the amount or type of acid present; it only measures the intensity of the acidity. Generally, pH measurements should be supplemented by chemical analysis, particularly when they are at undesirable levels. It should perhaps be mentioned at this point that concrete is itself alkaline in reaction, and therefore is unlikely to be affected by alkalis found in groundwater.

The acids occurring naturally in soils and groundwater are mostly organic, such as humic acids from peat, and carbonic acid from dissolved carbon dioxide from the atmosphere. However, in some marsh lands sulphuric acid is found and this is a much more serious matter. Groundwater from large open areas, such as moors and hills, may have a very low total dissolved solids (TDS) content. Such a water, even though the pH may be only slightly above 7·0 (say 7·5), could be aggressive to concrete because of its dissolving power. For the same reason, distilled water can be very aggressive to a wide range of materials.

It is not possible to lay down hard and fast rules for the protection of concrete against acid attack but, under most conditions found in practice, the provision of dense high-quality concrete, with the possible addition of backfilling with chalk or limestone to help neutralise the acidity, is sufficient. These measures can be supplemented by the provision of an additional thickness of concrete. The provision of a barrier of thick polyethylene sheeting (1000 gauge), PVC, or butyl rubber sheeting can also be very useful.

Attack by Sulphates in Solution in Groundwater

The sulphates most commonly found in groundwater are calcium sulphate (gypsum), magnesium sulphate (Epsom salts) and sodium sulphate. Calcium sulphate is less soluble than most other sulphates at normal temperature, and the solution is saturated at about 2000 ppm (2000 mg/litre). This is equivalent to about 1200 ppm of sulphur trioxide (SO_3). On the other hand, magnesium and sodium sulphates are much more soluble and thus the amount of sulphate which can be present in solution may be considerably higher. Magnesium sulphate is rather more aggressive towards Portland cement concrete than the other two sulphates previously mentioned, and this should be taken into account when deciding on the precautions to be taken.

In analysis, sulphates are usually expressed as the equivalent of sulphur trioxide (SO_3). If the figure in the analysis report is quoted as SO_4, then this can be readily converted to SO_3 as follows:

$$\text{ppm of } SO_3 = \left[\text{ppm of } SO_4 \times \frac{80}{96} \right]$$

Many clays contain sulphates in the form of crystals and they often appear in the clay as lenses or thin layers. If the sample for analysis is taken from such a layer or lens, the concentration may be very high; this is one reason why experienced interpretation of results is necessary. It must be remembered that the sulphates cannot attack the concrete unless they are in solution. In the author's opinion, this means, for well-compacted concrete, not merely damp soil conditions but a water table actually in contact with the concrete.

A much higher concentration of water sulphates can be tolerated in a well-drained soil than in groundwater. For more detailed information the reader is referred to the Bibliography at the end of this chapter.

CALCULATING THE YIELD OF CONCRETE MIXES AND THE QUANTITIES OF MATERIALS (CEMENT AND AGGREGATES) REQUIRED FOR CONCRETE, MORTAR AND GROUT

This section explains how to calculate the yield of concrete and mortar mixes and grouts, also the quantities of constituent materials required to obtain a specified quantity of concrete, mortar or grout. Information is given on the quantity of mortar required for brickwork and blockwork. While batching by volume is included, it must be emphasised that weigh batching should be adopted whenever possible, as a much more uniform mix (and, hence, more uniform quality concrete) results.

CONCRETE: BATCHING BY VOLUME
When the fine and coarse aggregate is measured separately, the volume of the mixed concrete is calculated as follows:

$$V = \tfrac{2}{3} \times (\text{vol. of cement} + \text{vol. of fine and coarse agg.})$$

When using volume batching, allowance must be made for the bulking of damp sand; the finer the sand the more it bulks. An average of 20–25 % is reasonable. No such allowance need be made in the case of the coarse aggregate.

CONCRETE: BATCHING BY WEIGHT

For practical purposes it can be assumed that $1\,m^3$ of compacted concrete weighs about 2385 kg, or $1\,yd^3$ weighs 4000 lb. On this basis the calculation of quantities is made as follows:

weight of concrete = total weight of constituent materials

$$\text{volume of concrete} = \frac{\text{wt. of concrete}}{\text{density of concrete}} = \frac{\text{wt (kg)}}{2385}$$

Example: A concrete mix per batch consists of:

cement	50 kg	w/c = 0·50
sand	84 kg	
coarse agg.	155 kg	
water	25 kg	
Total	314 kg	

$$\text{volume of concrete per batch} = \frac{314}{2385} = 0\cdot132\,m^3 \text{ or } 132 \text{ litres}$$

In Imperial measure, using approximate conversions, the figures would be:

cement	112 lb
sand	185 lb
coarse agg.	340 lb
water	56 lb
Total	693 lb

$$\text{volume of concrete per batch} = \frac{693}{4000} = 0\cdot173\,yd^3 \text{ or } 4\cdot66\,ft^3$$

The conversion factors used here are:
$1\,yd^3 = 0\cdot76\,m^3$; $1\cdot0\,m^3 = 1\cdot31\,yd^3$
$1\,lb = 0\cdot454\,kg$; $1\cdot0\,kg = 2\cdot2\,lb$
$1\,yd^3$ of concrete weighs 4000 lb or 1820 kg
$1\,m^3$ of concrete weighs 2385 kg.

MORTARS

There is no standard density for mortars and grouts, and so the best method of calculating volumes and densities of these two materials is to use what is known as the absolute volume method.

This is best explained by means of an example.

Example: The mix is 1 part cement and 3 parts dry sand by weight, with a w/c of 0·50; assume a 1 bag batch.

specific gravity of cement $= 3·12$
specific gravity of sand $\quad = 2·65$
specific gravity of water $\quad = 1·0$
then (using metric units):

$$\frac{50}{3·12 \times 1000} + \frac{150}{2·65 \times 1000} + \frac{25}{1·0 \times 1000} = \frac{16 + 56·5 + 25}{1000}$$

vol. of mortar $= 0·0975\,m^3$ or 97·5 litres

using Imperial units:

the density of water $= 62·5\,lb/ft^3$

$$\frac{112}{3·12 \times 62·5} + \frac{336}{2·65 \times 62·5} + \frac{56}{1 \times 62·5} = \frac{36 + 127 + 56}{62·5}$$

vol. of mortar $= 3·5\,ft^3$

(If $1\,ft^3 = 28$ litres, then $3·5 \times 28 = 98$ litres.)

BIBLIOGRAPHY

AMERICAN CONCRETE INSTITUTE, Committee 212. Admixtures for Concrete. *Proc. Am. Concrete Inst.*, **60**(11) (Nov. 1963). 1481–1526.

AMERICAN CONCRETE INSTITUTE, Guide for the protection of concrete against chemical attack by means of coatings and other corrosion resistant materials. Report by ACI Committee 515. *J. ACI* (Dec. 1966). 1305–1390.

BLACKLEDGE, G. F. *The Concrete Cube Test*, Cement and Concrete Association, London, 1972, Publication 45.005 1973, p. 9.

BLAKE, L. S., *Recommendations for the production of High-quality Concrete Surfaces.* Cement and Concrete Association, London, 47.019, 1967.

BRITISH STANDARDS INSTITUTION, CP110: *The Structural Use of Concrete*, 1972, p. 154.

BRITISH STANDARDS INSTITUTION, BS 5337: *The Structural Use of Concrete for Retaining Aqueous Liquids*, 1976, p. 16.

BUILDING RESEARCH ESTABLISHMENT, *Concrete in Sulphate-bearing Soils and Ground Waters*, Digest No. 174, HMSO, 1975, p. 4.

CONCRETE SOCIETY, THE, Admixtures for concrete. *Concrete* (Jan. 1968) 39–46.

GAGE, M., *Guide to Exposed Concrete Finishes*, Architectural Press, 15.334, London, 1970.

HALSTEAD, P. E., Behaviour of structures subjected to aggressive waters. Paper presented at Inter-Association Colloquium on Behaviour in Service of Concrete Structures, Liege, June 1975, p. 11.

LEA, F. M. *The Chemistry of Cement and Concrete*, 3rd edn (revised), Edward Arnold, London, 1970, p. 725.

ORAM, W. R., *Concrete Cladding*, Cement and Concrete Association, London, 1977.

ORCHARD, D. F., *Concrete Technology*, 3rd edn (3 vols.), Applied Science Publishers, London, 1976.

PERKINS, P. H., *The Use of Portland Cement Concrete in Sulphate-bearing Ground and Ground Waters of Low pH*, Cement and Concrete Association, London ADS/30, April 1976, p. 16.

PERKINS, P. H. *Concrete Structures: Repair, Waterproofing and Protection*, Applied Science Publishers, London, 1977.

RILEM COMMITTEE CRC-12, Corrosion of reinforcement in concrete. *Materials and structures*, **9**, No. 51 (May–June 1976) 187–206.

SHACKLOCK, B. W., Code 11.004: *Concrete Constituents and Mix Proportions*, Cement and Concrete Association, London, 1974, p. 102.

TEYCHENNE, D. C., FRANKLIN, R. E. and ERNTROY, H. C. *Design of Normal Concrete Mixes*, HMSO, 1975, p. 30.

TREADAWAY, K. W. J. and RUSSELL, A. D., *Inhibition of the Corrosion of Steel in Concrete*, Building Research Station Current Papers CP82/68, Garston, Dec. 1968, p. 5.

WILSON, J. G., *White Concrete with Some Notes on Black Concrete*, Cement and Concrete Association, 48.010, London, 1969.

WILSON, J. G., *Specification Clauses Covering Production of High-quality Finishes to in situ Concrete*, Cement and Concrete Association, 47.010, London, 1970.

CHAPTER 4

The Specification and Construction of Swimming Pools in In Situ Reinforced Concrete, Prestressed Concrete and Reinforced Gunite

INTRODUCTION

The majority of swimming pools larger than about 12·5 m × 6·0 m (41 ft × 20 ft) and with a depth greater than about 2·0 m (6 ft 7 in) are constructed in either *in situ* reinforced concrete or reinforced gunite. In the United Kingdom there is no Code of Practice for gunite, but in the United States there is the American Concrete Institute Code No. ACI-506-66 for Shotcrete.

A swimming pool is a water-retaining structure, and therefore, if it is built in reinforced concrete and unless it is quite small, the design and construction should comply with the relevant Code of Practice, namely, BS 5337: The Structural Use of Concrete for Retaining Aqueous Liquids. This is a revised version of CP 2007, and was issued in 1976.

The words 'design', 'specification' and 'construction' appear frequently throughout this book, and in this chapter in particular. It is always difficult to say exactly which operations belong to each of these words, and the author does not wish to attempt it here. As far as this book is concerned, the parts of 'design' which deal with the calculations to determine dimensions of the concrete members and the amount and details of reinforcement are not included. The reason is that there are many books which deal exclusively with reinforced and prestressed concrete design calculations.

COMMENTS ON BRITISH STANDARD BS 5337: 1976: CODE OF PRACTICE FOR THE STRUCTURAL USE OF CONCRETE FOR RETAINING AQUEOUS LIQUIDS

This new Standard replaced Code of Practice CP 2007, and is intended to cover the design and construction of all normal water-retaining structures, which includes swimming pools, in reinforced and prestressed concrete. The new Code contains a number of provisions with which some experienced engineers do not agree. These contentious provisions are:

(a) The alternative methods of design intended to deal with thermal contraction in the early life of the concrete.

(b) Clause 4.9 (Degrees of Exposure), and the design and specification criteria resulting from this classification.

(c) The limit state design concepts, with particular reference to permitted crack widths.

The author feels that it is too early to make complete and constructive comments on the new Code as these should await experience of its use in the design office and on site.

The site conditions under which the designer should select the degree of exposure are left rather open, and the author does not consider that the minimum cement contents recommended for class B exposure in Table 8, are adequate.

An unfortunately vague clause relates to aggregates (21.2.1), which requires that the drying shrinkage should be 'low', but gives no guidance on what this actually means. The maximum absorption has been raised from 2% to 3%, but the author has been unable to find any sound technical evidence that an aggregate with 4% or even 5% absorption would necessarily be unsatisfactory for a water-retaining structure.

Restrictions of this kind which are not based on valid technical reasons can result in a considerable waste of public money. The author knows of a case where the local flint gravel aggregate, which had been used for years for good-quality structural concrete, was found to have an absorption of $2\frac{1}{2}\%$, i.e. 0.5% above the Code recommendation. The import of aggregates from another source would add some £40 000 to the cost of the project. The author expressed the opinion that there was no technical justification for rejecting the local aggregates.

It is unfortunate that the concepts in the revised Code for determining crack widths, crack spacing and amount of reinforcement required to 'control' cracking (i.e. thermal contraction cracking) could not be based on actual site experience. However, water-retaining structures are now being designed in accordance with these new methods and it will be interesting, and no doubt instructive, to see the results. The author considers it a pity that 'partial' contraction joints have been retained in the revision, as he can see no use for these and feels that the carrying of the reinforcement across the joints will increase the risk of cracking at intermediate points.

The idea that cracks up to a certain width can be accepted without any remedial treatment appears to be promoted in Clauses 4.9, 5.1 and 5.3. Cracks due to thermal contraction invariably pass right through the member; therefore, irrespective of their width, the author recommends that they should be sealed in the most effective way possible in the circumstances of each case. This is dealt with in more detail in Chapters 6 and 8.

DESIGN AND CONSTRUCTION OF POOLS IN
IN SITU REINFORCED CONCRETE

GENERAL CONSIDERATIONS
It is felt that the most useful way of presenting information and recommendations is to divide swimming pools into two categories:

Category A: small to medium-size pools.

Category B: medium to large pools.

This division is of course rather arbitrary, but there are many problems with the small pool which do not arise with the large one. The basic principles of design and construction are applicable to both, but with the smaller pool (which is generally built for private clients) the amount of experience available for the design and the supervision of the construction is likely to be less than with a large pool, which is usually built for a public authority. However, there is one point of fundamental importance which applies to all reinforced concrete pools, and this is that the pool should be designed by an experienced civil or structural engineer, who should also be responsible for the specification and supervision of the work. Both should meet the criteria laid down in Chapter 1.

CATEGORY A: SMALL TO MEDIUM SWIMMING POOLS—
CONSTRUCTION METHODS

It is assumed that pools in this category have maximum dimensions of about:

16·33 m long × 8·0 m wide; water depth 1·0 to 3·0 m
(54 ft × 26 ft × 3 ft 3 in; 10 ft deep)

GENERAL
It is advisable to plan the work in advance so that one operation follows another in logical sequence and as rapidly as possible. This not only will reduce construction time and thus save money, but also may avoid the necessity of doing some of the work twice; for example, if the excavation is left open for a week or so waiting for the placing of the site concrete, the ground surface may be softened by rain, necessitating the removal of this soft soil and replacement by granular material or concrete.

All materials should be ordered well in advance and delivery dates agreed with the suppliers. Space must be provided for stacking materials on site, and access must be arranged for delivery of bulk materials so that double handling is avoided as far as possible. Although all the above factors are taken into account by an experienced contractor, it is surprising how many contractors do little or no pre-planning of the work.

EXCAVATION

It may be necessary to support the sides of the excavation, particularly at the deep end of the pool. If there is sufficient space, it is simpler and cheaper to batter the sides back so that they remain stable without timbering.

It is essential that the excavated area be kept free of water, and it may be necessary to provide a sump and a pump. The sump can be a simple affair consisting of an empty drum with perforated sides set in a hole at the lowest point and surrounded with shingle or gravel. Where ground conditions are difficult, more sophisticated methods of groundwater control will be necessary. Where the soil is not too fine-grained, well-point dewatering can be very effective.

PERMANENT SUBSOIL DRAINAGE

The provision of under-drainage is always worth while considering. On some sites the provision of a simple perimeter drain, 100 mm (4 in) diam., can effect a considerable improvement in the land drainage conditions. On other sites complete under-drainage may be required. Figure 4.1 shows a suitable layout of subsoil drains for a large pool. The inclusion of an adequate number of access manholes is considered by the author to be well worth the extra cost involved, since they not only enable any blockage to be cleared, but also provide for control of the flow in the system should a leak in the floor be suspected.

The pipes used can be:

Porous concrete to BS 1194.
Perforated dense concrete.
. Plain concrete with open joints to BS 4101.
Unglazed clayware to BS 1196.
Slotted plastic pipes.

The pipes should be surrounded with a graded gravel to act as a filter. In selecting the type of pipe consideration must be given to the presence of acids or sulphates in the soil and groundwater. For a more detailed discussion on the problem of durability of Portland cement concrete in aggressive soils, reference should be made to Chapter 3.

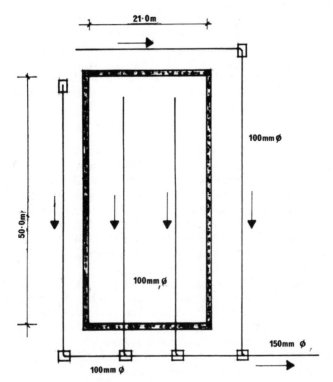

FIG. 4.1.   Diagram showing subsoil drainage of swimming pool site.

PRESSURE RELIEF VALVES

It is sometimes suggested that where there is a fluctuating or high water table, pressure relief valves should be installed in the floor. The basic idea of this is to prevent 'flotation', which is the upward movement of an underground structure due to groundwater pressure acting on the underside of the floor. It is essential to keep in mind the possible effect of groundwater pressure during the construction of the pool. Obviously pools with a diving pit are more vulnerable than a shallow pool used only for swimming.

If there is any likelihood of flotation occurring, even during construction (the possibility of groundwater level control pumping breaking down must be kept in mind), then necessary precautions should be taken. Pressure relief valves in the floor as a temporary measure during construction, and their sealing off on completion can be very useful. The author is not in favour of the provision of these valves as a permanent feature in swimming pools, except possibly pools constructed in reinforced gunite; this type of pool shell is discussed later in this chapter. Pressure relief valves, like all mechanical devices, can go out of order, and may jam in either the open or shut position. The provision of extra dead weight by thickening the walls and floor is the best solution. The extra cost of the additional concrete may be partly offset by a reduction in the amount of reinforcement in the walls.

THE FLOOR

As soon as possible after the excavation has been completed the whole of the excavated area should be covered with 50–75 mm (2–3 in) of 'oversite' concrete. This concrete can be a comparatively weak mix (an aggregate cement ratio of 8 or 9 would be suitable). It is recommended that this oversite concrete be finished with as smooth a surface as practicable, for two reasons: one is that this will assist in accurately locating and fixing the reinforcement which extends from the floor slab into the walls, and the other is that it will provide a smooth surface on which to lay the 'slip layer' of polythene sheet or bitumen.

In order to reduce the friction between the structural floor slab and the site concrete, one should either apply two coats of bituminous emulsion on the concrete or lay 1000 gauge polythene sheets well lapped to serve as a slip layer. This is important during the early life of the concrete floor slab, because thermal and drying shrinkage movements are then likely to be at their maximum, and the more restraint there is to this movement, the greater chance there is of the slab developing cracks. The reinforcement for the lower part of the walls which extends into the floor slab must now be accurately fixed in accordance with the drawings. It must be remembered that unless the reinforcement is in the correct place (as calculated by the designer), it cannot fulfil its purpose efficiently.

The drawings should show the position of the construction joints in the floor slab. There are no hard and fast rules for locating these. The width of the bays will be governed by the method of compaction employed: if poker vibrators are used, then the width can be equal to the length, i.e. square bays, but with hand-operated vibrating beams the width should not exceed 4·3 m (14 ft).

Another factor which is influenced by the bay shape and dimensions is the type of mesh reinforcement: for a square mesh there should be a square bay, and for a rectangular mesh a rectangular bay with the main wires running longitudinally. In the United Kingdom mesh reinforcement is usually 2·40 m (7 ft 11 in) wide, and there is an advantage in selecting the bay width so that cutting and waste is reduced to a minimum. For example, with a 150 mm (6 in) lap and 75 mm (3 in) cover at each side, two rolls of mesh will give a bay width of 4·35 m (14 ft). The reinforcement for concrete slabs uniformly supported on the ground is placed 40–50 mm ($1\frac{1}{2}$–2 in) from the top surface and, as previously mentioned, is usually in the form of high-tensile mesh (or fabric).

For rectangular bays up to 10 m (33 ft) in length, a rectangular mesh, reference No. C.385, weighing 3·41 kg/m² is usually adequate. For square bays, up to 6·0 m × 6·0 m (20 ft × 20 ft), a square mesh, reference No. A.252, weighing 3·95 kg/m² is suitable. Generally, the author feels that for swimming pool floors a bay length much in excess of 10 m (33 ft) should be avoided. If for any reason this length is exceeded, then the following mesh is recommended:

Bay length exceeding 10 m but not exceeding 15 m (33–49 ft), mesh B.503, weight 5·93 kg/m² (10·7 lb/yd²).

For bays exceeding 10 m in length the thickness of the concrete should be 200 mm (8 in).

A kicker around the perimeter of the floor slab is recommended, as this will greatly help in the fixing of the formwork for the walls.

There is now the question of the concrete mix. For ready-mixed concrete, the recommendations of the British Ready Mixed Concrete Association should be followed as far as the giving of information is concerned. The address of the BRMCA is given in Appendix 3. The order should be based on the following:

Cement:	Ordinary Portland cement, or sulphate-resisting Portland cement if sulphates are present in the subsoil or groundwater in injurious concentration (see Chapter 3).
Cement content:	Minimum cement content, 360 kg/m³ of compacted concrete (600 lb/yd³).
Water/cement ratio:	Maximum w/c ratio, 0·50.
Workability:	Slump, 60 mm ± 25 mm ($2\frac{1}{2}$ in ± 1 in).
Aggregates:	To comply with BS 882, maximum size 20 mm ($\frac{3}{4}$ in). If marine aggregates are used, the chlorides in the concrete must comply with CP 110.
Cube strength:	Characteristic (minimum) strength at 28 days, 30 N/mm² (4000 lbf/in²).
Admixtures:	Admixtures may be used with approval of purchaser, but must be 'chloride-free'.

It should be noted that if the concrete is to be placed by pumping, the workability (slump) would have to be increased but the w/c ratio should not be raised above 0·50. To obtain the necessary workability the use of a plasticiser would probably be necessary.

If the concrete is batched on site, it should be weigh batched for the reasons given in Chapter 3.

A suggested mix is given below. While the cement content and the w/c ratio should not be changed, the proportion of fine to coarse aggregate can be varied; generally, the sand content should be within the range of 35–40 % of total aggregate.

ordinary Portland cement:	50 kg (112 lb)
fine aggregate (a natural sand):	95 kg (210 lb)
coarse aggregate (a crushed rock or gravel 20 mm ($\frac{3}{4}$ in), maximum size):	155 kg (340 lb)
slump:	60 mm.$\pm$ 25 mm
maximum water/cement ratio:	0·50 = 25 kg (5·5 gal)

A simple calculation, as explained in Chapter 3, will show that the above mix has an aggregate/cement ratio of 5·0, and there will be 378 kg of cement in one cubic metre of the concrete (this is equivalent to about 640 lb/yd^3).

With the aggregates in general use in the United Kingdom, and the mix proportions given above, there should be no difficulty in obtaining the required workability. However, should difficulty arise which cannot be resolved by adjustment of the sand content, then a plasticiser should be used. Under no circumstances should the water/cement ratio be increased, and a plasticiser as mentioned in Chapter 2 is recommended.

It will be noted that the mix suggested for site batching is somewhat richer than that recommended when ordering ready-mixed concrete. This is because, provided the RMC firm is a member of the British Ready Mixed Concrete Association, who operate their own quality control scheme, the batching of the mix and the grading of the aggregates is likely to be of a rather higher standard than would be obtained on a small construction site.

After batching, the concrete has to be mixed, transported and placed. Thorough mixing is essential; it is usual for the aggregates to be put into the mixer first, followed by the cement; as the drum of the mixer revolves, the required (predetermined) quantity of water is added. For the standard type of tilting or non-tilting drum mixer, the mixing should continue for at least 2 min after the water has been added. If admixtures are used, they must be thoroughly mixed with the mixing water before the latter is added to the drum of the mixer.

The first batch in a mixer at the start of the day, or after concreting has been suspended, should either contain more cement than the usual batch, or some cement and a little water should be put in to the drum for a few revolutions before the first batch goes in. This will prevent the first batch coming out rather harsh.

The method of transporting the concrete from the mixer to the site where it has to be placed and compacted will depend largely on the size of the contract. For the pool itself, wheelbarrows are likely to be used. No matter what method is adopted, the object should be to get the concrete into its final position as quickly as possible.

It is perhaps worth mentioning that with ready-mixed concrete consideration may well be given to the use of a concrete pump. However, concrete for pumping needs to be specially designed for the purpose. The mix design put forward by the concrete pumping contractor must be checked against the basic requirements of the contract specification. This matter is referred to in more detail later in this chapter. In the United Kingdom concrete pumping has come into favour, and small efficient mobile pumps are now available. A number of specialist firms have been set up who will pump and place concrete as a sub-contract.

Compaction of the concrete in the floor slab can be done by two methods: either by hand-operated tamper working off the side forms, preferably with a vibrator attached (it then becomes a vibrating beam) or by poker-type vibrators. This has been discussed earlier in this chapter when the problem of bay size was considered. If poker vibrators are used, there must be an adequate number, i.e. at least three; it is quite useless for a contractor to send just one vibrator to the site, because the concrete will not be properly compacted in the event of a breakdown. Thorough compaction of the concrete is absolutely essential for watertightness. Poker vibrators should be used in addition to a tamper to ensure compaction at the edges of the bays.

When vibrating tampers are used, the side forms must be strong and rigid. The carrying of the mesh reinforcement across the longitudinal joints necessitates the side forms being split, and this weakens them and reduces the efficiency of compaction. With swimming pool floors the loading on the floor from the water is uniform and so load transfer devices are not generally required. If it is felt necessary to tie the bays together, then tie bars can be used. These are mild steel bars, 12 mm ($1\frac{1}{2}$ in) diameter, 1·20 m long, fixed in the centre of the slab at 400 mm (16 in) centres; one half length should be debonded.

The author recommends that all joints between bays in the floor slab should be contraction joints and be provided with a sealing groove. A section through floor bay joints is shown in Figs. 4.2 and 4.8.

It has been previously mentioned that the provision of a 'kicker' around the perimeter of the floor slab is recommended. This forms the base for the wall, and it is most important that the joint between the kicker and the wall should be watertight. There is no need to allow for shrinkage or thermal movement at right angles to this joint, and so the aim should be to obtain maximum bond between the old concrete in the kicker and the fresh concrete in the wall. To achieve this, the top surface of the kicker should be sprayed with water and brushed with a stiff brush to remove the laitance and

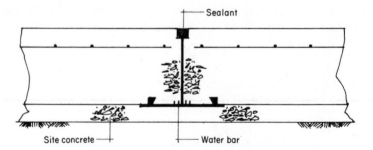

FIG. 4.2.   Contraction joint in floor slab.

expose the coarse aggregate a few hours after casting. There are other
methods of obtaining exposure of the coarse aggregate, such as bush
hammering, grit blasting, and high-velocity water jets. The latter leaves the
surface of the concrete clean and damp, while if percussion tools are used,
all grit and dust must be removed before the new concrete is placed. Figure
6.1 shows an exposed aggregate finish which will provide an excellent
mechanical key for the next layer of concrete.   It is unusual for a water bar
to be provided in the kicker, because with the correct preparation of the
surface of the 'old' concrete, and the weight of the new concrete in the wall, a
sound watertight joint should result. Flexible water bars such as PVC and
rubber are liable to be displaced when the concrete is placed and compacted
in the wall forms. If it is felt that a water bar is needed, then a mild steel flat
can be used. This should be at least 150 mm (6 in) wide and 3 mm ($\frac{1}{8}$ in) thick
and is usually vibrated into the top of the kicker an hour or so after placing
is complete. This type of bar is effective; the concrete bonds strongly to the
bar whereas with rubber and PVC there is no bond. Figure 4.3 shows the

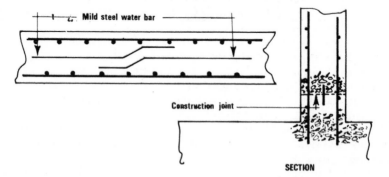

FIG. 4.3.   Metal water bar at junction of wall and floor.

method to be adopted where two lengths meet. Joints in the walls are dealt with later in this chapter.

Curing
Immediately after each bay is finished, it must be covered with either reinforced waterproof building paper, lapped 300 mm (12 in) and held down all around by timber boards or similar, or with 500 gauge polythene sheets, also lapped and held down in the same way as the building paper. This covering must be kept in position for 4 days.

The immediate covering of the fresh concrete is particularly important on hot sunny or windy days. If the specification calls for a curing membrane, which is resin-based and is applied by spray or brush, this will give satisfactory results, provided some physical protection is given to the surface on hot days. This protection usually takes the form of tentage, and it is kept in position for not less than 4 h, and preferably 8 h after casting; the actual time should be determined by weather conditions. The presence of the membrane on the concrete may interfere with the bond of subsequent layers such as a screed.

THE WALLS
Formwork: General
One of the most expensive items in connection with *in situ* concrete cast within forms is the formwork itself, especially when it is used only once. Steel formwork can be hired from a number of firms in the United Kingdom; the hire charges are modest and much less than the cost of even the cheapest timber forms.

If purpose-made formwork is used. then it is not advisable to try to save money by providing poor-quality forms. The formwork must be strong and rigid enough to resist undue deflection under pressure of the fluid concrete. It is now usual to cast walls in one lift, but this has the effect of considerably increasing the pressure on the formwork. If the forms deflect (bulge) seriously, this will cause difficulties with the subsequent rendering and tiling, and in some cases the bulges in the concrete have to be hacked off. This can result in the concrete cover to the reinforcement being reduced below the minimum of 40 mm ($1\frac{1}{2}$ in). Any joints in the formwork must be tight so as to prevent grout loss, which can result in honeycombing and leakage when the water test is applied. Grout-tight joints can be made by exercising care and using foamed polyurethane strip well compressed by tightening the forms.

The forms on each side of the wall panel have to be firmly held in position, and this is achieved either by using special through bolts or by the use of heavy walings and struts. The former method is the one usually adopted and can be quite satisfactory. Formwork without through tie-bolts is much more expensive and is not justified for swimming pools.

FIG. 4.4.   View of concrete blocks being laid as permanent formwork to RC wall of
pool (courtesy: Rutherford Ltd, Battle).

Precast Concrete Blocks as Permanent Formwork
In the United Kingdom precast concrete blocks are available as permanent
formwork for *in situ* reinforced concrete walls. Figure 4.4 shows these
blocks being laid.

Steel Formwork
There are many advantages in using steel formwork, the principal one from
a contractor's point of view being the very long life of the forms compared
with timber. Another is that this type of form can be hired. There are a
number of firms in the United Kingdom which operate a steel formwork
hire service, and the information which follows has been obtained from
Acrow Engineers Ltd of London.
    The panels are held together across the wall by special wall ties, part of
which remain in the wall while the two end pieces and cones are removed

and can be used again. The detailed design of these ties varies from one firm to another, but the principle, namely that the central part of the tie remains in the concrete wall, is the same. In most cases the ties can be supplied with plates on the central part to act as water stops.

Some architects and engineers place great importance on these water stops, but the author feels that if the concrete mix is cohesive and workable and is well compacted, there should be no leakage past the tie without the water stop. However, if there is some bleeding around the tie and lack of compaction, the water stop will not be able to prevent leakage. In any case, the cone-shaped hole on each face of the wall must be carefully sealed. A diagram of two types of through wall tie is shown in Fig. 4.5. The sealing of the bolt holes can be done in a number of ways; some engineers

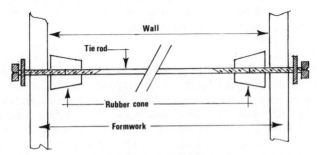

THREADED WALL TIES WITH RUBBER CONES
(RAPID METAL DEVELOPMENTS)

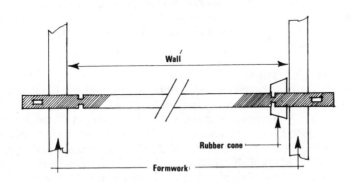

SNAP-OFF WALL TIE WITH AND WITHOUT
RUBBER CONE (ACROW ENGINEERS)

FIG. 4.5.   Formwork ties for pool walls.

use ordinary cement–sand mortar. The formula recommended by the author is as follows:

1 part ordinary Portland cement.
3 parts clean building sand.
9 litres (2 gal) styrene butadiene latex emulsion to each 50 kg (112 lb) cement.

Before the mortar is applied, the hole must be cleaned out and given a thin brush coat of grout consisting of 2 parts OPC to 1 part latex emulsion. The mortar should be as stiff as possible with just sufficient workability to enable it to be compacted into the hole. If the sand is wet, there will probably be no need for any additional mixing water apart from the latex emulsion itself. The mortar must be placed within 15 min of the application of the grout. Further details of the use of this type of latex in cement–sand mortars, screeds and renderings are given in Chapter 6.

POSITION OF JOINTS IN WALLS
As in the case of the floor, the position of construction and other joints in the walls should be decided at the design stage and marked on the drawings. At the same time, the position of these joints need not be looked upon as something which under no circumstances should be altered, since advice on this matter from an experienced contractor can be very useful and should always be given careful consideration. The whole subject of joints in the walls of water-retaining structures is one on which there is a wide divergence of views among experienced engineers and contractors. The subject of joints will be discussed in some detail later in this chapter.

Generally, the author recommends a comparatively short panel length of about 4·5 m (14 ft 6 in) with all joints provided with a sealing groove and properly sealed, and water bars if the thickness of the wall is not less than 300 mm (12 in).

FIXING REINFORCEMENT
Before the formwork is erected, the reinforcement in the walls must be fixed. In the United Kingdom the minimum cover to reinforcement is 40 mm ($1\frac{1}{2}$ in). For the purpose of crack control it is better if the horizontal distribution steel is fixed on the outside of the main vertical bars, because in this position it is as near the surface of the concrete as is allowed. Assuming 20 mm vertical bars and 40 mm cover, the distribution steel would be 60 mm (20 + 40) from the surface if it were on the inside, but only 40 mm if it were on the outside.

Small cement–sand spacer blocks should be wired to the reinforcement to ensure the correct cover. These are recommended in preference to plastic blocks, because the latter do not bond with the concrete and so there is some chance of water reaching the reinforcement via the perimeter of the spacer block. Calcium chloride must not be used in the mix for the cement–sand blocks.

CONCRETING THE WALLS

Once the reinforcement has been fixed and checked with the engineer's drawings, the formwork can be erected. Plain butt joints for the vertical construction joints between the panels are quite satisfactory; the use of rebated or joggle joints has nothing to recommend it. A good-quality release agent should be used on the formwork to secure quick release without damage to the surface of the concrete or the arrises at the joints. A mould cream emulsion made by a recognised firm is likely to give the best results.

The concrete mix can be similar to that used for the floor. The placing may be by crane and bucket or by wheelbarrows or by a concrete pump. If the contractor wishes to use a pump, the mix may have to be adjusted to give the degree of fluidity needed for efficient pumping. This can be accepted provided the basic requirements of the mix are maintained; in particular, the w/c ratio should not be increased. The concrete must be compacted by poker vibrators, with a panel length of 5·0 m. There should be a minimum of two vibrators working, with an extra one available as a stand-by.

The walls should be cast in one lift even in the deep end of the pool, as this eliminates horizontal construction joints. It is most advisable to cast the walls as soon as possible after the perimeter bays of the floor.

By careful organisation of the work, and perhaps a little overtime, it should be possible to start casting the wall panel 24–48 h after the casting of the kicker.

The ideal solution would be to cast the perimeter floor bay complete with kicker and the wall panel in one operation. This is sometimes done with reinforced concrete water reservoirs, and by using a cohesive mix the use of a top shutter on the floor slab is not required. By adopting this technique differential thermal and drying shrinkage movements between the 'old' concrete in the floor slab and the fresh concrete in the wall are avoided. Thermal and drying shrinkage stresses are thus substantially reduced and the risk of cracking correspondingly curtailed.

REMOVAL OF FORMWORK

The next problem, and one on which there is usually a great deal of argument on site, is how much time should elapse before the formwork can be removed. The contractor wants to remove it as soon as possible (perhaps after 16 h), and the Clerk of Works wants it left up for 48–72 h. It is the author's view that all the theoretical considerations involved cannot be satisfied on a construction site: the aim should be to reduce the temperature gradient across the section of the wall as much as possible. The most important factor is the maximum temperature reached at the centre of the wall, and the next is the amount of heat transmitted by the formwork, which is governed by the type of formwork used, the ambient air temperature, and the temperature of the concrete in contact with the formwork. It should be noted that the amount of heat transmitted by steel formwork may be 20–25 times that transmitted by 20 mm ($\frac{3}{4}$ in) plywood forms. The temperature at the centre of the wall is likely to reach its maximum 20–30 h after casting. From the point of view of strength, a period of 16 h is likely to be adequate, except in very cold weather.

The recommendations here are: first, that the factors mentioned above should be considered when deciding on the stripping time, and, second, that on most construction sites during the major part of the year in the United Kingdom steel formwork should not be removed before 24 h after the completion of the casting, and timber forms should be kept in position for at least 36 h.

CURING

As soon as the formwork is struck, the walls should be covered with 500 gauge polythene sheets or reinforced waterproof building paper held in position by a timber framework in such a way that there is no funnelling effect or current of air induced between the covers and the surface of the wall. The need to protect the concrete from rapid changes of temperature as well as to prevent the evaporation of moisture, for a period of 4–7 days after casting, is emphasised in the Code of Practice BS 5337. It is not advisable to cure what may be comparatively warm concrete by pouring cold water over it. The object of curing is to try to reduce drying shrinkage until the concrete has reached a strength sufficient to resist the stresses set up by the moisture changes. If the curing is 100 % efficient, there is no loss of moisture during the curing period (although there are other physical and dimensional changes). It is now agreed that thermal stresses in the early life of the concrete are more likely to cause cracking than drying shrinkage, except plastic shrinkage cracking on floor slabs.

Another method of curing often adopted is the spraying on to the concrete of a resinous compound which seals the surface and so prevents the escape of moisture. This is effective but it does not give any thermal protection. Furthermore, although the compound weathers off fairly rapidly, some may remain and can adversely affect the bond of rendering, which usually has to be applied to form a smooth even surface for the final decoration (whether paint or tiles).

BUILDING IN PIPEWORK

In a swimming pool there are a number of pipes which penetrate the walls and floor, mostly below top water level. The actual number will depend on the size of the pool and the system of water circulation adopted. A detailed discussion of water circulation systems is given in Chapter 7. Listed below are some factors which should be considered when deciding on the methods to be adopted for carrying the pipes through the structural shell of the pool:

(a) Degree of accuracy required in positioning the pipe.
(b) Location, i.e. whether above or below top water level.
(c) Diameter of the pipe and the material of which it is made.

To achieve maximum watertightness with pipes below water level the best method is to build in the pipe as the concrete is cast. The provision of a 'puddle flange' which has an external diameter at least 300 mm (12 in) greater than the nominal diameter of the pipe to which it is fixed will help to ensure a watertight connection. Special care is needed in the compaction of the concrete around the pipe.

Cast-iron and steel pipes are very robust, but copper pipes are thinner and more easily damaged. Copper is not attacked by fresh Portland cement concrete unless chloride ions are present. This is another reason why calcium chloride should not be used as an accelerator in the concrete of swimming pools. Copper pipes are often used for the outlets from scum channnels and for the purified water inlets.

In the case of the scum channel outlets, the copper pipes should be located with great accuracy: a tolerance of only ± 3 mm ($\frac{1}{8}$ in) is often the maximum which can be allowed. The reason for this is that they have to fit into the special glazed outlet scum channel units. Such accuracy cannot be obtained with pipes which are built in, and it is advisable to box out for these and then carefully fill in after the pipe is connected up, with a stiff mortar containing a styrene butadiene based latex to improve bond and reduce shrinkage.

When fixing copper pipes, one other matter must be watched: the copper pipe must not be fixed in contact with steel reinforcement, because these are dissimilar metals and galvanic action will be set up which will corrode one of the metals at the expense of the other. It is advisable to leave not less than 40 mm ($1\frac{1}{2}$ in) between the copper and the steel, and this must be filled with concrete or mortar. For positions where great accuracy is not required, as with outlet pipes through the floor, the pipes can be built in as previously described.

It should be noted that Portland cement is not aggressive to copper (see Chapter 2).

In most cases these days, PVC pipes are used for the outlets to scum channels, skimmer outlets, etc. A difficulty then arises on how to ensure a watertight joint between the outside of the very smooth PVC pipe and the concrete wall or floor of the pool. There is no entirely satisfactory answer to this, and it is recommended that the outside of the PVC pipe should be slightly roughened by careful wire brushing or rubbing with a file to remove the shiny surface, followed by the use of a special resin-based bonding agent, and then making good as suggested.

CATEGORY B: MEDIUM TO LARGE SWIMMING POOLS

GENERAL CONSIDERATIONS

Swimming pools which are 25·0–50·0 m and 12·0–25·0 m wide with a diving pit up to 5·0 m deep (82–165 ft long by 40–82 ft wide and up to 16 ft deep) can present special problems and may require rather different construction methods compared with the small to medium pools of Category A. The large pools are usually constructed by public authorities; they are designed by a team of professional men and tenders are invited from a selected list of contractors who are (or should be) experienced in the construction of swimming pools. 'Package deals' are now sometimes entered into by Local Authorities (see also Chapter 1).

In these cases the pool often forms part of a complex or group of buildings of 'prestige' character, so that, apart from the swimming pool itself, there is a great deal of high-class building work to be carried out. This involves the preparation of contract documents (in accordance with the standard forms set out by the Royal Institute of British Architects and/or the Institution of Civil Engineers) and full-time site supervision. The design and execution of the whole project will therefore be on a different basis compared with the smaller pools. More sophisticated equipment and different construction methods may be used and, with full-time site supervision, quality control of materials and workmanship will be at a higher level.

DESIGN OF THE POOL SHELL

One of the first matters to be considered in the design of the pool is whether the pool shell should be sunk into the ground, either partially or completely, or whether it should be elevated and use made of the space below. Each project will have to be investigated in detail and a decision taken in the light of all relevant factors. In view of the individual character of the problems involved, it is only practical to make a few general observations on the more important factors which must be considered. These factors may be grouped under two headings:

> Site position and layout conditions.
> Subsoil conditions.

Site Position and Layout

On a congested city site space may be at a premium, and by elevating the pool all ancillary equipment such as water treatment and heating and ventilating plant, and possibly a storage area, may be accommodated below the pool and the walkways around it. Even with these arrangements, if ground conditions are favourable, the walkways around the pool need not be above adjoining street level. However, with the pool shell sunk into the ground and the floor supported on the subsoil, the cost of the pool itself is likely to be less than where the floor is designed as a suspended slab.

The topography of the site must also be taken into account, as well as the regulations governing the maximum height of buildings. The proximity and support of the foundations of adjacent structures, and the presence of underground railways or deep sewer or water supply mains, are also important factors.

Subsoil Conditions

If the ground near the surface has poor bearing capacity, with or without a high water table, it may be more economical to do only nominal excavation and to design the pool shell as a suspended structure supported on piles. In this way expensive dewatering and cofferdam work may be avoided and the space beneath the pool floor utilised as previously mentioned.

In the case of floors for large pools, there is often the problem of possible differential settlement and how to deal with it. There is no general answer to this and the method adopted will depend on the assessment of the site conditions, based on an adequate number of trial borings, by the designing engineer. It is suggested that an RC flat slab with a sliding joint between the underside and the supporting members is worth considering. However, some thermal contraction cracking may be experienced. Precast post-tensioned concrete is another possibility worth considering.

THE FLOOR

Where the floor of the pool is supported on the ground, or where the space beneath the pool is utilised and thus a sub-floor is provided, under-drainage of the site may be needed. This subsoil drainage has been discussed earlier in this chapter, and a typical layout of subsoil drains is shown in Fig. 4.1. The problem of flotation has also been dealt with, but it must be realised that with a deep diving pit in water-bearing ground, the danger of flotation is increased, particularly during construction.

If the pool shell is suspended, then the floor will be designed as a suspended slab; this can be either a flat slab or a slab spanning between beams, at the discretion of the designer. However, the author would like to make one point clear with regard to slabs which rest on the ground but are in fact carried on ground beams spanning between stub columns or pile caps. Such slabs should be designed entirely as suspended slabs, which is quite different from slabs uniformly supported on the ground. The concrete mix should be a design mix, and this has been previously described.

Batching must be by weight, and, owing to the size of the job, the contractor may wish to pump the concrete, either from the site batching plant or from the discharge point of ready-mixed concrete trucks. Pumping can be quite satisfactory provided certain basic conditions are observed, and this is discussed later in this chapter.

The method of compaction of the floor slab can be by a vibrating beam if the slab is not more than 200 mm (8 in) thick and is supported on the ground. For thicker slabs and suspended slabs poker vibrators should be used. The author wishes to stress again the need for full compaction of the concrete to secure maximum impermeability. Careful curing is also essential.

THE WALLS

As with the floor, the concrete mix is likely to be 'designed'. Even at the deep end of the pool, it is recommended that the walls be cast in one lift. However, the higher the lift and the more rapid the casting of the concrete, the greater will be the pressure of the fluid concrete on the formwork. This is a very important factor in the design of the formwork, but is one which, unfortunately, is often overlooked.

PUMPING CONCRETE

The pumping of concrete has increased rapidly in the United Kingdom and there is now a fairly wide range of concrete pumps, including mobile units, from which the contractor can choose. The output of these pumps varies from about 6 to 60 m³/h (8 to 80 yd³), and the concrete can be pumped up to about 300 m (1000 ft) horizontally and to a height of 70 m (230 ft). It is not possible in this book to enter into a detailed discussion on the theoretical and practical aspects of pumping concrete, but a few observations on basic principles will be made.

The first and most important point is that for successful pumping the concrete mix must be specially designed. The procedure should be first to decide on the basic specification requirements of the mix from the point of view of the structure without regard to pumping. This specification is then passed to the pumping specialists, who put forward a design mix suitable for pumping which also meets the strength and durability requirements of the contract specification. As an example, the concrete specification given earlier in this chapter could probably be made suitable for pumping by an increase in slump to about 100 mm (4 in), but it must be made clear that the maximum water/cement ratio must not exceed 0·50. To obtain the increased workability and at the same time to avoid segregation, special attention would have to be given to the grading of the sand; it may also be necessary to use a plasticiser, and this could be agreed to, provided it did not contain calcium chloride. It cannot be emphasised too strongly that it is useless to think that a mix suitable for normal transporting and placing methods can be successfully pumped.

The second important point is that pumping is intended for transporting and placing both ready-mixed and site-mixed concrete in large volumes in a comparatively short space of time. In other words, the arrangements on site must be suitable for dealing with the volume of concrete which the pump will deliver. It is not good using a pump with an output of $20\,m^3/h$ if the contractor can only satisfactorily compact $15\,m^3/h$.

The third point is that the supply of concrete must be continuous and not intermittent. In the United Kingdom there is an Association of Concrete Pumping Contractors, and ready-mixed concrete firms also offer this placement service. The details of the mix design can be left to the specialists, subject to the overriding specification requirements, as has already been explained. Generally speaking, concrete for pumping must be workable and cohesive, and the grading of the fine and coarse aggregates is of the utmost importance. The sand content is usually rather higher than in ordinary concrete.

JOINTS IN FLOOR AND WALLS OF REINFORCED CONCRETE SWIMMING POOLS

GENERAL CONSIDERATIONS

All engineers know that joints are required, but the reason behind the selection of the type of joint, their location and detailing are often not fully appreciated. The structural design of the floor and walls must take into account the spacing and type of joint provided. Detailed consideration of the structural design criteria of the swimming pool shell is outside the scope of this book, but it is hoped that the following information will help to explain the recommendations given in respect of joints, and reference can also be made to the short Bibliography at the end of this chapter.

During the setting and early hardening process of concrete, considerable heat is evolved by the chemical reaction between the water and the cement, which results in a rise in temperature of the concrete. The actual rise, the peak temperature, and the time taken to reach the peak and then to cool down, will depend on a large number of factors, including the following:

(a) Temperature of the concrete at the time of placing.
(b) Ambient air temperature.
(c) The type of cement used, and the cement content of the mix.

(d) Type of formwork used (whether timber, plastic or steel) and the time the formwork is kept in position after the placing of the concrete.

(e) The thickness of the section cast, and the exposed surface area-to-volume ratio.

(f) Method of curing and provision, or otherwise, of thermal protection after the removal of the formwork. The peak temperature is probably reached before removal of the formwork, and so this item relates mostly to the cooling down period.

The behaviour and characteristics of the concrete as it hardens are not completely known and research on this is being carried out in the United Kingdom and other countries. As the concrete cools, it contracts and thermal stresses will be set up; these are generally tensile but in certain parts of a structural member they may be compressive. The magnitude of the stresses depends largely on the restraint imposed. It is the tensile stresses which are important, as the compressive stresses are unlikely to reach a critical level. Tensile stresses may (and often do) exceed the strength of the concrete in tension, and cracking may occur. The incidence of cracking can be reduced by the following measures:

(a) Properly located and detailed joints should be provided.

(b) Practical measures should be adopted to reduce the temperature of the concrete at the time of placing when concreting is carried out in hot weather.

(c) A minimum cement content should be specified sufficient for impermeability and durability, but this should not be exceeded unless there is a good reason to do so. This point has been discussed in Chapter 3.

(d) Formwork should be removed as early as practicable in hot weather, but precautions must be taken to avoid thermal shock. For example, it is not advisable to spray cold water on to hot or warm concrete.

(e) Adequate crack control steel should be provided in the walls and the floor. The amount is related to the type and spacing of the joints.

(f) The concrete should be carefully cured.

REASONS FOR PROVIDING JOINTS

There are a number of important reasons why joints are normally provided in the reinforced concrete shell of a swimming pool, and these include the following:

(a) Unless the pool is a very small one, the shell cannot be cast in one continuous operation, and even with small pools this does present certain practical difficulties.

(b) It may be necessary for structural reasons to make provision for movement in the shell of the pool.

The expression 'provision for movement' is used in this context in its widest sense and includes thermal contraction and drying shrinkage, which takes place as the concrete matures, as well as thermal expansion and contraction, creep and foundation movements which may occur during the lifetime of the pool.

TYPES OF JOINT
The following are the principal types of joint used in reinforced concrete swimming pools:

(a) Full movement joints; these are often called expansion joints.

(b) Partial movement joints, also known as contraction joints, semi-contraction joints and stress-relief joints.

(c) Sliding joints, where one structural member slides over an adjacent member with which it is in close contact.

(d) Monolithic joints, also known as construction joints and day-work joints.

Full Movement Joints
Full movement joints (often referred to as expansion joints) should accommodate both expansion and contraction of the concrete on each side of the joint. The basic features of this type of joint are that there is no structural continuity across the joint, which should be able to open and close with minimum restraint, and at the same time remain completely

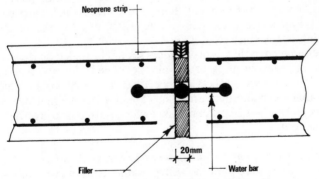

FIG. 4.6.   Full movement joint in RC wall.

watertight under all anticipated conditions of movement. It is essential for full movement joints to be continuous in one plane right through floor and walls of the pool. These joints are detailed so that there is a definite gap between one structural member and the next one; this gap is usually not less than 20 mm ($\frac{3}{4}$ in) wide, but seldom needs to exceed 25 mm (1 in) wide.

Figure 4.6 shows a full movement joint in a wall and Fig. 4.7 shows a full movement joint in a floor.

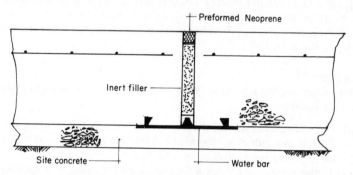

FIG. 4.7.   Full movement joint in RC floor.

The use of a centrally placed water bar is not recommended in a floor slab because of the difficulty in compacting the concrete underneath the bar. To ensure watertightness, the concrete must be well compacted all around the water bar, and steps taken to ensure that the bar is not displaced during concreting.

In vertical joints in walls a centrally located water bar can be used provided the wall is not less than 300 mm thick. This thickness is required so that there is room for the poker vibrators to compact the concrete around the bar. It can be seen that with 40 mm cover on both faces, 10 mm distribution bars and 16 mm main bars, and a 10 mm thick water bar, there is only 79 mm space each side of the water bar for the placing and compacting of the concrete.

It is recommended that joints in floors should be sealed on the water face and that in walls both faces should be sealed. *In situ* sealing compounds or preformed gaskets can be used, as described in Chapter 2. Figure 8.4 shows an alternative method of sealing the external face of a joint with a channel section Neoprene gasket which is fixed into grooves on each side of the joint.

Partial Movement Joints (*Contraction and Stress-Relief Joints*)
This is the basic type of joint the writer recommends between bays in floor slabs and between wall panels.

The provision of a properly detailed joint will allow the natural contraction of the concrete to take place during the first 24–48 h after casting without stresses in the concrete reaching a level which will cause the concrete to crack. The so-called 'partial contraction joint' in which the steel is carried across the joint is not recommended. If it is considered necessary to provide steel to resist shear, then properly detailed tie bars or dowels, bonded to the concrete on one side of the joint and debonded on the other, should be used. It is important that the joint be designed so that the concrete can contract as freely as possible on each side, i.e. so that the joint can open.

It is unfortunate that the effects of this early thermal contraction in concrete is often not recognised by designers and consequently proper allowance is not made for it. This omission leads to random cracking in floor slabs and walls, particularly the latter, because the temperature rise in the concrete in the wall is usually considerably higher than in the floor owing to the presence of formwork which acts as thermal insulation.

In floor slabs which are uniformly supported on the ground (which is the case with the majority of swimming pools) the fabric reinforcement in the top of the slab should be stopped about 50 mm from each side of the joint. An external type of water bar should be used and the joint should be sealed on the surface, as shown in Fig. 4.8. If a stop end is not used at these joints in

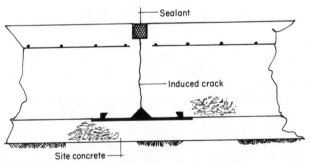

FIG. 4.8.   Stress-relief joint in floor slab.

the floor slab, then it is advisable to use a special type of external water bar which combines a crack inducer. Where a stop end is used, the surface of the concrete should not be prepared in any way, as the object is to ensure that the joint opens fractionally as the concrete contracts.

The detailing of joints in the floor slab of an elevated pool is difficult and it is not possible to give hard and fast recommendations. When the pool is elevated, it is usual for the space below to be used as plant rooms, as storage or by the public (weight-lifting, etc.). It is therefore essential for the pool shell, including the joints, to be completely watertight. The author feels that the use of the proprietary channel section Neoprene gasket shown in Figs. 4.9 and 8.4 has much to recommend it. When correctly installed, it is virtually impossible for leakage to take place. Later in this chapter some brief notes are provided on casting suspended floor slabs in large areas.

There are many advantages if the perimeter bays in the floor slab are cast with the walls in one continuous operation. This method of construction will help to reduce thermal contraction cracking in the walls. However, if this is required to be done, the contract documents must be prepared accordingly so that the contractor knows in advance what is required.

Figure 4.8 shows a stress-relief joint in a floor slab and Fig. 4.9 shows a stress-relief joint in a wall.

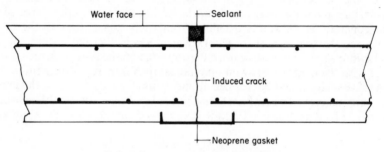

FIG. 4.9.   Stress-relief joint in wall.

One great advantage in using stress-relief joints in walls is that relatively long lengths can be concreted in one operation and the number of stop ends is substantially reduced.

The author recommends the cutting or stopping-off of the distribution steel across the joint so that this, together with the sealing groove on each face of the wall in line with the centre line of the joint, will ensure an induced crack at the joint. In walls which are more than about 450 mm (18 in) thick the provision of a vertical void in the centre of the wall is desirable to help with the formation of the induced crack.

It is better if the stress-relief joints in the floor slab are in line with those in the walls when it is intended that there will be transverse movement joints in the tiling, screed and rendering. If sufficient care is exercised, all these joints can coincide with each other. When there are only perimeter joints in the tiling, then there is no real need for the stress-relief joints in the structural floor and walls to line up. For more information on joints in tiling the reader is referred to Chapter 6.

In elevated pools thermal movement in the pool shell does take place during the normal operation of the pool. Investigations by J. R. Southern of the Building Research Station, East Kilbride, Scotland, and reported in a paper read at a Symposium in June 1973 (see Bibliography) showed the magnitude and importance of this movement. This occurs mainly when the pool is filled and emptied, and unless provision is made for it, cracking of the tiles can result.

A public swimming pool is usually kept filled with water at a temperature of at least 26 °C (76 °F) for a period of 4–8 years. It is then emptied for cleaning and general repair, usually in the middle of winter; at the same time, the opportunity is taken to repair all heating and ventilating equipment. This can result in an appreciable drop in temperature of an elevated pool shell, causing thermal stress in tiling, walls and floor.

The fine thermal contraction cracks which often occur in the walls and floor during construction invariably penetrate right through the walls and floor, thereby forming planes of weakness at those points. Sometimes the cracks are so fine that they are self-sealing, and/or are no wider than the 'minimum' accepted crack width in the Code of Practice. Nevertheless, if no steps are taken to repair the cracks, by some method which will help to restore the monolithic character of the concrete, or they are accepted as possible locations for future thermal movement and treated as such, they may open at some time in the future, particularly when conditions occur as outlined in the preceding paragraph. Suggestions for repairing cracks in swimming pool shells are given in Chapter 8.

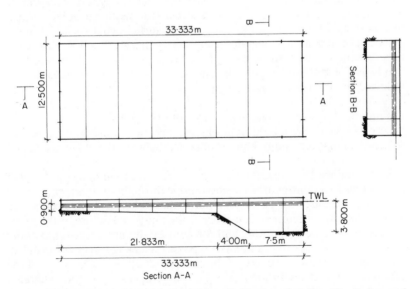

FIG. 4.10.   Possible arrangement of joints in floor and walls of in-the-ground swimming pool; dimensions are finished dimensions of tiled pool.

Swimming pools 'in the ground' are likely to experience appreciably less thermal movement during filling and emptying than elevated pools, owing to the small temperature range of subsoil and groundwater. The presence of a large service duct around the walls of the pool can influence the thermal gradient through the walls.

Figure 4.10 is intended to illustrate in diagram form a possible arrangement of joints (and therefore bay layout and panel lengths) in the floor and walls of an 'in ground' pool. The pool is shown to have a finished length of 33·33 m (110 ft) and a diving pit suitable for a 5·0 m (16 ft 4 in) fixed board. There are many other possible arrangements, and it is worth while to co-ordinate the joint spacing in consultation with the tile manufacturers, as some movement joints will be required in the tiling. Further information on joints in tiling is given in Chapter 6.

Sliding Joints
When a swimming pool is inside a building, the author recommends that the shell of the pool should be separated from the superstructure by a full movement joint. This is a general recommendation and should not be considered as mandatory in all cases. In some projects, depending on the detailed design of the structure, this movement joint may be a sliding one. A sliding joint should be detailed so that restraint is reduced to a minimum. The lower member on which the upper member is supported should be finished with as smooth a surface as possible. One method to achieve this is to trowel in a cement mortar on the concrete surface while the latter is still plastic. The mortar layer should be finished with a steel trowel. Before the upper member is cast, the surface of the lower one should be covered with two layers of 1000 gauge polyethylene sheets, or with bituminous enamel followed by one layer of polyethylene.

Monolithic Joints (*Construction or Day-Work Joints*)
Where it is decided to use this type of joint, the joint should be detailed and specified so that maximum bond is obtained between the old concrete and the new.

Some engineers feel that it is desirable to design a swimming pool so that the floor and walls are completely monolithic throughout; this idea is sound in theory, because it is generally known that, when leakage occurs in a water-retaining structure, it is usually at the joints. Therefore, if the joints are designed to be monolithic and the contractor can succeed in making them so, a considerable amount of possible leakage may be avoided. However, in practice, because of the stresses set up in the early life of the concrete and later on during fluctuations in temperature in the swimming pool it is very difficult indeed to achieve a completely monolithic shell. Reference has previously been made to the investigations carried out by

J. R. Southern and his findings that appreciable movement can take place in elevated pool shells when the pool is filled and emptied. A very heavy weight of distribution steel is required if the cracks are to be so distributed that none of them are wide enough to allow water to enter and reach the reinforcement. It therefore seems logical to the author that monolithic joints should be kept to a minimum in a swimming pool shell. The locations where monolithic joints can be safely provided in most swimming pools are:

(a) Between the kicker and the wall panel where the walls are designed as cantilevers at the base.
(b) Between lifts in walls.
(c) A joint formed in an emergency between predetermined bays in the floor slab or wall panel, or between predetermined lifts in the wall.

To form a monolithic joint the surface of the old concrete must be carefully prepared, either by water spray and brush before the concrete has hardened in order to remove laitance and expose the coarse aggregate, or by hacking or high-pressure water jets after the concrete has hardened. All reinforcement should be continuous across the joint. The surface of the old concrete should be checked before the new concrete is placed against it, to make sure that the surface is in fact clean. Wetting and coating with cement grout is not required if the surface is carefully prepared.

Generally speaking, the author does not feel that a water bar is required in the monolithic joint between the kicker and the wall panel. However, if the designer or contractor wishes to use one, a 150 mm or 200 mm (6 in or 8 in) mild steel flat has advantages over a standard PVC or rubber water bar. The mild steel flat can be easily vibrated into the concrete before the latter has hardened and a positive bond is obtained both in the kicker and in the concrete of the wall panel when it is placed. This is shown in Fig. 4.3.

Joints in the finishing of the swimming pool—that is, in the screed, rendering, and the tiling—are discussed in detail in Chapter 6.

TOLERANCES ON THE FINISHED INSIDE DIMENSIONS OF POOLS

For competitive swimming and diving, the distances and heights have to be correct within certain limits of accuracy. With the advent of industrialised building utilising precast concrete sections, it is beginning to be appreciated by architects and engineers that there is no such thing as an absolute dimension. In all cases where dimensions have to be particularly accurate, it is essential that this fact should be noted in both the contract documents and the drawings; in addition, the permitted tolerances must be clearly stated. In the author's view it is better if all tolerances are given as plus and minus, because it is impossible to ensure absolute accuracy in even one dimension. However, the tolerances permitted by the authorities controlling national and international swimming and diving competitions do not permit a minus tolerance on pool length. Tolerances which are allowed are as follows:

Pool Length. Permitted tolerance: plus 20 mm ($\frac{3}{4}$ in). There is no minus tolerance, and the measurement should be made with a steel tape with the water at 24 °C (75 °F). It should be noted that the tolerance is irrespective of nominal length—that is, there is a permitted tolerance of plus 20 mm on a 25·0 m, a 33·33 m and 50·0 m pool. The ASA do not indicate how this degree of accuracy should be obtained.

Diving Heights. Permitted tolerance: plus or minus $2\frac{1}{2}$% on the nominal height measured from the water surface to the top surface of the diving end of the board. This is necessary because of small fluctuations in the water level of the pool. The actual tolerances for the standard diving boards are therefore:

1·0 m spring board:	$\pm$ 25 mm	(1 in)
3·0 m spring board:	$\pm$ 75 mm	(3 in)
5·0 m high board:	$\pm$ 125 mm	(5 in)
10·0 m high board:	$\pm$ 250 mm	(10 in)

From the above it will be appreciated that great care must be exercised in the setting out and construction of the pool shell and the diving tower. This care must be taken at all stages of construction. It is no use being careful about the concrete shell of the pool and omitting the same care with regard to the rendering, backing for the tiles and the thickness of the tiles. Careless design or fixing of the formwork for the walls of the pool can result in movement of the forms when the concrete is placed which may quite easily be double the allowed tolerance.

To overcome this difficulty, which is a very real one, some designers make the pool 150–200 mm (6–8 in) longer than the specified length, and then provide special detachable and adjustable timing pads which can be accurately fixed in position for competitions. This has been done at the Olympic pool at Edinburgh. Some suggestions for general tolerances in construction are given in Appendix 5.

CONSTRUCTION OF SWIMMING POOLS ON THE UPPER FLOORS OF BUILDINGS

GENERAL CONSIDERATIONS

Sometimes a client wishes to have a swimming pool constructed on the upper floor of a building, which means that the pool shell is suspended and that the area below is used for various purposes depending on the type of building. This creates a number of special problems, of which the most important is the need to ensure that there is no moisture penetration into the areas below the pool. This is quite a different concept from passing the water test described in Chapter 6. The problem can be approached in two ways:

(*a*) To take all necessary steps to ensure complete watertightness of the pool shell and the surrounding walkways and other 'wet' areas, or

(*b*) To accept that some seepage or penetration of water will occur and to deal with it by providing 'drainage channels' below the pool, walkways and 'wet' areas.

There are two basic methods of completely preventing water and vapour penetration below and around the swimming pool shell and adjacent areas:

(1) To design and construct the pool in reinforced concrete with a sandwich-type membrane incorporated in the floor and walls; one method is shown in Fig. 4.11.

(2) To design and construct the pool shell as an independent structure located in a special void provided in the building frame for the purpose. The pool is supported on the building frame and an accessible working space is left right around the outside of the walls and below the floor of the pool. The pool shell can be constructed in reinforced concrete, precast post-tensioned concrete, reinforced gunite, or aluminium sheets. Figure 4.12 shows this method in diagram form.

Some general recommendations on each of these methods are given below.

Method 1: Reinforced Concrete Shell with Sandwich-Type Membrane
It is advisable for the pool shell to be structurally separate from the building frame on which it is supported. Although a watertight membrane is incorporated it is recommended that the pool shell is designed and constructed so as to be watertight in its own right. This means that the pool should be subjected to a water test as described in Chapter 6 and all leaks and damp areas repaired before the membrane is applied. The membrane must be carried under the floor surfacing of all adjoining wet areas, such as walkways, changing and shower rooms, etc.

There are basically two types of membrane which can be used: namely, sheet material (PVC, polyisobutylene, and butyl rubber), and *in situ* compounds such as epoxide and polyurethane resins. Whichever type is selected, it must be fully bonded to the base concrete and this will require correct preparation of the concrete, which is described in detail in Chapter 6.

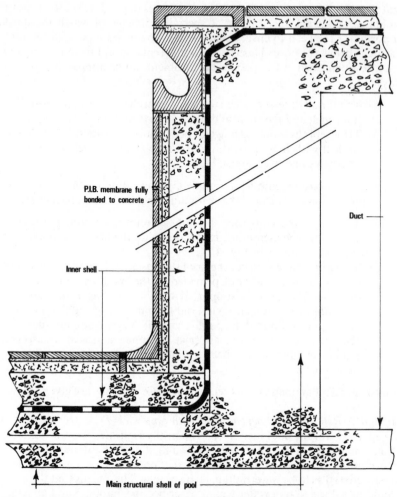

FIG. 4.11.   Detail of sandwich-type membrane for pool on upper floor of building.

The use of preformed sheeting introduces certain problems, the principal one being that subsequent layers (an inner concrete shell or screed and rendering) are not bonded to the membrane. Figure 4.11 shows how this is overcome as far as the pool shell is concerned, but the inner shell adds considerable dead load to the structure. The inner concrete floor should be dense impermeable concrete, otherwise water may penetrate it and accumulate on the membrane which could result in uplift and cracking of

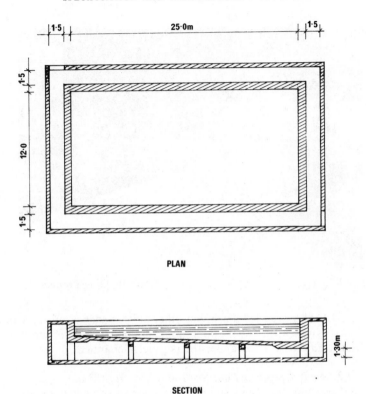

PLAN

SECTION

FIG. 4.12.   Pool on upper floor of building showing working space around walls
and beneath floor.

the tiles. The same of course applies to the walkways and floors of adjacent
wet areas and this is discussed in detail in Chapter 6.

The author feels that an *in situ* membrane of epoxide or polyurethane
resin has a number of advantages over sheet material. These organic
polymers bond well to concrete and they can be formulated to possess some
degree of flexibility. Cement mortar screeds and rendering can be effectively
bonded to the membrane; either by application while the membrane is still
'tacky', or later by the use of a bonding coat of similar resin. This method
was used in the hydrotherapy pool shown in Fig. 4.13.

If the concrete shell is finished with sufficient care and accuracy, there is
no reason why the tiles or mosaic finish should not be applied direct to the
membrane, thus saving both screed and rendering. The bedding and
jointing of the tiles would then have to be in a polymer resin.

FIG. 4.13.   Hydrotherapy pool (Courtesy: Tretol Building Products Ltd).

Figure 4.11 shows a tiled finish, but other finishes such as mosaic can be used. There is no reason why the pool should not be a deck-level one, but the membrane must be carried under the perimeter channel.

Method 2: An Independent Pool Shell in a Structural Void
It should be, and usually is, standard practice to provide a service duct around the perimeter of all indoor pools to carry the service pipes, cables, etc. The method now being discussed provides an access space below the floor as well as around the walls, as shown in Fig. 4.12. This access space must be large enough for men to enter for inspection and to carry out repairs if and when required. Permanent lighting and power points should be provided in this working space. The design of the pool shell must be given careful thought in relation to the building as a whole. The floor of the working space should be waterproofed with bitumen which should be carried up the surrounding walls to a height of 300 mm (12 in).

As previously stated in Method 1, the pool shell can be constructed in a variety of materials. For example, if the reduction of dead load is important, consideration can be given to the use of prefabricated aluminium sections as described in Chapter 5. Some information is given later in this chapter on the use of precast concrete swimming pool units which are post-tensioned together on site. The use of reinforced gunite is also described in this chapter.

The two methods so far described are expensive, but the author feels that the extra cost over what may be described as 'normal pool construction' is unlikely to be significant in relation to the cost of the whole building project. If a pool on the upper floor of an important building develops leaks which cause dampness in the areas below, the cost of putting this right can be very high indeed and can be very detrimental to the reputation of the designers and constructors. Clearly the client must be informed in writing of the alternatives which are available; as he pays it is reasonable that he should

FIG. 4.14.   Pool in London central YMCA building (Courtesy: Elsworth Sykes Partnership, Chartered Architects).

make the final decision. There is certainly nothing wrong in taking a calculated risk provided all concerned know what it is, and are prepared to accept it.

Figure 4.14 shows the swimming pool in the London YMCA which was completed at the beginning of 1977. The pool shell was designed on conventional lines and it was accepted that a limited amount of seepage might occur. Provision was made to intercept this and drain it away, thus preventing any dampness penetrating to the rooms below. An inspection by the author at the end of 1977 showed that the design concept had been successful after some ten months of use. A critical time will be when the pool is emptied for general maintenance, which is unlikely to be needed for several years; in public pools these intervals vary from three to eight years. The author is grateful to the Architects, Elsworth Sykes Partnership and the Consulting Engineers, Kenchington Little and Partners, for information on this outstanding project.

The swimming pool in the hotel in Zermatt, shown in Fig. 4.15, was constructed in reinforced concrete in accordance with the Swiss Code for water retaining structures and then lined with high quality PVC sheeting which formed the decorative finish to the pool as well as the waterproof

FIG. 4.15.   Pool on fourth floor of Hotel Nicoletta, Zermatt (Courtesy: W. Seeholzer, Manager, Hotel Nicoletta).

membrane. The pool was completed in about 1972 and, when the author visited the hotel in September 1977, no moisture penetration had occurred; the main lounge of the hotel is situated immediately below the pool.

Additional Requirements

In addition to the basic problems of watertightness of the pool shell, there are other matters which require careful attention if the project is to be completely successful from a technical point of view.

These are described below with recommendations for dealing with each.

(*a*) The pipework for the water circulation system should be designed so that there are the minimum number of pipes passing through the pool shell or membrane. A deck-level pool as described in Chapter 7 has obvious advantages.

(*b*) Special care should be taken in specification and construction to ensure that only the best materials are used and a high standard of workmanship achieved.

(*c*) The method of water treatment and sterilisation and the heating and ventilating services need careful consideration, and this is discussed in some detail below.

Arrangements must be made to reduce noise and vibration from plant and equipment and to prevent this, as well as noise from users of the pool, penetrating to other parts of the building. Sound insulation and antivibration techniques require careful study and a great deal of experience, and the engagement of specialist consultants for this is highly desirable. These problems must be dealt with early in the design of the building.

Chapter 7 deals with various methods of water treatment and sterilisation used in swimming pools, and it is mentioned that the usual sterilising agent is chlorine. Chlorine compounds have a very pungent odour and the human nose can detect them in exceptionally low concentrations. It is therefore most desirable that this smell should not be allowed to spread to other parts of the building. This can be achieved in several ways:

(*a*) By not using chlorine at all for sterilisation of the pool water, but adopting some other method, such as ozone, chlorine dioxide, bromine, metallic ions, or ultra-violet rays; all of these methods are discussed in Chapter 7.

(*b*) By an efficient system of mechanical ventilation which will discharge the 'contaminated' air at such a position that, irrespective of the direction of the wind, the smell will not be carried to other parts of the building.

(c) By complete aerial disconnection of the swimming pool hall from other parts of the buildings. This requires careful design and something considerably better than a small ventilated lobby is needed.

(d) By adding ozone to the ventilating system as described in Chapter 7; this will reduce considerably the smell of chlorine, but is unlikely to eliminate it completely.

(e) By some combination of methods (b), (c) and (d).

SOME SPECIAL PROBLEMS IN CONSTRUCTION IN REINFORCED CONCRETE

Many problems arise on construction sites during the course of the work. Some of these cannot be foreseen, however carefully the contract documents are prepared. However, there are a number of situations which occur fairly frequently, and it is these on which the following comments are made.

PLACING CONCRETE ON A STEEP SLOPE
It is sometimes necessary to place concrete on a slope exceeding about 20 degrees to the horizontal, and then misgivings arise as to the effect of this on the compaction of the concrete and whether a top shutter is needed. Experience suggests that with careful mix design (in order to obtain workable and cohesive mix) concrete can be laid successfully on slopes up to 35 degrees without a top shutter. Concreting should start from the bottom of the slope and proceed upwards. For the steeper slopes a climbing top shutter can be used. The compaction of the concrete is best obtained by poker vibrators and not by clamp-on vibrators on the formwork, as the latter are liable to result in a wave pattern on the surface of the concrete. Figure 4.16 shows concrete being placed on the slope to the diving pit in a private pool.

REMOVAL OF RUST FROM REINFORCEMENT
A frequent source of argument on site is whether rust should be removed from reinforcement before concrete is placed around it and to what extent a thin layer of rust improves bond between the concrete and the steel. In 1973 the Construction Industry Research and Information Association started an investigation into this problem. They published an interim report in 1974, entitled *Reinforcement, How Rusty Before You Start Using it?* A final report was published during 1977. The consensus of opinion among practically-minded engineers and contractors is that light powdered rust can remain on the steel and will do no harm but loose rust scale and loose mill scale should be removed.

FIG. 4.16.   Placing concrete on sloping floor of swimming pool (Courtesy: Rutherford Ltd, Battle).

It is obviously advisable that reinforcement should be properly stacked on site on either trestles or some other supports so that it is not lying on the ground becoming covered with water and mud. Bond, particularly in the early life of the concrete, is of special importance in the case of swimming pools as far as the distribution steel is concerned. The reasons for this have been discussed earlier. It is, of course, the borderline cases which are most difficult to resolve satisfactorily, but the author's advice is: 'When in doubt remove the rust'.

PLASTIC CRACKING
There are two categories of plastic cracking:

(a) The first, and most common, results from a too rapid evaporation of moisture from the surface of the concrete while the concrete is still plastic and is usually referred to as plastic shrinkage cracking.
(b) The second is plastic settlement cracking and is caused by the settlement of the plastic concrete as it is stiffening and after the completion of compaction.

Plastic Shrinkage Cracking

Investigation by various authorities has shown that when the rate of evaporation on the surface of the concrete exceeds the rate at which water rises to the surface (known as 'bleeding'), plastic cracking is very likely to result.

The rate at which the water in the mixed concrete reaches the surface and the total quantity involved depends on many factors, all of which are not yet completely understood, but the following are known to be important:

Grading, moisture content, absorption and type of aggregate used.
Total quantity of water in the mix.
Cement content.
Thickness of the concrete slab.
Characteristics of any admixtures used.
Degree of compaction obtained, and therefore the density and impermeability of the compacted concrete.
Whether the formwork (or sub-base) on which the concrete was placed was dry or wet.

The rate of evaporation from the surface will also depend on a number of factors which are much better understood, and these are:

Relative humidity.
Temperature of the concrete.
Temperature of the air.
Wind velocity.
Degree of exposure of the surface of the slab to the sun and wind.

Plastic shrinkage cracking shows itself as fine cracks which are usually fairly straight and can vary in length from about 50 to 750 mm. They are often transverse in direction. In some cases several of the cracks are parallel to each other and the spacing can vary from about 50 mm to 90 mm. The cracks are usually shallow and seldom penetrate below the top layer of reinforcement, although in severe cases they can extend to a greater depth and even right through the slab. They are generally fairly numerous. Figure 4.17 shows typical plastic cracking in a floor slab.

It is quite common for this type of cracking to occur in hot sunny weather or on days when there is a strong drying wind, and this can cause consternation to those who do not realise what it is. Unless it is very severe, when it may result in deep cracks and in a permanently weakened surface to the slab, it does no real harm. The cracks should, however, be grouted in with a Portland cement grout well brushed in and the treated surface should be covered with polythene sheets held down around the edges with planks and blocks for at least 48 h.

It has been found that the use of an air entraining admixture to give a

FIG. 4.17.   Plastic shrinkage cracking in floor slab (Courtesy: G. F. Blackledge).

total air content of the concrete of $4\frac{1}{2} \pm 1\frac{1}{2}\%$, will usually help considerably in reducing the incidence of plastic cracking. Prevention is always better than cure, and if the concrete is covered with plastic sheeting, well lapped down and held down around the perimeter immediately finishing operations are complete, it is unlikely that plastic shrinkage cracking will occur.

Plastic Settlement Cracking

The origin of plastic settlement cracking is quite different from that of the plastic shrinkage cracking which has been described above. It can be caused in two basic ways:

(1) By the resistance of the surface of the formwork to the downward settlement (compaction) of the plastic concrete under the influence of poker vibrators and the force of gravity. The resistance delays this movement, and when it occurs during the time that the concrete is stiffening, a crack is very likely to form. This is invariably a surface defect, and the cracks are wider at the surface and do not penetrate deeper than about 20–25 mm ($\frac{3}{4}$–1 in).

(2) By the concrete becoming 'hung-up' on either the reinforcement or the spacers, and a crack forming as the concrete stiffens. This is liable to occur in deep beams which have fairly heavy reinforcement

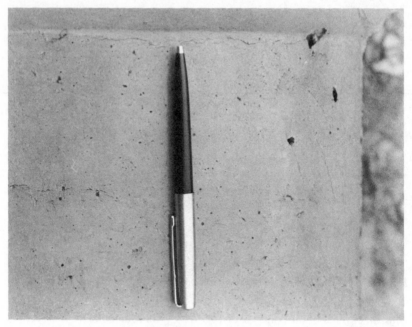

FIG. 4.18.   Plastic settlement cracking in mushroom head of RC column
(Courtesy: H. N. Tomsett).

and also in columns, usually in the upper third. This type of cracking is more serious, because the cracks penetrate at least to the reinforcement, they may be wider inside the concrete than on the surface and they may be associated with honeycombing underneath the reinforcement. Some changes in the mix proportions and greater care with compaction will usually solve the problem; the use of a plasticiser or an air-entraining admixture will also often prove to be beneficial.

Figure 4.18 shows this type of cracking near the head of a mushroom-headed column, while Fig. 4.19 shows in detail how the crack tends to widen as it proceeds inwards.

Information on methods of repair to this type of cracking is given in Chapter 8.

CASTING SUSPENDED SLABS IN LARGE AREAS
Contractors usually wish to cast suspended slabs in larger and larger areas as one continuous operation. Frequently the specification is very restrictive,

FIG. 4.19.   Close-up of core cut to show enlargement of crack inwards, from Fig.
4.18 (Courtesy: H. N. Tomsett).

and may limit the area to about 50 m². Arguments then develop on site as to
the reasonableness of the specification. The major problem which can arise
with casting large areas is cracking due to thermal contraction of the
concrete as it cools down, which may be aggravated by drying shrinkage. If
the slab is supported on frictionless bearings which do not induce any
restraint on the thermal movement of the concrete, then it is unlikely that
any stress will develop which exceeds the strength of the concrete in tension.
In practice, very considerable restraint is induced in floor and roof slabs by
supporting beams, walls and columns.

It is now not unusual to cast at least 400 m² of concrete suspended slab in
one continuous 'pour'. The problem is to try to assess the effect of the
restraints imposed by the supports in each particular case. For example, if
the slab is supported on walls or beams with a sliding joint, restraint will be
reduced compared with a monolithic or pinned joint in this position.
Similarly, massive beams on massive columns will introduce more restraint
than lighter beams on slim, flexible columns. Unfortunately, owing to the
large number of variables involved and lack of knowledge on how to
calculate the value of these variables, it is not possible at present to arrive at

a solution based on calculations. The most practical way to deal with the problem is to take the following precautions:

(a) Measures should be taken which will reduce the rise in temperature of the concrete during the first 36 h after casting.
(b) The whole concreting operation should be carefully pre-planned. If the concrete is ready-mixed, the understanding and co-operation of the supplier should be ensured by prior discussion, well in advance of the start of the operation.
(c) An adequate amount of experienced supervision should be provided on site.
(d) Within the area of each bay, i.e. one casting unit, there should be no part of the slab without adequate top reinforcement, preferably in the form of a fabric (BS 4483). The fabric is placed 40–50 mm ($1\frac{1}{2}$–2 in) from the top of the slab and is additional to the reinforcement required for normal design purposes. It is required to control cracking due to thermal contraction.
(e) Depending on the area involved and the degree of restraint imposed, it may be desirable to provide stress-relief joints at selected locations. These are in reality vertical planes of weakness purposely formed in the slab in positions where their presence will not reduce the resistance of the slab to imposed loads under the worst conditions of loading. Their location should be determined as a separate design problem.
(f) The detailing of the stress-relief joints mentioned in (e) above will depend on the duty which the slab has to perform, e.g. roof, floor of normal rooms or floor of shower rooms, etc., and on whether there is likely to be movement across the joint during the normal operation of the building.

SWIMMING POOLS CONSTRUCTED IN REINFORCED GUNITE

GENERAL CONSIDERATIONS
Gunite may be defined as a mortar or concrete conveyed through a hose and pneumatically projected at high velocity onto a surface; the force of the impact compacts the material. Swimming pools constructed of reinforced gunite are very popular in the United States, Australia and South Africa and the use of this method of construction is increasing in the United Kingdom. There are a number of advantages in using reinforced gunite as compared with reinforced concrete; there are also some disadvantages. These may be summarised as follows:

Advantages

(a) High speed of construction; a swimming pool 18·0 m × 12·0 m with a depth of 1·0 m–2·5 m (60 ft × 40 ft × 3 ft 3 in–8 ft 6 in) can be constructed from a prepared excavation in about 20 working days. This is all the work necessary for the structural shell, but does not include finishings and pipework, etc.

(b) The pool can be built on a congested site where access for equipment and materials is severely restricted because the delivery hose to the gun can be at least 100 m (330 ft) long.

(c) The only joints in a normal gunite pool are plain butt joints which do not require sealing.

(d) For pools larger than about 12 m × 6 m (40 ft × 20 ft) it is often cheaper than reinforced concrete.

(e) It is cheaper than reinforced concrete for 'free-formed' pools.

(f) Little or no formwork is required.

Disadvantages

(a) For a successful job it should only be entrusted to specialist firms.

(b) Size for size, a gunite pool is appreciably lighter than one in reinforced concrete and is therefore more liable to flotation unless special precautions are taken.

(c) The usual design, and probably the most satisfactory one structurally, incorporates a wide cove angle between the wall and floor. If the pool is to have a finish of ceramic tiles, this cove angle must be changed to a right angle.

There is no British Code of Practice for gunite, but there is an American Code, prepared by the American Concrete Institute, entitled Recommended Practice for Shotcreting, No. ACI 506–66. In the US gunite is known as shotcrete. In British Standard BS 5337: The Structural Use of Concrete for Retaining Aqueous Liquids, gunite is mentioned as suitable for the cover coat for prestressing wire in prestressed concrete tanks, and as reinforced concrete.

In the opinion of the author properly designed and constructed gunite is an excellent structural material for swimming pool shells. It has been used quite extensively for private pools in the United Kingdom and in recent years its use has been extended to public pools.

There are two guniting processes in general use, but of these, only one, the dry-mix, is used for swimming pools in the United Kingdom. The other process, known as wet-mix, is comparatively new and is used for both structural gunite as well as linings, principally in the United States.

In the dry-mix process the cement and sand is weigh batched and thoroughly mixed in a special piece of plant. The mixture is forced along the delivery hose to the nozzle by compressed air, and at the nozzle water is admitted by the gun operator. The nozzle is so designed that the water and the cement–sand mix are thoroughly mixed before they are discharged onto the surface being gunited. The water/cement ratio is about 0·35.

In the wet-mix process the cement and sand (and coarse aggregate if it is a concrete) and the water are weigh batched and then thoroughly mixed. The mix is then projected along the delivery hose to the discharge nozzle by compressed air. Additional compressed air can be admitted at the nozzle if required, to increase the velocity of impact. The mortar when it is discharged from the nozzle must be cohesive and capable of supporting itself on vertical (and in special cases on overhead) surfaces. The water/cement ratio is generally about 0·35.

The properties and performance of gunite depend largely on the skill of the operator, but mix proportions, grading of the sand, type of equipment used and site conditions are also important. It should be noted that the mix proportions of the gunite in place are likely to be different from proportions at the time of batching. This is due principally to rebound, but other factors such as water/cement ratio, grading of the sand, placement velocity and site exposure conditions, are important to a greater or lesser degree. Generally, there is a tendency for the mortar in place to be rather richer than the mix as batched.

Figures given for rebound vary, but the following are quoted from United States experience:

floors: 10–15%
walls: 15–30%

While this section is concerned with the construction of swimming pools in gunite, it is relevant to remark that this method of construction is used widely for shell roofs, sewage tanks and the repair of damaged and deteriorated concrete structures. Gunite is also used as a structural lining for many types of structures and as the protective coating to circumferentially wound prestressed concrete tanks. The use of gunite for repairing swimming pools is discussed in Chapter 8.

EXCAVATION
This should be carried out as carefully as possible and must be kept free of water. It should be noted that while most gunite pools are constructed entirely or partly below ground, they can be built on the ground surface.

REINFORCEMENT
High-tensile steel is generally used; often in the form of a fabric (BS 4483) for smaller pools, with vertical bars to hold the mesh in position. The cover to reinforcement is usually accepted as 25 mm instead of the 40 mm

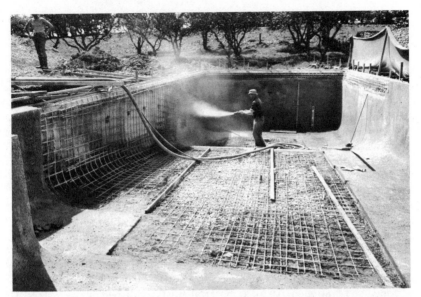

FIG. 4.20.   Construction of swimming pool in reinforced gunite (Courtesy: Cement
Gun Co. Ltd and Gunite Swimpools Ltd).

required for reinforced concrete. In the opinion of the author, cover in
excess of 30 mm ($1\frac{1}{4}$ in) is undesirable, as crack control is reduced with
increase in distance from the surface. The wall reinforcement must be
securely anchored into the floor slab and carried up into the ring beam at
the top of the wall. Figure 4.20 shows reinforcement fixed and 'gunning' in
progress.

EXECUTION OF THE WORK
One of the most difficult, but at the same time most important, matters is
to ensure that the gunite is of uniform density throughout and that there are
no voids or sand pockets behind the reinforcement. Corners require special
care in this respect. When reinforcing bars are lapped, it is advisable for the
bars to be spaced at least two diameters apart so that they can be fully
embedded in the gunite.

   In swimming pools it is usual for the walls and the adjoining bays of the
floor to be gunited first. When these are complete, the central portion of the
floor is gunned. The walls are usually gunned in panels to their full height
and thickness together with the adjoining floor bay in one operations. This
means that to a large extent the length of the panel is governed by the
capacity of the equipment and the output of the operator. Formwork is not

used for the wall panels, but only for the ring beam at the top and for any intermediate beams which are often inserted in deep pools.

On the outside of the reinforcement, stout hessian is fixed to timber supports spaced at about 1·0 m centres, and this forms the background to which the gunite is applied. The hessian also acts as a dividing layer between the structural shell and the sides of the excavation. Prior to the commencement of the gunning the hessian is given a coat (or spray) of gunite or cement grout to stiffen it. Hardboard and plywood can also be used, but plaster board should not be used as it is composed largely of gypsum (calcium sulphate) and the sulphate may become embedded in the gunite.

The floor is usually formed of large shingle—known as 'rejects'—laid to a depth of 150–200 mm (6–8 in). On this the gunite is applied to the required thickness, which may vary from 250 mm (10 in) next to the walls to 100 mm (4 in) in the centre part of the floor. Apart from the reinforcement from the walls, a mat of reinforcing bars or a mesh is provided in the gunite floor slab. (See Figs. 4.20 and 4.21.)

If for any reason a panel has to be increased in thickness after it has been gunned, then the first layer must be allowed to take its initial set before the second layer is applied. All loose material must be brushed off the surface. If the lower layer has already hardened, then it is advisable to grit blast the surface and dampen it with a water spray.

FIG. 4.21. 'Gunning' in progress for club swimming pool (Courtesy: Rutherford Ltd, Battle).

All pipework passing through the floor and wall must be fixed in position and gunited in with the wall and floor. The author recommends the use of puddle flanges on these pipes but, for reasons previously given, great care must be exercised to ensure that there are no voids or sand pockets behind them.

Generally, skimmer outlets rather than scum channels are used in gunite pools, and these are formed by boxing out as the wall panels are gunned. If scum channels are provided, these are bedded on the ring beam, which is then L-shaped with the channel supported on the horizontal leg. The different types of outlets for swimming pools and methods of water treatment are dealt with in Chapter 7, but, in the author's opinion, a properly laid scum channel is more efficient than skimmers for larger pools.

PRESSURE RELIEF VALVES

The thickness of both floor and walls of gunite pools is less than that of reinforced concrete; also, the density (weight per unit volume) of gunite is lower than that of well-compacted concrete made with normal aggregates. Because of this, the total weight of the shell of a gunite pool is appreciably less than that of a pool of the same size in reinforced concrete. This is the reason why the majority of gunite contractors strongly recommend the provision of pressure relief valves in the floor. The author has given his views on pressure relief valves earlier in this chapter, but he does agree that with gunite pools there is a strong case for their use.

JOINTS

Full movement joints are not provided in normally designed gunite pools. However, even the smallest private pool is unlikely to be gunned in one continuous operation and therefore day-work or construction joints are required. The method of dealing with these joints varies. The US Code (ACI 506–66) recommends feather edging, but a leading firm of gunite contractors in the United Kingdom does not consider this satisfactory. They prefer a plain butt joint down to the reinforcement; below this, the joint is tapered.

In view of what has been said earlier in this chapter about joints in reinforced concrete walls and floors, a natural question is why should gunite be satisfactory without any contraction or stress-relief joints. It is not easy to give a completely clear unambiguous answer to this, but the factors involved are:

(a) Usually the walls of a gunite shell are thinner than with *in situ* concrete. This, together with the absence of formwork at least on one side, results in less build-up of heat and consequently lower thermal stresses are developed.

(b) Gunite is generally reinforced with heavy high-tensile fabric and the amount of horizontal (distribution) steel is therefore likely to be greater than normally provided in a reinforced concrete wall.

(c) Good-quality gunite has a low water/cement ratio, about 0·33–0·35, while concrete has a w/c ratio of 0·45–0·50.

(d) The compressive strength of high-quality gunite is likely to be in the range 55–65 N/mm^2 (8000–9500 lbf/in^2) with equivalent tensile strength. That of *in situ* concrete is likely to be 30–40 N/mm^2 (4000–6000 lbf/in^2).

All the above factors reduce the tendency to thermal contraction cracking.

The above remarks are not intended to suggest that cracking in gunite pools is unknown. It does occur, but in high-grade gunite it is less frequent and usually takes the form of fine surface cracks which do not penetrate below the level of the reinforcement.

CURING

In the opinion of the author, the curing of gunite is as important as for concrete, but is often neglected by even the good contractors. Curing is best effected by the use of polyethylene sheets securely fixed in position so that there is no funnel effect behind the sheets. The curing should be continued for 4 days. The freshly placed gunite should also be shielded from the direct rays of the sun on hot summer days; also from heavy rain and, in cold weather, from the effect of freezing temperatures. High-quality gunite is probably rather less vulnerable to low temperatures than concrete owing to its high cement content, which is between 450 and 500 kg/m^3 (750–880 lb/yd^3).

FINISHING

Gunite can be left 'straight from the gun' or the surface can be worked over with a wood float or steel trowel, depending on what subsequent treatment is required. It is usual to apply a coat of rendering prior to tiling, mosaic or marbelite. In this case a wood float followed by combing the surface to form a mechanical key should be adequate.

SWIMMING POOLS CONSTRUCTED IN *IN SITU* PRESTRESSED CONCRETE

Prestressed concrete is in many ways an ideal material for water-retaining structures because the concrete remains in compression even when under maximum load. Therefore, with proper design and construction, there is no tendency to crack formation.

In view of this it is somewhat surprising that so few swimming pools have been constructed in this material. The main reason appears to be the rectangular shape which is more or less compulsory for pools in which there will be competitions, unless the pool is very large indeed. The rectangular shape and the fact that in the majority of pools the floor slab is supported on the ground, makes it difficult to analyse the stresses in the walls and floor accurately. This reasoning seems to be borne out by the fact that large numbers of above-ground circular water reservoirs have been constructed in prestressed concrete but very few rectangular ones.

A circular shape for a small swimming pool can be very attractive, and quite suitable for private houses, hotels and clubs. If the pool is situated on the upper floor of a building, a circular shape and construction in prestressed concrete is well worth consideration. The problems of pools in this position have been considered in detail in another section of this chapter.

Another position where prestressing may provide the answer to a somewhat difficult problem is where one or more walls of the pool are completely exposed to the public view, with large windows in them for underwater viewing. In such a case not even the smallest crack or seepage can be tolerated, and so a design which keeps the wall under permanent compression is one solution.

Because of the small number of prestressed pools constructed, there is very little published information on the design criteria and construction techniques employed. From the little that has been written, it is clear that both design assumptions and construction methods vary and have evolved with the experience of the designers. In some pools in Denmark the two long walls were concreted first and partially stressed; this was followed by the two short walls, then the floor. The completion of the stressing was carried out in the same order. As the walls and floor were stressed separately, mild steel reinforcement was provided to secure structural continuity between walls and floor. In the Olympic pool (50 m × 21 m) at Rødovre the short end wall at the deep end was provided with counterforts, and a horizontal reinforced concrete slab entered the wall near the top.

In these Scandinavian pools great importance was attached to reducing friction between the floor of the pool and the subsoil. Also, owing to the absence of mild steel reinforcement in the floor slab to control cracking, special precautions were taken with the curing, and partial stressing was carried out as soon as possible after casting, in this case 3 days. The floor was cast in one operation, working from both ends, and 160 m³ (210 yd³) of concrete was used.

POOLS WITH FLOORS OF EITHER *IN SITU* REINFORCED CONCRETE OR REINFORCED PRECAST CONCRETE AND WALLS OF REINFORCED PRECAST CONCRETE UNITS POST-TENSIONED TOGETHER

A number of very attractive swimming pools have been built in Germany consisting of precast concrete units post-tensioned together. The principal system in use is covered by the patents of the firm IBACO of Velbert, who work in association with the contracting firm of Dyckerhoff and Widmann of Munich. In many cases the precast pool is part of a sports or other building which is also constructed in precast concrete units. As far as the author is aware, this method of swimming pool construction has not been used in the United Kingdom.

This type of pool can either have an *in situ* reinforced concrete floor and reinforced precast wall units or both floor and walls can be in reinforced precast units. In both cases the walls are cast with a foundation slab and provision is made for post-tensioning through the walls and the floor. The wall units are brought to the site complete with wall tiling and pipe connections cast in. These units can have either skimmer outlets or scum channels; underwater windows and lighting units can also be incorporated. The scum channels are cast separately in units the same length as the wall panels and placed in position after the wall panel has been erected. Another

FIG. 4.22.   Factory made prefabricated post-tensioned concrete swimming pool units being erected on site in Germany (Courtesy: Dyckerhoff and Widmann GmbH, München).

FIG. 4.23. Factory made prefabricated post-tensioned concrete swimming pool units being erected on site in Germany (Courtesy: Dyckerhoff and Widmann GmbH, München).

feature which is often incorporated in this type of pool is a movable floor; this considerably increases the use to which the pool can be put and its flexibility of operation. A detailed description of the movable floor system is given in Chapter 6.

The post-tensioning system used introduces permanent compression into both floor and walls, with the result that the pool shell is a prestressed post-tensioned structure with all the advantages which this gives in ensuring watertightness. The residual prestress is particularly useful when ground conditions are poor and differential settlement may occur. In addition to the structural advantages of prestressed concrete, there is the improved quality of the concrete and the finishes which are produced under factory conditions. Figures 4.22 and 4.23 show precast units being erected.

BIBLIOGRAPHY

AMERICAN CONCRETE INSTITUTE, *Shotcreting—A Symposium of* 13 *Papers*, Publication SP-14, Detroit, USA, 1966, p. 223.

AMERICAN CONCRETE INSTITUTE, *Recommended Practice for Shotcreting*, ACI Committee 506–66, Detroit.

BRITISH STANDARDS INSTITUTION, BS 5337: *The Structural use of Concrete for Retaining Aqueous Liquids*, 1976.

BUILDING RESEARCH ESTABLISHMENT, *Concrete in Sulphate-bearing Soils and Ground Waters*, Digest No. 174, HMSO, 1975, p. 4.

JACKSON, P., Shutter ties in unlined concrete water retaining structures. *The Structural Engineer*, **44**(4) (April 1966), 135–8.

MURPHY, F. G. The effect of initial rusting on the bond performance of reinforcement. CIRIA Report No. 71, Nov. 1977, p. 26.

PERKINS, P. H., Specification and construction of swimming pool shells. Paper at Symposium at East Kilbride Building Research Establishment, June 1973, p. 13.

PERKINS, P. H., Some problems in the design, specification and construction of concrete swimming pools with particular reference to joints. *Build International* (6) (1973), 161–81.

PERKINS, P. H., Swimming pool shells and walkways. Paper presented at Symposium given by British Ceramic Tile Council and Sports Council, London, July 1975, p. 12.

PERKINS, P. H., *The Use of Portland Cement Concrete in Sulphate-bearing Ground and Ground Waters of Low pH*, Cement and Concrete Association, ADS/30, London, April 1976.

PERKINS, P. H., Concrete Structures: Repair, Waterproofing and Protection, Applied Science Publishers, London, 1977.

RASMUSSEN, SV. AA., Swimming pools in prestressed concrete. *Ingenioren International*, **5**(2) (June 1961), 47–51.

SHACKLOCK, B. W., Code 11.004: *Concrete Constituents and Mix Proportions*, Cement and Concrete Association, London, 1974, p. 102.

SOUTHERN, J. R., Joint movements. Paper at Symposium at East Kilbride Building Research Establishment, June 1973, p. 6.

TEYCHENNÉ, D. C., FRANKLIN, R. E. and ERNTROY, H. C., *Design of Normal Concrete Mixes*, HMSO, London, 1975, p. 30.

TOPALOFF, B., Prestressed concrete swimming pool. *Beton und Stahlbeton*, **53**(2) (Feb. 1958), 48–52 (in German).

TYLER, I. L. and ERLIN, B., A proposed simple method of test for determining the permeability of concrete. *J. Research Development Laboratories*, Portland Cement Association (Sept. 1961), 2–7.

CHAPTER 5

The Specification and Construction of Swimming Pools Built of Materials Other than Reinforced and Prestressed Concrete and Reinforced Gunite

INTRODUCTION

Chapter 4 dealt with the construction of swimming pools in reinforced and prestressed concrete and reinforced gunite. These materials and corresponding methods of construction are used for the vast majority of medium and large swimming pools. There are, however, other materials which can, in appropriate circumstances, be used successfully for building small to medium-size pools. These materials, together with methods of construction, are described in this chapter.

It is important to remember that there are definite restrictions on the size and depth of pools which can be built satisfactorily in these 'other' materials; in addition, site conditions must be taken into account. The author has a high opinion of many contracting firms which offer design and construction all-in package deals. But he also feels that in cases where quite large sums of money are involved the relatively small extra cost of taking independent professional advice is worthwhile. In the long term this is better for both the contractor and the client. For further information on how to get a pool built the reader is referred to Chapter 1.

SWIMMING POOLS CONSTRUCTED WITH AN *IN SITU* REINFORCED CONCRETE FLOOR AND PLAIN CONCRETE (GRAVITY-TYPE) WALLS

In theory there is no limit to the size of pool which can be constructed by this method. However, owing to the thickness of the walls and the number of joints or crack-inducers required, a size larger than about 10·0 m × 6·0 m with a depth or 1·0 m–1·5 m (33 ft × 20 ft × 3 ft 3 in–5 ft) is unlikely to be an economic proposition.

EXCAVATION
General advice on the excavation, including subsoil drainage, has been given in Chapter 4 and will not be repeated.

THE FLOOR
The floor of the pool should be constructed in *in situ* reinforced concrete not less than 150 mm (6 in) thick. The requirements for bay size, weight of reinforcement and joints are all the same as those described in Chapter 4 for small to medium pools, and these are summarised as follows:

(*a*) Oversite concrete to be 50–75 mm (2–3 in) thick with an aggregate/cement ratio 8·0 or 9·0.

(*b*) A slip layer to be provided consisting of 1000 gauge polythene sheets or two coats of bituminous emulsions.

(*c*) The floor slab should have a minimum thickness of 150 mm (6 in) and be laid in bays of convenient size to suit the pool dimensions. If the wall is constructed on the floor slab, the slab should be thickened below the wall to 250 mm. The reinforcement should consist of high-tensile mesh, placed 40–50 mm ($1\frac{1}{2}$–2 in) from the top surface of the slab. The mesh should be rectangular, with minimum weight of 3·41 kg/m², (6·21 lb yd²) and the main wires running longitudinally.

The placing of the concrete, compaction, finishing and protection and curing of the slab should all be as previously recommended in Chapter 4. It should be noted that because the walls derive their stability from their mass, there is no reinforcement connecting the floor slab with the walls, as was the case with walls of reinforced concrete. This, of course, greatly simplifies the construction of the floor slab. All joints should be provided with a sealing groove and properly sealed. If the depth of water exceeds about 2·0 m (6 ft 6 in), an external type water bar should be used below the joint, as shown in Fig. 4.2.

THE WALLS
The external and internal loading is resisted by the weight (or mass) of the wall itself. This is the theoretical idea; in practice, the end walls provide some restraint to the side walls and the materials used do possess some tensile and shear strength, as well as considerable compressive strength.

The graphical stability analysis is shown in Fig. 5.1. The basic factors used are:

Density of concrete: 2385 kg/m³ (4000 lb/yd³).
Density of water: 1000 kg/m³ (62·4 lb/ft³).

The wall is 1·20 m (4 ft) high, with water on one side at a height of 1·0 m (3 ft 3 in) above the floor; there is no support on the other side of the wall. The

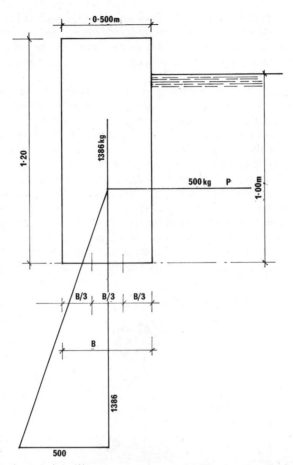

FIG. 5.1.   Diagram of forces acting on mass (plain) concrete wall of pool.

diagram shows that, even with a thickness of 500 mm (19½ in), the resultant falls outside the middle third of the base and therefore, theoretically, the wall is unstable. In practice, the following factors would be acting together and would make the wall stable; there would be considerable support from compacted backfilling on the outside of the wall; the restraint from the end walls and the tensile strength of the concrete, together with the bond developed at the junction of the wall and the floor, would all help to prevent overturning or slipping.

It is assumed that steel formwork will be used, and as this has been dealt with previously, only the casting of the wall will be discussed here. The surface of the part of the concrete floor on which the wall will be cast must be prepared so that there is a maximum bond between this concrete and the wall. What is required is an exposed aggregate finish for the full width of the wall. This surface preparation has been described in detail earlier in this chapter.

In view of the fact that there is no reinforcement in the wall to take thermal and drying shrinkage stresses (there is a detailed discussion on these stresses in Chapter 4), the wall must be cast in short lengths to its full height; the length of the wall panels should not exceed 3·0 m (10 ft). The joints between the panels should be considered as contraction or stress-relief joints, as discussed in Chapter 4. The provision of a water bar, and sealing grooves on both faces of the wall, is recommended. The stress-relief joints can be detailed with crack inducers so as to reduce the number of stop ends and thus speed up the casting of the wall. This type of joint is shown in Fig. 5.2. The vertical ducts extend for the full height of the wall and can be formed by an inflatable former such as a Ductube. The holes should be carefully plugged as soon as the former is removed, and the final filling of the voids should be carried out as late in the construction process as possible.

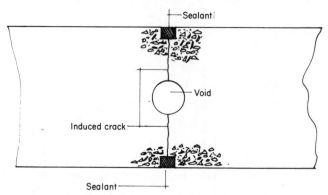

FIG. 5.2.   Stress-relief joint in plain concrete wall of pool.

The water bar between the wall and the floor slab can be a mild steel flat 150 mm × 3 mm (6 in × $\frac{1}{8}$ in).

The concrete mix for the walls should be weight batched with mix proportions as follows:

Cement: Ordinary Portland, 50 kg.
Coarse aggregate: 20 mm ($\frac{3}{4}$ in) maximum size, 150 kg.
Fine aggregate: a clean concreting sand, 100 kg.
Water/cement ratio: 0·50.

Detailed information on the ordering of ready-mixed concrete has already been given in Chapter 4. In the present case the only changes would be:

(a) The cube strength should be 25 N/mm^2 (3500 lbf/in^2) minimum at 28 days.

(b) The minimum cement content should be 330 kg/m^3 (550 lb/yd^3).

(c) The slump should be 25–75 mm (1–3 in).

The concrete should be compacted with poker-type vibrators so as to obtain the maximum density. The wall panels can be cast one after another in the most convenient order; there is nothing to be gained by a 'hit and miss' procedure. The formwork should be left in position for at least 48 h after completion of each panel, and when it is removed, the same procedure should be followed as previously recommended for *in situ* reinforced concrete walls.

On completion of the wall panels the bolt holes should be filled in by the method previously described. This should be followed by cleaning out and sealing the grooves at all joints. The pool is then ready for testing, but this should not be carried out earlier than 28 days after the casting of the last wall panel. The method of testing is described in Chapter 6. The important point here is that with the type of pool described the water test should be carried out before any rendering or decorative finish is applied; in other words, the floor and walls should be watertight in their own right.

SWIMMING POOLS BUILT WITH AN *IN SITU* REINFORCED CONCRETE FLOOR AND WALLS OF HOLLOW CONCRETE BLOCKS WITH THE VOIDS FILLED WITH *IN SITU* REINFORCED CONCRETE

GENERAL CONSIDERATIONS

There is a divergence of views as to whether this method is a sound one. On theoretical grounds it is not satisfactory, but many contractors specialising in the construction of swimming pools use it and claim that they have done so successfully for many years. The objections which are usually raised can be summarised as follows:

(a) The concrete blocks are less dense than well-compacted good-quality *in situ* concrete, and are more permeable to water under pressure. Therefore, although the hollows are in effect *in situ* reinforced concrete columns, the webs of the blocks between the columns and the mortar joints between the blocks are comparatively porous. Reliance for watertightness has to be placed on the internal rendering or a special watertight membrane.

If the groundwater level is above the floor of the pool, external rendering or membrane is also required.

(*b*) Owing to the natural permeability of the blocks they are liable to greater moisture movement than dense *in situ* concrete. If the pool is kept empty for any length of time, this moisture movement (drying shrinkage) can result in cracking of the wall and the rendering.

(*c*) Ordinary concrete blocks have a low crushing strength compared with good-quality *in situ* concrete.

(*d*) Owing to the presence of the horizontal and vertical mortar joints, the wall cannot be assumed to act monolithically under the bending moment stresses imposed on it by internal water pressure and external ground pressure.

(*e*) The reinforcement has to be placed practically in the centre of the wall, which is structurally the most unsuitable position. Generally, when the pool is full, the maximum tension is on the inner (water) face of the wall, whereas when it is empty, the maximum tension is on the outer face.

(*f*) This type of construction does not satisfy the requirements of British Standard Code of Practice BS 5337 for concrete water-retaining structures. The most vulnerable point in the pool is the junction of the walls and floor, where the stress and pressure are at a maximum, and it is here that the best possible rigid joint is required. It is doubtful if the required standard of rigidity can be achieved with a concrete block wall built on an *in situ* concrete floor slab. However, the watertightness of the joint can be improved by raking out the mortar and sealing the joint with a preformed Neoprene strip.

In the opinion of the author, even under very favourable conditions the limit to size should be $10 \cdot 0$ m $\times$ $6 \cdot 0$ m $\times$ $1 \cdot 0$ m–$1 \cdot 5$ m deep (33 ft $\times$ 20 ft $\times$ 3 ft 3 in–5 ft 0 in deep); in unstable ground or where a high water table exists, the method is best avoided. One further point is that, owing to the inherent porosity of the blocks, rendering is required on the outside walls as well as on the inside, if the water table is at any time likely to rise above floor level. If this external rendering is not provided, the water pressure from the outside may force the internal rendering off the walls when the pool is empty. There is an advantage in using special mortars with high bond characteristics for the rendering in this type of pool.

As previously stated in Chapter 1, a pool with a water depth less than $3 \cdot 0$ m is not suitable for use with a $1 \cdot 00$ m spring board.

THE FLOOR
The floor slab is constructed as previously described, but the reinforcement which is located in the hollow blocks for the walls is anchored in the floor slab; this reinforcement must be accurately and securely fixed in position

before the floor bays are cast. It is advisable for the position of the bars to be checked immediately prior to the casting of the floor. The surface of the floor slab around the perimeter must be prepared as a construction joint (exposed aggregate finish), as previously described.

THE WALLS

A section through a wall is shown in Fig. 5.3. The walls are built in hollow concrete blocks complying with British Standard BS 2028, 1364: 1968: Concrete Blocks. Type A blocks should be used with a minimum compressive strength of $10 \cdot 5 \, N/mm^2$ ($1500 \, lbf/in^2$). It is recommended that every effort be made to ensure that the vertical reinforcing bars are as near as possible to the centre of the voids in the blocks, so that there is the maximum possible cover of *in situ* concrete around each bar. A further requirement for the blocks is that the total chloride content of the concrete should not exceed $0 \cdot 06 \%$ by weight of cement.

If the length of the pool exceeds about $7 \cdot 5 \, m$ ($25 \, ft$) or the depth of water exceeds $1 \cdot 20 \, m$ ($4 \, ft$), reinforcement of the horizontal joints is advisable. This reinforcement can be in the form of expanded metal complying with British Standard BS 405, or special reinforcement such as 'Brickforce' or 'Bricktor', or small diameter mild steel bars. It is recommended that the bedding mortar should incorporate an artificial rubber latex of the styrene butadiene type. The mortar should be batched by weight, if at all possible, and the proportions should be:

1 part ordinary Portland cement.
3 parts clean plasterers sand.
9 litres of latex to 50 kg cement in the gauging water (2 gal to 112 lb of cement).

As the latex is a powerful plasticiser, the following procedure is recommended for mixing:

The latex should be added to the cement and sand in the mixer. If the mortar is still too stiff, water can be added slowly until the required workability is obtained. The amount of water required usually corresponds to a free water/cement ratio of about $0 \cdot 30 - 0 \cdot 35$; this includes the water in the sand, the water in the latex emulsion and the water added at the mixer. A fine sand may hold so much water that no additional water is needed to obtain correct workability.

The joints, both vertical and horizontal, should be raked out as the work proceeds, to provide a key for the rendering. Details of the rendering are given in Chapter 6.

During the building of the wall care must be taken to keep the voids clean and prevent mortar falling down the voids onto the concrete floor, as this

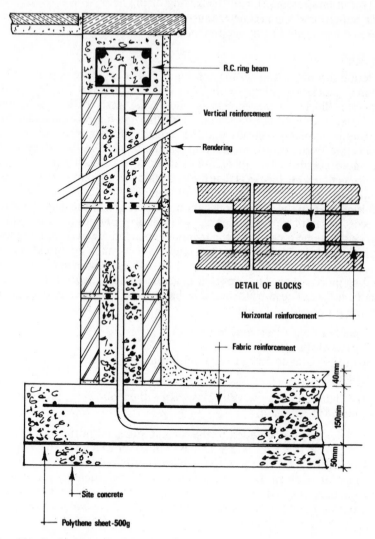

FIG. 5.3.   Section through reinforced hollow concrete block wall and *in situ* RC floor.

will reduce the bond between the floor and the *in situ* concrete which has to be placed and compacted in the voids.

The recommended mix for the *in situ* infill concrete is:

Ordinary Portland cement: 50 kg (112 lb).
Clean concreting sand: 100 kg (224 lb).
Coarse aggregate-gravel or crushed rock, 10 mm ($\frac{3}{8}$ in) maximum size: 110 kg (246 lb).
The slump should be about 75 mm (3 in).

It is preferable to build the wall to its full height before the voids are filled with the *in situ* concrete. The concrete should be well rodded down around the vertical reinforcing rod in each void, and each void must be filled in one lift.

The provision of a reinforced concrete ring beam along the top of the wall cast monolithically (if possible) with concrete infilling, is recommended. If the beam is not cast with the filling, then the surface of the latter should be brushed while it is still plastic, so as to remove the laitance and provide a good bond with the concrete in the ring beam. This ring beam will help tie the walls together and increase resistance to thermal and moisture movement.

It must be remembered that the top of the wall is exposed to the sun, while the remainder is immersed in water with a temperature many degrees lower. The vertical reinforcement in the wall should be carried up into the ring beam. This is shown in Fig. 5.3.

SWIMMING POOLS WITH WALLS OF PLAIN *IN SITU* CONCRETE AND BLOCKWORK AS PERMANENT FORMWORK

This method of building a small private swimming pool is described in detail in the booklet issued by the Cement and Concrete Association, entitled *Building a Concrete Block Swimming Pool*. The technique is a simple one, but even so, to ensure a watertight pool requires considerable experience and care. A brief description follows.

The maximum recommended dimensions are 8 m × 5 m with 1 m depth of water (approximately 26 ft × 16 ft × 3 ft 3 in deep). The ground conditions should be good, with a low water table. The floor is constructed first and consists of a 50 mm (2 in) thickness of site concrete, followed by 1000 gauge polythene sheet as slip layer. On this is laid 150 mm (6 in) of high-quality concrete with reinforcing fabric 40–50 mm (1$\frac{1}{2}$–2 in) from the top of the slab. If the floor slab is laid in two bays, the joint should be provided with an external type water bar and sealed on the surface, as shown in Fig. 4.8. A sheet steel water bar is used to help ensure a watertight joint between the floor slab and the *in situ* concrete core wall (see Fig. 4.3). The walls are built on the floor slab and consist of two skins of 102 mm (4 in) thick dense concrete blocks, with 100 mm *in situ* concrete core wall. The two skins of blockwork are tied together with wall ties. Nominal reinforcement is used in the corners; there is no vertical reinforcement. The top of the wall should be finished with a coping. The inside surface of the concrete blocks (water face) should be sealed either by rubbing in a cement–sand grout or by rendering. The final surface should be a cement-based paint or chlorinated-rubber paint. Information on finishes to swimming pools is given in Chapter 6.

POOLS WITH SLOPING SIDES, GUNITED DIRECT ON TO THE GROUND

This method is widely adopted in the United States, Canada and Australia. It is particularly suitable where subsoil conditions are good and the water table is well below the floor of the pool. The method is structurally sound provided the subsoil is stable, but the sloping sides create some hazard to people diving from the edge of the pool, and for this reason such a pool could not be used for competitions. A detailed discussion on minimum requirements for diving in private and public pools has been given in Chapter 1.

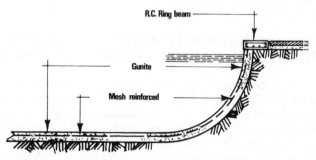

FIG. 5.4.   Part section of swimming pool with wall and floor gunited direct to natural ground.

The actual method of construction varies somewhat. In some cases hessian is spread over the excavated ground and pegged down, and the gunite is applied to that. In others the gunite is applied direct to the ground. If, during the period of construction, there is likely to be rain, then the sides and the floor should be stabilised by a thin layer of gunite, as soon as the excavation is complete. The gunite is reinforced with a medium mesh

$3.06 \, \text{kg/m}^2$ (about $5.5 \, \text{lb/yd}^2$) and the thickness should not be less than 75 mm (3 in). Figure 5.4 shows a section through such a pool.

POOLS IN ROCKY GROUND WITH GUNITE LINING

On those rare occasions when the site of the swimming pool is rocky, all that is needed is a gunite lining to the carefully trimmed rock face, provided there is no seepage of water from the rock. If there is seepage, then this must be either sealed off first or piped away so that the gunite can be placed in the dry and pressure does not build up behind it.

The instruction to trim the rock face carefully sounds rather simple but, in practice, this may prove quite difficult. It may therefore be easier and cheaper to fill the holes with a fine concrete or mortar, so as to bring the walls and the floor to a reasonably level surface. In this way the minimum amount of gunite will be used. Assuming the rock is stable, the gunite need not be more than 50–60 mm (2–$2\frac{1}{2}$ in) thick. The insertion of a light mesh reinforcement is strongly recommended.

POOLS WITH BRICK, BLOCK OR STONE WALLS WITH AN INNER LINING OF REINFORCED GUNITE

In this case the walls must be stable by their own weight when under pressure from the ground when the pool is empty, and from the water in the pool when it is full; in other words, they are gravity-type retaining walls and the gunite provides a structural watertight lining. This type of wall built in mass concrete has already been discussed earlier in this chapter, and the basic principles of stability set out there also apply here. With mass concrete the wall itself should be watertight, but with bricks, blocks or masonry reliance for watertightness must be placed on the gunite.

Either the walls can be built on independent foundations, and the floor constructed separately, or the floor can be of *in situ* reinforced concrete and the wall supported on that. In the latter case the edge of the slab should be thickened. Sections through the two types of wall support are shown in Fig. 5.5.

Pools built in this way can be very successful provided the water table does not rise much above the floor of the pool. A small external head can be tolerated because, if the work is properly executed, the gunite lining will bond strongly to the walls, and with a large cove angle and mesh reinforcement quite considerable pressure would be needed to force it off the wall.

The gunite lining should be applied to a thickness of 75 mm, reinforced

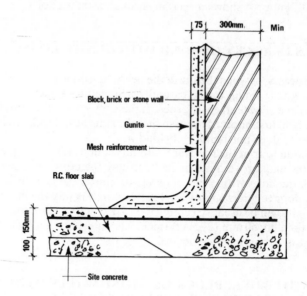

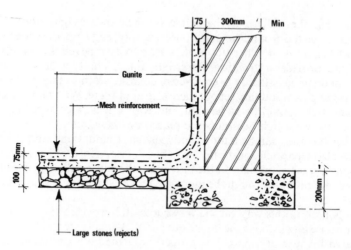

FIG. 5.5. Pools with mass (gravity-type) walls and reinforced gunite lining.

with a medium-weight steel fabric (say $5\cdot5\,\mathrm{lb/yd^2}$). It is usual to fix the reinforcement with steel pins driven into joints in the wall and for the joints in the wall to be raked out to assist bond. In fact there is no objection to the wall being built as a dry stone one (without mortar). The cover to the reinforcement should be about 25 mm (1 in). If the walls are on an independent foundation, then it is better to construct the floor of 'rejects', covered with 150 mm of gunite, and to bring the wall reinforcement down round the cove and into the floor. The gunite floor should also have a similar layer of steel fabric to the walls. One of the attractions of this method is that a considerable part of the whole job can be carried out by a comparatively inexperienced contractor, and only the gunite lining need be put on by a specialist firm.

SWIMMING POOLS WITH BLOCK, BRICK OR STONE WALLS, COMPACTED SAND FLOOR AND INNER LINING OF PVC SHEETING

GENERAL CONSIDERATIONS

In this type of pool the floor usually consists of carefully excavated, trimmed and levelled ground covered with a layer of fine washed sand not less than 50 mm (2 in) compacted thickness. Some contractors in the private swimming pool sector recommend the use of vermiculite instead of, or in addition to, the sand, to provide thermal insulation. As all subsoil in the United Kingdom is invariably damp and often quite wet, the thermal insulating properties of the vermiculite will be considerably reduced. The walls are solid or hollow concrete blocks, concrete or clay bricks or stone masonry, built on a concrete foundation. The walls must be designed to resist the pressure of the ground when the pool is empty and the pressure of the water when the pool is full. These are mass-gravity-type walls, and some information on design has been given at the beginning of this chapter.

In the type of pool now under consideration the vinyl or other plastic liner makes the pool watertight and also forms the inside finished surface, and so no decoration is required. The type of ground, particularly the presence or absence of a water table above the floor level, has an important bearing on whether the pool can be constructed satisfactorily.

It is sometimes claimed that pressure relief valves can be installed in the floor of this type of pool to enable it to be built with the floor below water table level. The use of pressure relief valves has been discussed earlier in this chapter, and the author's opinion is that the risk of relying on such a mechanical device to prevent destruction of the pool floor is too great and should not be taken. If the pool is emptied when the groundwater level is above the floor of the pool, then there is a serious risk that the pressure of the water will force the sand layer and vinyl liner upwards and the whole floor would have to be relaid. In such a case it is doubtful if the liner could be got back into position satisfactorily.

Setting Out, Excavation, Foundations to Walls and Building Walls

The setting out and excavation is carried out as previously described except that trenches must be excavated for the concrete foundations for the walls. Unless the subsoil is particularly stable, such as chalk or gravel, the concrete foundation should be 150 mm (6 in) wider on each side than the base of the wall. The mix proportions for the concrete should be 1 part ordinary Portland cement to 6 parts of aggregate by weight. With a 'one bag batch' the actual weights are likely to be:

Ordinary Portland cement: 50 kg (112 lb).
Clean concreting sand: 115 kg (250 lb).
Coarse aggregate, 20 mm ($\frac{3}{4}$ in) maximum size: 185 kg (400 lb).
The slump should be 50–75 mm (2–3 in).

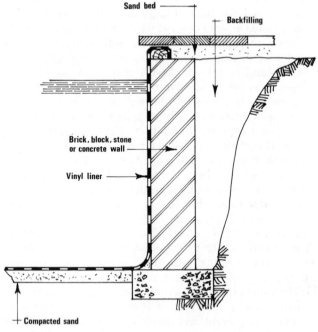

Fig. 5.6.   Pool with mass (gravity-type) walls and floor of compacted sand with coloured vinyl liner.

The concrete should be well compacted and cured for not less than 4 days by covering with waterproof reinforced building paper or polythene sheets, well lapped and securely held down. The walls can now be built in any of the materials mentioned, to the thickness designed to resist the forces which will act on them when the pool is full and when it is empty.

The formation of a cove at the junction of the wall and floor is recommended, but this must be executed carefully and feather edged to the wall and floor. A reinforced concrete ring beam can be cast along the top of the walls as described for gunite pools and this helps to tie the four walls together. Figure 5.6 shows some details of this type of pool.

THE PLASTIC SHEET LINING
These liners are usually PVC and can now be obtained in an attractive range of patterns and colours. The author does not recommend a liner thinner than 0·75 mm (0·030 in). Liners of this type are made to measure, and there are some advantages in constructing the pool first and then ordering the liner, giving the exact dimensions which have been carefully measured on site with a steel tape and checked. The suppliers of the liner will give detailed directions for its installation, and these must be followed.

There are a number of methods of fixing the liner around the top of the walls. One of these is to carry the liner over the top and down the back of a smooth rounded timber plate which has been Rawlplugged to the wall at about 1·25 m (4 ft) centres. It is an advantage if all coping and paving around the pool is completed before the liner is fixed, because this helps to avoid accidental damage. If the paving is done later, then it is advisable for the pool to be kept filled with water while this work is in progress, because hard sharp objects dropped into the pool are then less likely to damage the liner.

POOLS WITH FLOOR AND WALLS OF RIGID MATERIALS AND WATERPROOFED WITH BONDED DECORATIVE MEMBRANE

Since the first edition of this book was published in 1971, the use of fully bonded decorative PVC sheeting to waterproof the walls and floor of swimming pools has been introduced into the United Kingdom. This method has been used on the Continent for many years and has proved successful and popular there.

It is more expensive than the 'loose bag' type of PVC liner, but in the opinion of the author has a number of advantages when used in the right way.

The floor is usually constructed of *in situ* reinforced concrete and the walls in concrete blocks, bricks or other structurally sound durable

FIG. 5.7.   View of large open-air pool in Germany with bonded PVC liner (Courtesy: Alkor
Plastics (UK) Ltd).

FIG. 5.8.   Close-up view of end wall of pool in Fig. 5.7 (Courtesy: Alkor Plastics (UK) Ltd).

materials. The finished surface on which the PVC sheeting is to be bonded must be reasonably true and smooth. It is important that there should be no ingress of water from the ground; otherwise, when the pool is empty, the lining may develop blisters and in extreme cases be forced out of position. This means either that the pool shell must be watertight in its own right or the groundwater should not rise above the level of the floor of the pool. The sheeting is applied to the floor and walls by means of a special water-resistant adhesive. The individual sheets are lapped and solvent-welded. The author recommends that the sheeting should not be less than 0·75 mm (0·030 in) thick, and 1·0 mm (1/25 in) is better.

This type of sheeting can be obtained in an attractive range of colours and patterns. Figures 5.7 and 5.8 show a large open-air pool in Germany lined in this way.

POOLS WITH A COMPLETE MEMBRANE LINING SANDWICHED BETWEEN THE STRUCTURAL SHELL AND AN INNER LINING OF RIGID MATERIAL

This method of construction is seldom adopted in the United Kingdom, because it is more expensive than the methods so far described. Also, it is generally considered by designers of swimming pools that the structural shell should be watertight in its own right and reliance should not have to be placed on waterproof membranes except in very special cases. However, on the continent, and particularly in Germany, the method is obviously popular, judging by the number of pools which use it.

One of the best-known methods is 'System Karnatz' or 'Mammut Haut', executed by the firm of Mammut Bäderbau of Trier. The undoubted advantage of such a system is that, if it is properly executed, the pool is completely water- and vapourtight; also, the designers and constructors do not have to worry with the precautions required to ensure watertightness in the concrete walls and floor. Provided the pool shell is structurally stable, the membrane takes care of the watertightness.

In the System Karnatz, the membrane can be either a sandwich type or on the water face of the pool. In the latter case the decoration, usually a special paint, is applied direct to the membrane. In both cases the membrane is fully bonded to the structural shell of the pool. The essential feature of such a membrane is that it must be continuous over the whole of the walls and floor, and all joints in the sheeting must be absolutely watertight. Pipework passing through the membrane needs careful detailing, and great care must be exercised to ensure that it is not punctured by the fixing of steps, etc.

The promoters of this method of construction make a point of emphasising that the provision of the membrane in the floor and walls improves the thermal insulation of the pool shell, thereby reducing heat losses and giving a saving in heating costs. Further details of the principles of membrane construction for swimming pools are given in Chapter 4 and in Chapter 8, which deals with repairs to pools.

POOLS WITH A COMPLETE MEMBRANE LINING BETWEEN THE STRUCTURAL SHELL AND THE NATURAL GROUND

GENERAL CONSIDERATIONS

One of the disadvantages of pools with the plastic liner on the water face serving both as the waterproof layer and the internal decorative finish to the pool is that it is liable to damage by the bathers and to general deterioration by the chemicals in the water and ultra-violet light. A further disadvantage is that if the groundwater table is above the floor level and the structure is not watertight (which it need not be if a plastic liner is used), then there is a distinct likelihood of a 'blow' when the pool is emptied for cleaning.

In view of these possible difficulties, a number of firms on the Continent who specialise in plastic-lined pools recommend that the liner be placed between the natural ground and the structural shell of the pool. With the liner in this position the disadvantages mentioned above do not apply. The floor and walls must be structurally sound and stable both when the pool is full and when it is empty. The inside surface of the walls and floor require a decorative finish.

METHOD OF CONSTRUCTION

The excavation is carried out in the usual way, but as the waterproof liner will be laid on the ground, special care must be taken to ensure that all stones and other sharp objects are completely eliminated because these may puncture the membrane. A layer of fine well-compacted sand over the whole area is recommended if there is any doubt about complete elimination of all stone, flints, etc. The sand layer should not be less than 50 mm (2 in) thick. When this is done, the membrane can be laid. This may be a preformed membrane, made in the factory to measurements supplied by the client, or it may be fabricated on site.

When using a butyl rubber membrane, it is generally better to have it made up in the factory because of the superior quality of the factory-made joints; but with polyisobutylene the site joints, if carefully made, are entirely satisfactory. The reasons for this are detailed later in this chapter and in Chapter 8. Once the membrane is in position over the whole of the floor, the concrete can be placed, but again care must be taken to ensure that the membrane is not damaged.

The author recommends that the floor be cast over the whole area and the

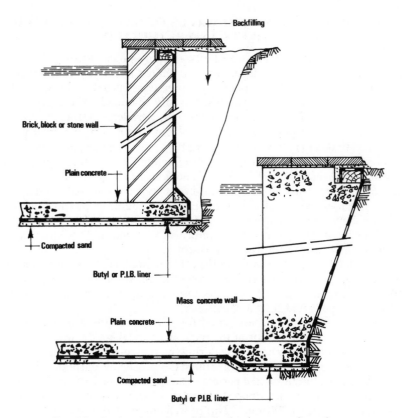

Fig. 5.9. Section through pool shells showing external membrane.

walls built around the perimeter, as shown in Fig. 5.9. The walls can be constructed in any durable material provided they are stable under all conditions of internal and external pressure. Neither the floor nor the walls have to be watertight so that all problems with joints in the concrete are eliminated. The batching can be by volume, and a mix of 1 part OPC, $2\frac{1}{2}$ parts concreting sand and 5 parts coarse aggregate is suitable. The floor slab can be 125–150 mm (5–6 in) thick, laid in bays about $4·0$ m $\times$ $4·0$ m, and reinforcement is not needed for this size of bay. Correct compaction and curing is recommended as previously described.

The floor and walls have to form the background for the final decoration of the pool. In order to obtain a decoration of a high standard, the floor must be screeded and the walls rendered. Complete recommendations for this work and for the decorations themselves are given in Chapter 6.

SWIMMING POOLS WITH WALLS OF GALVANISED MILD STEEL SHEETS AND PLASTIC LINER

The use of galvanised mild steel sheets, suitably stiffened with galvanised angles and tees, was introduced into the United Kingdom from Canada, and since then a number of pools have been constructed in this way. The information which follows has been mostly obtained from the United Kingdom agents of the Canadian company, Fernden Contractors Ltd.

The size of the pool offered varies from about 5·20 m × 2·60 m to 20·0 m × 10·00 m (17 ft × 8 ft 6 in to 66 ft × 33 ft). The height of the wall sections is 1·10 m (3 ft 6 in), which, with a freeboard of about 150 mm, gives a water depth of about 0·90 m (3 ft). The floor of the pool is the natural ground finished with 50–75 mm (2–3 in) of washed and well compacted sand. The pool can be of uniform depth throughout, or provided with a hopper-shaped section at one end to form a diving pit. The whole of the inside of the pool is lined with a preformed vinyl sheet. The liner can be obtained in a range of attractive colours.

Clear and detailed directions for the construction of the pool are given by the licensees, who are also willing to construct the whole pool. They offer a 10 year guarantee, under certain specified conditions, for the galvanised walls of the pool and for the vinyl liner.

Pools of this type are best suited for sites where the groundwater is permanently below the floor of the pool. In cases where the water table is higher than floor level at any time during the year, effective means must be provided to keep the groundwater around the pool below the floor. This can usually be done by cut-off and perimeter land drains which discharge either by gravity or to a pump sump. In the case of clay soils it is the author's opinion that at least 300 mm (12 in) of well-compacted granular material should be laid over the whole of the excavated area; 50–75 mm (2–3 in) of washed sand should be laid and compacted on this. It must be appreciated that the floor of the pool is not structural in the way that a concrete or gunite floor is, and, therefore, no upward movement can be tolerated.

If a diving pit is provided, the sides of the pit must slope at approximately the angle of repose of the subsoil. In Chapter 1 there is a detailed discussion on pool dimensions and general recommendations for diving in private and public pools. The reason for the recommendations given is to avoid accidents to people who are not experienced swimmers. The author feels that a hopper-shaped diving pit is unlikely to meet these recommendations. Figure 5.10 shows, in diagram form, the layout for small and medium-size pools of this type. Figure 5.11 shows a completed pool.

FREE-STANDING POOLS

Another pool made of the same basic materials, namely mild steel sheet for walls, a specially prepared bed of soft soil for the floor and made waterproof

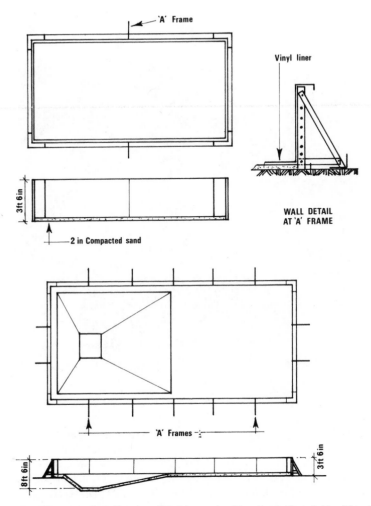

FIG. 5.10. Diagrams of small and medium-size pools with galvanised steel sides (Courtesy: Fernden Contractors).

with a vinyl liner, is marketed in the United Kingdom by Cranleigh Pools Ltd. The pool originated in the United States, and the parent company is Coleco Inc. of Hartford, Conn. These pools are erected on the surface of the ground, so that no excavation is required. It can therefore be considered as a portable pool, and the suppliers claim that planning permission to erect the pool is not needed.

FIG. 5.11.   View of completed pool constructed with galvanised steel sides, compacted floor
and waterproofed with vinyl liner (Courtesy: Fernden Contractors Ltd).

The walls are corrugated steel, electrically galvanised, and are finished
on both faces with a vinyl acrylic paint. The vinyl sheet liner is imported
with the pool from the United States. Complete erection instructions are
supplied with each pool. The suppliers state that erection time varies from
2 h for a 3·6 m (12 ft) diameter pool to 8 h for a 8·2 m (27 ft) straight-sided
oval pool holding 50 m³ (11 200 gal) of water. Important matters for
attention include careful preparation of the base for the pool, which must
be absolutely level. A layer of soft resilient material is recommended, and
sand and gravel should not be used.

ALUMINIUM SWIMMING POOLS

One of the most attractive of the new materials for swimming pools is sheet
aluminium. The author had the opportunity of inspecting a number of

these pools in Switzerland, where they are very competitive with traditional materials. The pools visited were made and erected by Hulftegger and Co. AG of Stäfa near Zurich. Another well-known continental firm supplying aluminium pools as well as aluminium and stainless steel pool halls, is Karl Richter and Co. AG of Augsburg.

The description and information which follows refers to pools in Switzerland supplied by Hulftegger and Co. The pools are supplied in a range of standard sizes varying from 6·0 m × 3·0 m to 12·0 m × 7·0 m; they can be either of uniform depth of 1·5 m or with a sloping floor of 1·3 m to 1·7 m depth.

The firm can supply pools larger and deeper than the standard range to special order, and have designed and erected aluminium pools up to 50·0 m × 20·0 m with a maximum depth of 2·0 m.

The method of construction is as follows:

(1) The site is excavated to the required depth and the base is carefully levelled and covered with at least 75 mm of sand, which, in turn, is levelled and rolled.

(2) The partly fabricated pool is brought to site, and the units are set up in position and then welded together. The amount of prefabrication depends on the size of the pool and the accessibility of the garden in which the pool is to be erected. For pools in the smaller sizes the sides are prefabricated in the factory and the floor in as large units as possible. For a pool 6·0 m × 3·0 m it could be in one piece. On site the sides are welded together at the corners, the floor sections are likewise welded and the walls are welded to the base.

(3) The whole of the outside of the walls and floor is given a minimum of two coats of bituminous paint and welded areas are made good with the paint as the work proceeds.

(4) The inside of the pool and the special non-slip aluminium coping is given three coats of epoxide resin or polyurethane paint. The life of the former is estimated at 8–10 years provided the pool is properly maintained.

It should be noted that concrete foundations and special backfilling around the walls is not required in stable ground conditions, including clay, for the standard range of pools. With larger pools a concrete strip foundation and external concrete buttresses are recommended to support and stiffen the walls. Figure 5.12 shows an isometric sketch of a pool in the standard range size.

In addition to the standard rectangular shape, pools of other shapes— circular, oval, etc.—can be obtained from suppliers in both Switzerland and Germany, to special order. A further use for aluminium pools is to use them as a new watertight lining for pools which are too deteriorated to be economically repaired. This is dealt with in Chapter 8.

Swimming pools with the walls made of patented extruded aluminium

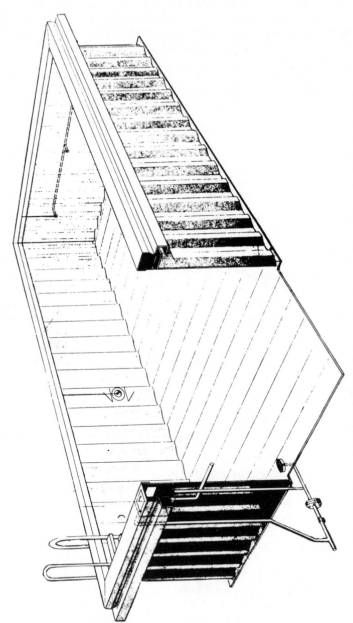

Fig. 5.12. Isometric drawing of aluminium swimming pool (Courtesy: Hulfteger AG, Zurich).

FIG. 5.13.   View of swimming pool under construction using proprietary aluminium wall panels (Courtesy: Sunpools Ltd, Eynsham).

sections are now available on the United Kingdom market. These pools are, in general, constructed in a similar way to those with galvanised mild steel sheets; the walls are aluminium and the floor is either rolled sand or about 50–75 mm of a cement–sand mortar or a cement–vermiculite mortar. The whole of the inside of the pool is lined with prefabricated PVC sheeting. Figure 5.13 shows such a pool under construction, and Fig. 1.8 shows a completed pool.

SWIMMING POOLS OF GLASS-FIBRE REINFORCED CEMENT (GRC)

Glass-fibre reinforced cement is now used for a number of building components. This is a composite material composed essentially of Portland cement and patented alkali-resistant glass fibres. The fibres and composite were developed jointly by Pilkington Bros. and the Building Research Establishment; the fibre is marketed under the name of CemFIL. The special characteristic of the glass fibres is that they are resistant to the caustic alkalis in the cement paste. The bulk density of GRC is about 2100 kg/m^3, compared with about 2380 kg/m^3 for good-quality concrete. For swimming pools, the walls are made of the GRC panels and the floor of either rolled sand, cement–sand mortar or cement–vermiculite mortar. On completion, the pool is lined with preformed PVC sheeting.

TIMBER SWIMMING POOLS

Another attractive and economic pool from the Continent is the vinyl-lined timber swimming pool supplied by the Arizona Pool Company of Zwingen, Switzerland. These pools are made with capacities from $13 \cdot 1 \, m^3$ to $54 \cdot 5 \, m^3$ (2900 gal to 12 000 gal); the depth is uniform for all sizes and is approximately $1 \cdot 10 \, m$ (3 ft 6 in). The suppliers claim that it can be erected on a prepared base in just over two hours.

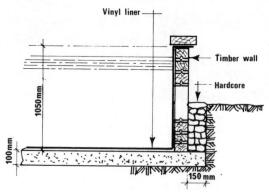

FIG. 5.14.   Section through pool with timber walls and concrete floor, waterproofed with vinyl liner (Courtesy: Arizona Pools Ltd).

The pool is sunk into the ground to a depth of about $0 \cdot 50 \, m$ (1 ft 6 in) and the base on which it stands is carefully levelled. A layer of fine sand 150 mm (6 in) thick is spread over the excavated area and levelled and rolled. The timber walls are then erected in accordance with the detailed instructions of the suppliers. The insertion of the vinyl liner and fixing of the coping around the top of the walls completes the pool. A section through such a pool is shown in Fig. 5.14.

GLASS-FIBRE REINFORCED PLASTIC SWIMMING POOLS

In recent years glass-fibre pools have come on to the market in the United Kingdom and other countries. These pools are generally built up layer by layer by hand in the factory and consist essentially of glass fibres embedded in a synthetic resin, usually of the polyester type. Inlet and outlet connections are incorporated as the walls and floor are formed. The resins are pigmented in a limited range of colours, of which blue is the most popular, and on completion they do not require any further decoration. The colour changes somewhat as the pool ages, owing to the action of ultraviolet light on the pigments, but this occurs with all pigmented coatings.

The author has heard complaints from some owners of these pools that algal growth is very difficult to remove and that sometimes the pool shell suffers from cracking. One of the best-known manufacturers of these pools, F. J. Buckingham of Kenilworth, strongly challenges these claims and has told the author that some of their pools are now more than ten years old and are still in first-class condition. They simply need care and regular maintenance in the same way as any other type of pool.

The method of installation is comparatively simple and may be briefly described as follows:

(1) The excavation is prepared in accordance with the drawings supplied by the manufacturers. All stones must be removed and it is better if the whole of the base is covered with a 100 mm (4 in) layer of fine sand levelled and rolled.

(2) The pool is then lowered into position on the sand bed and the space between the walls and side of the excavation is backfilled concrete or cement mortar. The thickness of this backfilling is 150–200 mm (6 in–8 in), and this has to be allowed for when setting out the excavation. The concrete or cement mortar is carefully placed and compacted in 300 mm (12 in) layers, and as this is being placed, the pool is slowly filled with water. It is most important that the water level inside the pool and the level of the backing outside should coincide, so that the pressures are more or less equalised. The reason for this is that the pool shell depends largely for its structural stability on the support it receives from the backing material around the walls and the uniform support from the carefully levelled sand base.

The sizes available in the United Kingdom are in the range 5·0 m × 2·5 m × 1·0 m deep holding about 11 m³ to 12·0 m × 6·0 m with the depth varying from 1·0 m to 2·0 m and holding 100 m³. In Imperial units this is 16 ft 6 in × 8 ft × 3 ft 3 in holding 2400 gal to 40 ft × 20 ft × 3 ft 3 in–6 ft 9 in deep holding 22 000 gal.

SWIMMING POOLS WITH THE FLOOR AND SIDES FORMED IN THE NATURAL GROUND AND LINED WITH A PLASTIC SHEET

Pools of this type are in many ways similar to the pools described earlier in this chapter which have sloping sides gunited onto the natural ground. In the case now under consideration the plastic sheet replaces the gunite lining, but there are a number of important differences. The most significant one is that with the plastic lining the walls and floor are non-structural and non-rigid (flexible). This means that the ground must be stable and self-supporting and that groundwater must be permanently below the level of the floor of the pool. The latter difficulty can be partly overcome by the insertion of pressure-relief valves; the installation of these valves has been discussed in some detail in Chapter 4.

The sides of the pool must be sloped to the angle of repose of the soil, and are formed either by the excavation or by a well-compacted embankment. The floor and sides must be carefully trimmed and all stones and other sharp objects removed. If the ground is rather stony, then a layer of fine sand 50–75 mm (2–3 in) thick must be spread over the whole area. This sand layer should be watered and rolled. When this is complete, the pool is ready for lining. In the opinion of the author the lining should be either butyl rubber or polyisobutylene, 1·5 mm (0·060 in) thick. Basic information on these two materials is given in Chapter 2. Both materials suffer from the disadvantage of being black in colour, but they can be painted with a limited degree of success.

The lining can be either made up in the factory to the dimensions given by the purchaser or it can be brought to the site partly fabricated or in sheets, the joints being made there with an adhesive. In the case of butyl rubber sheeting the factory-made joints are much stronger since they are heat-welded, while the site joints rely on the surface adhesion imparted by the adhesive used. Polyisobutylene is different in this respect, because there is chemical action between the adhesive and the sheeting and this forms a very strong joint.

The lining must be securely fixed around the sides at the top of the pool, and one method of doing this is shown in Fig. 5.15.

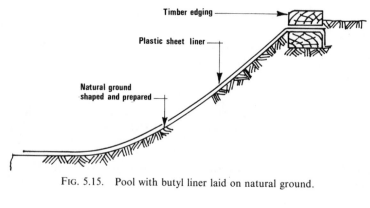

Fig. 5.15.   Pool with butyl liner laid on natural ground.

It should be noted that pools of this type are usually very small and do not lend themselves to the installation of water-treatment equipment. In the opinion of the author they should be considered either as a temporary measure, pending the construction of a pool with water treatment, or as a permanent pool where the flow-through method of water circulation can be adopted. Details of water treatment and circulation are given in Chapter 7.

SWIMMING POOLS WITH FLOOR AND WALLS OF WELDED MILD STEEL SHEETS

Since the first edition of this book was published, a number of public swimming pools have been constructed in the United Kingdom of welded mild steel sheets, stiffened with structural steel sections. In almost all cases the pool shell is suspended and the space below is usually utilised for storage, plant rooms, etc. The walkways around the pool are in reinforced concrete. The pools are finished internally with ceramic tiling or mosaic, but in spite of precautions to protect the steel from corrosion, rusting has occurred to a greater or lesser degree in many of these pools. The author feels this is an example where, in theory, the selected material (mild steel) should have proved satisfactory but experience has been otherwise.

THERMAL INSULATION OF SWIMMING POOL SHELLS

In recent years many package-deal contractors in the private swimming pool market have recommended the use of a thermal insulating layer below the floor slab (or PVC sheet liner) of the pool shell. Some information on heat losses from swimming pools and a brief discussion on the heating of open-air pools are given in Chapter 7. The greatest loss of heat is from the surface of the water, and only a small percentage is through the walls and floor, probably not more than 20% of the total heat loss. Under the most favourable conditions, using a minimum thickness of 75 mm (3 in) of a high-grade insulating material such as vermiculite, which is permanently maintained in a dry condition, the U-value of the floor would be reduced by about 60%. Unfortunately, if the insulation below the floor slab becomes saturated by ground moisture, its thermal insulating properties will be substantially reduced, so that the U-value would revert almost to that of ordinary concrete or mortar. Therefore, unless the thermal insulation can, by special detailing, be kept permanently dry, there is little point in providing it. An alternative, if the cost is considered justified, is to use insulation which is impermeable to moisture. Some proprietary materials based on extruded polystyrene and polyurethane are claimed to be very resistant to moisture penetration.

GENERAL NOTES ON THIN FULLY BONDED LININGS AND COATINGS TO SWIMMING POOL SHELLS

The most common defect which occurs with thin bonded linings and coatings to swimming pool shells is loss of bond with the base material. This debonding usually takes the form of large or small blisters, flaking, or, in extreme cases, loss of bond over large areas of lining, resulting in rocking and cracking. This is why it is essential to ensure that the material used is compatible with the substrate and that the substrate is correctly prepared. It is most important that the directions of the suppliers of linings or coatings are carefully followed. For large pools, it is advisable, in order to avoid divided responsibility, that the supplier of the material should be made responsible for the preparatory work and the application of the lining or coating.

Surface adhesion is usually not good enough; the adhesive or primer should penetrate into the surface layers of the substrate.

When trouble develops, many varied and ingenious arguments are sometimes advanced. The suggestion may be made that the failure of bond is due to osmotic pressure. Osmotic pressure can be developed through a material which acts as a semi-permeable membrane, when one side of the membrane is in contact with a liquid of lower total dissolved solid (salt) content and the other side is in contact with a liquid of higher total dissolved solid content. The pressure will then be exerted from the side in contact with the liquid of lower dissolved solid content.

All these quite exceptional conditions (the semi-permeable membrane separating two liquids of differing total dissolved solid contents, sufficient to generate the necessary osmotic pressure), must be present at the time of failure. The author has not come across an authentic case of osmotic pressure occurring in a swimming pool and causing bond failure of the lining or coating.

Sea Water Pools and Pools Containing Saline (Spa) Water

High quality Portland cement concrete is not adversely affected by normal sea water in temperate climates. However, cement mortar for rendering, screeds and bedding for tiles is more permeable than concrete and may be vulnerable to attack by sulphates in solution in sea water. Therefore, for sea water pools sulphate-resisting Portland cement should be used for such mortar. For screeds and tile bedding in walkways, shower and changing rooms subject to wetting and drying, proprietary resin-based mortars are recommended. In the case of pools containing saline (spa) water, specialist advice should be obtained due to the wide variation in the chemical composition of such waters.

CHAPTER 6

Part 1: *Testing and Finishing the Pool*

TESTING THE POOL FOR WATERTIGHTNESS

A swimming pool is a water-retaining structure and must be watertight. This means

(a) That the structural shell of the pool must retain the water in the pool without leakage.

(b) If the pool is wholly or partly below groundwater level, there must be no ingress of water into the pool from the surrounding ground when the pool is empty.

To ensure that condition (a) is complied with, a leakage test must be carried out; the details of this test are given later. Condition (b) can be checked by keeping the pool empty and stopping all groundwater pumping which may have been necessary for the construction of the floor and walls; this is referred to again under the conditions of test.

There is a difference of opinion among engineers, architects and contractors as to whether the leakage test should be carried out before or after the application of the internal rendering and floor screed. It is the author's opinion that where the pool shell is constructed of material which should be watertight in its own right (as is the case with *in situ* reinforced concrete and reinforced gunite, and pools with reinforced concrete floor and mass *in situ* concrete walls), then the leakage test should be carried out before any rendering or screed is applied.

To avoid any misunderstanding of terminology, in this book a cement–sand mortar applied to walls is called 'rendering', while a cement–sand mortar applied to a floor slab is referred to as a 'screed'. This may sound rather academic, but there are some important differences in the grading of the sand for the rendering compared with the screed. There are also differences in method of application and in the thickness which can be applied.

Reinforced concrete and gunite pools are usually rendered and screeded on the inside to obtain the necessary true and level surface required for the satisfactory application of the decorative finish. The decoration may take the form of paint, tiles, mosaic or a special *in situ* finish such as Marbelite, which is a type of terrazzo. In the case of pools constructed of materials which, while being structurally sound, are not completely watertight in their own right, such as concrete block walls, then the rendering must be applied before the leakage test is carried out. In any case, the leakage test should be carried out and the pool passed as satisfactory before any decorative finish is applied.

When the pool has been designed by an engineer or architect, the method of test is usually laid down in the specification. In the case of 'package deal' or 'turnkey' jobs, it is advisable for the contractor in his own interest to test the pool, but this is often not done. A test based on clause 32 of BS 5337 would generally be considered as satisfactory. The author's suggestions which follow are based on the Code requirements.

One point should be made clear at the start and this is that if at the time of test the groundwater level outside the pool shell is higher than the floor of the pool, then any leakage outwards may be interfered with—that is, the extent of the leakage may be reduced, because the water pressure inside will tend to be balanced by the pressure from outside. There is, therefore, good reason to keep the groundwater level down below floor level during the water test. If it had been allowed to rise to its normal level while the pool was still empty, this would then impose some degree of test on the pool shell from outside. The actual test procedure should be as follows:

(*a*) All valves on outlet pipes should be closed.

(*b*) It is important to check that all bolt holes and joints have been properly sealed.

(*c*) The pool should be filled slowly: say 600 mm (2 ft) depth in 24 h.

(*d*) When the top water level has been reached, it should be allowed to stand for about 7 days; this period can well be increased to 10 days if the pool has been empty for a considerable period. The water level will drop during this initial 'soaking' and it should therefore be kept topped up.

(*e*) At the commencement of the test the water surface should be brought up to the correct level and recorded in some satisfactory way, since the permitted drop in level should be quite small.

(*f*) The test should last for 7 days and during this period the level should not drop more than 10 mm ($\frac{3}{8}$ in) from causes other than evaporation. Many experienced engineers feel that this figure (10 mm) is unnecessarily generous and that with a properly designed and carefully constructed pool shell the loss of water over the 7 day period should not exceed 6 mm ($\frac{1}{4}$ in). When the pool is under test, slight seepage, showing as moisture at joints and damp patches, often occurs. Sometimes these are self-sealing, but in many cases the wet areas persist throughout the test. An attempt to measure the water lost through such defects will show that the quantity is very small and hardly shows at all as a drop in water level in the pool. In a pool 25 m × 12 m (82 ft × 42 ft) a drop in level of 10 mm ($\frac{3}{8}$ in) represents a loss of 3·0 m³ (660 gal), so that a 1 mm ($\frac{1}{25}$ in) drop would amount to a loss of 0·3 m³ (66 gal).

(g) During the period of the test the drop in water level, if any, should be recorded each day at the same time. Also, any ducts around the pool and manholes on any land-drains under the pool should likewise be checked each day.

Regarding evaporation losses, the author has not seen any published figures relating to swimming pools. When the result of a water test is satisfactory (the drop in level not exceeding the specified figure), no arguments arise. However, when the test result is not satisfactory, then there is certain to be a discussion about allowance for evaporation. This leads to delay, and it is therefore recommended that a method be adopted to measure evaporation in a practical way during the test period. This can be done by immersing a steel drum in the pool; the drum should be filled with water to within about 50 mm (2 in) of the rim. The drop in level in the drum can be taken as representing evaporation from the pool.

Lapworth, in a paper published in the *Journal of the Institution of Water Engineers* in March 1965, described investigations into evaporation from a large open reservoir near London. He reported that the annual evaporation over a 7 year period was about 26 in (600 mm), with the monthly average varying from 0·6 in (15 mm) in January to 4·2 in (107 mm) in July. The water temperature varied from 41 °F (5 °C) in January to 64 °F (18 °C) in July.

FINISHES TO WALLS AND FLOORS OF SWIMMING POOLS

During the preliminary soaking and the water test itself, the surface layers of the concrete or rendering become saturated, and therefore, when the test is over, some time must be allowed to elapse before any decorative or other coatings can be satisfactorily applied. This is to enable the background to dry out to some extent. Although this delay may be rather exasperating, particularly when the contract is behind schedule, it is nevertheless advisable to accept this drying-out period. This applies equally to pools which are tested before the application of any rendering; in other words, the concrete should be allowed to dry out before any rendering is applied.

Some authorities specify a 'waterproof' rendering, apparently on the assumption that this provides an additional line of defence against future leakage even when a pool has already passed the water test. One disadvantage which can arise with some of these 'waterproofers' in either the concrete of the shell or the rendering is that they may impart a degree of water repellency (which is mistaken for impermeability) and this water-repellent characteristic may interfere with the bond between the 'waterproofed' concrete or rendering and the backing mortar for the tiling.

There is a wide range of finishes which can be applied to the inside of swimming pools. The type of finish selected should be appropriate to the background to which it is to be applied. For example, the author would not recommend the use of glazed ceramic tiling or mosaic for the walls of a pool constructed with concrete blocks. Such rigid materials should be fixed only to mass or reinforced concrete or reinforced gunite.

Apart from this, the type of finish will depend to a large extent on how much money the client is prepared to spend; the saying that one gets what one pays for and pays for what one gets is particularly appropriate to finishes for swimming pools. It really revolves around the question of whether a comparatively high capital cost for a long-lived material such as glazed ceramic tiles or mosaic, can be accepted, or whether a lower initial investment and higher maintenance costs are preferred.

Unless the pool has a coloured vinyl lining or is constructed of glass-fibre (as described in Chapter 5), some form of decoration is required. Generally, in order to obtain the best results, the inside of the walls should be rendered and floor screeded to provide a smooth level surface on which the decoration can be applied.

CEMENT–SAND RENDERING TO WALLS OF SWIMMING POOLS

Introduction

Rendering in Portland cement–sand mixture will be considered in relation to three types of walls:

(a) *In situ* concrete (reinforced and plain).
(b) Concrete blocks, bricks and masonry.
(c) Gunite.

Since the first edition of this book was published in 1971, the author has been involved in a number of cases of chemical attack on the mortar joints between ceramic tiles and on the bedding, screed and rendering. By the time an investigation starts the pool is invariably found to be empty and so it is impossible to check the chemical composition of the pool water; also, it is usually found that there are no full chemical analysis reports of the pool water available. When the mortar was examined by an experienced chemist, the result showed clear evidence of attack by sulphates, sometimes with signs of acid attack as well. The most likely source of the aggressive chemicals was the pool water, as in all cases alum (aluminium sulphate) had been used as a coagulant. This chemical gives an acid reaction in solution and also provides sulphate ions in the water. While, in the overall context of the number of swimming pools in operation in the United Kingdom, these cases of chemical attack are rare, they do give rise to some concern.

In view of the above, the author considers that the use of a high-quality, dense impermeable mortar is most desirable. Sulphate-resisting Portland cement will give greater resistance to attack by acid sulphates than ordinary Portland. High-alumina cement would also be resistant to sulphates and to dilute acids. Both these cements are darker in colour than ordinary Portland, particularly the HAC.

Impermeability and general resistance to attack will be further improved if a styrene butadiene latex emulsion is used as the gauging water for the mortar.

PREPARATION OF CONCRETE TO RECEIVE RENDERING/SCREED

It is essential to obtain maximum bond between the base concrete and the rendering, as bond failure is probably the most frequent cause of trouble with rendering. At the present time, it is generally accepted that the most effective way of obtaining a high standard of bond is to prepare the concrete surface so that the coarse aggregate is exposed. This type of surface is shown in Fig. 6.1, and can be obtained by the following means:

(a) Percussion tools, i.e. scabblers, bush hammers.
(b) Grit blasting.
(c) High-velocity water jets (see Fig. 6.2).

A depth of exposure of 3–5 mm ($\frac{1}{8}$–$\frac{1}{4}$ in) is adequate. Method (a) gives rise to noise, vibration and dust, while the objection to (b) is the dust which is created. The author prefers method (c), as there is little noise, no dust and no vibration, and the surface of the concrete is left damp and clean. With methods (a) and (b), all grit and dust must be removed before the first coat of rendering is applied. If percussion tools are used, the work should not be started sooner than about 21 days after completion of casting of the concrete, but grit blasting and high-velocity water jetting can start after 7 days or even sooner. With high-pressure water jets, the nozzle pressure is likely to be in the range of 300–500 atm (5000–8000 lb/in^2).

There are two other methods which are sometimes used for providing a 'keyed' surface to the concrete. One is to use retarders on the formwork, and then when the forms are stripped, the surface of the concrete should be thoroughly washed down with a stiff brush to remove all friable material. It is very difficult to obtain reasonably uniform exposure of the coarse

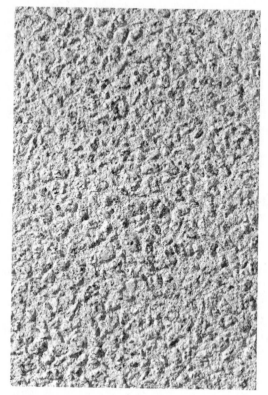

Fig. 6.1.   Example of exposed aggregate finish to provide mechanical key for rendering or
screed (Courtesy: Cement and Concrete Association).

aggregate; there is also the danger that a too generous application of the
retarder on the forms will result in honeycombing at kicker level.

There are proprietary systems for forming indentations or keys in the
concrete by means of special formwork linings. The surface of the concrete
between the indentations is relatively smooth, and the same applies to the
surface within the indentations themselves. Weak laitance is not removed
and the overall result is not as satisfactory as correct exposure of the coarse
aggregate by methods (a), (b) or (c).

It must be pointed out, however, that with the introduction some ten
years or so ago of artificial rubber latex emulsions based on styrene
butadiene for use in grouts and mortars, there is a growing weight of
experience which suggests that, when correctly used, this type of latex may
render it unnecessary to expose the coarse aggregate to obtain good bond.

A satisfactory bond has been obtained in a number of swimming pools by thorough cleaning down and removal of all weak laitance followed by the application of a grout composed of Portland cement and the latex in the proportion of 2:1. As an additional precaution, the latex can be incorporated in the mortar mix for screed and rendering.

FIG. 6.2.   View of high-velocity water jet used to form key on RC wall to receive rendering (Courtesy: J. M. Dykes).

The use of a PVA-based bonding agent is not recommended in swimming pools, walkways, changing and shower rooms, as under conditions of continuous saturation or continuous partial saturation the PVA may re-emulsify. This can result in serious reduction in bond and weakening of the mortar, leading to failure of large areas of tiling/mosaic.

Spatter Dash Coat
A spatter dash coat is not required if the concrete has been prepared by exposure of the coarse aggregate as described above. It is necessary, however, if rendering is applied to a relatively smooth dense concrete. Before the spatter dash is applied, the concrete should be thoroughly brushed down to remove all dirt and friable material, and the remains of any curing membrane or retarder.

The object of this coat is to provide a firm rough surface on which the first coat of rendering can be applied. The mix proportions by volume for 'spatter dash' should be:

1 part ordinary Portland cement.
$1\frac{1}{2}$–2 parts clean sharp dry sand (if a damp sand is used, allowance must be made for 'bulking' up to 25%). The grading of the sand should comply with Table 1 of BS 1199: Building Sands from Natural Sources, for External Rendering; or sand to zones 2 or 3 of BS 882.

The cement and sand should be mixed with sufficient water to give a consistency of a thick slurry. The concrete should be thoroughly brushed with wire brushes to remove all weak and friable areas or traces of mould oil (release agent) left from the formwork; after this the concrete should ·be lightly dampened immediately before the spatter dash is applied. To ensure adequate hydration (because the coat is not more than about 2 mm thick), the spatter dash should be lightly sprayed with water about an hour after application, and also protected from hot sun and strong winds by properly fixed covers, as recommended for rendering. When the spatter dash coat has dried out, about 36–48 h after application, the first coat of rendering can be applied.

First and Subsequent Coats of Rendering
The number of coats and to some extent the thickness of each will depend on the total thickness of the rendering.

If, owing to inaccuracies in the base concrete, the rendering has to exceed about 25 mm (1 in) in thickness, it is advisable for a light-weight mesh to be provided as reinforcement. Stainless steel is best for this purpose, as in the course of a few years it is more than likely that the rendering will become completely saturated with pool water. This water usually contains chlorine compounds which are aggressive to mild and high tensile steel. If stainless steel is considered too expensive, then a heavily galvanised mesh must be used. The fixings for securing the mesh to the wall must be of the same metal as the mesh. Care should be taken to avoid the fixings coming into contact with the reinforcement in the concrete if the former are stainless steel.

The thickness of the rendering on the short end walls is critical when the pool will be tiled and used for competitions. In the United Kingdom the Amateur Swimming Association require an accuracy in the length (finished surface to finished surface) not exceeding plus 20 mm ($\frac{3}{4}$ in) with no minus tolerance. Unfortunately the ASA do not say how this should be measured.

The batching of rendering is still done by volume in spite of the known inaccuracies involved. The author considers that those responsible for specifying rendering and screeds for swimming pools should require all batching to be by weight to help ensure uniform quality of the mixed material. All mixing should be by mechanical mixer.

The recommended mix proportions for the first coat of rendering are (weigh batching):

1 part ordinary or sulphate-resisting Portland cement.
3 parts clean dry sand, to Table 1 in BS 1199.

The thickness of the first coat is usually 10–12 mm ($\frac{3}{8}$–$\frac{1}{2}$ in). If a greater thickness than 12 mm is required, this should be built up in two or more coats. Each coat is considered as providing the backing for the following coat and the surface should be combed or scratched to form a key for the next coat. Each coat should be allowed to mature as long as possible before the next coat is applied, and this period must be at least 48 h. It is most important that each coat is no stronger, and preferably slightly weaker, than the preceding one. The reason for this is that if a stronger coat is applied to a weaker coat, the former will tend to pull the lower one off. Examples of mix proportions by volume used in good practice are:

First coat: 1:3   12 mm thick ($\frac{1}{2}$ in)
Second coat: 1:3$\frac{1}{2}$ 8 mm thick ($\frac{1}{3}$ in).

The final coat should be floated with a wood float to give a dense level and even surface. A tolerance of ± 3 mm under a 3·0 m straight edge should be achieved. If the rendering is to receive tiling, which is bedded in cement–sand mortar, the final coat should be combed or scratched to form a key for backing mortar. However, if a proprietary adhesive is used to fix the tiling, the final coat of rendering should be finished with a wood float. If the tiles are fixed with what is termed a 'thin bed' adhesive, where the thickness of the bed does not exceed 3 mm, great care must be exercised in the finishing of the final coat of rendering.

Panel Sizes
All full movement joints in the pool shell must be carried through the rendering. This type of joint, which is rather unusual in pools less than 50·0 m (165 ft) long, is 20–25 mm ($\frac{3}{4}$–1 in) wide, and this width should be maintained through rendering, screed and tiling. Movement joints are referred to in more detail later in this chapter.

While full movement joints are rare in swimming pool shells, partial movement joints (also known as contraction, semi-contraction and stress-relief joints) are used in most pools. In addition, construction (or day-work) joints have to be used in certain locations in the walls and floor of the shell of every pool. The problems relating to the selection of the type of joint and its location and detailing in the pool shell is covered in Chapter 4.

Research work carried out at the Building Research Station by J. R.

Southern and reported in a paper at the BRE Symposium at East Kilbride in June 1973 shows that significant movement does take place in the elevated shells of swimming pools when they are filled and emptied during normal operation. The paper states that the major movement occurs at full movement joints, which is, of course, quite logical, and the movement across contraction joints, etc., is very much smaller. However, in pools where full movement joints are not provided there would clearly be greater stress developed, resulting in greater movement across contraction, stress-relief and construction joints than there would be in a pool where a full movement joint is provided. It is difficult to ensure that joints in the pool shell line up exactly with joints in the tiling. This problem is discussed later in this chapter.

Regarding the rendering, it is advisable that the length of a panel rendered in one operation should not exceed about 4·5 m, but the panel length could correspond with the length of the concrete wall panels, provided these do not exceed about 5·0 m.

Curing and Protecting the Rendering

There is no need to wet-cure rendering apart from the application of the spatter dash coat as previously recommended. However, it is most important that each coat, as it is applied, should be protected from hot sun, drying winds and rain for a period of not less than 48 h, or until the next coat is applied, whichever is the shorter. The author strongly recommends that rendering should not be carried out in very cold weather, as a 10–12 mm thickness of cement–sand mortar applied to a cold concrete background is very vulnerable to the effects of low temperature.

Many swimming pools are inside buildings, and some architects and contractors consider that this is protection enough and therefore there is no need to cover up the work as recommended above. The fact is that in buildings which have unglazed window openings and probably no doors a funnel effect may be created; the resulting blast of air through the building can have a most adverse effect on the rendering. Therefore the author recommends that all specifications should include a clause requiring the contractor to allow in his tender price for protecting each coat of rendering immediately it is completed, for a minimum period of 48 h, and this may be increased if weather conditions are adverse.

CEMENT–SAND SCREEDS TO THE FLOORS OF SWIMMING POOLS

Screeds are laid to provide a true and level surface with good suction to receive the ceramic tiles. The high-quality dense impermeable concrete floor slab is considered to give insufficient suction when tiles are bedded directly on it. Apart from this, however, there are many advantages in omitting the screed and taking special care with the surface finish of the concrete. The author considers that in view of the problems so often encountered with screeds in general, and in swimming pools in particular, consideration should be given to providing an accurate finish direct to the floor slab and then bedding the tiles in a polymer mortar. If the joints were also pointed with a similar resin, this would reduce any possibility of deterioration by unforeseen chemical attack from the pool water. The surface of the concrete floor should be prepared as previously described for rendering.

Screeds are usually 30–65 mm ($1\frac{1}{4}$–$2\frac{1}{2}$ in) thick, and should be laid to their full thickness in one operation. If for any reason the thickness has to exceed 75 mm (3 in), then a fine concrete should be used and finished with a 20 mm ($\frac{3}{4}$ in) thick screed laid monolithically with the topping. The mix for the topping concrete should be:

360 kg OPC per m^3 of concrete (600 lb/yd^3).
The coarse aggregate should be 10 mm ($\frac{3}{8}$ in) maximum size.
The w/c ratio should not exceed 0·5.
The sand content is usually 45–50 % by weight of total aggregate.
The concrete should be batched by weight.

For reasons previously given for rendering, the mortar for the screed should be batched by weight, and this requirement should be included in the specification. In addition, all mixing should be by machine. The recommended mix proportions for the screed are:

1 part OPC or SRPC to 3 parts clean concreting sand graded to zones 1 or 2 of BS 882: Aggregates from Natural Sources for Concrete. This means that a concreting sand should be used for the screed and not a plasterer's sand.
The w/c ratio should not exceed 0·5. If this does not give sufficient workability for full compaction, a plasticiser can be used; this should not be a stearate type, as these tend to impart some degree of water repellency to the screed which can adversely affect bond with the bedding mortar for the tiles.

The screed should be laid in bays of 2·0–3·0 m (6 ft 6 in–10 ft) width and thoroughly compacted between screeding boards. The length of the bay should not exceed about 1·5 times the width. However, in determining the length and width of the bays, the location of joints in the structural shell should be taken into account, as well as the need to thoroughly compact the screed.

All full movement joints in the pool shell must be carried through the screed. The importance of proper compaction cannot be overemphasised, as this imparts density, strength and impermeability to the screed. It is surprising that specifiers and contractors recognise the importance of compacting concrete, but often completely neglect this when dealing with screeds. The screed should be finished with a wood float if the tiles will be bedded in a resin-based adhesive; if cement mortar is used for the bedding, then a slightly rougher texture is desirable.

The screed must be cured for a minimum period of 4 days after laying. The use of polyethylene sheets (500 gauge), well lapped and held down around the edges, will be satisfactory. The sheets should be placed in position as soon as screed has hardened sufficiently to prevent the surface being damaged.

RENDERING TO CONCRETE BLOCKS, BRICKS AND MASONRY
To ensure watertightness the walls must be rendered on the inside, and if the water table is likely to rise above the floor level of the pool, then the outside of the walls should also be rendered. The outside rendering should be carried up to a height of at least 600 mm (2 ft) above the highest estimated water table level. The rendering can be either a standard cement–sand mix or a similar mix with a styrene butadiene-based artificial rubber latex added. The advantage of the latex rendering is that it bonds very strongly to the background, and has low drying shrinkage characteristics and good impermeability to water under pressure. It should be noted, however, that due to the possible movement in concrete block walls of swimming pools, a rigid lining such as cement–sand rendering and Marbelite may crack. Hence, there is some advantage if a material which possesses some degree of flexibility is used, such as a glass-fibre polyester resin laminate or high-quality sheet vinyl. However, with these linings there is still the need to ensure watertightness on the outside of the wall against groundwater.

Preparation of the Background
The surface of the blocks should be well brushed down to remove all dirt, dust and loose particles, and dampened just before the spatter dash coat is applied.

Tack Coat (Spatter Dash)
The tack coat is about 2–3 mm ($\frac{1}{12}$ to $\frac{1}{8}$ in) thick. Detailed directions for the application of this coat were given in a previous section.

First Coat of Rendering
When the tack coat has dried out (about 24–48 h after application), the first coat of rendering can be applied. This should have a thickness of 10–16 mm ($\frac{3}{8}$–$\frac{5}{8}$ in). Detailed recommendations for this coat have been given in a previous section.

Final Coat of Rendering
The first coat must be allowed to dry out before the next one is applied, and this drying out is likely to take anything from 48 to 96 h. Second and subsequent coats should be slightly leaner (containing less cement) than the previous coat. Detailed directions for this have already been given.

Curing and Protection of the Rendering
This should be carried out as previously recommended.

RENDERING INCORPORATING STYRENE BUTADIENE-BASED LATEX
The author considers this type of rendering particularly suitable for the walls of swimming pools which are built in concrete blocks, bricks or masonry. The following are recommendations for application.

Preparation of Background
The same as for the standard cement–sand rendering just described.

Tack Coat (Spatter Dash)
This can be omitted because a strong bond is provided by the incorporation of the latex in the first coat.

First Coat of Latex Rendering
The thickness need not be more than 10 mm ($\frac{3}{8}$ in) and the mix proportions should be:

1 part ordinary Portland cement.
3 parts clean well-graded sand, to Table 1 of BS 1199.
9 litres (2 gal) of latex to each 50 g (112 lb) of cement.

The cement and sand are usually proportioned by volume, and allowance should be made for the bulking of the sand. As mentioned with the bedding mortar for block walls in Chapter 4, the latex is a powerful plasticiser, and so it should be added to the cement and sand and well mixed before any water is added. If the sand is very wet, it may be that no additional water is needed at all. The surface should be combed or scratched to form a key for the second (final) coat.

Final Coat
The mix proportions should be 1 part ordinary Portland cement and $3\frac{1}{2}$ parts clean dry, well-graded sand, with 9 litres of the latex in the mix. The same precautions are required with the mixing as described for the first coat. The thickness of this coat is 5–7 mm ($\frac{3}{16}-\frac{1}{4}$ in). The coat should be well trowelled with a wood float to give a dense even surface.

Curing and Protection
The same as for ordinary rendering, except that it is generally considered
advisable to delay covering up the work for at least 12 h.

GENERAL
Whichever type of rendering is used, it should be carried down to form a
cove angle at the junction of the wall and floor.

RENDERING ON TO A BACKGROUND OF GUNITE
Properly applied gunite makes a waterproof shell, but may not provide an
acceptable surface on which the final decoration (whether it is paint or tiles)
can be directly applied. A levelling coat of cement–sand rendering may
therefore be required. The natural surface of gunite forms an excellent key
for hand-applied rendering, and so very little surface preparation should be
needed. The surface of the gunite should be well brushed down and checked
for any hollow spots or weak areas, and these should be cut out and
repaired. It is usually desirable to lightly spray the surface with water just
before the rendering is applied, to ensure uniform suction. The thickness
will be governed by the depth required to provide a level and even surface or
to ensure that the inside dimensions of the completed pool are within the
tolerances laid down in Chapter 4 and mentioned earlier in this chapter. A
thickness less than 10 mm ($\frac{3}{8}$ in) is undesirable if the wall is to be tiled. The
general method of application, mix proportions, panel sizes and curing are
all as recommended for rendering on to reinforced concrete.

CERAMIC TILING

GENERAL CONSIDERATIONS
For open-air pools only a frost-resistant (fully vitrified) tile should be used.
It is the opinion of the author that ceramic tiles and mosaic are the two most
durable and attractive finishes which can be given to swimming pools.
Ceramic mosaic is much less popular in the United Kingdom than on the
Continent.
   The previous sections in this chapter have given detailed information on
screeds and rendering, which are the usual background materials (or
substrate) to which tiles are fixed. Complaints and enquiries about 'failures'
of tiling seem to be on the increase, although this may be due to the large
number of new swimming pools which have been built during the past 10–15
years. Investigation usually shows that it is very seldom that the fault lies
with the tiles themselves. The trouble usually arises from the screed,
rendering, bedding, jointing or movement joints in the tiling. The most

common fault is loss of bond between the substrate and the concrete shell of the pool, which shows as lifting and cracking of the tiles. It is often difficult to give satisfactory and detailed reasons why the trouble has occurred. It is invariably a combination of circumstances, each one of which would not have caused the failure on its own.

In the opinion of the author, the tiling should include the provision of a ceramic scum channel around the full perimeter of the pool unless it is a deck-level pool. In the case of deck-level pools, the scum channel is replaced by a large collecting channel and for some unaccountable reason the author has found that many of these channels are just left as bare concrete. The recommendation here is that all such channels should be lined with ceramic tiles or mosaic, or finished with a high-quality epoxide resin.

There are two basic categories of ceramic tiles used for swimming pools in the United Kingdom. The differences arise from the method of manufacture, and they are usually described as pressed tiles and extruded tiles. In each category there are many divisions, and full details should be obtained from the manufacturers because of continuous development in the industry. The imported tiles for pools are mostly extruded. Generally, pressed tiles are thinner and the body of the tile is relatively absorbent, but the dimensional tolerances are small, which means that there is very little variation in the declared size of the tiles. The extruded tiles tend to be thicker and the body is usually fully vitrified, resulting in almost zero absorption, but the dimensional tolerances are relatively large. The thicker tiles generally have deeper 'frogs' or indentations on the back.

The differences in the principal characteristics of the two categories of tile are reflected in the methods for laying and jointing. The pressed tiles are laid with comparatively narrow joints, usually 3 mm ($\frac{1}{8}$ in) wide, while the extruded tiles are laid with 10 mm ($\frac{3}{8}$ in) wide joints to allow for the variation in tile dimensions.

The difference in water absorption is likely to affect the recommendations for the number and location of movement joints in the tiling, and this is discussed in detail later in this section.

A number of pools built 40 or more years ago were finished in glazed clayware bricks; although they proved to be very durable, they are no longer used in swimming pools. Also, at one time, some pools were finished with fiance tiles, but these have gone off the swimming pool market in the past 10–15 years.

Tile Laying

Both types of tiles, pressed and extruded, can be laid successfully with a cement–sand bed, but proprietary adhesives have now largely replaced this material, particularly for the tiles which have shallow recesses on the back. The thicker, fully vitrified extruded tiles with deep frogs are still often

FIG. 6.3. View of tile laying in progress in public swimming pool (Courtesy: Shaw
Hathernware Ltd).

FIG. 6.4. View of tiling of set-in steps in wall of pool (Courtesy: Pilkingtons Tiles Ltd).

bedded on cement and sand mortar; but even here adhesives are slowly entering the market.

The most important point in considering the bedding of tiles is to follow the detailed recommendations of the supplier of the tiles. While there are some differences of opinion between the various suppliers, they are unanimous on certain points, which are given below:

(1) With cement–sand bedding, the tiles should be given a preliminary soaking in water, and the water should be allowed to drain off before the tiles are laid.

(2) When adhesives are used, the tiles should be dry and not dipped in water.

(3) Irrespective of whether thick bed (10 mm) or thin bed (3 mm) is used, the tiles must be fully bedded and all necessary precautions taken to ensure this.

(4) The structural shell of the pool and all other structural concrete which will receive tiling should have been completed at least 28 days

FIG. 6.5.   View of well-designed and well-finished public pool (Courtesy: H. S. Fairhurst, Architects, and Pilkingtons Tiles Ltd).

before any rendering or screeds are laid. The rendering and screeds should be completed at least 14 days before tiling is commenced.
(5) Tiles should not be laid over hollow-sounding areas of screed or rendering.

Figures 6.3 and 6.4 show tile laying in progress, and Fig. 6.5 shows high-quality tiling in a well-designed public pool.

THE PROVISION OF MOVEMENT JOINTS IN THE TILING
All reinforced concrete pools have joints; these are either monolithic or partial movement joints, i.e. contraction, semi-contraction or stress-relief joints. In addition, in certain special cases there may be one or more full movement joints in the pool shell. Joints in the pool shell were discussed in detail in Chapter 4. Where there is a full movement joint in the pool shell this must be carried through all applied rigid finishes, i.e. screed, rendering and tiling. Pools which do not have full movement joints in the shell must nevertheless have movement joints in the tiling, and these joints should be carried down through the screed and rendering to the base concrete. The problem is whether these movement joints should be located so as to line up with joints in the pool shell, and where these joints should be positioned. There is no simple answer to this and many differences of opinion exist. The author's views are summarised below:

(a) Movement joints in the tiling need not be lined up with monolithic joints in the pool shell.
(b) Movement joints in the tiling should ideally be lined up with partial movement joints in the pool shell. However, whether this should be insisted on in all cases depends on what movement is anticipated in the pool shell during normal operation, including filling and emptying. Therefore a decision on joints in both the pool shell and the tiling should be taken at the design stage. This requires close liaison and co-ordination between the structural engineer, architect and tile supplier in the early stages of the project. It is difficult to ensure that the spacing of joints in the pool shell will coincide exactly with the joint lines in the tiling, and cutting of tiles may be required. Whenever tiles are cut, the cut edge should be rounded off, otherwise hands and feet of bathers can be cut.
Unless this line-up of joints in shell and tiling is to be achieved, then the movement joints in the tiling should be determined according to the type of tile used, as discussed later in this section, i.e. independently of joints in the shell.
(c) Where the pool shell is elevated so that use is made of the space below, there is greater need to ensure a line-up of the joints in shell and tiling than where the pool is sunk in the ground. The reason for

this is the temperature changes and resultant strain in the pool shell, which occur when the pool is emptied (usually in winter) after being kept filled with water at about 26 °C (79 °F) for 3–8 years.

The reason for the provision of movement joints in the tiling screed and rendering is that experience has shown that these are needed to allow movement to take place during the normal operation of the pool. Differential movement can and does occur between the tiling, the substrate (rendering and screed) and the concrete shell of the pool. This movement can be caused by:

(a) The thermal gradient through the tiling, substrate and shell.
(b) Moisture changes (i.e. absorption of moisture) by the tiles, screed and rendering, and to a considerably lesser extent the pool shell.

Research on long-term moisture movement in ceramics has been carried out at the Building Research Station, and Reports on this are contained in the Bibliography at the end of this chapter. Actual measured movements in elevated pool shells were reported by Southern and Hodson at the BRE Symposium on Swimming Pools, in East Kilbride, in June 1973.

In theory the joints between the tiling should be impervious to the passage of water, but in practice watertightness is never achieved. The total length of plain butt joints in a tiled pool 33·33 m × 12·5 m (110 ft × 41 ft) with an average depth of 1·5 m (4 ft 10 in) is about 6 km ($3\frac{3}{4}$ miles). It is therefore not surprising that areas of screed and rendering become saturated in the course of time. The tiles also absorb water (slowly), the amount depending on the category of tile; pressed tiles absorb appreciably more than the extruded, fully vitrified tiles.

This slow absorption of water causes dimensional changes in tiles and substrate, resulting in the build-up of stress. If this movement (dimensional change) cannot take place owing to the absence of an adequate number of correctly located movement joints, trouble is likely to develop in the form of cracked tiles and debonding of screed and rendering.

The lower part of the joint—that is, the part in the bed and screed—should be filled with a filler, sometimes called 'back-up' material. Materials in common use include expanded polystyrene, expanded polyurethane and Neoprene-bonded cork granules. Of these, the author favours Neoprene-bonded cork granules. Information on joint fillers is given in Chapter 2.

Trouble seldom arises from the filler, but there is considerable disquiet among baths managers and architects over the unsatisfactory performance of sealants immersed in swimming pool water. The sealants in general use are polysulphides (one- and two-pack) and silicone rubbers. The author's experience is that the useful life of these compounds is unpredictable. The reasons for 'failure', i.e. lack of durability, are difficult or impossible to determine, even with the active co-operation of the manufacturer, which is not always forthcoming. One of the difficulties is that the manufacturer does not fix the material on site, so that there is immediately divided responsibility, and this is the first point for argument when something goes wrong. A material which has proved very durable in other conditions, including sewage treatment works, is preformed Neoprene. Preformed Neoprene gaskets, which are imported, can be obtained in a range of sizes and in black and light grey. When correctly installed, they give a watertight joint. A new *in situ* sealant is a flexible epoxide, which is potentially very durable.

In Chapter 4 mention was made of the optimum dimensions of the sealing groove in concrete structures, and it is recommended that the same principles should be applied to joints in tiling. This means that the width of the joint should be greater than the depth of the sealant. For tiles which are 10 mm ($\frac{3}{8}$ in) thick the joint should be 12 mm wide.

LOCATION OF MOVEMENT JOINTS IN TILING
The tile manufacturer should be consulted on the location of movement joints in the tiling, but the following comments are based on the experience of the author.

Pressed Tiles (not Vitrified Throughout)
Joints should be provided at the ends of walls and also at about 3·5 m–4·5 m centres (11 ft 6 in–14 ft 9 in), bearing in mind the previous comments on lining up the joints with movement joints in the pool shell. There should also be a joint between the wall and the floor. In some cases a joint is also provided at the top of the wall below the scum channel. It is open to question whether there should be movement joints in the scum channel to line up with the joints in the wall tiling. The author feels this is not necessary; failure of scum channel units due to absence of movement joints, except at the four corners, is very rare. In the floor, movement joints should be in line with those in the walls, and at major changes of gradient; for example, at the top and bottom of the slope down to the diving pit. As previously stated, a full movement joint in the pool shell must always be carried through the screed, rendering and tiling.

Extruded Tiles (Fully Vitrified)
Joints should be provided at the ends of walls, and also between the wall and floor. If the length of the pool exceeds 33·33 m (110 ft), a central transverse joint in the walls and across the floor is probably desirable. Reference should be made to the discussion on lining up these joints with movement joints in the pool shell. In the floor, a movement joint should be provided at all major changes of gradient (as described above for pressed tiles) and at all full movement joints in the pool shell.

Fiance Tiles

These are seldom used now in swimming pools, but if they are, movement joints should be located as for pressed tiles.

REINFORCED CONCRETE WALKWAY SLABS AND FLOORS OF CHANGING AND SHOWER ROOMS

These concrete floor slabs can be *in situ* or precast. Walkway slabs are often cast monolithically with the top of the wall of the pool, but in some designs they are simply supported on the wall of the pool on one side and the frame of the superstructure on the other. In some projects the walkway slabs and the floors of changing and shower rooms form the ceiling of plant rooms, stores or public rooms below. It is then essential that the slabs be completely watertight to the same standard as the roof of a building.

The structural slab is usually finished with a screed on which ceramic non-slip tiles are laid in the usual way, to fall to drainage channels which discharge to the drainage system of the building. The author is not in favour of finishing these floors with concrete slabs or tiles owing to the absorbent nature of the concrete surface compared with ceramic. A non-absorbent surface is essential to reduce the risk of foot infections. While the swimming pool is in use, these floors are constantly wet, but they tend to dry out during the night. However, experience shows that, in the course of time, the screed below the tiles is likely to become saturated. The result is that if the structural slab is itself not completely watertight, water will penetrate through. Not only will this cause consternation to designer and client, but also, if water drips onto electrical equipment, there may be serious trouble. Designers and builders should therefore take all precautions to ensure that this type of floor is completely watertight when there are working areas or stores beneath. There are approximately 2.8 km (1·75 miles) length of joints between 150 mm × 150 mm (6 × 6 in) tiles on a walkway 2·5 m (8 ft) wide around a 25 m × 12·5 m (82 ft × 41 ft) pool. Leakage through these slabs usually occurs at construction joints and fine cracks. The slab can often be cast in bays about 5·0 m (16 ft) long, spanning from the pool to a beam at the back of the walkway. With a plain butt joint between each section (the distribution steel is not carried across the joint), intermediate cracks are unlikely to form. The joints (which are in effect contraction joints) can be readily sealed. The joint should be carried through the screed and tiling; it is much easier to reseal such a joint than to remove tiling and screed and locate and repair a crack in the slab below.

On the Continent precast slabs, complete with tiling, are often used, the levels in the supporting structure being such as to provide the necessary drainage falls.

The surface of all these 'wet' areas must be finished to adequate falls and be provided with correctly sized channels to carry away the water. The author considers that a gradient of 1 in 40 is adequate. There are many advantages in having the gradient in the slab itself, and when a membrane is used to waterproof the slab, this is essential for the reasons given in (2) below.

Complete watertightness of these slabs in certain cases is essential, and there are various ways of achieving this which are set out below.

(1) The structural slab is designed so as to be watertight in its own right. In this case it should be checked for leakage by being ponded before the screed–tiling is laid on it. No seepage or even damp spots should be accepted.

(2) The slab is designed in the ordinary way (CP114 or CP110) and a waterproof membrane is laid on it. All joints in the membrane should be hot- or solvent-welded and it must be terminated in such a position that water cannot penetrate down behind it; also, it must not be damaged during subsequent operations (screed and tile laying). Provision must be made for draining this membrane, because the screed will eventually become saturated. If the water accumulates on the membrane, this is likely to result in 'rocking', and partial disintegration of screed and cracking of the tiles.

(3) The slab is designed in the usual way and laid to the required falls. This will necessitate extra care in finishing the slab, because in this method the tiles will be bedded directly on the slab in an epoxide resin which will ensure complete watertightness. It would be prudent for the surface of the concrete to be prepared and treated with one coat of resin prior to the bedding of the tiles. This is the method which the author considers is likely to be most satisfactory in the long term.

THE FINISHING OF SWIMMING POOLS CONSTRUCTED IN REINFORCED GUNITE
Details of reinforced gunite for the construction of swimming pools are given in Chapter 4. There are certain special features of gunite pools which affect tiling.

The usual design incorporates a large cove angle, having a radius of about 1·0 m (3 ft 3 in), at the junction of the wall and floor. Normal pool tiles cannot be applied to such a cove, and so gunite pools are usually finished in mosaic (generally ceramic, but sometimes glass). An alternative is Marbelite, which is much favoured by package deal contractors, and is described later in this chapter. A third alternative is some form of coating, such as cement-based paint, chlorinated rubber paint, etc. (also discussed later).

It is, however, possible to design and construct a gunite pool with a right angle at junction of floor and wall. This is often required in public pools, and then the shell can be tiled in the usual way.

Gunite pools seldom contain movement joints of any type. There are joints, because the shell is not 'gunned' in one continuous operation, but these are monolithic joints.

It is usual practice to finish the gunite with a wood float, and then comb or scratch the surface to provide a key for the rendering–screed. All loose material should be brushed off and, if necessary, the surface slightly dampened (to give uniform suction), immediately before the rendering is applied. The principles of applying rendering and laying the floor screed are the same as in a reinforced concrete pool. There is also no difference in the tile laying. Movement joints should be provided in the tiling to suit the type of tile used.

MOSAICS

Ceramic mosaic as a finish to swimming pools is very popular on the Continent. In the United Kingdom its use seems to be largely confined to pools constructed in reinforced gunite. The reason for its use in gunite pools is that the usual large cove at the junction of the wall and floor precludes the use of tiles. In the opinion of the author, ceramic mosaic is equal to high-quality ceramic tiling. Glass mosaic provides an attractive and durable finish, but has been used only to a very limited extent, and is confined to private and hotel pools in the United Kingdom.

The basic requirements for successful laying of mosaic are similar to those for ceramic tiles, but prospective users should obtain detailed directions from the suppliers. Movement joints should be provided in the same positions as for extruded fully vitrified tiles.

GLASS MOSAIC

This material is made in the United Kingdom, but some is imported from Italy. The mosaic is stuck to strong brown paper in squares of about 300 mm × 300 mm (12 in × 12 in). As in the case of ceramic tiles, a sound level background of high-grade rendering is required on which to bed the mosaic. The rendering must be of the same quality and mix as that previously described; also, it must be fully bonded to the concrete shell as recommended.

The bedding mortar mix proportions should be as recommended by the suppliers of the mosaic. For example, importers of the Italian mosaic, recommend:

$\frac{1}{4}$ part slaked lime.
1 part ordinary Portland cement.
4 parts clean dry plasterers sand.

The bedding is applied to the cleaned and damped surface of the rendering about 6–10 mm ($\frac{1}{4}$–$\frac{3}{8}$ in) thick. The panel of mosaic is given a thick coat of slurry of white cement and, while the bedding is still plastic, it is firmly pressed and tamped into position. Special care must be taken to clean off the edges of adjoining panels so that there is an even spacing of joints. The joints should be a minimum of $1\frac{1}{2}$ mm wide and a maximum of 3 mm ($\frac{1}{8}$ in). The backing paper (which covers the front surface of the mosaic) is then well damped and stripped carefully off. The panel is again tamped and levelled. When the backing coat begins to harden, the joints should be grouted with a grout of white cement of the same consistency as was applied to the back of the panel; all surplus slurry is removed with a damp cloth.

Not earlier than 48 h after the completion of the fixing of the panels, the surface can be washed down with a dilute solution of hydrochloric acid (1 part acid to 10 parts water). This acid wash must be carried out with care, using rubber gloves and eye shield, and the panels must be well washed down with plenty of water. Expansion joints should be provided in the same basic positions as recommended for ceramic tiling, and also detailed in the same way.

The preceding notes are intended as a brief description of the method which should be used for the fixing of the mosaic, but a first-class job is only likely to be obtained from experienced and skilful setters.

The cost of the mosaic depends on the quantity ordered, the colour and the size of the tesserae (mosaic pieces). The darker colours and the larger tesserae are the most expensive. The standard sizes are 20 mm × 20 mm and 25 × 25 mm ($\frac{3}{4}$ × $\frac{3}{4}$ in and 1 × 1 in), but a wide range of other sizes can be obtained as well as special bull-nosed edge pieces. The tesserae are frost-resistant in the same way as ceramic mosaic and fully vitrified tiles, and can therefore be used in open-air pools. Because of the very smooth surface, particularly when wet, glass mosaic should not be used for walkways around the pool, or on steps leading down into the pool. If used on the floor in the shallow end, notices warning the pool users of slipperiness should be clearly displayed.

IN SITU FINISHES

MARBELITE

This consists of a mixture of white Portland cement and marble chippings graded 3 mm ($\frac{1}{8}$ in) down, and free from dust, with mix proportions of about 1 part cement to 2 or $2\frac{1}{2}$ parts chippings. The proportions are not fixed and vary from one sub-contractor to another. Some specialists use a mix as rich as 1:1. A plasticiser is often added to improve workability. The Marbelite is really a type of *in situ* terrazzo.

The pool walls and floor must be rendered and screeded to obtain a level and even base on which to apply the Marbelite. The surface of the base should be combed or scratched to provide a key for the Marbelite, which is usually applied in one coat to a thickness of 6–10 mm ($\frac{1}{4}$–$\frac{3}{8}$ in). The Marbelite should not be applied earlier than 14 days after the completion of the base (rendering or screed). The Marbelite is usually applied by specialist sub-contractors and in the opinion of the author it is not advisable to entrust this work to an ordinary plasterer. The method of application is generally as follows:

(a) The background is brushed down to remove all dirt, dust and loose particles and slightly damped immediately prior to the application of the Marbelite.

(b) The Marbelite mix is then applied in one coat to the required thickness (6–10 mm) and worked up to a smooth even surface with a trowel. The finished area is covered with damp sacking, polythene sheets or similar for at least 48 h to help prevent too rapid drying out or sharp temperature changes.

(c) About 2 days after completion, the surface is lightly ground using a coarse abrasive stone. The surface is then washed down with plenty of water. Immediately after this a coat of white cement grout is well brushed into the surface. Careful curing is essential.

After this the surface is again covered for about two days to maintain humidity and reduce temperature changes. The final grinding is done by means of a fine abrasive stone. While the walls can be given a very smooth finish, and in fact are often highly polished, it is not advisable to impart too smooth a finish to the floor in the shallow end of the pool because this makes it very slippery. Figure 6.6 shows Marbelite being cleaned after final grinding and polishing.

Marbelite tends to stain easily, and for this reason it is usual to provide two courses of glazed ceramic tiles or a band of mosaic 300 mm (12 in) wide at the water line, which is the place in the pool where most staining occurs. Because of its tendency to stain, Marbelite should be used only in pools which will be well maintained; if the pool is of the open-air variety, it should be covered in the winter and the water treatment plant kept in operation.

Another point which should be kept in mind is that, because Marbelite is composed entirely of marble chippings and white Portland cement, it is particularly susceptible to acid attack, which can occur if the pH of the water in the pool is not maintained consistently above 7·0. It is emphasised in Chapter 7 that for efficient water treatment the pH should be kept in the range 7·2–7·8; mention is also made of the need to measure the pH correctly. Water from upland gathering grounds often contains organic acids and carbon dioxide in solution which results in a pH below 7·0.

FIG. 6.6.   Final cleaning of Marbelite finish to pool (Courtesy: Rutherford Ltd, Battle).

Staining can occur if the water contains iron or manganese salts in solution, and organic colouring matter from leaves.

PAINTS
Cement-based Paints
These paints are based on white or pigmented Portland cement, to which are usually added accelerators, waterproofers and extenders. As normally used, they give a matt finish and are available in a range of about nine colours, including white. By the addition of a glaze, a gloss can be imparted to the surface. The base to which the paint is applied must be clean, sound and relatively dry.

This type of paint is particularly suitable for cementitious backgrounds, such as concrete and concrete blocks and rendering. In the case of dusty or absorbent surfaces it is advisable to apply a priming coat or stabilising liquid supplied by the manufacturer of the paint.

The manufacturers always give detailed directions for the mixing and application of the paint, but the following general recommendations are common to most brands. First, the powder should be mixed with a little water to the consistency of a smooth paste and then more water should be added until the final proportions of 3 parts of powder to 2 parts of water by volume are reached. It is better to mix sufficient for application for one hour's work rather than a larger volume.

A minimum of two coats is recommended. The first coat should be well scrubbed into the surface with a stiff brush. The second coat can be applied as soon as the first has thoroughly hardened, but there should be a minimum period of 24 h between successive coats even in summer. A period of at least 48 h must elapse between the completion of the final coat and the filling of the pool with water. The covering capacity varies according to the porosity of the background, but with good-quality *in situ* concrete or rendering 50 kg (112 lb) should cover between $150 \, \text{m}^2$ and $180 \, \text{m}^2$ ($180–220 \, \text{yd}^2$) with two-coat brush work.

It is not possible to say how long such a coating will last, since it depends on both the conditions of use and the standard of maintenance adopted. For example, an open-air swimming pool which is not covered in winter and given considerable use in summer may need decorating each year, while another pool which is well maintained and is covered during the winter may keep an excellent appearance for several years.

This type of paint is generally used for small private and club pools; it has the great merit of cheapness and ease of application and can be applied over existing decorated surfaces provided these are clean and sound.

Chlorinated Rubber Paints

These paints are particularly useful both for the inside of swimming pools and for decoration and protective coatings in the swimming pool hall. The problems of the pool hall will be discussed later in this chapter. The paint consists of chlorinated rubber and a plasticiser together with inert pigments. High-build chlorinated rubber paints (which is the type to be used for swimming pools and pool halls) should contain a thickening or thixotropic agent and should be capable of giving a dry film $0·10 \, \text{mm}–0·15 \, \text{mm}$ (100–150 μm or 4–6 mils) thick. When correctly applied the paint is resistant to weak acids and alkalis, and particularly chlorine; it can be obtained in an attractive range of colours and produce a gloss finish.

These paints give the best results when they are applied to good-quality cement–sand rendering which has been finished with a wood float; the wood float gives a dense even surface without laitance. The paint is supplied mixed and ready for use except for stirring. The surface of the base must be clean and dry, and the complete removal of all dirt and mould growths is essential.

In the case of new pools, it is advisable to neutralise the surface of the concrete or rendering by washing down with a dilute solution of hydrochloric acid. Some paint manufacturers recommend 1 part of commercial acid to 2 parts of water, which is a very strong solution. The author suggests a much weaker solution, 1 part acid to 8 parts water, and to repeat the wash if necessary. The surface should be well washed down with water immediately prior to the application of the dilute acid, since this will help prevent the acid being absorbed into the base. The acid wash is applied by a soft brush in one or two coats, the second following straight after the first. After about 5 min, the surface should be well washed down with fresh water and then tested for pH by a suitable indicator. The pH should be not lower than 6·5 and not higher than 7·5.

One disadvantage with chlorinated rubber paints is that for the best results they should be applied within a fairly narrow range of air temperature and relative humidity. A warm dry day without too much sun is ideal, and the surface to be painted must be dry. For outdoor pools such conditions are difficult to obtain in the United Kingdom and other countries with similar unsettled weather conditions.

It is the author's opinion that when results of painting with chlorinated rubber paints are disappointing, the cause is usually either bad weather or inadequate preparation of the background or a combination of both. Three-coat work is recommended, and the coverage on a good background is 8–12 m² (10–15 yd²) per gallon in three-coat work (or 2–3 m² per litre). The first coat should be well brushed in, but the second and third coats are best applied lightly. An absolute minimum of 24 h must elapse between the coats, and 48 h is better. After the final coat, a period of 14 days is recommended before the pool is filled. The above information is intended as a general guide, and the detailed directions of the manufacturers should be carefully followed.

Epoxide Resin Paints
Epoxide resin paints can be obtained in a range of standard colours and are eminently suitable for the decoration of swimming pools, provided the following conditions are fulfilled:

(a) The paint must be of the highest quality and a statement should be obtained from the manufacturer on the percentage of resin in the paint.

(b) The preparation of the background and the application of the paint should be as detailed in Chapter 8, where the use of epoxide coatings for the repair of swimming pools is described.

Subject to the above, the paint should have a life of at least 10 years.

SYNTHETIC RUBBER FLOOR TILES
In recent years, synthetic rubber floor tiles with a patterned non-slip surface have come onto the swimming pool market. They have been used successfully on walkways around the pool, on staircases, corridors,

changing and shower rooms and saunas. The material is soft to the feet, resilient and hard-wearing. The tiles vary in size from about 750 mm × 750 mm to 1·00 m × 1·00 m (2 ft 6 in sq. to 3 ft 3 in sq.), and are usually 4 mm–5 mm thick ($\frac{1}{6}$ in–$\frac{1}{5}$ in). Full bond to the substrate is required for satisfactory service, and they are usually laid with a Neoprene or epoxide adhesive. The substrate should be firm, clean, strong and smooth. A high-quality cement–sand screed (1:3) finished with a steel float is likely to provide a satisfactory surface on which the tiles can be laid.

GLASS FIBRE–POLYESTER RESIN LINING TO SWIMMING POOLS

This type of lining has now been in use for probably 10 years in the United Kingdom. Originally it was used to line small private and club pools, but the use has now been extended to large public pools, and the pools in the leisure centres at Whitely Bay, Rotherham and Swindon have been finished with this material. The results are not up to the original expectation in most cases.

It is important that the pool shell should be tested for watertightness before the lining is applied. It is also desirable that there should be no infiltration of groundwater into the pool when the pool is empty. In the opinion of the writer, the latter requirement is more important than the former, because the lining itself should form a watertight membrane against escape of water from the pool, but if the pool is empty and groundwater can pass through the pool wall, then pressure will be exerted on the lining and may cause serious trouble.

Linings of this type are normally fully bonded to the base concrete, and the comments which follow are intended to apply to how this work is generally carried out. There are, of course, variations according to the ideas of the specialist contractor who carries out a particular job. These small variations may, in fact, be important because they make the difference between success and failure.

There are four stages in the work, as follows:

Stage 1. The preparation of the surface of the concrete. This is to ensure that the resin–glass-fibre laminate will bond properly to the concrete. Light exposure of the coarse aggregate followed by the removal of all grit and dust should prove satisfactory.

Stage 2. The polyester resin, the catalyst, and the glass-fibre are applied to the concrete through a three-nozzle gun; one nozzle takes the catalyst, one the resin and the centre one the glass-fibre. The first coat is approximately 1 mm ($\frac{1}{25}$ in) thick; as it is applied, it is consolidated by metal rollers to ensure that all the glass fibres are completely covered by the resin.

Stage 3. This consists in the application of a thin glass tissue sheet about 0·3 mm ($\frac{1}{75}$ in) thick; the object of this is to seal in any ends of glass-fibre which may be left projecting through the resin. It should be noted that stages 2 and 3 follow each other immediately until the whole pool is completed.

Stage 4. This really consists of two substages. The first is the application by spray of a gel-coat which is a modified polyester resin without any glass-fibre in it. This is applied direct to the glass tissue which has been laid at the end of stage 3. The gel-coat is finished with a rubber squeegee. This gel-coat is allowed to semicure, and the time taken depends on the formulation of the resin and also on the planning of the work (the curing time can be modified within a fairly wide limit). The second substage consists of the application of a further gel-coat which is a modified polyester resin also without glass-fibre. These two gel-coats usually contain pigments, but in some cases the pigments are confined to the second gel-coat, in which case it can be applied some months after the application of the first gel-coat. In this way, damage by contractors' labour can be avoided. The overall thickness of the polyester resin–glass-fibre laminate is about 3 mm–5 mm ($\frac{1}{8}$–$\frac{1}{4}$ in), and therefore, to achieve the best results, it is important that the background should be as smooth as possible (subject, of course, to the preparation of the concrete as described briefly in stage 1).

Certain facts should be kept in mind when considering the use of this type of lining, particularly for large pools; these are summarised below:

(a) Polyester resins have high shrinkage characteristics (about 2% linear) and this can result in the build-up of stress at angles, corners and points of entry of pipework. These stresses can cause crazing and cracking in the areas of stress concentration.

(b) There is a significant difference in the coefficients of thermal expansion of the polyester resin and the glass fibres. Pools are filled initially with water at mains temperature, say 10 °C (50 °F), and when this is raised to operating temperature of about 26 °C (79 °F), considerable stress will develop within the laminate and at the interface of laminate and substrate.

(c) Should the lining be damaged so that water penetrates into the laminate, delamination can occur. As there is more than one type of polyester resin, it is important that a resin with low water absorption characteristics should be used.

(d) Experience with these linings suggests that it is difficult to obtain really good bond between the laminate and the base concrete, screed–rendering. One of the results of poor bond is that if the laminate cracks and water penetrates behind the lining, debonding can occur and spread over a considerable area. The final result may be a failure of a large part of the lining.

(e) The final gel-coats are usually highly pigmented and are therefore of different composition compared with the main body of the laminate to which they are applied. It is the gel-coats which often give trouble such as blistering, flaking, loss of pigment and general wear. This occurs particularly in areas of heavy use such as the shallow ends of pools.

Briefly: while polyester–glass-fibre laminate linings to swimming pools have in some cases performed well and given good service, there have been instances of serious trouble. It is therefore advisable to ensure that there is an adequate guarantee of satisfactory performance in the contract documents.

Reference should be made to the section at the end of Chapter 5 on fully bonded lining to pools.

FILLING AND EMPTYING SWIMMING POOLS

The remarks which follow apply to covered, heated pools.

The pool should be emptied as infrequently as possible, compatible with proper maintenance. With public pools, practice differs: some authorities empty the pool every 4–8 years, while others consider this should be done every 3–4 years. It is the author's opinion that if the pool requires emptying more often than once in three years, then some aspects of the maintenance, and operation and functioning of the equipment should be carefully scrutinised. Generally, the frequency of emptying depends on the loading of the pool, the efficiency of the water treatment plant, the characteristics of the raw water supply, the standard of daily cleaning and the need to carry out repairs to the tiling.

The usual arrangement of the water treatment and heating installation is such that the heating only starts when the pool is full and normal water circulation is in operation. This results in the pool being filled with water at mains temperature, perhaps as low as 5 °C (40 °F). This water then has to be raised to about 26 °C (79 °F) or even higher. Pools are usually emptied in the middle of winter (when demand for swimming is at a minimum), and the opportunity is then taken to carry out servicing to the other mechanical and electrical equipment. This can result in a rapid fall in temperature in the pool hall. It is recommended that the pool should be kept empty for as short a period as possible. Refilling should take place slowly, the water level rising about 600 mm (2 ft) every 24 h. The water temperature should also be raised slowly, by about 2 °C/h.

Part 2: Finishes to Swimming Pool Halls, Fitting Out and the Provision of Ancillary Equipment

INTERIOR FINISHINGS TO SWIMMING POOL HALLS

GENERAL CONSIDERATIONS

The selection of attractive and durable finishings to the interior of swimming pool halls presents certain problems which require careful consideration. The walls around the pool are usually tiled or finished in similar material (mosaic) to a height of about 2·0 m (6 ft 6 in). However, apart from this there are the remainder of the walls, the ceiling, windows, doors and metal work. The conditions under which these finishes have to function are severe. The air temperature can be in the range 25–28 °C (77–83 °F), the humidity is high and, in addition, there is a small amount of chlorine compounds in the air. The chlorine concentration is likely to be about 0·5 ppm by volume (0·5 cm^3/m^3). These three factors together make the atmosphere much more corrosive to steel than normal air. To avoid maintenance costs, the finishes should be specially selected for long life under the specific conditions in which they will have to function.

In many modern swimming pool halls one or more external walls may be fully, or almost fully, glazed. In these cases the glazing should be double to improve the heat insulation characteristics of the windows, and a safety barrier should be provided for extensive areas of glass which extend down to within 1·50 m (5 ft) of the surface of walkways, corridors, etc.

The finishes may be divided into four main types:

(a) The natural surface of the structural material such as fair-faced concrete blockwork, off the form concrete or other special high-quality finish, fair-faced brickwork. Unpainted hardwood, such as oiled teak or mahogany.

(b) Preformed materials such as ceramic tiles, ceramic mosaic, glass mosaic.

(c) *In situ* finishes such as terrazzo.

(d) Applied coatings.

From the above it can be seen that the designer has a wide choice, and the final effect will depend on his artistic ability. The aesthetic merits of various finishes and their combination are outside the scope of this book, but the author hopes that the information and comments which are given will help designers with the most important factor, namely durability. Thermal and sound insulation is also very important. Special finishes which possess properties of thermal insulation, sound absorption and anti-condensation are dealt with in Chapter 7.

THE USE OF THE NATURAL (UNPROTECTED) SURFACE OF THE STRUCTURAL MATERIAL

The increase in cost of both labour and materials has in recent years led to an intensive search for surfaces which can be produced on basic structural materials which will be aesthetically satisfying and have a long maintenance-free life. This applies particularly to *in situ* and precast concrete. Good-quality *in situ* Portland cement concrete will be unaffected

FIG. 6.7.   View of untreated concrete blockwork walls to interior of pool hall. This type of finish is not recommended for reasons given in the text.

throughout the lifetime of the building by the atmosphere in swimming pool halls. The slight (although to most people, unpleasant) smell associated with chlorine will have no erosive effect on the concrete. Some staining will undoubtedly occur, but this is unavoidable, no matter what kind of material is used. The application, at about 5 year intervals, of a good-quality silicone water-repellent will help in reducing staining to a minimum, and this applies both inside and outside the building.

The author wishes to make it clear that he does not advise the use of untreated concrete surfaces in positions where people will come in direct contact with them, since this will certainly result in serious staining by grease and dirt from hands; such staining will be very difficult indeed to remove (see Fig. 6.7). The provision of a smooth impervious surface, such as glazed tiles or mosaic to a height of 1·5 to 2·0 m (5 ft to 6 ft 6 in) above floor level, is recommended for all wet areas, including shower rooms, changing rooms, toilets and walkways around the pool. The same remarks about staining applies to fair-faced clay brickwork; stains and grease on bricks will be even more difficult to remove than from concrete. Any unpainted timber should be oiled; teak or mahogany, properly maintained, will last a very long time indeed.

MATERIALS SUCH AS CERAMIC TILES, MOSAIC AND TERRAZZO

Materials such as glazed ceramic tiles, glazed and unglazed ceramic mosaic and glass mosaic, provided they are of good quality and properly applied, will last as long as the building. It may be necessary to replace a broken tile or piece of mosaic, but apart from this, and possible fresh grouting and sealing of the joints after 15 years or so, no maintenance other than cleaning should be required. These materials are ideal for wall areas which will come into contact with water. The important thing is for the designer to insist on high-quality products. Appreciable differences in the price of the material are a clear indication of differences in quality. The experience of the author is that quality generally varies directly as the price.

The correct mix of bedding mortar and fixing procedure are also important. The author has seen cases where tiles have crazed badly owing to bad fixing technique. Apart from the inconvenience and cost to the client, the need to retile the walls of a swimming pool hall a few years after completion is most embarrassing to the designer. Recommendations for rendering and bedding and fixing tiles and mosaic have already been given earlier in this chapter for the pool itself, and if these are followed, the result should be satisfactory.

Terrazzo, both *in situ* and tiles, makes a very attractive, durable and easily cleaned wall finish. For reasons given in Chapter 1, terrazzo is not recommended for floors which will be walked on by bathers with wet feet, because there is a danger of slipping.

APPLIED COATINGS

These coatings may be divided into three basic types:

(1) Paints applied by brush and spray.
(2) Special plastic and other proprietary materials.
(3) Sprayed and other metallic coatings.

Paints of many different types can be applied successfully to all categories of background, such as concrete, clay brick, timber and metal. For the best results, only first-quality materials should be used; the paint and primer should be from the same manufacturer and must be selected to suit both the background to which it will be applied and the environment in which it will exist. Paints which contain pigments will slightly change colour in the course of time owing to the action of ultra-violet light on the pigment: some pigments (blues and greens) are more sensitive in this respect than others.

It is obviously impossible in the course of one section of a single chapter to discuss in detail the techniques of painting on all types of materials used in swimming pool halls and ancillary buildings, but a few basic considerations will be mentioned. A great deal of useful information is contained in the two Codes of Practice, CP 231: Painting and BS 5493: Protection of Iron and Steel Structures from Corrosion. Paint manufacturers will always give detailed advice on specific problems. The important thing to remember is that the problem is a serious one and needs expert advice to solve it satisfactorily.

Careful preparation of the background and skilled application of the primer and various coats of paint are essential for the success of any painting job. The following types of background will be considered briefly: concrete, asbestos-cement, timber, steel and aluminium.

CONCRETE SURFACES AND ASBESTOS-CEMENT

All the paints and coatings mentioned earlier in the chapter as being suitable for the decoration of the pool shell are suitable for use above the water-line in the pool hall. However, as previously stated, all walls adjacent to the pool and all other wet areas are best finished with glazed ceramic tiles or similar. Of the paints, probably the most widely used is chlorinated rubber, since it is resistant to chlorine, which is usually present in the building, even though the concentration is very low. The background should be dried out very thoroughly unless one uses specially formulated epoxide resins which will bond to damp surfaces. The author does not recommend the use of ordinary oil paints, because they are unlikely to be resistant to chlorine; however, if for any reason they are used, a special alkali-resistant primer must be applied first.

TIMBER

As mentioned previously, the use of tropical hardwoods, particularly teak and mahogany, which only need regular applications of oil, is recommended. If soft woods are used, then they have to be painted for decoration and protection. The preparation and priming of the base surface is of great importance. The paint should be strongly adherent, water-resistant and flexible. Timber such as pine, and hardwoods, can be stained and varnished, and this type of treatment is both decorative and protective. In view of the arduous conditions in swimming pool halls, all joinery should be primed before assembly and the members assembled while the primer is wet.

EXTERIOR FINISHES TO SWIMMING POOL HALLS AND ANCILLARY BUILDINGS

Some very brief notes on finishes to the outside of concrete structures have been included in Chapter 3, and a number of references were given in the Bibliography at the end of that chapter. The subject of external finishes to concrete is a very wide one and is essentially the province of the architect. However, the author suggests that architects need guidance in what can be reasonably achieved on a building site. The vast majority of disputes on site over surface finishes revolve round whether a particular finish is to a reasonable standard or not. It was stated in Chapter 3 that samples of the type of finish required must be made and agreed by the parties to the contract. On important projects such as sports centres and leisure centres it is also necessary to have full-size mock-ups prepared on site. Large areas of plain concrete, however well finished, can be very disappointing in overall effect. There are a number of unfortunate examples of this type of finish in the United Kingdom in London and the provinces. Figure 3.2 shows a well-designed and well-executed concrete structure for a new sports centre.

There are now on the market a large number of proprietary coating materials which provide a high-class durable decorative finish to concrete, brick and stone. The emphasis is on the use of ready-mixed materials, as this eliminates the uncertainties and errors of site mixing. Apart from cement-based paints, oil paints and chlorinated rubber paints, the owner can choose from Tyrolean finish, Sandtex, Cullamix and Cullaplast. These can all be used on new structures as well as old. Of special interest for those responsible for the renovation of old buildings with uneven surfaces is a new resin-based multitexture coating known as 'High Build'. Figure 3.1 shows a typical finish using Sandtex Matt.

THE PROTECTION OF FERROUS METALS IN SWIMMING POOL BUILDINGS

Mild and high-tensile steels corrode in normal atmospheres unless a protective coating is applied. The performance (durability) of coatings depends on:

(a) The standard of surface preparation of the metal.
(b) The characteristics of the coating material.
(c) The thickness of the coating.

It has been estimated that 20 % of the annual steel production in the United States is lost by corrosion and that the annual cost of this loss in 1969 was $600 million.

A great deal has been written about the protection of steel, and if the choice lies between first-class preparation with a second-class coating material or a second-class preparation with a first-class coating, then the former alternative will give the better results. High-quality preparation can be achieved by shot or grit blasting, the use of high-velocity water jets, flame cleaning, acid treatment followed by neutralisation, and wire brushing. It is important that the coating should follow immediately after the surface has been prepared.

Protective coatings can be divided into four main groups:

(1) Paint systems.
(2) Plastics dip-coatings.
(3) Galvanising.
(4) Sherardising.

PAINT SYSTEMS
There are literally hundreds of proprietary paints, and it is very difficult for an engineer or architect to have sufficient knowledge and experience to select the best one. The sensible procedure (until adequate experience has been gained) is to carefully list the requirements which must be met, including the details of the environment in which the protected steel will have to operate. This list should be sent to some of the well-known manufacturers as well as a few formulators/applicators of polymer coatings (epoxides and polyurethanes) and a quotation requested, including a guarantee of satisfactory performance.

Paints are normally applied by brush, roller, air-spray or airless spray. In recent years the technique of plastic dip-coating has been developed. Powder coatings are also used, but must be factory-applied and are expensive.

With all types of paint systems there should be a minimum of three coats, consisting of primer, undercoat and finish; alternatively, there can be a primer and two finishing coats. The thickness will depend on the conditions of use, but in areas where the steel work will be exposed to a humid atmosphere containing chlorine (as in the case of swimming pool halls and adjoining areas), a minimum thickness of 0·4 mm (0·016 in) is required. In absolute terms this thickness is very small, but reliable instruments are available for measuring such a thickness. These 'thickness meters' can measure the thickness of a coating within the limits of 0–2·5 mm.

The author's experience suggests that epoxide resins and polyurethanes will provide excellent protection for a long period, provided, of course, there has been first-class preparation of the steel and the coating is correctly applied.

PLASTIC DIP-COATINGS
Plastic dip-coatings are applied over a special adhesive primer in order to ensure maximum bond between the coating and the steel. The plastics commonly used are PVC or nylon (polyamide). The PVC coatings are approximately 0·5 mm thick and the nylon slightly thinner (0·38 mm). Both materials give good service under normal conditions, as they are resistant to atmospheric corrosion and sea-water spray.

GALVANISING
There are two methods of galvanising, electrodeposition and the hot-dip process; the latter gives the more durable coating and is the one normally used. The steel section is submerged in hot acid and then after neutralising is submerged in a bath of molten zinc. The hot zinc and hot steel bond together, forming a series of zinc–iron alloys. The coating of zinc has good impact and corrosion resistance except in severe industrial conditions, when the galvanised surface must itself be protected by an adequate paint system; the author considers that swimming pool halls come within this category.

SHERARDISING
This consists of heating a properly cleaned steel member in an environment of zinc dust. This forms a coating of zinc–iron alloys on the surface of the steel which is metallurgically bonded to the steel. The steel is best prepared by acid pickling followed by neutralising; the castings should be cleaned by sand or shot blasting. Sherardising is mainly used for small items owing to limitation on size of containers and the furnace required. The cost is rather higher than that of hot-dip galvanising.

ALUMINIUM AND ALUMINIUM ALLOYS
While aluminium and aluminium alloys are resistant to attack under normal atmospheric conditions, they are vulnerable to corrosion by acrds,

chlorides and caustic alkalis. Therefore, in the atmosphere of a swimming pool hall and near the sea, aluminium requires protection. This protective treatment can take the form of painting or anodising. The author recommends the latter whenever this is practicable.

With painting, pretreatment in the factory is to be preferred; if this is not done, special etching primers must be used. The priming paint recommended is a zinc chromate, and this should be followed by normal oil, synthetic or bituminous paints. The presence of chlorine in the atmosphere must be kept in mind in selecting the paint.

Anodising is an electrolytic process which builds up a dense film of aluminium oxide on the surface of the metal. There are two British Standards dealing with anodising, BS 1615: Anodic Oxidation Coatings on Aluminium and BS 3987: Anodised Wrought Aluminium for External Architectural Application. Aluminium in swimming pool halls should comply with BS 3987, and the anodised coating should be not less than 0·025 mm (25 μm or 1 mil) thick.

Because aluminium is liable to attack by caustic alkalis, it should not be in direct contact with concrete and rendering or asbestos-cement or plaster in the presence of moisture. It will not be attacked in the dry. Two good coats of bituminous paint on the contact surface will give lasting protection. This does not apply if the aluminium has been anodised to the recommended thickness.

MOVABLE FLOORS IN SWIMMING POOLS

Reference has been made in Chapter 1 to the conflicting requirements of the various types of swimming activities in sports centres, which may be summarised as follows:

(1) Teaching (learners) pool with depth varying from 0·80 m to 1·00 m or 0·50 m to 0·90 m (2 ft 8 in to 3 ft 3 in or 1 ft 7 in to 3 ft).

(2) Ordinary swimming pool with a shallow end for non-swimmers, also for the considerable number of adults who are not at all anxious to swim out of their depth; this means a large expanse of water with the depth varying from 0·80 m to, say, 1·50 m (2 ft 8 in to 5 ft).

(3) Water polo, which requires an area of 20 m long and a width of at least 8·0 m—maximum 20·0 m; the depth throughout this area must not be less than 1·80 m.

(4) A separate diving section of deep water, the dimensions and depth depending on the height of the diving boards, but with a 1·0 m and 3·0 m spring board and a 5·0 m and 10 m fixed board, the dimensions would be about 18·0 m (59 ft) × 15·5 m (51 ft), with a depth of 4·5–5·0 m (14 ft 8 in–16 ft 6 in).

To provide four separate pools would involve high capital expenditure which may not be available and which the ratepayers may not consider justified. Requirements for pools (1), (2) and (3), can be met satisfactorily by the installation of a movable floor and hydraulically operated separating wall in one large pool. Diving should always be carried out in a separate pool. Several hundred pools with movable floors have been built in Germany, The Netherlands, Austria and Luxembourg. One of the well-known firms which design and erect such floors is E. Piesker and Co., Gretchenstrasse 36, Hanover 3, and the author is indebted to this firm for the information which follows. The licensees in the United Kingdom are F. J. Buckingham of Kenilworth. This information has been condensed and it is only intended to give an outline of how the whole thing works.

(1) The floor extends for the full width of the pool and for either the full length of the pool (if it is a small one not exceeding 20 m (66 ft) long), or for some part of the length. For example, in a 33·33 m (110 ft) pool the movable floor could be 16·00 m (52 ft) long.

(2) By providing four hydraulically operated lifting pistons the floor can be given a slope, if so desired. This is illustrated in Fig. 6.8. The floor can be raised to its full height or to any part of it, according to the use to which the shallow section will be put.

(3) The movable floor when in the lowered position rests on the normal floor of the pool. It is recommended that this lower floor be constructed and finished with glazed tiles in the usual way.

(4) The movable floor itself can be either steel, aluminium, glass-fibre or reinforced concrete. The top surface should be finished to a high standard, and for large pools the author recommends a reinforced concrete slab, finished with tiles in exactly the same way as the rest of the floor, even though this is more expensive in first cost. With steel, corrosion presents serious problems; and aluminium also requires protection. A further objection is that tiles (which is the best finish to a swimming pool), cannot be readily fixed to base materials other than concrete.

(5) Provision must be made for water to pass through the floor as it is raised or lowered, and the perimeter of the floor adjacent to the walls of the pool is usually perforated. No one should be allowed in the pool when the floor is being moved. The rate of lift (and retraction) is about 0·30–0·60 m (1–2 ft) per minute.

(6) It is important that when the floor is in the raised position, the space below should not form a dead pocket of water. To this end inlets should be installed below the level of the floor when it is raised. These can be in addition to those in the normal position.

(7) Provision is made for cleaning below the floor, and this cleaning must be carried out to a strict schedule.

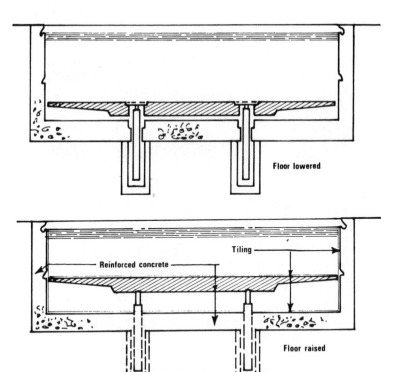

Floor lowered

Tiling

Reinforced concrete

Floor raised

FIG. 6.8.   Diagram of movable floor to swimming pool.

FIG. 6.9.   View of pool looking towards deep end with movable floor in foreground and movable separating wall in middle distance (Courtesy: E. Piesker and Co., Hanover, and F. J. Buckingham, Kenilworth).

FIG. 6.10.   View of movable floor in raised position (Courtesy: E. Piesker and Co., Hanover, and F. J. Buckingham, Kenilworth).

(8) A special safety barrier must be provided along the side of the floor adjacent to the deep water. In large pools this can be a solid barrier raised hydraulically, in the same way as the movable floor. Such a hydraulically operated division wall is described in the next section.

There are, of course, various problems connected with movable floors, but the author is convinced that it is a most useful piece of equipment which many local authorities would do well to consider seriously when planning new public pools. Figures 6.9 and 6.10 show two swimming pools with different types of movable floor.

HYDRAULICALLY OPERATED DIVISION WALLS IN SWIMMING POOLS

Another feature which the author recommends for the consideration of baths managers and architects dealing with the planning of new swimming pools is the hydraulically operated separating (or division) wall. This can be used in conjunction with a movable floor as shown in Fig. 6.9 or on its own to divide a large pool into two distinct areas, one for swimmers with a depth of, say, 1·50 m and over, and the other for the more timid swimmers and non-swimmers. The great advantage of such a wall is that it provides a completely safe barrier between the shallow and deep sections of the pool. The wall can be reinforced concrete finished in ceramic tiles (which is undoubtedly the best), or aluminium or steel suitably protected and decorated.

SWIMMING POOLS WITH ARTIFICIAL WAVES

On the Continent swimming pools with artificial waves have been popular for many years. This applies particularly to The Netherlands, Germany, Switzerland and Austria. In the United Kingdom, up to about 1973, the only pool with operational wave-making equipment was the Porto Bello open-air baths in Edinburgh. It is interesting that the equipment in this pool was installed in about 1936.

When writing the first edition of this book, the author had to obtain information on wave machines from the Continent, where one of the leading manufacturers is Friedrich Koster KG of Heidi-in-Holstein, West Germany. Another well-known continental firm is Imhof and Co. GmbH of Hamburg.

The position in the United Kingdom has changed dramatically in the past seven years as a number of new public pools are now equipped with wave-making machines (see Fig. 6.11).

Fig. 6.11.   View of waves in main pool at Swansea Leisure Centre (Courtesy: Cement and Concrete Association).

While in theory there may be many methods of creating artificial waves in swimming pools, the author only knows of three which have been put to practical use:

(1) The 'swing arm' type of equipment.
(2) Compressed air.
(3) The reaction of a falling column of water.

From published reports, it appears that only the first two methods have been used for indoor pools. A brief description of the above methods is given below.

WAVES BY MEANS OF SWING ARM EQUIPMENT

The information which follows has been obtained from Friedrich Koster KG. This firm normally makes a model of new baths in order to assess all important hydraulic features such as wave height, location of 'breaking' point, backwash, cross-currents, etc. Figure 6.12 shows a plan and section of a typical pool using this type of equipment. The trapezoidal shape and uniformly sloping floor create the effect of a shelving beach with the waves breaking naturally. This shape also provides maximum area of shallow water for non-swimmers. In the pool shown, there is a hydraulically operated submerged wall which can be raised to divide the pool into two sections. This wall is not required for the effective operation of the wave machine. The wave-making equipment consists of two swing arms or wings, known in German as 'Schwingflügel', which operate together but not in complete unison; one moves at 17·5 oscillations per minute and the other at 18·0. A total of 80 brake horsepower is required. A screen is provided in front of the wings. The design of this screen is important for the optimum operation of the machine.

COMPRESSED AIR

Since about 1973 a number of the new leisure centres built in the United Kingdom have been equipped with wave-making machines. These include Whitley Bay, Rotherham, Bletchley and Swindon; a number of new public pools under construction in the north-east of England will be similarly equipped.

Patented systems creating artificial waves by means of compressed air (as opposed to the swing arm just described) include the Imhof system, marketed under licence by Biwater Treatment Co. Ltd, the Armfield Engineering Ltd system and the Barr and Wray Ltd system. Figure 6.13 shows a pool with artificial waves in Germany. Each firm provides special features covered by patents, but basically the waves are initiated in a concrete chamber extending along one side (a short side) of the pool. The admission of compressed air onto the surface of the water, followed by

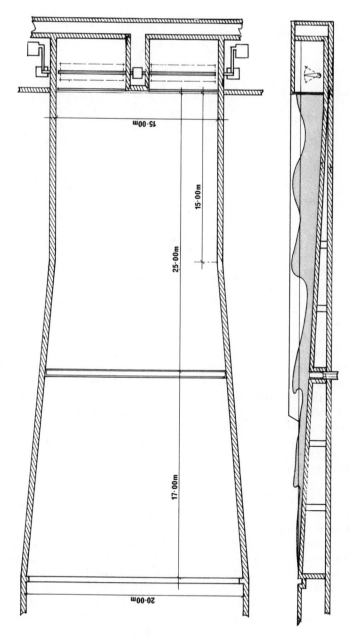

FIG. 6.12.   Plan and section of swimming pool designed for artificial waves (Courtesy: K. Koster KG Heidi Holstein, Germany).

FIG. 6.13.   View of pool with artificial waves (Courtesy: Imhof GmbH, Germany, and
Biwater Ltd, Dorking).

suction, starts the oscillation of the water in the chamber which manifests
itself as waves in the pool. Figure 6.14 shows in diagram form the general
arrangement for wave making by compressed air.

As mentioned for wave-making with swing arm equipment, the correct
design of the pool to ensure waves of the desired height and length (i.e.
distance from crest to crest) is not a simple matter. The shape of the pool,
the slope of the floor and the design of the grill in front of the wave chamber
are all relevant factors. In many cases the production of a scale model with
tests is required before the design can be finalised. In the Rotherham leisure
centre, where the wave machine is an Imhof patent (licensee Biwater
Treatment Co.), the waves are stated to be about 800 mm (2 ft 8 in) high and
11 m (36 ft) crest to crest.

The author is indebted to both Biwater and Armfield for the basic
information given above.

REACTION OF A FALLING COLUMN OF WATER

The only published information on this which the author could find was in
the US journal *Swimming Pool Weekly*. It appeared that the method was first
used by Big Surf Inc. of Arizona, in a large lagoon at Tempe. The lagoon
was about 400 ft (122 m) × 300 ft (92 m), with a maximum depth of 9 ft
(2·7 m), and was provided with water treatment equipment. The waves were
5 ft (1·5 m) high, so that surf riding could be indulged in. The water is
pumped to a prearranged height (not given in the article) at one end of the

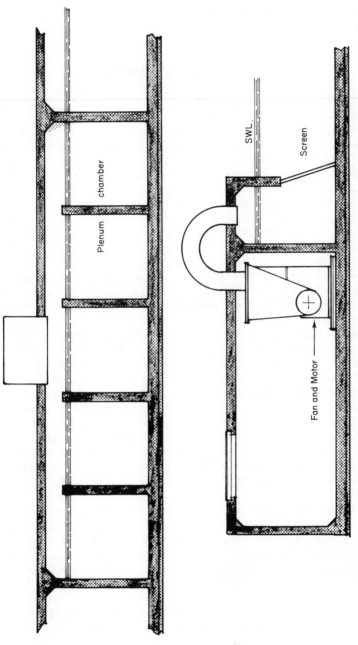

FIG. 6.14.   Diagram showing general arrangement for making artificial waves by compressed air (Courtesy: Armfield Engineering Ltd).

pool. It is released through underwater gates and then flows over a weir (reef), thus forming the waves, which sweep across the lagoon.

ANCILLARY EQUIPMENT

DIVING BOARDS AND DIVING STAGES

These can vary from the single platform or board fixed 1·0 m (3 ft 3 in) above the water level to multistoried diving towers with the fixed platform 10·0 m (33 ft) above water level. The more simple units, suitable for private house pools and hotels and clubs, are usually constructed of 38 mm (1½ in) stainless steel tubing with either stainless steel or teak treads.

It should be noted that by merely specifying 'stainless steel' complete freedom from rusting and corrosion is not necessarily assured. The atmosphere in a swimming pool hall is highly corrosive to a wide range of metals, particularly the ferrous ones. The author has seen a number of cases where stainless steel handrails and steps to diving stages have shown definite signs of rusting within a few years of installation. Admittedly, this rusting was superficial, but it was nonetheless there and caused considerable annoyance to the pool owners, who were under the impression that 'stainless steel never rusts or corrodes'.

The author recommends that the type ordered should be Type 316 S 16: austenitic chromium–nickel, rust-, acid- and heat-resisting steel. This will cost more than the ferritic type steel, but a very long corrosion-free life will be assured, which may not be the case with the ferritic steel.

When made-up diving stages and steps are ordered, the supplier should be required to state the type of stainless steel used. The board or platform can be either teak or glass-fibre. The vertical members of these platforms must be securely fixed at the base and so should either be grouted into the pool surround or fixed in sockets which have been themselves grouted-in or cast-in. It is essential that they be absolutely rigid, and to this end the detailed instructions of the suppliers should be followed. All reputable suppliers are only too willing to give full information for fixing, including drawings.

Coconut matting is often used to ensure a non-slip surface to steps and boards and platform, but the author does not recommend it, since it is very unhygienic and tears and rucks easily. Special plastic material which is far superior to coconut matting is now on the market; one such material is 'Treadmaster AF/DB', supplied by Contemporary Industries (Engineering) Limited. This material has the added advantage that it can be used direct on reinforced concrete staging.

The most widely used piece of diving equipment is the spring board, and this varies in length from 4·25 m to 4·8 m (14 ft to 16 ft) and is usually 0·50 m

(20 in) wide. Information on the International Regulations for diving stages which were in force when this book was written are given in Chapter 1. An extra piece of equipment which is recommended for all pools with spring boards, except private house pools, is a safety clamp with automatic catch for holding the board end in the raised position when for any reason diving is not permitted.

Spring boards should be covered with non-slip material except when they are made with Duraluminium or glass-fibre, since these two materials can be used without matting if so desired. Spring boards for international events should be provided with movable fulcrums which can easily be adjusted by the diver. Spring boards can be installed at an angle of not more than 1 degree with the horizontal.

The fixed diving platforms must be rigid and covered with non-slip material. The back and sides of each platform must be provided with a handrail, and access to the platforms must be by means of stepped ladders and not rungs. Diving towers which are hydraulically operated can also be obtained; these are described in the next section.

Diving stages incorporating 1·0 and 3·0 m spring boards can be obtained 'free-standing': that is, they are not permanently fixed to the pool surround, but are secured for the period they are in use by some other means such as fixing to rear walls, or to steel or reinforced concrete beams spanning between columns.

The 3 m boards must have access ladders, and guard rails 1·0 m high, and while these are supplied complete with shop-fabricated diving stages, all these requirements must be met when reinforced concrete diving towers are designed. Some of these are extremely elegant, but, as with the ready-made stages, special care must be exercised to ensure maximum rigidity; this can often be achieved by anchoring the tower to the structural frame of the building or to a massive rear wall. If access to the various stages is by means of a ladder, then this must not be vertical but should be inclined to the vertical by an angle not less than 15 degrees. The ASA recommend that under a static load of 540 kg (1200 lb) on the diving end of the board (spring board or firmboard), the maximum deflection of the platform in any direction shall not exceed 3 mm ($\frac{1}{8}$ in). The ASA speak very strongly of the merits of the 1·0 m spring board and state that 85 % of all diving techniques can be taught and learnt on the 1·0 m board. If this is accepted, and there is no reason why it should not be, the considerable expense involved in the provision of the higher boards can seldom be justified, except for competitions. For international events diving platforms should incorporate take-off positions at 1·00 m, 3·00 m 5·00 m, 7·50 m and 10·00 m (3 ft 3 in, 10 ft, 16 ft 5 in, 24 ft 7 in and 32 ft 10 in) above water level. The permitted tolerance on these heights is ±100 mm.

The positioning of the diving tower in relation to the spectator

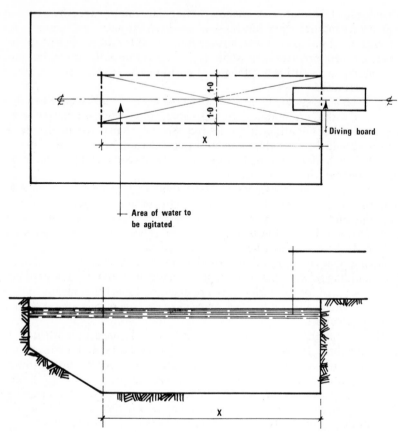

FIG. 6.15.   Diagram showing area of water to be agitated in diving pit for competitions.

accommodation and the judge's box, to ensure maximum vision, is of great importance. Means should be provided to agitate the surface of the water in the diving pool so that divers can readily see the surface. This is shown in Figure 6.15.

For group training in diving a teaching platform can be provided. This can be opposite to the main diving stage. The height from this teaching platform to the water surface is usually in the range 300–350 mm (12–14 in). It should be located at least 2 m (6 ft 6 in) away from the end wall of the pool.

HYDRAULICALLY OPERATED DIVING PLATFORMS
These are used on the Continent for coaching and for teaching difficult dives. The take-off position can be varied in height above water level in the

range 0·50–3·00 m (1 ft 8 in–10 ft). The same basic requirements apply to these as to fixed platforms, and, in addition, there must be an automatic locking device to secure the platform at each position. One of the main firms supplying this type of equipment is Meyer-Hagen GmbH of Hagen/ Westfalen.

STARTING BLOCKS

These should be covered with a resilient non-slip material and, if required, can incorporate electrically operated touch pads. The electrical connection must be completely sealed and absolutely safe; it is usual for these devices to operate under a non-lethal voltage. Water depth in front of the blocks must not be less than 1·80 m (5 ft 11 in) over a minimum length of 6·0 m (20 ft).

POOL MARKING

There are two types of permanent marking in swimming pools:

(a) Marking for depth of water.
(b) Marking for swimming lanes.

The varying depths of water should be clearly marked on the walls of all pools which have a water depth greater than about 1·5 m (5 ft). This marking should be on the walls in positions easily visible to both swimmers and non-swimmers. At the present time in the United Kingdom it is usual to mark the depth vertically down the side of the pool in 1 ft (300 mm) intervals. However, when the metric system is fully adopted, the markings are likely to be at 250 mm (10 in) intervals. The markings should be at certain defined depths such as 3 ft, 5 ft, 6 ft 6 in, etc. (0·09 m, 1·50 m and 2·0 m).

Swimming lanes are marked on the bottom of the pool and are often terminated about 2·0 m (6 ft 6 in) from each end, the end of the marking lane being emphasised by either a T or a square. The marking should not be less than 75 mm wide (3 in), and as most baths which are used for competitions are finished in white tiles, the lane markings are usually in black. Distances should be marked in figures along the length of the pool. Special glazed ceramic tiles are available for both the lane marking and the numerals.

One point should be noted in connection with the marking of lanes on the floor of the pool, and that is that the swimmers swim along the marked lanes and not between them. Guide ropes on floats, fixed at each end of the pool, mark the boundary of each swimming lane, and these are positioned mid-way between the black marker lanes.

POOL LADDERS AND STEPS, AND SAFETY LINES

Ladders and Steps

In all pools used for competitions the steps must be recessed and there must be no projections inside the swimming area. The steps must be provided with handrails at bath surround level, and the handrail is brought down to the water level; the treads must be non-slip. The manufacturers of glazed ceramic tiles produce all the necessary specials for this work.

For the smaller private hotel and club pools it is usual to find ladders provided at the pool side instead of the recessed steps, as the latter are considerably more expensive. Ladders usually consist of stainless steel (previous remarks in this chapter on the use of stainless steel for diving stages should be noted) or other non-corrosive metal side rails, and the treads can be of the same material or of teak. If the treads are metal, they should have a non-slip pattern, and the teak is often covered with coconut matting. However, as already recommended in the section on Diving Stages and Boards, special plastic material is to be preferred. Entirely satisfactory steps can be purchased ready-made and there is seldom any need to fabricate them on site, which, of course, costs a lot more. Recommended dimensions for stairs are 1·0 m (3 ft 3 in) wide, with 300 mm (12 in) treads and 150 mm (6 in) rises. Steps and ladders should have a maximum step height of 300 mm (12 in), a depth of 150 mm (6 in) and a width of 600 mm (24 in).

The point which needs care, but which is often neglected, is the fixing of the side rails into the paving on deck level. There are few things more annoying to the client than to find that the pool steps have become loose after a few months' use. The ends of the rails should either be fixed with special anchors which are sometimes sold with the steps or by flanges welded on and carefully set in *in situ* concrete. To cut holes in the paving and try to grout-up with mortar usually proves unsatisfactory.

Safety Lines
If for any reason safety lines are required in the pool, then cup anchors should be fixed into the pool wall at the water line or just above. The cup anchors are usually made of brass, heavily chromed, or stainless steel. Either the holes can be preformed or the hole is drilled in the completed wall. The hole should be larger at the bottom than on the surface, and a good-quality low-shrinkage mortar should be used to fix the anchor. In the case of tiled pools with a scum channel, special channel units incorporating a safety line fitting are supplied by most tile manufacturers. Racing lane marker ropes must also have anchors, and these also are provided in special channel units.

UNDERWATER LIGHTING AND OBSERVATION WINDOWS
Underwater lighting in swimming pools increases the safety of the users because it improves the visibility below water level. Lights can be installed in pools of almost any size and depth. Observation windows are only provided in large, deep pools and diving pits, and the wall containing the window(s) is

exposed on the outside to public view. Lights can be fitted in a recess on the inside of the wall, and is the method usually adopted in open-air pools. This is appreciably cheaper than providing access from the outside by means of a duct or special chamber. The usual intensity of lighting is 1000 lm/m^2 of water surface (100 lm/ft^2). In large pools the lights are usually on both long walls, and staggered, the distance apart being 2·0 m–3·0 m (6 ft 6 in–10 ft). In deep pools and diving pits it is usual to install two horizontal rows of lights; the top row should be not less than about 1·0 m (3 ft 3 in) below the water surface.

The voltage must be non-lethal, and therefore a transformer is required. 12 V is often used, but anything up to 30 V should be safe. The whole unit and cable must be completely watertight, and they are usually sold as complete units with detailed instructions for fixing. The lights are 400–600 mm (16–24 in) diameter. All metal parts must be corrosion-proof, such as stainless steel (austenitic type 316.S16), phosphor-bronze, gunmetal, etc. It is important that bolts for fixing should be kept at least 50 mm from any steel reinforcement in the pool shell because of the danger of galvanic action starting corrosion of one of the metals.

Observation windows should be fitted between two lighting positions. The dimensions of the windows in swimming pools is about 1·5 m (5 ft) long and 0·50 m (20 in) high, while in diving pools they are somewhat smaller. The windows are finished flush with the inside surface of the walls and should be constructed of toughened safety glass, fixed in corrosion-resistant frames. The necessary openings in the pool shell must be carefully detailed so as to ensure complete watertightness. The wall containing the observation window(s) is exposed to public view and must therefore be completely watertight. Seepage, however slight, is usually unacceptable, and special precautions must be taken.

OTHER ANCILLARY FITTINGS AND EQUIPMENT

These usually consist of a pool brush, telescopic pole, hose to wall fitting, white vacuum hose and a vacuum head for fitting into the vacuum point in the wall about 150 mm (6 in) below the water line. When not in use, the vacuum point is closed with a plug. All metal parts should be of non-ferrous metal, but the telescopic pole is usually anodised aluminium and the vacuum hose is plastic. For open-air pools a leaf rake is also desirable.

The above equipment, and brushes for cleaning the paving around the pool, are all that is needed for the daily cleaning of most pools. All the equipment is readily obtainable from a number of suppliers, who issue complete operating instructions with each item sold.

For small private pools which have been built without provision for water treatment and circulation, a 'skimmer-step filtration unit' can be obtained. The side rails of the steps act as the flow and return pipes to the filter, which is located at a convenient place nearby. The top step is about 50–75 mm (2–3 in) above top water level, and below this step is a skimmer weir in a box. This is a floating weir—as in all skimmer outlets—and adjusts itself to the water level. The water is drawn into the skimmer box through the opening in the front, up one of the tubular side rails to the filter and chlorinator, and then is circulated back and enters the pool through the other tubular side rail. The vacuum point for the cleaning equipment is located in the draw-off side rail.

FIG. 6.16. View of high-velocity jet ('Jet Stream') in private house pool (Courtesy: Unterwasser-Electric GmbH and Co KG, Germany).

Mention has already been made of the advantages of providing a movable cover to an open-air pool. These are of various types and are made by a number of firms. In covered pools, particularly large ones, a difficult problem is that of access to high-level lights and other fittings, windows, etc. For this type of maintenance work a useful piece of equipment is a light alloy scaffold made by John Rusling of Hitchin, Hertfordshire. This scaffold includes special braces in the lower section which automatically lock into position, thus ensuring rigidity and safety.

Another interesting piece of pool equipment which has been popular for many years on the Continent has recently been introduced into the United Kingdom. It consists of a twin jet of high-velocity water which is injected into the pool by a special device. There is more than one proprietary installation, and the following is a general description of the equipment.

Water is pumped into the pool through two adjustable jets which can be adjusted to produce either a concentrated jet or a broad stream of turbulent water. The regulator allows accurate adjustment of the pressure to suit strong or weak swimmers, learners or children. The jets deliver about 880 litres per min (200 gal/min). Provision is made in the equipment for aerating the water so that it is fresh and bubbly. The low-voltage switches are fully protected and can be located so as to operate from the pool or from the

FIG. 6.17.   View of 'Badu-Jet' in operation (Courtesy: Interpool Equipment and Liners Ltd, Stockport).

surround. The jets can be used for training for fast or slow swimming, and provide vigorous or mild underwater massage. The equipment is complete with pump, motor, valves, regulator and main switch.

Figure 6.16 shows a 'Jet Stream' unit in operation in a private house pool, and Fig. 6.17 shows a 'Badu-Jet' in operation.

BIBLIOGRAPHY

BLAKE, L. S. *Recommendations for the Production of High-quality Concrete Surfaces*, Cement and Concrete Association, London, March 1967, p. 38.

BRITISH CERAMIC TILE COUNCIL. *The Laying of Ceramic Floor Tiles and Mosaics*, Stoke-on-Trent, 1972, p. 45.

BRITISH STANDARDS INSTITUTION, *Wall Tiling*, Code of Practice CP 212, Parts 1 and 2.

BRITISH STANDARDS INSTITUTION, *Painting*, Code of Practice CP 231.

BRITISH STANDARDS INSTITUTION, *Suspended Ceilings and Linings*, Code of Practice CP 290.

BRITISH STANDARDS INSTITUTION, *Protection of Iron and Steel Structures from Corrosion*, British Standard BS 5493.

BRUCE, W. E., Preserving timber for constructional work. *Civil Engineering and Public Works Review*, Oct. 1972, pp. 1049–55.

CHANDLER, K. A., Structural steelwork coatings. *Civil Engineering and Public Works Review*, Oct. 1972, pp. 1043–8.

DEESON, A. F. L., Sherardizing steel. *The Contractor*, Dec. 1969, p. 14.

DEPARTMENT OF THE ENVIRONMENT, Plastics dip-coatings for metalwork. *DoE Construction*, June 1972, **2**, pp. 37–9.

FREEMAN, I. L., *Moisture Expansion of Structural Ceramics*, Building Research Station Garston, Research Series No. 61, p. 20.

GREATER LONDON COUNCIL, Slip resistance of ceramic floor tiles. *Bulletin No. 57*, Item 2, July 1972, p. 3.

HALL, J. R., Galvanizing steel. *The Contractor*, Dec. 1969, pp. 6–8.

HARDEMANN, J. H. E. The adjustable swimming pool floor. *Inst. of Baths Management*, 39th Annual Conference Report, London 1969, pp. 126–33.

HODSON, H. A. Glazed ceramic tiling. Paper presented at Symposium at East Kilbride, Building Research Establishment, June 1973, p. 7.

INTERNATIONAL BOARD FOR AQUATIC SPORTS AND RECREATION FACILITIES, International Standards for Swimming Pool Construction Pool Engineering and Pool Operation 1976—Part B: Construction, Finish & Equipment. Published in *Sport Bader Freizeit Bauten*, Feb. 1977, pp. 133–60.

LAPWORTH, C. F., Evaporation from a reservoir near London. *J. Inst. Water Engrs*, **19**(2) (March 1965) 165–81.

LOWREY, K. W., Protective coatings for structural systems. *Civil Engineering and Public Works Review*, Oct. 1972, pp. 1059–67.

PERKINS, P. H., *Floors—Construction and Finishes*, Cement and Concrete Association, London 1973, p. 132.

PERKINS, P. H., Swimming pool shells and walkways. Paper presented at Symposium in London, July 1975, British Ceramic Tile Council and Sports Council.

SMITH, R. G., *Long-term Unrestrained Expansion of Test Bricks*, Building Research Establishment, Garston, Current Papers CP/16/73, 1973, p. 5.

SOUTHERN, J. R., Joint movements. Paper presented at Symposium at East Kilbride, Building Research Establishment, June 1973, p. 6.

WILSON, J. G., *Exposed Concrete Finishes*, Vols. 1 and 2. CR Books Ltd London, 1962 and 1964, pp. 144 and 184.

CHAPTER 7

Engineering Services for Swimming Pools: Water Treatment and Sterilisation, and Water Circulation. Notes on Heating and Ventilation

GENERAL ENGINEERING SERVICES

The engineering services of the pool and ancillary buildings will vary according to the size and complexity of the whole project. At one extreme there is the private house open-air pool and at the other the sports and cultural centre of a city involving a capital investment of several million pounds sterling. However, if the recommendations given in this book are accepted, even the smallest pool will require the following services:

(*a*) Water supply.
(*b*) Drainage.
(*c*) Power (electricity, gas or oil).
(*d*) Water treatment and sterilisation equipment.

For covered pools, additional services would include some or all of the following:

(*e*) Heating and ventilating, including energy conservation equipment.
(*f*) Lighting, normal, and battery-operated emergency lighting.
(*g*) Fire and burglar alarms.
(*h*) Fire-fighting installations.
(*i*) Fuel storage.
(*j*) Telephones.
(*k*) Public address system.
(*l*) Refuse storage.
(*m*) Anti-vandalism devices (unfortunately!).

It is obviously impossible to give detailed requirements for all these services, but a few general comments will be made on the more fundamental ones.

WATER SUPPLY

This is usually taken from the mains of a public supply, and in this case it can usually be assumed to be satisfactory. However, it must be pointed out that although the pH, alkalinity and colour may be suitable for drinking, chemical treatment may be needed to ensure satisfactory filtration and sterilisation when the water is used in a swimming pool. Water when viewed through a glass tumbler may appear to be quite clear, but the same water several metres deep in a swimming pool may look most unattractive.

If the source is a private one from a well or borehole, it should be tested chemically and bacteriologically at regular intervals. Such a source of supply would only be used in the country, where there is often no drainage and, consequently, the sewage goes to a cesspool or septic tank. These disposal units can cause contamination of a nearby water supply; hence the need for regular testing. Apart from quality, the supply must be adequate in quantity for topping up the pool and washing the filters.

DRAINAGE

Some satisfactory arrangement must be made for the disposal of the wash water from the filters, and from the pool itself when it is emptied for cleaning and maintenance. The quantities of water to be disposed of (and, of course, required in the first place), will vary according to the type, size and number of filters installed, but it would be prudent to allow for the flows given in Table 7.1, assuming that each filter is washed separately (which is

TABLE 7.1

Filter diameter	Wash water flow
1·10 m (3 ft 6 in)	540 litre/min (120 gal/min)
1·40 m (4 ft 6 in)	900 litre/min (200 gal/min)
2·0 m (6 ft 6 in)	1 800 litre/min (400 gal/min)
2·60 m (8 ft 6 in)	2 700 litre/min (600 gal/min)

the usual procedure), and that the filters are standard pressure sand filters without air scour. If air scour is provided, the quantity of wash water will be approximately two-thirds of these figures.

These are based on a requirement of 400 litre/m^2/min (8 gal/ft^2/min) with air scour and 600 litre/m^2/min (12 gal/ft^2/min) without air scour. The drain pipes must be of adequate size and laid to a gradient which will ensure the discharge required. The drain must discharge to a public

TABLE 7.2

Pipe diameter	Gradient	Discharge
100 mm (4 in)	1 in 50	520 litre/min (117 gal/min)
150 mm (6 in)	1 in 100	1 000 litre/min (220 gal/min)
200 mm (8 in)	1 in 150	1 860 litre/min (415 gal/min)
225 mm (9 in)	1 in 120	2 800 litre/min (630 gal/min)
250 mm (10 in)	1 in 220	2 760 litre/min (620 gal/min)

sewer or water course. Pipes up to about 150 mm (6 in) diameter are usually either asbestos cement or glazed clayware. For pipes of larger diameter, asbestos cement or precast concrete is used.

Table 7.2 indicates the range of pipe diameters and gradients required for the wash water discharge given above.

POWER (ELECTRICITY, GAS OR OIL)

Electricity would normally be used for power, but gas or oil or even solid fuel may be used for heating the pool. For lighting, the electrical supply in the United Kingdom is 220 V, AC, 3-phase; for circulating pumps, particularly the larger units, and for air compressors, the supply required would be 440 V.

Since any voltage above about 50 V is considered dangerous, special care must be taken in detailing and executing electrical installations; reference should be made to the Electricity Council and the detailed specifications of the Institution of Electrical Engineers. Electrical connections below water level in the pool should be of non-lethal voltage, and it is recommended that 12 V be used for this purpose; in this case a transformer is required. For gas installations reference should be made to the British Gas Corporation.

PLANT ROOMS FOR LARGE POOLS

For large swimming pools the planning of the plant room(s) is of great importance. Few things can be more frustrating to a baths manager than to find that the maintenance and repair of the expensive and complicated equipment under his control is seriously hampered by poor layout of the plant room. Large pools, particularly indoor ones which include mechanical ventilation, require large pieces of equipment, and it is essential for these to be housed in a plant room of adequate size and suitable shape with proper access and with a well-drained floor. It is therefore obvious that the selection of the various items of plant and the planning and layout of the plant room should be the responsibility of one authority.

FIG. 7.1.   View of plant room of large public swimming pool (Courtesy: Wingfield-Bowles
and Partners, Consulting Engineers).

For small installations the procedure of obtaining 'design and erect'
quotations for the various items of equipment from the manufacturers
may, in favourable circumstances, yield satisfactory results. However, for
large projects the whole of the engineering services should, in the author's
view, be the responsibility of a firm of experienced consulting engineers.
Their job is not only to select the most suitable items of plant and
equipment, but also to co-ordinate all the services and plan the complete
installation. The whole installation must work in harmony and the various
items of equipment must be in correct balance. Figure 7.1 shows a well-
planned plant room for a large municipal baths establishment in London.

WATER TREATMENT

GENERAL CONSIDERATIONS
The necessity for the treatment and purification of water in public
swimming pools is now recognised, and no public authority would consider

constructing a swimming pool without a properly designed plant to maintain the water at an adequate standard of purity. However, as stated in Chapter 1, legislation directly relating to the purity of water in swimming pools in the United Kingdom is contained in local authority by-laws and is only applicable to pools which are open to the public and for which a charge is made. Therefore the owner of a swimming pool for which a charge is not made, such as a school, club or hotel, is not under legal obligation to provide purification equipment. While certain sections of the Public Health Acts can be considered as applying to swimming pools which are in such a state as to be dangerous or injurious to health, there are no clear unambiguous standards for the purity of the water laid down by law which apply to all classes of swimming pools.

There can be no doubt, however, about the moral obligation of every one concerned with the operation of a swimming pool to ensure that the water is clear, sparkling and free from pathogenic bacteria. It may be of interest to note here that some managers of public swimming baths estimate that about 40 % of bathers urinate in the pool. In the opinion of the author every swimming pool, irrespective of size, whether public or private, must have some reliable means of maintaining the water in a pure and clear condition. The method adopted will depend on a number of factors: some methods are better than others, but they may be classified under two main headings:

(1) Continuous flow-through, or intermittent flow-through, without treatment.
(2) Continuous circulation with filtration and treatment.

The latest edition of the official publication, *The Purification of Swimming Pool Water* (see Bibliography), contains a wealth of useful and practical information and advice. It should be read by all who are interested in the treatment of swimming pool water. The author does not agree with all that is written in the booklet. In particular, the brief comments on the use of ozone and bromine do not do justice to the excellent qualities of these two methods of purifying water. Ozone is being used to an increasing extent on the Continent, particularly in Germany and Switzerland. No one who has visited public swimming pools in these countries can fail to agree that concern for public health and safety is at least as great as in the United Kingdom. In addition, the standard of hygiene and maintenance is well above what is achieved here.

CONTINUOUS FLOW-THROUGH OR INTERMITTENT FLOW-THROUGH WITHOUT TREATMENT

With this system the swimming pool is connected either to a stream or lake or to the sea.

The stream may be diverted through the pool either to give continuous flow, or by means of valves, penstocks or some similar device to give intermittent flow. With tidal pools pumping is usually required either to empty the pool or to fill it. The fill and empty arrangements can be such that, as the tide comes in, fresh sea-water flows into the pool at one end while the pumps empty the used (dirty) water out at the other; alternatively, the pool is emptied by gravity as the tide goes out and simultaneously filled at the other end by pumping. However, whether the water is obtained from sea, lake or river, it is generally free (i.e. not charged for on a quantity basis), but there may be the cost of pumping, and owing to the frequent changes of water in the pool, there can be no question of heating as the cost of this would be prohibitive.

Compared with continuous circulation and treatment, there is saving on capital for the treatment plant and its operation. Provision may have to be

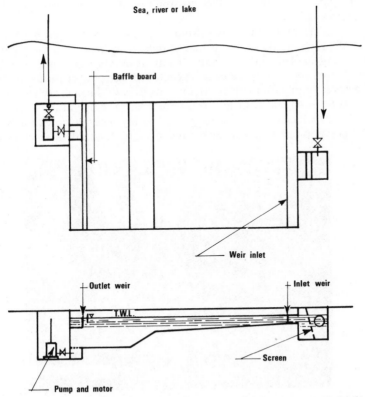

FIG. 7.2. Layout of swimming pool with continuous or intermittent flow-through without treatment.

made to ensure that the water entering the pool is clear and, in the case of sea-water, that seaweed and jellyfish are excluded as well as excessive amounts of sand. A settling tank between the sea and the pool on the intake pipeline is advantageous and may often be essential. Where water is drawn from a stream or lake, investigations must be made to ensure that the water will be pure throughout the bathing season; means must be provided to settle out mud in suspension, and to exclude floating debris such as leaves, etc., particularly after heavy rain. Some streams may receive sewage effluent above the intake to the pool; another source of pollution is drainage from farmyards, manure pits and refuse dumps.

Before deciding to rely on the purity of the stream or lake, enquiries should be made of the Health Authority and/or River Authority responsible for the area. Even in the case of the sea, information should be obtained on the location of sewer outfalls.

The layout of one of the possibilities discussed above is shown diagrammatically in Fig. 7.2.

Very occasionally one finds a swimming pool formed largely by nature as part of a river or lake. A beautiful example of such a pool is the Eden Roc swimming pool at Salvin, about 10 km from Martigny in Switzerland. Apart from the man-made walls at each end, the pool is entirely natural. The water supply is an alpine stream which flows through the rock basin. The water is crystal-clear and in summer has a temperature of 18–20 °C (64–68 °F), which is very refreshing on a hot day. The pool and the environs are very popular and well kept, and a high standard of cleanliness is

Fig. 7.3.   View of 'Eden Roc' natural swimming pool at Les Marécottes, near Martigny, Switzerland (Courtesy: Edward Schwarz, Stäfa, Switzerland).

maintained. As the water is continuously flowing through the basin (pool), it is not treated in any way. Figure 7.3 is a view of the pool.

WATER TREATMENT AND STERILISATION WITH CONTINUOUS CIRCULATION
General Considerations
The actual equipment selected will depend to a large extent on the size of the pool and the use to which it will be put; this latter is sometimes referred to as the pool loading. The essential items for even small pools are as follows:

(1)   Pipework for water circulation, water supply and drainage.
(2)   Strainer.
(3)   Electrically driven centrifugal pump.
(4)   Filter(s).
(5)   Means for continuously sterilising the water.
(6)   Electrical installation.
(7)   Plant room to accommodate items (2)–(6) above.

Additional items which may be needed for medium-size pools and which would certainly be required for large public pools include the following:

(8)   Coagulant dosing apparatus.
(9)   Alkali dosing apparatus.
(10)   Automatic residual chlorine and pH controller.
(11)   Chlorine cylinder storage or equivalent for other methods of continuous sterilisation of the water.
(12)   Store for chemicals used in items (8) and (9) above.
(13)   Possibly an automatic chlorine leak detector and alarm.
(14)   Boiler.
(15)   Heat conservation equipment.

Figure 7.4 shows an arrangement in diagram form, of the various items of equipment for a medium-size swimming pool in which chlorine is used for sterilising the water. Where there is more than one swimming pool in a sports centre, it is recommended that separate equipment for each pool should be provided—that is, items (1)–(5) and (8)–(10) inclusive. This will enable each pool to function on its own. Flexibility can be introduced by interconnecting certain items so that in the event of a breakdown equipment from one pool can assist in the operation of another.

However, the whole of the equipment can with advantage be located in one large well-laid-out plant room. The area of the plant room should be dictated by the dimensions of the items of equipment and their most advantageous disposition from the point of view of operating efficiency and ease of maintenance and replacement.

The continuous circulation of the whole of the water in the swimming

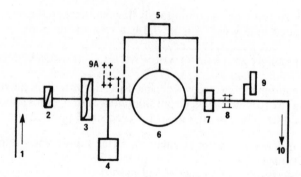

FIG. 7.4.   Layout of treatment plant: 1, outlet main from pool; 2, strainer; 3, circulating pump; 4, coagulant dosing; 5, pH regulator; 6, filter(s); 7, heater; 8, aerator; 9, water sterilising equipment; 9A, alternative position for sterilising equipment; 10, treated water main to pool.

pool, combined with filtration and sterilisation, is the only satisfactory method of ensuring that the water is maintained at the required standard of clarity and bacteriological purity. The object of the treatment plant must be to produce and maintain in the pool at all times a clear and bacteriologically pure water which has no irritating or harmful effect on the bathers. Strange as it may seem, water of drinking quality may not be entirely satisfactory. For example, the colour of many potable supplies is such that it appears quite clear and colourless to the consumer, but when viewed through a depth of 2·0 m or more, the colour and clarity can be poor. Figure 7.5 shows water of high clarity in a public swimming pool. Also, the chemical characteristics required of the water are different from potable water in that high chlorine residuals are required (to prevent infection), as well as comparatively high alkalinities and pH values to prevent unwanted side reactions. An interesting historical review of the treatment of water in the United Kingdom is given in the 4th edition of the *Manual of British Water Supply Practice*, compiled by the Institution of Water Engineers.

Apart from the decision on the items of equipment required for the complete treatment plant, there is also the problem of the overall design from the point of view of the size (capacity) of each piece of equipment. The design on this basis is empirical, so much so that if three firms are asked to prepare a scheme for, say, a school pool having dimensions of 20·0 m × 12·0 m with a depth varying from 1·0 m to 1·5 m, the result would be three different schemes with a wide range in capital and running costs. The possibility of this occurring must be anticipated when inviting tenders on a design and construction basis.

The way to obtain a reasonable measure of uniformity is to specify clearly the basic requirements; it will then be possible to compare one tender with

FIG. 7.5.   View of public pool showing clarity of water (Courtesy: Wallace and Tiernan Ltd, Tonbridge).

another. The items which will have an important effect on the treatment plant may be summarised as follows:

Pool type (private house, school, club, hotel, public).

Pool use, the whole year or intermittent (as at some country hotels and houses).

Open-air or indoor.

Shape and dimensions, including volume of water.

Main services available or to be made available, such as water, electricity, gas, fuel oil, drainage.

Whether or not the pool is to be heated.

Information on estimated pool loading, including peak loads and frequency.

Turnover period for treatment plant. If more than one pool is involved, then the turnover period for each pool should be defined.

Requirements for method of water circulation, types of inlets and outlets.

Chemical analysis of the water supplied to the pool.

Location of plant house and approximate size (unless the latter is to be left to the discretion of the treatment plant contractor).

Any requirements or restrictions on the type and design of the filters.
Requirements for chemical dosing and pH control.
Requirements for method of sterilisation.
Standard of purity, including clarity, required for the treated water.
A statement from tenderers on their recommendations for maintenance
and operational control and detailed analysis of estimated running cost
of the whole installation.

While the author is in general favour of leaving as much discretion as
possible to the specialist contractors, it is only fair that, when considering
the tenders, like should be compared with like.

Plant Rooms for Small Pools
Before discussing in detail the various items of equipment mentioned
above, some general recommendations will be given on plant rooms for
small installations, including those for open-air pools. The latter are used
only in the summer and thus remain closed during the whole winter, which
may be a period of 6–8 months. The treatment plant is expensive, as is the
heating installation, and both must be properly cared for during the long
period when they are not in operation. In view of the capital investment
involved, the following points are considered essential for the plant house:

(1) It must be of adequate size and properly built with concrete
foundations and concrete floor and walls of concrete blocks or clay bricks.
The roof should be of durable materials and completely weathertight.

(2) It should be designed and built with easy access so that all plant and
equipment can be removed without difficulty; this means pump and motor,
filter, chlorinator and boiler (if heating is included).

(3) It must be well lighted and ventilated. In addition to door and
window, at least two louvred openings about 250 mm × 75 mm covered
with wire mesh should be provided, one near the floor and the other near the
ceiling.

(4) Assuming that the water is chlorinated, special precautions must be
taken to protect all metal fittings, and special paint must be used which is
resistant to chlorine (in large installations the chlorinator is often kept in a
separate room).

(5) All electrical equipment and installations must be of the most robust
type and highest quality, complete with accessible control panel.

(6) The floor must be drained.

Some notes on each item of equipment previously mentioned are given
below.

Recommendations for maintenance including winterisation are given in
Chapter 8.

Strainers
The strainer usually consists of a cast-iron box with an inner basket of perforated heavy-gauge copper. This basket is removable for cleaning and can be replaced by a spare one. It is required to intercept leaves and coarse suspended matter which could eventually choke the circulating pump, and in any case would reduce the efficiency of the filter.

Circulating Pumps
The pumps used for the circulation of swimming pool water are the centrifugal type with directly coupled electric motors. It is obviously advantageous to have the pump and motor in duplicate but this is only justified in large installations. For these large installations a number of alternatives are possible, and these are:

(*a*) Two pumps each capable of 75 % of the maximum duty required.
(*b*) Two pumps each of 100 % of the maximum duty to be run alternately for some fixed period.
(*c*) Three pumps, each capable of 50 % of the full duty. Two of these will always work in parallel, with the third in reserve. The reserve pump and motor should be put into service on a regular time schedule to rest the others and ensure that they are all in full working order.

In cases where there is more than one pool in the same building or group of buildings it is recommended that each pool should have its own treatment plant complete, but the separate plants can be interconnected so that in an emergency the equipment belonging to one pool can be used to help with the treatment of water from another. In such a case great care must be exercised with the interconnection of circulating pumps, since these are designed to operate under certain specific hydraulic conditions (rate of flow and head). In the opinion of the author, the interconnection of circulating pumps is best avoided. It is far better to give adequate reserve for each pool in the manner previously described.

For larger pumps it is an advantage if the pump is of the split casing type because this gives maximum accessibility to the impeller. The top half of the casing can be completely removed, and if the top half of the bearing shells is also removable, the impeller and shaft can be readily lifted out.

The 'characteristics' of the pump should be such that delivery does not fall off significantly when the filters are showing signs that they require cleaning, i.e. the increase in delivery head caused by the accumulation of deposits in the filters should not greatly reduce the output of the pump. The pump should be self-priming. Circulating pumps are driven by a directly coupled electric motor operating on AC, 3-phase, and usually 440 V; the very small units may operate on 220 V.

With covered pools the installations invariably include water heating equipment which is housed in the main plant house which helps to ensure that the whole plant room area is dry and warm. For small and medium installations, a typical range of centrifugal pumps is the Sulzer low-lift NCP whole-casing pump operating at 1450 or 2900 rev/min, with capacities from 0·50 to 100 litre/s (6 to 1300 gal/min). The 'duty' of the pump in this context may be taken as the quantity of water to be pumped and the head against which the pump must work. The quantity of water pumped depends on the size of the pool and the 'turnover' period, i.e. the time taken to circulate the whole of the water in the pool. The turnover period varies according to the use to which the pool is put, but typical figures are:

Public swimming pools:
  separate diving pools, 6 h;
  swimming pools with and without diving pits, $2\frac{1}{2}$–4 h;
  learner pools, 2–3 h.
School pools, 4–6 hours.
Club and hotel pools, 3–6 h depending on bathing load.
Private house pools with light bathing load, 6–8 h.

There are a number of formulae available which can be used for determining the turnover period; these formulae include a 'factor' relating to the use to which the pool will be put, so, in the end, the calculation is purely empirical and the author prefers to use the generally accepted figures given above.

Filtration Plant

There are three main types of filter used for the treatment of swimming pool water; and these are:

Rapid (gravity) sand filters.
Pressure sand filters.
Diatomaceous earth pressure filters.

A newcomer to the swimming pool filtration field is the ultra-high rate filter operating at about 50 000 litre/m² per hour (1000 gal/ft² per hour).

Rapid (Gravity) Sand Filters

The rapid sand filter occupies considerably more space than the pressure filter for the same throughput of water. It is hardly ever used for covered pools but can be useful for large open-air pools, particularly those near the sea.

This type of filter operates under atmospheric pressure, the filter medium being graded sand, and the water passes down through the filter under the head created by the depth of water over the top of the filter. The rate of filtration depends on the head; the rate of operation is usually expressed as the rate at which the water flows downward through the filter. A speed of 1 ft/h being equivalent to $6\frac{1}{4}$ gal/ft^2 per hour; in metric units this would be 1000 litre/h for a flow of 1·0 m/h. As designed in the United Kingdom, rapid gravity filters operate at about 5000 litre/m^2 per hour (100 gal/ft^2 per hour).

Probably the largest rapid gravity filter installation for a swimming pool in the United Kingdom is the open-air pool at New Brighton, for the County Borough of Wallasey, Cheshire. In this plant about 1 700 000 gallons (7700 m^3) are circulated through the filters every 6 h.

Pressure Sand Filters
Pressure filters using sand as the filter medium are the type most widely used for swimming pools, in both the United Kingdom and other countries in Europe, the United States, Australia, etc. They are made to suit pools of the smallest to the largest size.

The main manufacturers in the United Kingdom recommend rates of 10 000–15 000 litre/m^2 per hour (200–300 gal/ft^2 per hour). The Department of the Environment, in the publication *The Purification of Swimming Pool Water*, recommend flow rates towards the lower end of the scale, but make it clear that there is nothing absolute about the figure. They go on to say that at present there is insufficient information based on careful experimental work to enable them to be more precise. It is perhaps rather surprising that the official regulations in the State of California, which were referred to in Chapter 1, permit a maximum of only 180 gal/ft^2 per hour (9000 litre/m^2 per hour).

Needless to say, there is a wide divergence of views on the safe rate at which pressure sand filters can operate. Filters installed for use with municipal swimming pools usually operate at the rate of 12 500 litre/m^2 per hour (250 gal/ft^2 per hour). The same type of filters installed for private clients and schools may be found to operate successfully at 15 000–25 000 litres/m^2 per hour (300–500 gal/ft^2 per hour). Some manufacturers consider that if the filter medium consists of carefully graded high-quality limestone chippings, a rate of 25 000 litre/m^2 per hour (500 gal/ft^2 per hour) may give better results than using graded sand.

In spite of the intensive sales campaign mounted by suppliers of extra-rapid high-pressure filters operating in the range 25 000–50 000 litre/m^2 per hour (500–1000 gal/ft^2 per hour), the author considers that the safe maximum for private pools is 25 000 litre/m^2 per hour (500 gal/ft^2 per hour). For hotel, club and public pools, 17 000 litre/m^2 per hour (350 gal/ft^2 per hour) should be the safe maximum filtration rate, with a lower figure for heavily loaded pools.

It seems to the author that carefully controlled research over a reasonable period of time should resolve many of these problems. This may result in more economic design of the filters and would certainly help to introduce some uniformity in performance specifications, and last, but not least, the results of such research carried out by a competent independent organisation would inspire confidence when using the recommended flow rates.

The object of efficient filter design is to secure maximum reduction in suspended and colloidal matter, long runs between washes, rapid and effective cleaning, minimum attention and maintenance, and a long life for the filter material itself. This is achieved by careful selection of the sand, design of the washing equipment and design of the underdrainage (collecting) system.

Pressure sand filters utilising graded sand as the filter medium are often classified according to the method used in cleansing the filter medium, but all have one feature in common—a reverse flow of water. The sand has to be agitated so that the wash water (reverse flow) will carry away all particles of suspended matter, and this agitation is achieved in one of three ways:

(a) By mechanical agitation of the sand, usually by revolving rakes.
(b) By compressed air.
(c) By the pressure of the wash water itself.

The filter consists of a circular steel shell with graded sand inside; this is in effect a pressure vessel and the operating pressure is usually about 2 atm ($2 \, kg/cm^2$ or $30 \, lb/in^2$).

For efficient operation the filter medium must arrest the passage of suspended matter in the water to the maximum possible degree but at the same time allow a high rate of filtration. The method of collection of the water after it has passed through the sand bed must be carefully designed so that there are no 'dead' pockets.

The sand used must be specially selected and graded. In this context the term 'graded' means that the grain size is selected, which is rather different from the meaning used in concrete technology. Some filter manufacturers use single size grading, while others use different sizes in layers with the finer grading at the top increasing in grain size to the coarsest at the bottom. Each type has advantages and disadvantages. The single size for the full depth of the bed is easier to clean and much easier to replace in whole or part; on the other hand, the graded sand bed gives rather better filtration. The sand grading often used has a grain size which will pass through a No. 16 sieve but be retained on a No. 30 sieve (sieves to BS 410). The sieves mentioned have nominal mesh apertures $1 \cdot 0 \, mm$ ($1/25 \, in$) and $0 \cdot 50 \, mm$, respectively.

The filters can be either horizontal or vertical, i.e. the axis of the circular filter may be horizontal or vertical, but in both cases the water flows from the top to the bottom; in other words, the water flow is vertically downwards. Filters vary in diameter from about 0·50 m to 2·60 m (1 ft 6 in to 8 ft 6 in) and the height (or length) from about 1·0 m to 7·50 m (3 ft 3 in to 24 ft). The capacities of these filters are within the range 1·7–180 m^3 (380–40 000 gal) per hour.

The mechanically agitated filter is usually the most expensive in initial cost of the three types mentioned earlier in this chapter. Figure 7.6 shows such a filter. The next in order of capital cost is the filter utilising compressed air to agitate the sand, with the plain reversal of flow the lowest. Mechanical agitation is provided only for vertical filters and therefore requires more headroom than a horizontal filter of the same capacity. It is often easier to increase the floor area of the plant room than the height; this applies particularly when the equipment is located below the pool floor.

For compressed air agitation, about 1·22 m^3 (43 ft^3) of air is required per m^2 of filter bed, at a pressure of about 0·35 kg/cm^2 (5·2 lb/in^2); the air scour operation lasts about 1$\frac{1}{2}$–3 min. The author considers that, taking all relevant factors into consideration, filters utilising compressed air for the agitation of the filter medium are the most suitable for medium to large swimming pool installations. Figure 7.7 shows a pressure sand filter.

All sand filters have to be back-washed irrespective of the method used to agitate the sand. The quantity of water used is about 400 litre/m^2 of filter medium per minute (8 gal/ft^2 per min) for a wash period of between 3 and 8 min, using air scour to first agitate the sand. If air scour is not used (as in small installations), the amount of wash water required is increased by about 50 %. As an example, a swimming pool holding, say, 370 m^3 (80 000 gal) with a turnover period of 4 h would probably need two pressure sand filters, each 2·0 m (6 ft 6 in) diameter and about 1·5 m (5 ft) high, and these would require about 1·8 m^3 (400 gal) of wash water per minute. This wash water has to be disposed of and, as mentioned earlier in this chapter, the drainage system must be designed with these figures in mind. This rate of flow may for various reasons prove difficult to handle and then the use of a balancing tank may be necessary. This tank will hold back the flow and release it at a much slower rate. An alternative is to use horizontal filters which can be divided into two compartments by vertical steel partitions and each half back-washed separately, thus reducing the rate of flow by 50 %.

An obvious question arises as to how often a filter should be back-washed and on what criteria the decision to back-wash rests. The decision is taken on the record of the pressure drop through the filter, and a differential pressure gauge should be installed for this purpose. A sight glass is installed in the discharge pipeline so that the clarity of the wash water can be observed. All filter manufacturers supply a complete set of operating instructions and these must be followed. The observations given in this book are intended as a statement of general principles.

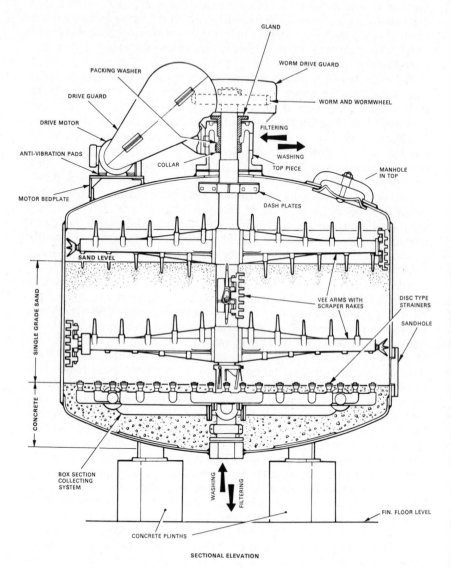

FIG. 7.6. Pressure filter with mechanical agitation equipment (Courtesy: Bell Bros. (PCI Ltd)).

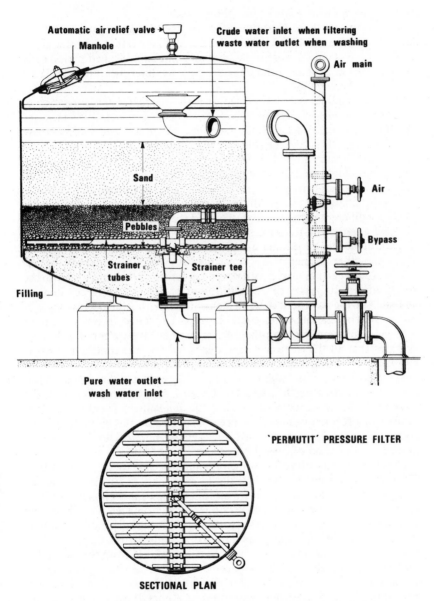

FIG. 7.7. Pressure filter with air scour (Courtesy: Permutit Co. Ltd).

Diatomaceous Earth Filters (Diatomite Filters)

Diatomaceous earth or diatomite filters are also known as pre-coat filters; the basic difference between this type and sand filters is that in the latter the filter medium (sand) is more or less permanent and is cleaned periodically by back-washing, while in the pre-coat filter the filter medium is replaced when it has become dirty.

The filter medium is a diatomaceous earth; this material is composed of the siliceous shells of diatoms, which are unicelled plants of microscopic size. It usually occurs in beds a few feet thick, but in the United States there is a bed several thousand feet thick. The majority of the beds were formed during the Tertiary period, many millions of years ago. Diatomaceous earth is light-coloured and looks rather like chalk but it is a silica compound and does not react with most acids as does chalk. In Europe it is known as kieselguhr. Diatomaceous earth should not be confused with Fuller's earth, which is a different material altogether and is a fine clay used for industrial and civil engineering purposes.

A diatomaceous earth filter usually consists of a vertical steel cylinder in which the filter elements are suspended. A specified quantity of the diatomaceous earth is mixed with water in a tank and then pumped into the steel cylinder. It passes through the filter elements and in so doing is deposited on the outside of these elements, thus coating them with a layer of the earth. The diatomaceous earth slurry is circulated through the filter until the liquid coming from the filter is comparatively clear. This clarity indicates that all the earth has been deposited and the coating process is complete, and the filter ready for use. The appropriate valves are now closed and others opened, and water from the pool is circulated through the filter. The diatomaceous earth coating acts as a strainer and removes the suspended matter in the same way as the sand filter. There are a large number of proprietary makes of pre-coat filters on the market, and the description given here is intended as a general one to indicate the basic features and method of operation of this type of filter.

The cleaning procedure is in principle similar to that used for sand filters. When the pressure drop through the filter reaches a certain preselected value, the filter is considered due for cleaning. The cleaning is carried out by a reversal of flow of water, which dislodges the diatomaceous earth coating from the filter elements and carries it away with the suspended matter in the pores. Suitable arrangements have to be made for the disposal of the wash water, which contains not only the dirt removed from the swimming pool water, but also the diatomaceous earth. The whole sequence of operations is shown in the diagram in Fig. 7.8. When the back-wash water is seen to be clear, the reverse flow of water is stopped; more diatomaceous earth is mixed into a slurry and the whole operation is repeated as previously described.

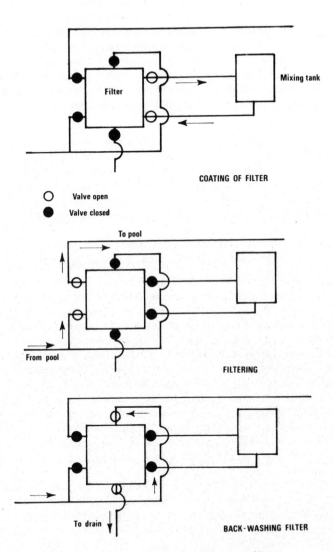

FIG. 7.8. Diagram of operation of pre-coat filters.

This type of filter, when carefully operated and properly maintained, will give water of maximum clarity, but it is more sensitive to careless operation than pressure sand filters and is rather liable to clogging. Grease in the water (from hair and face cream) is particularly bad for the filter.

Diatomite filters are popular with swimming pool contractors who offer a complete design and construct package-deal service for the small to medium-size pool. They are seldom used for public pools, and independent consultants tend to avoid specifying them; the reasons given for this vary from one consultant to another, but generally they are based on the following:

(a) The head required to circulate a given volume of water through the filter in a given time (and thus the head under which the circulating pump has to work) is considerably higher than for pressure sand filters. In other words, the initial pressure drop through the filter when it is first put into operation is much higher. This increases the current consumed by the pump and so the pumping costs are higher. One consultant estimated this at about 50%.

(b) The cost of renewing the diatomaceous earth each time the filter is cleaned costs about four times the equivalent sand renewal.

However, the above two factors may be partly offset by the fact that the amount of wash water used is comparatively small compared with an equivalent sand filter. Also, if this water has to be paid for (it may be a metered supply), the cost can be set against the items mentioned.

It should also be noted that some small installations use a type of filter in which the filter medium is washed by the backflow of water and then re-used, but this is not as satisfactory as renewing the diatomaceous earth at each wash. The filter after such a wash does not perform as efficiently as when the filter medium is new. Needless to say, these statements are strongly challenged by the makers of proprietary pre-coat filters, so that in the end the designer or client has to decide himself. Before reaching a decision however, it is most advisable to visit a few pools of the same class as it is proposed to build, and discuss with the owners the advantages and disadvantages.

Two of the largest installations of pre-coat filters are at Richmond-upon-Thames, Surrey, and Sheaf Valley, Sheffield. The Richmond installation consists of 'Meta' filters and deals with a total bath capacity of about 200 m^3 (400 000 gal), while at Sheaf Valley the filters were supplied by Schumacher and will filter some 125 m^3 (276 000 gal) of pool water. Three new public pools (one for water polo, one for bathing and swimming and one for teaching) are under construction at Varley Street, Manchester. The whole of the water in the three pools will be filtered through pre-coat filters of Dutch design. The results are awaited with interest.

The Committee which prepared the latest revision to the official publication *The Purification of the Water of Swimming Pools* (1976 edition) say on p. 9 of the booklet: 'It is probably sufficient to say that, so far, there seems no reason to prefer them [i.e. pre-coat filters] to the far better established sand filters. . . .'

Pad filters. From information available it appears that filters of this type are only suitable for small installations, such as private house, club, hotel and school pools. In brief, they consist of a metal tank or cylinder, containing a series of pads of varying coarseness, the water flowing through under pressure. The pads are now usually made of man-made fibres and are replaceable as they become dirty. They are relatively cheap and simple to operate. Information on their performance in terms of removal of suspended and colloidal matter, improvement in clarity, etc., is scarce. Until this is available, it is unlikely that this type of filter will be used for public swimming pools.

Clarity of Swimming Pool Water
From the point of view of public safety, the clarity of pool water is of greater importance than bacterial purity. Outbreaks of water-borne disease formally traced to swimming pools hardly ever occur in the United Kingdom and other developed countries with a similar climate. The author has been unable to find a single authentic case of death arising from infection in a swimming pool in the United Kingdom during the past thirty years. Unfortunately the same cannot be said about deaths from drowning where substandard clarity of the pool water was a contributory cause.

It is very difficult to define clarity and to produce a standard method of measuring it. The suggestions in Sections 6.7–6.25 in *The Purification of the Water of Swimming Pools*, are useful and practical. The Technical Unit for Sport (Bulletin No. 1) recommend that clarity, as measured by the test in the DoE booklet, should not fall below 12·2 m. On the Continent it is required that the bottom of the pool must be clearly visible at all times when viewed from the edge of the bath at walkway level. In the early part of 1974 it was reported in the American journal *Swimming Pool Weekly* that turbidity standards were to be set. The National Sanitation Foundation Committee on Swimming Pool Standards approved an acceptable turbidity level, for pools up to 12 ft (3·5 m) deep, of 0·5 Jackson Turbidity Units. The requirement will contain a provision that, while this limit (0·5 JTU) can be slightly exceeded during times of peak load, the water treatment system must be capable of reducing the level to the 0·5 JTU during one turnover period. A level higher than 1·0 JTU would be unacceptable at any time.

CHEMICAL DOSING EQUIPMENT

It is beyond the scope of this book to go into the chemistry of water treatment, since this would require a volume by itself, but some information on basic principles will be given. The first thing to note is that chemical dosing in this context is quite different and distinct from the addition of chemicals for sterilisation of the water. The object of chemical dosing is twofold:

(a) To create a 'floc' to assist the filters in removing suspended and colloidal matter; this is sometimes termed 'coagulant dosing'.

(b) To ensure that the pH of the water is maintained between 7·2 and 8·0 so that the water is alkaline in reaction. This is also known as 'alkali dosing' or 'pH regulation'. (Some explanation of the term 'pH' has been given in Chapter 3.)

The best pH values for floc formation are well below those found in swimming pool water. Good floc formation would be due to the depression of the pH by the action of the acid aluminium sulphate. Aluminium sulphate is normally added intermittently, e.g. for 2–3 h after back washing the filters at a dose of about 20 ppm. The period of dosage is often for one complete cycle (turnover period).

For the control of the pH, sodium carbonate (soda-ash) is added. Sodium hydroxide and sodium bicarbonate are also used. These chemicals must be added in the correct amount, and the recommendations of the firm supplying the treatment plant must be followed. It is important that the soda-ash be completely dissolved before it is injected in the pumping main, and mechanical feed equipment is recommended for this purpose.

The amount of chemicals required for optimum conditions depends on the chemical characteristics of the water. For example, a slightly acid moorland water would require different dosing compared with a hard water derived from boreholes in the chalk. To form an effective 'floc', the aluminium sulphate has to react with an alkali to form aluminium hydroxide, which is a gelatinous precipitate; this precipitate carries down the fine suspended and colloidal matter in the water and it is deposited on to the filter medium.

While at first sight the formation of the floc may appear to be essential for efficient filtration, the author was informed by water treatment specialists that this is not the case. The fact is that with correct treatment and correctly designed filters it is not necessary for an aluminium hydroxide gel (floc) to form on the top of the filter. Alum is added to remove colour by floc formation and to produce conditions in the filter media conducive to the precipitation of colloidal matter, so that the improvement in filter performance is not exclusively due to floc formation.

According to the *Manual of British Water Engineering Practice*, 4th edition (Vol. 3), most waters in the United Kingdom fall into three main classes:

(a) Soft acid water, with a pH between 5·0 and 6·5, and alkalinities of less than 50 mg/litre (50 ppm); these waters are often rather highly coloured by organic matter.

(b) Waters with a pH between 6·5 and 7·0, with alkalinity of about 200 mg/litre,

(c) Waters with a pH between 7·0 and 8·4; these are generally considered as alkaline waters.

While the soft acid waters definitely require the addition of an alkali for efficient coagulation, the waters under category (c), particularly those in the higher part of the range, are difficult to coagulate and may require massive doses of aluminium sulphate.

The coagulant must be added before the filters, but the alkali dosing may take place either before or after filtration, depending on the chemistry of the water and to some extent on the ideas of the treatment plant designers. As already pointed out, water does not need to be alkaline for floc formation, and waters with pH values well below 7·0 give the best flocs. The water, however, must contain some 'alkalinity'. The addition of alkali to pool water is basically for breakpoint chlorination and not for floc formation (efficient coagulation). The total alkalinity of pool water should be about 150 mg/litre (150 ppm). This is to act as a buffer to prevent pH change on the addition of chlorine.

The pH control, usually by soda-ash, is generally necessary to ensure the alkaline reaction of the water for the floc formation, and for breakpoint chlorination; in addition, an acid water is likely to attack any cementitious materials with which it comes into contact and is more aggressive to ferrous metals than one which is alkaline. It should be noted that, in general, the addition of an alkali to raise the pH is not required when sodium hypochlorite solution is used for sterilisation, since this compound is itself alkaline in reaction. On the other hand, with the use of hypochlorite there is a tendency for the alkalinity of the water to rise to undesirable levels which can cause irritation of the skin and eyes. Regular checking of the pH is therefore necessary, and arrangements must be made to correct the pH (to lower it to, say, 7·8). This downward correction of the pH is not easy to achieve in practice and is one of the reasons why sterilisation with hypochlorite solution is not as popular as it might otherwise be.

A fairly new method of pH correction (for increasing the alkalinity) is to use a material sold under the name of 'Akdolit'. This is a granular material which can be placed on the top of the filter medium. As the water passes through it, the pH is raised to a certain level; the process is self-adjusting, since the lower the pH of the incoming water the more of the Akdolit will be dissolved. Thus the pH of the water leaving the filter is kept approximately constant. The Akdolit does not, and is not intended to, take part in the filter process; it is used simply for pH control, and can be located in the filter or in a separate container.

The pH of the water can be determined approximately by indicator solutions. These are sold with complete test kits which include comparators for assessing the amount of free chlorine in the water. The determination of the pH is made by comparing the colour resulting from the addition of a set quantity of standard solution to the water in a test tube with a range of coloured discs; each colour of disc represents a certain pH.

Mention has been made of the possible aggressive effects of pool water which is slightly acid—that is, has a pH below the neutral point of 7·0. It is usual for the pH value to be checked and recorded at least once a day. This is often done using phenol red indicator or diphenol purple. Chlorine reacts with both these indicators to give a colour which corresponds to pH values higher than the correct ones. Even when special tablets are used to eliminate the chlorine, high readings may still be obtained; the error can amount to as much as plus 0·5, which means that a comparator reading of 7·1 would read 6·6 if an accurate pH meter were used.

One point which cannot be emphasised too strongly is that water treatment is a highly specialised subject and changes should not be made in the quantities of chemicals or in the type of chemicals recommended by the water treatment consultant or the manufacturers of the installation. Over- or under-dosage can have serious results on the efficiency of the filters and on the purity of the water, as well as resulting in attack on metal and concrete. The formation of a floc to assist the work of the filters can be achieved without the use of chemicals; electrically charged copper plates liberate copper ions into the water. This is dealt with later in this chapter.

CHEMICAL ATTACK FROM SWIMMING POOL WATER
Fears are sometimes expressed that the chlorine and/or chlorine compounds in the pool water will attack the cement mortar joints between the tiles and that these compounds in the air in the pool hall will attack unprotected concrete. If the concentration of these compounds in the water or in the atmosphere reached a level which was significantly aggressive to Portland cement products, the unfortunate users of the pool would become seriously ill in a matter of minutes. However, conditions in the pool water (apart from the chlorine and associated compounds) can become aggressive to Portland cement mortar owing to incorrect dosing with the water treatment chemicals. These are usually aluminium sulphate and soda-ash (sodium carbonate). It is the aluminium sulphate which can cause the

trouble, as this is acid in solution and produces sulphate ions. Both the acidity and sulphate ions in certain concentrations are aggressive to cement mortar, and in extreme cases to concrete. It should be remembered that mortar, owing to its higher permeability, is more vulnerable to attack than dense concrete; also, the temperature of the pool water—say 25 °C—intensifies chemical attack.

It is therefore most important that the measurement of the pH of the water should be by means of an accurate pH meter, and the pH level should not be allowed to fall below 7·2. The sulphate concentration should not exceed 250 ppm expressed as SO_3. Assuming that aluminium sulphate is used as the coagulant, the calculation for equivalent SO_3 concentration is:

$$Al_2(SO_4)_3 = 2(27) + 3(32 + 64) = 54 + 288 = 342$$
$$SO_4 = 96$$
$$SO_3 = 80$$

Therefore the equivalent sulphate content of aluminium sulphate $(Al_2(SO_4)_3)$, expressed as SO_3, is:

$$\frac{80}{96} \times \frac{288}{342} = 0·70$$

Hence, mg/litre of aluminium sulphate $\times$ 0·70 = mg/litre of SO_3.

WATER FOR PRIVATE SWIMMING POOLS SOFTENED BY THE BASE-EXCHANGE PROCESS

Most domestic and small industrial water softeners operate on what is known as the base-exchange or ion-exchange process. In this process the active material is a natural or artificial zeolite, a sulphonated carbonaceous material or a synthetic resin which has ion-exchange properties.

Hardness is due principally to bicarbonates and sulphates of calcium and magnesium in solution in the water, and softening is the process required to remove this hardness. Water flows through the bed of the active material, and the calcium and magnesium ions leave the water and become associated with the insoluble ion-exchange material. This can be shown in a simple way as follows:

sodium zeolite + calcium bicarbonate
$\rightarrow$ calcium zeolite + sodium bicarbonate

sodium zeolite + magnesium sulphate
$\rightarrow$ magnesium zeolite + sodium sulphate

After a time all the sodium zeolite is used up and the softener has to be regenerated by the application of concentrated common salt solution (sodium chloride):

calcium zeolite + sodium chloride
→ sodium zeolite + calcium chloride

magnesium zeolite + sodium chloride
→ sodium zeolite + magnesium chloride

The calcium and magnesium chlorides are in solution in the wash water, which goes to waste.

From the above it can be seen that there is no change in the total dissolved solid (tds) content of the water. Provided the water is not acid and does not contain any dissolved carbon dioxide and the Langlier Index is positive, it should not be aggressive to good-quality Portland cement concrete and mortar.

Water of zero hardness can be obtained from an ion-exchange softener, but for various reasons this can be undesirable, and so it is usual to blend the softened water with a percentage of the hard water to give the required degree of hardness.

THE STERILISATION OF SWIMMING POOL WATER

Some authorities use the word 'purification' or 'disinfection' rather than 'sterilisation', but the author prefers the latter. The reason is that purification is really the function of the whole treatment plant, while one section only of the plant is intended to actually destroy bacteria in the water; although, as stated later, the effectiveness of the sterilising agent is considerably influenced by the other treatment processes and the water circulation system. It cannot be reasonably claimed that the water is completely sterilised in the strict medical sense. However, the Department of the Environment in their booklet *The Purification of the Water of Swimming Pools* (1976 edition), conclude that: '... when coliforms are absent and a satisfactory level of free residual chlorine is maintained, the risk of infection to bathers ... is minimal. ...' The booklet goes on to say that when filtration and disinfection is properly operated, coliforms and *Escherichia coli* will not normally be detectable in 100 ml samples of the pool water. The absolute need for proper purification including destruction of pathogenic bacteria in pool water has been mentioned earlier in this chapter.

It is the considered official opinion in the United Kingdom that destruction of harmful bacteria in water as it passes through the treatment plant is not enough and that a sterilising (disinfecting) agent must be injected into the water so that its potency remains active in the pool itself. In this way, it is argued, continuous destruction of pathogens brought in by the bathers is assured, and the health of the pool users safeguarded. It is, however, a fact that on the very rare occasions when there is an outbreak of infectious disease which may be spread by swimming pool water, all public swimming pools in the area are promptly closed for the duration of the epidemic. Thus there seems to be some lack of confidence in the real effectiveness of the 'free residual chlorine' requirement.

CHLORINATION

There are three basic methods of chlorinating water:

(a) The injection of chlorine gas by means of a gas chlorinator.
(b) The addition of sodium hypochlorite or chloride of lime (bleaching powder), from solution feed apparatus.
(c) The addition of other compounds which liberate chlorine or chlorine-containing compounds when dissolved in water.

The use of chlorine gas is considered the most efficient method of chlorination because the dosage can be accurately controlled; this is the method employed in most modern public swimming pools and many medium to large private pools as well. However, owing to the advent of the Health and Safety at Work legislation, some objections have been raised to the use of chlorine gas cylinders. The chlorine, whether it is injected into the water or liberated by special chemical compounds, is the active sterilising agent and is used up by bacteria and organic matter in the pool water. It therefore follows that with wide fluctuations in the number of persons using the pool at any one time there is a corresponding fluctuation in the amount of bacteria and organic matter being deposited in the water.

A satisfactory level of chlorine in the bath water at all times under these fluctuating bathing load conditions is anything but a simple matter. Under-chlorination is potentially dangerous, and over-chlorination can give rise to complaints from the bathers due to irritation of the eyes, nose and throat. Some of the adverse features of chlorine as a sterilising agent are:

(a) It is highly poisonous.
(b) It is very corrosive to many structural and engineering materials, particularly metals.
(c) By reaction it can give rise to objectionable smells which may cause irritation to the eyes and sometimes to the nose and throat as well.

In view of these by no means insignificant objections, it is surprising that chlorination has maintained its place for a half-century as the number one sterilising agent for swimming pool water in all countries of the world. Considerable efforts have been made to find a substitute which is economic and simple to dose, will maintain its sterilising effect for a reasonable period, and is such that its presence in the water in the required concentration can be detected by quick and simple tests.

The basic chemistry of the chlorination of swimming pool water is extremely complex, and even today there are a number of features which are not completely understood. It may be expressed in approximate and simple terms as follows. Chlorine gas dissolves in water and forms hypochlorous acid and hydrochloric acid:

$$Cl_2 + H_2O = HOCl + HCl$$

The hydrochloric acid will be neutralised by any alkalis present in the water, while the hypochlorous acid (which is a strong bactericide) will react with organic and nitrogenous compounds. Because ammonia is usually present in some form or other, the hypochlorous acid will also react with it

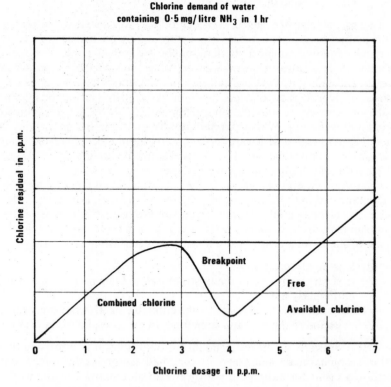

Fig. 7.9. Diagram of breakpoint chlorination (Courtesy: J. F. Malpas, Wallace and Tiernan Ltd).

and forms complex compounds known as chloramines. Chloramines are not as powerful or as rapid in destroying bacteria as free chlorine, but they are more stable and last longer than free chlorine; in some cases this may be advantageous.

If chlorine continues to be fed to the water, it will cause the chloramines to break down into nitrogen and hydrochloric acid, and the surplus chlorine will form hypochlorous acid. The chlorine concentration at which the chloramines are broken down and hypochlorous acid starts to form again is called the 'breakpoint', and the technique of achieving this is known as 'breakpoint chlorination'. This is shown in diagrammatic form in Figs. 7.9 and 7.10. It must be remembered that this reaction is occurring continuously in a swimming pool in that pollution in the form of ammonia is continually being added. Hence, it will not normally be possible for the pool water to contain only free chlorine, since the reaction of chlorine with ammoniacal compounds is a relatively slow one.

The basic reason for breakpoint chlorination is to create a free-chlorine

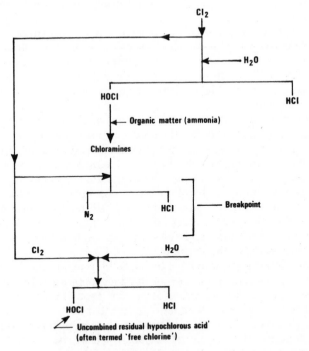

FIG. 7.10.   Diagram of chemistry of breakpoint chlorination (Courtesy: A. Elphick, Wallace and Tiernan Ltd).

residual, and this can only be maintained by the continuous decomposition of ammonia. The chemical reactions which take place at the breakpoint are largely controlled by two factors, viz. the pH of the water and the amount of chlorine in the water (the dosage). For various reasons, the only practical way of determining the required dosage is by measuring the chlorine residual. Some bath managers maintain a free-chlorine residual of 1 mg/litre (1 ppm) at the deep end of the pool, when the fresh-water inlets are concentrated at or near the shallow end. This is because the heaviest bathing load and consequently heaviest contamination is at the shallow end.

The term 'combined residual chlorine' is for all practical purposes the chloramine content of the water. In many cases, especially where heavy bathing loads are experienced, this chloramine will be due to the reaction of chlorine with organic substances in the water rather than with ammonia. These organic chloramines are very stable indeed and so may build up after heavy loading. These compounds appear, during chemical tests, in the dichloramine fraction, and so it is important that, for control of breakpoint, the monochloramine concentration only is compared with the free chlorine level.

Irritation to the eyes is usually associated with the formation of nitrogen trichloride at low pH values or very high chlorine residuals. However, high combined-chlorine residuals are not desirable. Hypochlorous acid is not only a much stronger and swifter germicide than chloramine, but can also be tolerated in much higher concentrations, which are in the range 1–3 mg/litre (ppm).

Chlorine gas is added to the water by means of a chlorinator. This can be a fully automatic model so that the predetermined quantity of chlorine in mg/litre (ppm) of water flow will be maintained irrespective of variations in the actual flow. Automatic chlorine control maintains a chlorine level not only irrespective of the water flow (which is often constant anyway), but also irrespective of the quality of the water, i.e. depending on the degree of pollution in the returning water and on the free residual chlorine in that water. In other words, the actual quantity of chlorine delivered will vary with the volume of flow, and the parts per million figure will remain constant over a wide range of flow.

The point in the installation at which the chlorine is injected varies from one treatment plant manufacturer or designer to another. It may be after the aerator, just before the water enters the pool. If chlorine is injected before filtration, then the alkali must be injected at the same point in the system. Otherwise, local pockets of water with a low pH may form, leading to the production of nitrogen trichloride, which will be released when the water enters the pool. Also, the alkali should be dosed in proportion to the dosage of chlorine.

If the chlorine is applied before the filters, there are some advantages and, contrary to popular thought, the chlorine is not 'wasted'. The contact time in the filters allows the chlorine to react with pollution in solution before the water enters the pool. The water entering the pool is therefore in a more stable condition and attains a higher degree of purity. This pre-filter chlorination also helps to keep the filters in good condition and may increase the time between back-washing.

When a gas chlorinator is used, the cylinders of chlorine gas and the dosing apparatus must be kept in a well-ventilated room, preferably separate from the other installations. There should be vents near the floor terminating in the outside air or extract fans. The door of the room must open outwards direct to the external air. The cylinders should be securely fixed so that they cannot fall or be accidentally knocked over. A reliable type of gas mask must be kept in a locked cupboard outside the chlorinator room but close to it. The whole of the equipment must be of robust design and all metal parts must be of an alloy which is not affected by chlorine gas. Since there are always small quantities of the gas present in the air (this can be smelt), the decorative materials must be selected accordingly. Regular inspection and maintenance is essential.

The smallest gas chlorinator commercially available would deliver about 0·0125 lb of chlorine per hour; this would treat approximately 5 m^3 (1100 gal) of water per hour with a concentration of 2 mg/litre (2 ppm). With a turnover period of 6 h, the smallest pool which could use a gas chlorinator would therefore hold about 30 m^2 (6600 gal). This represents the extreme range, and it is doubtful whether in practice a pool smaller than 50 m^3 (11 000 gal) would use a gas chlorinator.

Other methods of chlorination involve the addition in solution form of compounds containing a considerable quantity of chlorine which is released when the substance is dissolved in water. Two of the most widely used compounds are sodium hypochlorite and calcium hypochlorite; the latter is known as bleaching powder. The sodium hypochlorite can be obtained in solution form or as a powder which can be made into a solution on site. The essential feature of the equipment for dosing is that the solution feed must be accurate and adjustable. The addition of bleach direct to the water of the pool should never be adopted except in an emergency and then only for a short period.

Chlorine compounds, available in tablet form, have come on to the market in recent years and are used to an increasing extent for small private pools. These tablets are generally trichloroisocyanurates which slowly liberate chlorine into the water. For the reasons already given, the author does not favour this method of chlorination except for pools of the smallest size. They are, however, very useful for children's paddling pools and the inflated dinghy type of garden swimming pool.

For small installations equipment is available which combines the injection of chemicals for floc formation and pH control. For medium and large installations, the provision of an automatic cylinder changeover unit is recommended. One cylinder may become empty while the baths staff are fully occupied with a heavy bathing load, and this is the time when there is the maximum demand for chlorination.

It has been previously mentioned that the water in the pool should be checked frequently for residual chlorine; this applies particularly to public pools and pools belonging to clubs and hotels, where there are wide fluctuations in the bathing load. This can be done by simply taking samples by hand from the pool and testing them in a comparator; an alternative and, in the author's opinion, better method is to install an automatic residual controller. A typical piece of equipment is manufactured by Wallace and Tiernan Ltd, Tonbridge, Kent. This will automatically and continuously control the amount of chlorine injected and the amount of the alkali solution.

The sample of water is taken from near the inlet to the pool (after filtration, chemical dosage and chlorination), and is passed through a measuring cell, where the residual chlorine is determined and, if necessary, the pH as well. A signal is then transmitted to a V-notch chlorinator and an alkali solution feeder to increase or decrease the chlorine or alkali, or both. In this way the residual chlorine and the pH of the water returning to the pool can be maintained at predetermined figures irrespective of the bathing load. It should be noted that the measurements are made on the purified water returning to the pool and not on the water in the swimming pool itself. Additional, but rather complicated, equipment can be installed for monitoring the water in the pool, but very few pools in the United Kingdom have this sophisticated equipment. Although the equipment is used almost exclusively with gas chlorinators, it can be adapted for use with hypochlorite chlorinators as well.

Orthotoluidine is no longer permitted to be used for industrial purposes in the United Kingdom and, therefore, should not be used for chlorine residual determination. The reason for this ban is that the compound is considered to be carcinogenic. However, there are now other equally accurate and rapid methods which, in addition, are quite safe to use. Palin's DPD method is one of the best-known.

OTHER METHODS OF STERILISATION (DISINFECTION) OF POOL WATER

Methods other than those employing chlorine as the active agent are in use in public and private pools outside the United Kingdom. Some have been used extensively and have replaced chlorine, while others have found less favour and their use has been largely confined to hotel and private pools.

The principal alternatives to chlorine are:

(a) Ozone.
(b) Bromine.
(c) Chlorine dioxide.
(d) Metallic ions.
(e) Ultra-violet radiation.

The important features of any satisfactory method of water sterilisation for swimming pools should include all or most of the following:

(1) The compounds or elements used must possess strong germicidal properties and should effect a massive 'kill' with great rapidity.
(2) The method should be reasonably competitive in first cost and operation with other comparable methods. All relevant factors must be taken into account in making this cost comparison.
(3) The germicidal effects should last for a reasonable period so that fresh contamination introduced into the pool by bathers is effectively neutralised.
(4) The dosage must be easily controlled.
(5) It must be non-irritating to pool users and should not impart unpleasant odours to the water or to the air above the pool surface.
(6) It is advantageous, but not essential, if simple and rapid tests can be carried out to check the presence of the active agent in the pool water, or to check its effect; for example, the Redox potential which is used extensively on the continent, but not at all in the United Kingdom; this is a measure of the oxidising action of the sterilising agent.

The two factors on which opinion is most strongly divided are (3) and (6) above, particularly (3). In considering these differences it is important to ensure that all aspects of the water treatment and water circulation systems, as well as pool loading and the habits of the pool users, are taken into account. Unless this can be done, wrong conclusions are likely to be drawn.

In preparing the brief notes which follow on the five methods of water sterilisation listed above, the author has endeavoured to be as impartial as possible. When deciding on which method to adopt in a particular case, different authorities place varying emphasis on the importance of the factors listed under (1) to (6) above. On the Continent considerable importance is attached to pre-cleansing (showers and footbaths), and a highly efficient water circulation system which often involves the daily addition of fresh water to the extent of 10 % of the pool capacity.

Mention was made of the Redox potential, which is a method of measuring the oxidising action of the sterilising agent. The higher the potential the more effective the agent. Standard Redox potentials of halogen and ozone are given below, and the author is indebted to Professor Ing. K. E. Quentin of the Munich Institute of Technology for this information, which was taken from one of his papers, 'Ozone in the Purification of Swimming Pool Water'.

Hypochlorous acid	1·49V
Elemental chlorine	1·36V
Chlorine dioxide	0·95V
Hypochlorite ion	0·94V
Ozone	2·10V

The above readings were taken at 25 °C in 1 molar solutions. The higher the redox potential the more organic matter is oxidised, and this in turn indicates the effectiveness of the sterilising agent in the pool water to destroy pathogens. It has been stated in a German paper by BBR, May 1975, that a slight excess of ozone will give a Redox potential E, of $+800$ mV, against a saturated calomel electrode at pH 7·0.

Ozone

After chlorine, this is the most widely used method for sterilising water in swimming pools. It is particularly popular on the Continent; it is claimed that more than 600 public pools use ozone, and all new public pools in Switzerland use it. In the United States there is considerable enthusiasm for ozone-treated pool water; its growing success there is due largely to the work of the International Ozone Institute.

In the United Kingdom the position is quite different; in 1977 there was only one public pool using ozone, and this was the Valley Leisure Centre at Newtownabbey, near Belfast. However, the author is optimistic that a change is on the way and that during the next decade many public pools will change over to ozone and new pools will be designed with ozone equipment. In fact, four new pools now under construction for the Grampian Regional Council will have the water sterilized by ozone. The three pools in the Andersonstown Leisure Centre, Belfast, originally designed for chlorine sterilisation, will be changed over to ozone; five further pools will be converted during the next few years. Figures 7.11 and 7.14 show the equipment at the Newtownabbey pools.

The author has swum in many pools on the Continent where ozone was used as the sole sterilising agent, and found it a very pleasant experience compared with the heavily chlorinated pools in the United Kingdom.

The following are the principal factors in the use of ozone:

(1) Ozone is a powerful and rapid oxidising agent, more so than chlorine, bromine and metallic ions. Organic contamination in the pool water is therefore oxidised and rendered harmless.

FIG. 7.11.   View of control panel, booster pumps, air drier, etc., at Valley Leisure Centre, Newtownabbey, N. Ireland (Courtesy: Barr and Wray Ltd, Glasgow).

(2) Ozone destroys bacteria and viruses very quickly; this is shown in Fig. 7.12.

(3) The water comes from the treatment plant clear and sparkling, and there are no unpleasant smells and no irritation to the eyes, nose and throat of bathers.

(4) By using ozone as the main sterilising agent, considerable savings can be effected in the cost of operation of the main ventilating and heating system of the pool hall. This is discussed later in this chapter.

(5) The capital cost of the equipment to produce ozone is much higher than that required for effective chlorination.

(6) As ozone is not very soluble in water, and in any case is unstable in water, there is no effective 'residual'. This means that while the water returned to the pool is in a higher state of purity than when chlorination is used, no further disinfection takes place in the pool itself. This can be overcome by the injection of a small quantity of chlorine, and is discussed later in this section.

It must be stated that ozone is highly poisonous but no more so than chlorine, a point which is often omitted in discussions on the relative merits

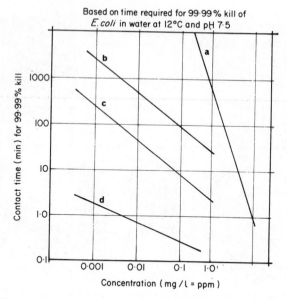

FIG. 7.12. Diagram showing comparison between different methods of disinfecting water; after Butterfield, Ridenour and Wuhrmann (Courtesy: Electricity Council). a: monochloramine. b: silver ions. c: chlorine dioxide. d: ozone.

of the two methods of water treatment. The 'smell threshold' of ozone is about 0·02 ppm.

Ozone is an allotropic form of the element oxygen; the molecule of ozone contains three oxygen atoms instead of the two which comprise the oxygen molecule. It can be produced in various ways, but for water sterilisation it is formed by the passage of an electric current in a special machine; a silent electric discharge through air or oxygen will form ozone. It is not proposed to go into the details of ozone production but some general information is given below. The actual design of the equipment varies considerably from one manufacturer to another, but the basic items are:

(a) Electrodes.
(b) Insulators (or dielectrics).
(c) Equipment for drying the air between the dielectrics.
(d) A fan or water-cooling equipment to reduce the temperature.

The ozone generator operates at a high voltage, often between 5000 and 20 000 V, so that a transformer is required. However, the actual power consumption is small; one figure quoted (by Wallace and Tiernan Ltd) is

1 kWh for the production of 3 g of ozone per hour. As the concentration may be about 1 mg/litre, 3 g would be sufficient for $3 m^3$ of water.

Ozone is also formed from oxygen by high-energy (ultraviolet) radiation. This is how the ozone layer in the upper atmosphere (altitude of 15–30 km) was formed and maintained. This action of ultraviolet radiation on oxygen has been utilised in proprietary equipment to produce small quantities of ozone for the sterilisation of swimming pool water. For maximum ozone production a specific ultraviolet wavelength must be produced by the equipment.

The main argument about the use of ozone for the sterilisation of swimming pool water revolves around the absence of an effective 'residual' in the water in the pool itself. It is accepted that if you start with a pool of clear, pure water, the first bather will introduce contamination even though he may have taken a shower, etc., before entering the pool. In a paper by Alois Heinz, 'Hygiene and disinfection of baths, requirements and practical solutions' (in German), it is stated that each bather introduces into the pool:

(a) Urine: 50 ml.
(b) 0·5–1·0 g of other organic matter.
(c) Micro-organisms: 600 million, including 1–10 million colon bacteria. In healthy people these organisms are harmless; however, no one is medically examined before entering the pool!

The natural reaction to the above is that some form of effective residual disinfectant is needed in the pool itself. However, some authorities (particularly in Switzerland) claim that if the pool is provided with a correctly designed and operated water circulation system, a residual is not essential. The Swiss allow a small excess of ozone to remain in the water as it enters the pool, on the basis that with really efficient circulation the short-lived ozone residual will do all that is required. They are clearly not worried by minute quantities of ozone getting into the air above the pool water surface. On the other hand, in Germany it is required that sterilisation by ozone must be followed by removal of any excess by activated carbon or similar, and then a very small quantity of chlorine (about 0·5 ppm) is injected into the water before it is returned to the pool, so as to give a 'free chlorine residual' of about the same amount, as the water has already been sterilised by the ozone.

Figure 7.13 shows in diagram form the general arrangements of a modern water treatment plant incorporationg ozone generators and associated equipment. A photograph of a complete plant is shown in Fig. 7.14.

It should be noted that the upper part of the multilayer filter (Fig. 7.13) acts as a contact zone to ensure complete oxidation of organic matter and destruction of bacteria and viruses. In the upper part of the filter is a layer of

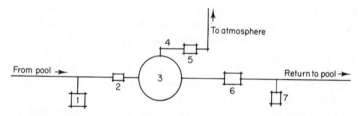

FIG. 7.13. Diagrammatic layout of water treatment plant: 1, ozone generator; 2, mixing device; 3, filter/deozoniser; 4, air vent; 5, activated carbon; 6, heater; 7, hypochlorite dosing (Courtesy: Barr and Wray Ltd, Glasgow).

hydroanthracite which removes excess ozone in the water, and below this is the normal sand filter. The filter is ventilated and the air from the filter passes through activated carbon before being discharged to atmosphere. The hydroanthracite is not used up during the de-ozonising process, but the activated carbon is and therefore has to be renewed from time to time. Chlorine in the form of hypochlorite is injected as shown, and this tends to raise the pH of the water. To correct this, and maintain the pH in the range 7·2–7·8, provision is made for dosing with acid as required. The author feels

FIG. 7.14. View of complete treatment plant incorporating ozone generators, air driers, deozonisers, etc., at Valley Leisure Centre, Newtownabbey, N. Ireland (Courtesy: Barr and Wray Ltd, Glasgow).

that this is a conservative approach to the use of ozone, but there seems little doubt that it is the correct one in the circumstances.

The presence of ozone in pool water can be checked in a similar way to that used for free residual chlorine. Because ozone is unstable in water, the test must be carried out immediately the sample is taken There are two possible tests, one using DPD and the other potassium iodide. Ozone reacts instantaneously with DPD in the presence of potassium iodide to give a stable red colour. With the second practical test, ozone in an acid solution reacts with potassium iodide to release some iodine into solution. The colour of the iodine solution is proportional to the amount of ozone present. Simple comparator discs are available from such firms as Tintometer Ltd. It should be noted that both ozone and chlorine react in exactly the same way with DPD and an acid solution of potassium iodide, and therefore, if chlorine is injected, it will not be possible to determine which is being measured.

Bromine

Bromine is in the same group of elements—the halogens—as chlorine, which it closely resembles in chemical properties. While chlorine is a gas at normal temperature and pressure, bromine is a liquid; its melting point is $-7.3\,°C$ ($18.5\,°F$) and its boiling point is $58.8\,°C$ ($137.8\,°F$). Bromine has a pungent smell and is very soluble in water. It was first used on an experimental scale for the sterilisation of swimming pool water in the early 1930s, but little interest was shown and no real progress made until the middle 1960s. It is now claimed that it is used successfully in many public pools on the Continent and in the United States. In the United Kingdom it has been claimed that bromine forms the sterilising agent for over 300 small to medium pools belonging to private houses, clubs and hotels. So far, no public pools in the United Kingdom use bromine.

Bromine is a strong oxidising agent and a powerful germicide. In solution in water it reacts with ammonia and organic compounds to form bromamines (in a similar way to chlorine forming chloramines). However, it is claimed that the bromamines are equal to bromine in their power to destroy bacteria, whereas chloramines are much slower in their action. In the concentrations used in swimming pools bromine does not cause any irritation to nose, throat, eyes or skin, and gives rise to no objectionable odours. The germicidal effect of bromine and its compounds in water is influenced by the pH. Activity increases with a fall in pH value below 7.0 but there is a marked decrease above a pH of 8.5.

Bromine can be used in swimming pools in two main ways:

(1) By means of liquid bromine dispensed into the pool water through patented equipment. In France this is the 'Bromostat', produced by the Mines de Potasse d'Alsace.

(2) By means of stabilised compounds which liberate bromine when dissolved in water. One such compound is 'Bromalsace SP' (from the manufacturers of the 'Bromostat'); another originates in the United States and is called the 'DI-halo Brominator'.

The use of liquid bromine is only suitable for large installations such as public swimming pools under the control of a trained plant manager. The stabilised compounds can be used quite safely in a similar way to sodium hypochlorite solution. It is claimed that, because of the strong germicidal action of the bromamines, the bromine dosage can be lower than with chlorine, as it is not necessary to use breakpoint bromination. The Conseil Supérieur d'Hygiène Public de France recommend that the bromine level at the outlets of the pool farthest from the inlets should be maintained at 0·4 mg/litre (0·4 ppm). This level can be substantially increased to cope with heavy bathing loads without causing any discomfort to the bathers.

Chlorine Dioxide
In its pure form chlorine dioxide is a heavy yellow gas which is very unstable and can explode violently when heated. Its considerable oxidising properties have been known for more than forty years, but, owing to its instability, this useful characteristic has not been exploited in the field of water sterilisation until fairly recently. The change has come about through patented methods of preparing stable solutions. Chlorine dioxide is usually prepared by the action of hydrochloric acid on sodium chlorite. To ensure that there is no surplus of chlorine and that the maximum amount of chlorine dioxide is obtained from the reaction, an excess of hydrochloric acid is used. For those interested in chemistry, the equations are:

$$2HCl + 4NaClO_2 = 2ClO_2 + NaClO_3 + 3NaCl + H_2O$$

$$5NaClO_2 + 4HCl = 4ClO_2 + 5NaCl + H_2O$$

Two well-known stable forms of ClO_2 are marketed under the names of Ultrazon and Dichlor.

For very small pools it is advisable to use the stable liquid form, and, because of its stability, it is claimed that continuous dosing is not essential. Periodic doses as high as 20 ppm can be used and will remain effective until it is used by reaction with organic matter, etc., in the pool water. However, the author does not favour periodic dosing of any main sterilising agent, as the time for the 'next dose' is often forgotten; continuous injection should always be used.

It is claimed that chlorine dioxide has the following advantages over chlorine:

(*a*) Its oxidising power is greater.

(*b*) It does not form chloramines and gives rise to no unpleasant smell or taste.

(*c*) It does not cause irritation to the eyes, nose and throat.

Some of these claims are disputed: for example, oxidising potential and germicidal properties depend on methods of test. Also, the large quantities of fresh water which are introduced into public swimming pools in Germany and Switzerland are likely to influence the results obtained with chlorine dioxide.

Close pH control is not required, as chlorine dioxide acts in a wide range of pH values (3·0–9·0). However, pH control is likely to be necessary to ensure optimum conditions for filtration. It is usually recommended that the dosage should be such that a residual of 0·1 ppm is maintained in the pool water; this should be increased to 1·0 ppm if there are problems of algae growths.

While chlorine dioxide has a pungent smell, somewhat like chlorine, it is not detectable in concentrations lower than about 50 ppm (the smell threshold).

If chlorine dioxide is used alone, there is a tendency for the pool water to become rather cloudy, the colour varying from 'milky' to 'yellowish-green'. To overcome this, it is normal practice to dose with chlorine from time to time. The frequency of chlorine dosing depends on the bathing load, and can vary from once in a month for a little-used hotel pool to nightly for a heavily loaded public pool. In Switzerland it has been found that an overnight dose of chlorine is sufficient to restore a high standard of clarity. The author has used two pools in Switzerland (one hotel and one public) in which chlorine dioxide with periodic dosing with chlorine was used. In both cases he found the water clear and sparkling without any smell or taste; in other words, very pleasant indeed to swim in.

From the above it can be seen that there are reasonable differences of opinion on some of the practical aspects of the use of chlorine dioxide in public swimming pools in the United Kingdom. It is therefore of particular interest that the new public baths in Varley Street, Manchester, use chlorine dioxide as the sole sterilising agent.

Metallic Ions

The first reference the author has found for the use of metallic ions for the sterilisation water was work by a Dr Krause of Munich in 1929, on what came to be known as the 'Catadyn Silver' process. An account of experimental work on this process is contained in a paper by E. V. Suckling in the *Proceedings of the British Water Works Association* in 1932. It seems to have been used to a limited extent on the Continent for purifying small quantities of water. In the 1960s the author found it being used in a more sophisticated way in the Vellos-Casanovas process for the purification of swimming pool water in a large hotel pool in Switzerland. Swimming in this pool was very pleasant indeed, and a detailed description of the pool was given in the first edition of this book. A brief description of the process follows.

Water is drawn from the pool, and passes through a strainer and then through a series of copper or aluminium plates. A pulsating electric current passes through the plates, which operate on the principle that, owing to the difference in electric potential between the plates, metallic ions are liberated into the stream of water. (Ions are atoms or groups of atoms carrying an electric charge.) The suspended and colloidal matter in the water is attracted to the ions and forms what the patentees term a 'micro-floc'—that is, a much finer floc than that formed by chemical coagulants. This micro-floc penetrates into the body of the filter and does not just form a blanket on the surface, as occurs with a chemically produced floc. The filter is thus used much more efficiently (or so it is claimed) and so the rate of flow can be considerably increased. The standard pressure sand filter operates at 10 000–15 000 litres/m² per hour (200–300 gal/ft² per hour), while by using a micro-floc the same filter can be safely operated at 24 000 litres/m² per hour (500 gal/ft² per hour).

After filtration the water is passed through a battery of silver plates, which are similar to the copper plates for floc formation. The electric current passing through the silver plates liberates silver ions, which have a strong sterilising effect. It is claimed that these silver ions not only effect a 'first kill' of bacteria, but also remain in the water after it has returned to the pool and continue to sterilise the water as fresh contamination occurs from the bathers. In other words, the claim is that they have the same effect as residual chlorine.

This method of treatment does not appear to have been used to any extent in the United Kingdom; in fact, the author knows of only one pool from personal experience. It appears that for effective flocculation and sterilisation the pH of the water must be controlled within fairly narrow limits, and for the average private pool owner this can present problems. However, when properly installed and operated, this method does provide a pool with clear water without any objectionable smell, taste or irritation to the eyes, etc.

There is no simple test for detecting the presence of the metallic ions of copper and silver. It has been claimed that the equipment will ensure that there is about 1 ppm of copper and 0·1 ppm of silver present in the pool water and that this is adequate to deal with bacteria and control algal growths.

Figure 1.10 (p. 18) shows a hotel pool in Switzerland where the water was treated and sterilised by this method.

Ultraviolet Radiation

The fact that ultraviolet radiation is destructive to bacteria has been known since the beginning of this century and was reported in a paper by Cernovodeanu and Henri (in French) in 1910. Since then various papers have been written on the sterilisation of water by ultraviolet radiation, and a few are included in the Bibliography at the end of this chapter.

An essential feature of successful sterilisation is that the ultraviolet radiation must obtain maximum penetration of the water which is being treated. In addition, there is an optimum wavelength band for effecting maximum 'kill' of bacteria and viruses, and this has been established as 2500–2800 Å, which is approximately 250–280 μm.

The advantages of this method are that no chemicals are added to the water; overdosage is impossible; the application is perfectly safe; and, when correctly designed, a very high percentage (over 90 %) 'kill' is obtained. The principal disadvantage is that there is no residual to continue with the disinfection of the water in the pool itself, and the effect of the ultraviolet radiation on the organic compounds introduced by the bathers has not been fully investigated. Nevertheless, the author feels that ultraviolet radiation is an attractive method for private pools, as the smell and irritation due to chlorine does not arise.

The ultraviolet radiation is normally produced by three models namely, low-, medium- and high-pressure mercury vapour discharge lamps. In the United Kingdom models are available which can effectively sterilise water at a flow rate of 2–45 m^3/h (450–10 000 gal/h). It is important to remember that the condition of the water must be such that maximum penetration of ultraviolet radiation can take place. This means that the water must be low in suspended and colloidal matter and very low in certain dissolved salts such as iron and nitrates. Therefore the chemical characteristics of the incoming fresh water must be checked and a highly efficient filter located before the ultraviolet radiation point.

AERATORS

The aerator is a piece of equipment on which there is a wide divergence of views among the 'experts'. Some consider it a most useful and beneficial item in the treatment process, while others feel that it is best avoided and that its alleged benefits are largely illusionary. The object of aeration is to improve the appearance of the water and to give it a bright, fresh and sparkling appearance.

The disadvantages are stated to be:

(a) It reduces the amount of free chlorine in the water (this is open to question).

(b) It may cause corrosion in the heating unit.

(c) There is no detectable difference in the appearance of the water in the pool when the aerator is not working compared with when it is in operation.

Items (a) and (b) can be eliminated if the aerator is located after the heating unit and before the chlorination point. With closed (indoor) pools the aerator generally consists of a closed steel or cast-iron cylinder with an air release valve at the top. The water enters through a Venturi tube (a taper pipe of special dimensions) at the inlet of which there is an intake of compressed air. The vent from the air release valve must discharge to a position where no nuisance will be caused, because in some cases the issuing air contains a higher than average concentration of chlorine. Many managers of public swimming pools have discontinued the use of aerators for this reason and because they tend to get out of order rather easily. In the case of open-air pools the aerator often consists of an attractive fountain or series of fountains or cascades which have some sort of aesthetic appeal to the bathers.

WATER CIRCULATION IN SWIMMING POOLS

There is a great variety of methods for bringing fresh water into the pool and taking the contaminated (dirty) water out. These inlet and outlet arrangements are known collectively as the water circulation system. The most convenient way of describing the various methods is to take the different types of pool and discuss the usual circulation systems used in them.

CONTINUOUS OR INTERMITTENT FLOW-THROUGH WITHOUT TREATMENT
This type of pool is described earlier in this chapter. In pools of this category the flow of water into and out of the pool is generally continuous throughout the whole period the pool is in use. It is just this continuous flow-through of fresh water which enables this type of pool to be used safely. The flow of water may be stopped during the night or at other times when the pool is not in use. The inlet can be a fixed weir for the full length of the short side at the shallow end (assuming the pool is rectangular) or some other convenient place at the shallow part of the pool if the shape is irregular. The important thing is that the weir should be at the shallow part of the pool, where the bathing load will be heaviest; furthermore, the longer the weir the better, since this will give a slower but more even flow. If the intake is from a stream, a lake or the sea, it is then worthwhile to fit a baffle board on the intake side of the weir. The outlet can be either a fixed weir at

the deep end, and as far as possible from the intake weir, or a number of skimmers located at suitable places in the walls. Either of these outlet arrangements can be combined with an outlet through the floor at the deep end (usually in the sump).

Outlets in the floor, because they operate under the head of water in the pool, must be of special design, and are sometimes known as anti-vortex outlets. It is advisable for all outlets except weirs to be fitted with gratings. The outlet weir should be protected by a baffle board. Some details of skimmers are given later in this section (p. 294).

POOLS WITH CONTINUOUS CIRCULATION AND FULL TREATMENT
General Considerations
In these pools the water is continuously circulated through the pool and treatment plant during the whole period the pool is in use. Many authorities recommend that the circulation, including chlorination, should continue even when the pool is not in use (at night). By continuing the circulation in this way the water will be brought to the highest pitch of purity and a 100% 'kill' of bacteria ensured.

It is essential that the inlets and outlets be designed and located so that the circulation is as complete as possible and that pockets of 'dead' water and short-circuiting are eliminated. There should also be no objectionable currents. The methods adopted to achieve this will depend on the size and shape of the pool and the use to which it is put—that is, whether it is a pool used by members of one family and their friends, where the maximum bathing load is likely to be very light, or whether it is a club, school or public pool with very heavy peak loading. Success depends largely on the practical experience of the designer. The system must be in reasonable balance—that is, the withdrawal of water must keep pace with the inflow and vice versa. With heated pools, particularly open-air ones, the even distribution of the heated water throughout the whole pool is most important for the comfort of the bathers.

CIRCULATION SYSTEMS FOR SMALL POOLS
The outlets are either what are known as skimmer-weirs or a scum channel which runs continuously along one or more sides of the pool, combined with an outlet in the pool floor. The author recommends that the circulation should be designed so that not less than 50% of the outflow from the pool is by means of the skimmer-weirs or scum channel, since the maximum contamination is likely to be in the surface layers of the water.

In pools with a clearly defined deep end the heavier bathing load, and, hence, maximum contamination of the water, occurs at the shallow end, and this is the best position for the inlets. It therefore follows that the outlets should be towards the deep end to ensure sufficient circulation in the pool and prevent short-circuiting.

A third method, which in spite of its popularity the author does not recommend, consists of one outlet on the centre line of the pool at the deep end with two or more inlets on the short wall at the shallow end.

Skimmer-weirs (or skimmers) are openings in the walls provided with a fixed or hinged floating weir and a perforated basket or strainer. This is shown in the diagrams in Fig. 7.15. Skimmers also discharge to concealed

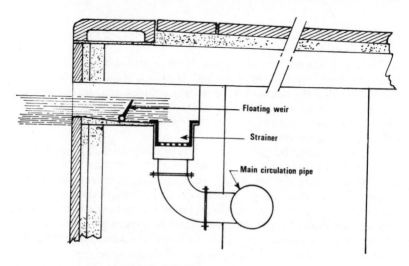

DIAGRAM OF SKIMMER OUTLET

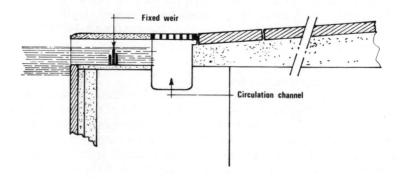

DIAGRAM OF SKIMMER WITH FIXED WEIR FOR DECK LEVEL POOL

FIG. 7.15.   Diagrams of skimmer outlets.

channels which, in turn, discharge to the main circulating pipework. The following are suggestions for number and location of skimmer outlets:

Pool capacity up to 60 m^3 (13 000 gal)
    minimum: two numbers, one on each long wall near the deep end.
Pool capacity 60–85 m^3 (13 000–19 000 gal)
    minimum: three numbers, one at about the centre point of each long wall, and one about the middle of the short wall at the deep end.
Pool capacity 85–125 m^3 (19 000–27 000 gal)
    minimum: four numbers, either two on each long wall towards the deep end, or one about the middle of each long wall and two in the short wall at the deep end, spaced equidistantly.

In addition to the skimmer-weirs, there are sometimes one or more outlets on the longitudinal centre line of the pool, one of which is at the deep end; this is generally located in the sump but must be fitted with an anti-vortex device. A minimum of one floor outlet fitted with an anti-vortex device is recommended.

The author considers that skimmer-weirs are satisfactory only where the peak bathing is not heavy; with a heavy peak load, scum channels should be used. However, there is no doubt that skimmers have definite constructional advantages in free-formed pools of irregular shape, and the initial cost of installation is lower than with scum channels. With irregular-shaped pools, the location of outlets and inlets require special care and experience if an even distribution of incoming and outgoing water is to be obtained.

Scum Channels

The other method of withdrawal of water from the pool is by means of scum or overflow channels. This is the method adopted in most large pools. For the small pools now being considered, a scum channel along the two long walls would be adequate. The scum channel acts as a continuous weir and so provides a very even draw-off. Scum channels can be obtained in various shapes and sizes, and are made in glazed clayware.

The outlets from the channel are usually 50–75 mm (2–3 in) diameter, depending on the length of the channel and its size. Glazed clayware channels have good flow and self-cleaning characteristics. As with skimmer-weirs, at least one outlet in the floor, fitted with an anti-vortex device, is recommended.

Inlets for Small Pools

The recommendations which follow are intended to indicate in a general way suitable numbers and locations of inlets to ensure an even and efficient distribution of purified water in the part of the pool where the bathing load is likely to be heaviest.

The inlet velocity must be low; a figure of $0 \cdot 300 \, m/s$ (1 ft/s) is often recommended, and this requires care in the selection of the diameter of the inlet and design of the spreader:

Pool capacity up to $60 \, m^3$ (13 000 gal)
   minimum: two numbers, located either in the short wall at the shallow end or one on each of the long walls towards the shallow end.
Pool capacity $60-85 \, m^3$ (13 000–19 000 gal)
   minimum: four numbers, two in the short wall at the shallow end and one in each of the long walls towards the shallow end.
Pool capacity $85-125 \, m^3$ (19 000–27 000 gal)
   minimum: eight numbers, two in short wall at the shallow end and three in each of the two long walls.

The recommendations are based on rectangular pools where the length is usually about twice the width. With pools having different length-to-width ratios, or of irregular shape, or shallow pools in which the bathing load is likely to be uniformly spread over the whole pool, different distribution of the outlets would be required to ensure efficient circulation and avoidance of 'dead' pockets and short-circuiting.

CIRCULATION SYSTEMS FOR LARGE POOLS

POOLS FOR CLUBS, HOTELS, SCHOOLS AND LOCAL AUTHORITIES
As mentioned previously, the method adopted for distributing the purified water to the pool and the withdrawal of the contaminated water is of the utmost importance in maintaining the whole of the water in the pool at the required standard of purity, and temperature, if the water is heated.

The need for really efficient circulation within the pool itself is, unfortunately, not generally recognised or accepted in the United Kingdom. Even the latest edition of the official booklet on swimming pool water purification issued by the Department of the Environment deals with circulation as a subject of little real importance. It appears to suggest that shortcomings in the design of inlets and outlets resulting in poor circulation within the pool need cause little concern, as this will be automatically adjusted by the agitation of the water by the swimmers themselves! The author is forced to conclude that the ideas put forward in Section 7 of the booklet do not make a serious contribution to this important and difficult problem.

By contrast, designers of public swimming pools on the Continent pay a great deal of attention to the provision of inlets and outlets to el as this is practical, that:

(a) There are no 'dead' pockets of water.
(b) The surface water (which is known to contain the greatest amount of contamination), is drawn off quickly and efficiently.

In the United Kingdom there is great emphasis on the 'free residual' chlorine; in many cases this requires massive doses of chlorine, with all that this entails in the form of strong smell and smarting eyes. If the polluted surface water is drawn off as quickly as possible, the need for the residual is proportionately reduced. In one public pool in the North of England visited by the author, he found only two outlets, both at the deep end, one in the floor taking about 80 % of the outflow, and the other in the short cross-wall below water level, taking the remainder. On enquiry, he was told that this was part of the 'basic standard design' of the client's architect.

Some fundamental research is obviously needed in the United Kingdom on water circulation in swimming pools; until acceptable methods can be established in this way, the author recommends for public pools:

(a) The outflow should be in the form of a continuous weir extending around the full perimeter of the pool, designed to take not less than 60 % of the circulating water. In addition, there should be at least one outlet in the floor at the deep end to take the remaining 40 %.
(b) An adequate number of inlets, located in the two long walls of the pool, designed so that a comparatively strong jet issues from each. These inlets need not necessarily be all at the same depth below water level; there should be more at the shallow end than the deep end.
(c) An alternative to (b), which may not be so efficient, is to have the inlets positioned longitudinally along the centre line of the pool floor.

For the above to be really effective, information is needed on the circulation induced by the inlets and the perimeter overflow weir.

Provided there are an adequate number of reasonably spaced inlets, deck-level pools are likely to possess a much higher standard of circulation than the normal type of pool. It is obvious that water circulation in free-formed pools will present a more difficult problem than with rectangular pools. It should be possible to produce a practical method of test for the efficiency of a water circulation system. This and all the matters mentioned above require impartial investigation by an organisation such as the Water Pollution Research at Stevenage, the Water Research Association at Medmenham, or the Hydraulics Research station at Wallingford.

The author considers that all pipework should, as far as practicable, be fixed in accessible ducts. If the pool is elevated, this should present no difficulty, but with pools in the ground serious problems can arise. The extra cost of providing the ducts is less than having to tear a pool almost to pieces to get at defective pipework.

With deck-level pools a balancing tank is required to even out variations in the quantity of water leaving and entering the pool. There is no generally recognised method for calculating the size of the balancing tank. Each treatment plant manufacturer produces his own design, and some firms are most unwilling to divulge the details. A reasonable basis for calculation follows:

(a) Allow 70 litres (16 gal) per person for the estimated maximum number of persons using the pool at any one time. Information on methods of calculating pool loading has been given in Chapter 1.

(b) Allow for the quantity of water required to back-wash one filter.

(c) To the total of (a) and (b) add 10 % to cover overflow from the pool due to wave action.

The total of (a), (b) and (c) will give the nett capacity of the balancing tank, and the dimensions can be worked out in the usual way, but an allowance of 300 mm (12 in) should be made for freeboard above top water level in the tank.

The perimeter channel to deck-level pools is large and is covered with a removable grill. This channel should be finished in the same way as the pool itself, i.e. glazed ceramic. The balancing tank can be finished with two coats of chlorinated rubber paint.

The author has given his personal views on water circulation and inlets and outlets to swimming pools. Needless to say, there are many different opinions on this, and water treatment plant manufacturers, tile manufacturers and consulting engineers have all produced designs which are claimed to meet all reasonable requirements. Some of these include special design for the perimeter scum channel.

All gratings and fittings in the pool should be of non-ferrous metal, such as phosphor-bronze, gunmetal or stainless steel (austenitic, type 316 S.16).

With deck-level pools, it is important that the walkways around the pool should drain to a separate channel which discharges to the foul drainage system of the building.

HEATING OF SWIMMING POOLS

GENERAL CONSIDERATIONS

There are very few indoor swimming pools in the United Kingdom and other countries with a similar climate which are not heated, but many open-air pools are without heating. The reason for this is that open-air pools are intended for use only in the summer and apparently the designers (and owners) consider that swimming in nice cool (cold?) water is very pleasant; there is the additional consideration that heat losses from an open-air pool are likely to be appreciably higher than from a covered one. From this it follows that the capital investment for the heating will be utilised for not more than 50% of the period of a covered pool and the operating (principally fuel) costs will be higher per unit of pool capacity (expressed as kilocalories per cubic metre of water or therms per 1000 gallons).

On the other hand, there is no doubt that the provision of heating in an open-air pool not only adds enjoyment to the use of the pool, but also enables it to be used in comfort for a longer period. Since the capital cost of the heating installation is unlikely to be more than 12–15% of the overall cost of the pool (and may well be only 10%), this means that the 85–90% of the capital invested can be utilised for 25–50% longer than if the pool is not heated.

An open-air swimming pool which is provided with an adequate heating system can be used in comfort for 5–6 months of the year in the United Kingdom, whereas a similar pool without heating will have a season not exceeding 3–4 months; and certainly the pleasure of swimming and bathing in such an unheated pool will be appreciably reduced.

In this book 'pool heating' is intended to mean a properly designed and installed heating system connected to the water circulating system of the pool, and this applies irrespective of the size of the pool. This is mentioned because for small private pools it is sometimes suggested that the placing of specially designed heating elements in the pool itself is adequate, but the author is against this, since it is potentially dangerous and very inefficient.

Open-Air Swimming Pools

The calculation of heating requirements for open-air swimming pools is best made on an empirical basis. Any attempt to carry out a refined mathematical analysis is likely to result in a boiler which is either unnecessarily large, or too small for the purpose.

By far the greatest loss of heat is from the surface of the water, with only a small percentage through the walls and floor to the surrounding ground. However, this latter percentage may be substantially increased if the water table is high and is moving. In such a case insulation of the floor and those parts of the walls which are in direct contact with the groundwater may well be justified. The provision of such insulation is even more desirable in cases where a special thermal insulating cover is used over the pool at night and on wet days.

The loss of heat from the water surface depends on a large number of factors all of which are closely associated with weather conditions, such as ambient air temperature, hours of sunshine, wind velocity and relative humidity. These all change not only from day to day, but also from one part

300 SWIMMING POOLS

of the day to another. Therefore, so many assumptions and approxi-
mations have to be made when using formulae which take all these factors
into account that the end result is likely to be appreciably more inaccurate
than using, say, one or two factors put together in one simple formula.

As will be mentioned later, there are two basic methods of providing the
heat energy: direct from the sun's rays (solar heating) or by electricity or
other fuel. The author has never seen detailed calculations for a solar
heating unit, and, therefore, the only calculations given in this book will
relate to heating by electricity, gas and petroleum oil.

The selection of the fuel to use, and, therefore, the type of heating
installation, is usually one of economics.

A simplified calculation will be given to illustrate how to assess the
thermal capacity of the boiler required for a medium-size pool, such as item
2 in Table 1.10. This has a water surface of 133 m² (1436 ft²) and the volume
of water is 160 m³ (35 200 gal). The conversion factors and coefficients used
are given in Appendix 2. The calculation will be presented in Imperial and
SI units, and will show:

(a) Suitable capacity (rating) for the boiler.
(b) Heat input per day to maintain the required water temperature.

Many papers have been written on the various methods which can be
used for determining the size (capacity or rating) of the boiler. The author
prefers to adopt a simple approach by basing this on the heat required to
raise the whole volume of water in the pool at 1·5 °F/h (0·75 °C/h). If it is
assumed that the temperature of the pool water drops 3 °F (1·5 °C)
overnight, then it would take approximately just over 2 h to reach the
required temperature. If a more rapid response is desired, or if it is felt that
the drop in temperature will be greater than 3 °F, and some allowance is
required for heat loss during the heating-up period, then the rating can be
based on a 2 °F (1 °C) rise per hour. This will increase the boiler capacity by
$33\frac{1}{3}\%$, with about a 20 % increase in capital cost. It should be remembered
that at the beginning of the season, or after any significant shut-down
period, the time required to heat the pool to the required temperature will
be proportional to the difference between the initial and final water
temperatures, plus an allowance for heat loss during the warming-up
period. The thermal capacity of the boiler (assumed efficiency of 80 %) is:

Imperial units: $\dfrac{35\,200 \times 10 \times 1\cdot5}{0\cdot80} = 660\,000$ Btu (6·6 therm)

SI units:

$$\frac{160 \times 1000 \times 0\cdot75}{0\cdot80} \times \frac{4\cdot18}{1} = 626\,000\,\text{kJ} = \frac{626\,000}{3600} = 175\,\text{kWh}$$

Add 10% for heat loss during warming-up period; this will give a required heat output from the boiler of 190 kW or 730 000 Btu.

There are two types of gas- and oil-fired boilers, the direct-heating and the indirect or non-storage calorifier. With the direct-heating, the water coming from the boiler should have a temperature not exceeding about 110 °F (43 °C), while with the calorifiers, the water in the calorifier tubes may be 250–350 °F (120–177 °C). For boilers and calorifiers, reference should be made to the following British Standards:

BS 779: Cast-iron Boilers for Central Heating and Hot Water Supply.
BS 853: Calorifiers for Central Heating and Hot Water Supply, Part 1, Mild steel and Cast-iron, and Part 2, Copper.
Code of Practice CP 332, Parts 2 and 3: Central Heating Boilers (Gas-fired).

SOLAR HEATING
In recent years a great deal has been said about the 'energy crisis' and the urgent need to conserve conventional supplies of fuel. This has led to investigations into alternative sources of heat energy, of which the most obvious is the sun. In Israel it has been the practice for many years to use a

FIG. 7.16. View of private pool with solar heating panels (Courtesy: Robinsons Development Ltd, Winchester).

simple type of solar heater, fixed on the roof, to supplement the heat source (electricity, gas or oil) for domestic hot water. The use of solar energy for heating open-air swimming pools has followed as a natural step.

The water in the swimming pool is circulated through a special piece of equipment which is designed to receive and store heat energy from the sun. While it obviously operates at maximum efficiency when the sun is shining from a clear sky, a surprising amount of heat can be obtained on even a cloudy day. This is because the heat rays are able to penetrate through the cloud layer better than radiation in other sections of the solar spectrum.

Various methods have been developed and patented to act as 'solar energy collectors', and the use of solar heating for private open-air pools is increasing fairly rapidly. The real problem is that if a pool owner wishes to be sure that his pool will have a temperature of, say, 24 °C (75 °F) from 08.00 to 20.00 daily throughout the summer season (May to September), then a conventional heating installation (electricity, gas or oil) must be provided in addition to the solar heating. This means increased capital investment, but the solar heating will reduce the fuel consumption by a significant degree. The amount of heat energy required to start up and maintain a small private pool has been calculated approximately in a previous section, and in a good summer it should be possible to save up to 75 % of the fuel bill by the use of solar heating. To obtain the maximum efficiency from such a dual installation, thermostatically operated control valves would be required interconnected with switches controlling the conventional heat source.

Figure 7.16 shows solar heating panels for a private swimming pool.

HEATING THE WATER IN COVERED SWIMMING POOLS
The temperature of the water in covered pools is usually rather higher than in open-air pools. In private house, club and hotel pools the water temperature is often 30 °C (85 °F), but in public pools in the United Kingdom it is usually 26 or 27 °C (78 or 80 °F); on the Continent 28 °C is considered a minimum. The heating of the water and the heating and ventilating of the pool hall are all part of the same problem, and detailed calculations are outside the scope of this book. Some figures on the heat requirements of public swimming pool establishments are given later in this chapter together with some very brief comments on energy conservation.

For comfort, the air temperature in the pool hall should be kept at least 1 °C (about 2 °F) above the water temperature, assuming this is not lower than 26 °C (78 °F). All pool halls are mechanically ventilated (or should be) and the air movement, about 0·20 m/s (40 ft/min), although very slow, does tend to increase evaporation from the skin and so reduce body temperature.

Because the major heat loss from the pool water is from the surface, it is not the practice in the United Kingdom to provide thermal insulation to the walls and floor of the pool itself.

Ventilation and Heating of Swimming Pool Halls and Adjoining Areas

The efficient heating and ventilation of swimming pool halls and the surrounding and connected parts of the building present many problems, not least of which is the capital cost of the necessary equipment and the operating expenses. Owing to the rapid rise in the price of all types of fuel in recent years, attention is now being given to ways and means of reducing energy consumption. This is discussed briefly in the next section. One thing, however, is clear: increase in capital investment in the form of energy-saving equipment should always be given careful consideration, because such equipment may well pay for itself in a matter of a few years.

Another matter of importance is that in the United Kingdom the standard method of sterilising the water in swimming pools is to use chlorine. This creates unpleasant smells in the pool water and also in the air which penetrates to almost all parts of the building and to the outside. The use of ozone in the ventilating system will substantially reduce the air-borne smell, but the air cannot be recirculated, resulting in a great waste of heat.

No one likes to see condensation on walls, windows, etc., but it is an expensive business to eliminate it. Condensation takes place when the temperature of the building surfaces falls below the dew-point of the surrounding air. The principal factors involved are air temperature and pressure and amount of water vapour present in the air. Warm air can contain much more water vapour than cold air, yet appear to be drier.

Mention was made in the preceding section of the need (for the comfort of bathers) to keep the hall air temperature above that of the water. However, a survey carried out by G. D. Braham in 1974/75 showed that only 20 % of the pools sampled maintained a hall air temperature above that of the water. This, combined with the relatively low water temperature, confirms the discomfort experienced by the author when using public swimming pools in the United Kingdom. More important, however, is the fact that this standard of air temperature will increase risk of condensation, which can result in fairly rapid deterioration of roof structures (steel and timber).

To increase the comfort of users of public swimming pools in the United Kingdom, attention should be given to the provision of heated benches around the pool and under-floor heating to the walkway slabs and changing room floors. Under-floor heating in these conditions requires special design and great care in installation.

The details of the mechanical heating and ventilating system vary from one building to another and from one designer to another as it is highly specialised. One system provides for the full heating of the incoming fresh air close to the intake, the heated air being carried by well-insulated ducts to the discharge points. Another system reduces or eliminates the insulation on the main ducts and operates the main heaters at a lower temperature with booster heaters near the discharge points.

The position of inlets and outlets varies greatly. In some designs on the Continent outlets are provided near the water surface of the pool so as to draw off the maximum amount of moisture-laden air; this is of particular importance when chlorine is used as the sterilising agent for the pool water. Generally, in pool halls the inlets for the fresh air are at high level, with the suction outlets at low level. In spite of wide differences in design approach, it is generally agreed that the following basic principles apply:

(a) Condensation should be reduced to the maximum practical extent.

(b) The air pressure in the pool hall should be slightly lower than in the adjoining areas, so as to induce a flow of air towards the pool hall. This will help prevent, but will not eliminate, the diffusion of chlorine smells to other parts of the building when chlorine is used in the pool water. It should be remembered that what is smelt is not free (elemental) chlorine, but chlorine compounds, mostly nitrogen trichloride.

(c) When chlorine is used as the main sterilising agent, the air should not be recirculated, but must be discharged to waste.

(d) In conventional systems heat loss is reduced by double glazing and thermal insulation of external walls and roof, and can be further reduced by means of a 'heat wheel'.

(e) The air changes per hour (ventilation rate) will vary in different parts of the building. For the pool hall the Technical Unit for Sport, in *Design Bulletin No. 1*, suggest that the ventilation should be based on the area of the water surface and surrounding walkways, as it is from these that evaporation takes place. They put forward a figure of $0.015 \, \text{m}^3/\text{s}$ per m^2 of water surface and wet surround. For changing rooms, sanitary accommodation, etc., about eight changes per hour is recommended.

The dangers of condensation have been mentioned before, and roof structures of timber and steel are particularly vulnerable unless special precautions are taken. The author is not in favour of the use of a 'pressurised' roof space which is based on the assumption that air pressure in this space will always be maintained above that in the hall below. The designer cannot control what happens after the building is complete and put into operation. The baths manager has to carry out the instructions of his Committee, who may decide, for reasons of economy, to reduce heating and ventilating costs by shutting down the equipment at night.

When roof structures are hidden behind a ceiling, as is often the case, deterioration can continue unnoticed for a considerable period. There have been a number of failures of roofs over pool halls due to the combined effects of high temperature and humidity and the absence of regular inspections.

HEAT CONSERVATION BY MEANS OTHER THAN THERMAL INSULATION

The Survey of public swimming establishments by Braham, mentioned in the previous section, showed that the pools sampled used on the average 6500 kWh/m^2 of pool surface area per annum. For a pool 25 m × 12·5 m (82 ft × 41 ft), the annual energy consumption is 2 × 10^6 kWh. (6·8 × 10^9 Btu). Many other facts of great interest and importance were brought to light by the Survey and are set out in the paper. The present method of conserving thermal energy in buildings in the United Kingdom and many other countries is to provide thermal insulation in the building structure. So far comparatively little real progress has been made in reducing energy consumption by means of heat reclamation techniques. However, there is a 'wind of change' in this matter, and the next decade will undoubtedly see many developments aimed at conserving and reclaiming heat in buildings of all types.

G. D. Braham has written a number of papers on practical methods of energy-saving and the following information is taken largely from his paper 'Conservation and management of energy'. Two swimming pools in Germany were used as examples of how considerable savings in energy consumption can be effected by the installation of heat pumps. The pools were of identical size and building design. One, at Sinsheim, used a conventional heating and ventilating installation, while the other, at Vaihingen Enz, included internal and external heat pumps. The energy consumption of the two pools was:

(1) Sinsheim: 10 618 kWh/m^2 of pool surface (29·2 × 10^7 Btu/ft^2).
(2) Vaihingen Enz: 2272 kWh/m^2 of pool surface (6·1 × 10^7 Btu/ft^2).

The pool at Vaihingen Enz showed a saving of 78·6% in energy consumption compared with the pool at Sinsheim. Unfortunately, information on the increase in capital investment due to the installation of the heat pumps was not given.

Braham also briefly discusses the question of capital investment for the provision of heat recovery equipment in connection with existing swimming pools. A figure of £7000 per annum at 1975 prices is mentioned as the probable saving on the heating costs for a pool having an area of 400 m^2 (4300 ft^2).

Earlier in this chapter the author discussed in some detail various methods for sterilising swimming pool water, with particular reference to chlorine, ozone and chlorine dioxide. With ozone and chlorine dioxide there are no 'chlorine' smells and therefore the air in the pool hall can be recirculated. The resulting saving in heat output can make a significant

305

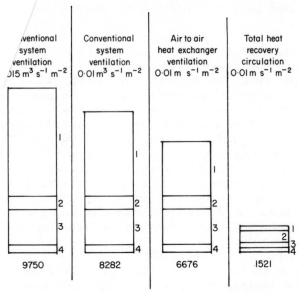

FIG. 7.17. Comparison of annual heat energy losses (kWh m^{-2}) from 25 m covered pool; 1: ventilation loss, 2: fabric transmission loss, 3: hot water service, 4: backwash. (Courtesy: G. D. Braham, Electricity Council).

contribution to the annual fuel bill. This fact should be taken into account when considering the extra capital cost of ozone equipment compared with that required for chlorine.

Figure 7.17 shows annual heat energy losses for a 'standard' swimming pool.

THERMAL INSULATION, ANTI-CONDENSATION, ACOUSTIC TREATMENT FOR SWIMMING POOL HALLS

These three subjects are closely bound together in the materials used for the inside surfaces of walls and ceilings of swimming pool halls. For a height of about 2·0 m (6 ft 6 in) above deck level, the walls should be tiled with glazed ceramic or mosaic, but above this level a different treatment is desirable.

It is most important that the temperature of the surfaces of walls and ceilings should not fall below the dew-point, and this requires good thermal insulating properties (or anti-condensation characteristics). In addition, echo and reverberation must be controlled, and for this to be achieved, the surfaces must possess good sound absorption properties. The presence of large areas of water, glass and hard polished surfaces, such as glazed tiles, causes echo and reverberation, and, of course, the high humidity is ideal for condensation.

In public swimming pools the problem of the transmission of noise from one part of the building to another is generally of less importance than the prevention of echo and reverberation in the hall itself. However, this is not the case with pools in clubs, hotels and, sometimes, schools, when it may be essential to reduce noise transmittance by the maximum possible degree. In some respects the reduction of sound being transmitted from the pool hall to other parts of the building is an easier problem than prevention of echo and reverberation in the pool hall itself. Density and mass are the two main factors in preventing or reducing sound transmission from the hall to other parts of the building.

It is fortunate that many materials which have good heat insulation properties also possess good sound-absorbing characteristics. The whole subject is highly specialised and only a few brief notes and general recommendations can be given here.

All materials used for thermal insulation and acoustic purposes must be unaffected by moisture, heat and chlorine compounds in the atmosphere and condensation water when these are used to sterilise the pool water. For acoustic treatment special blocks of thick perforated ceramic have been used very successfully in many pools on the Continent. If acoustic ceiling tiles are fixed with an adhesive, it is most important that the adhesive should be unaffected by moisture, i.e. it must not be water-sensitive. Any materials which are used for acoustic and thermal insulation are rather easily damaged but are otherwise very effective, and if such a material is chosen, it should only be used at a level of at least 2·0 m (6 ft 6 in) above floor level.

The roofs of public swimming pool halls are often steel trusses, and the space between the ceiling and the rafters is used for the accommodation of ducts and other services. The need for the greatest care and maximum protection of all steelwork has already been emphasised in Chapter 6. It is important that there should be no condensation in this space.

There are a large number of proprietary materials on the market for construction of the ceiling; they should be completely resistant to the air conditions prevailing in the hall and have good acoustic properties. All windows should be double-glazed, because this will reduce heat losses and help considerably in preventing condensation.

Regarding external walls, the use of structural lightweight concrete, either *in situ* or in the form of precast panels, is well worth considering. Another good technique is to use ordinary structural concrete or load-bearing concrete blockwork on the outside with an inner leaf of high-grade insulating material. The value of the use of thermal insulation can be illustrated by one example; a 275 mm (11 in) cavity wall of concrete blocks would have a U-value of, say, 0·35, but the addition of 16 mm ($\frac{5}{8}$ in) of vermiculite plaster would bring this down to 0·26, and 50 mm (2 in) wood wool slabs bonded to the blockwork with 12 mm ($\frac{1}{2}$ in) cement–sand mortar and plastered two coats, would reduce the overall U-value by about 60 % to 0·15. Expressed in simple terms, under the same conditions of internal and external temperature, there is two and a half times as much heat lost through a wall with a U-value of 0·37 as there is through a wall with a U-value of 0·15.

For internal finish, there is a large number of proprietary materials on the market which can be applied by trowel, brush, roller or spray.

Many of these are now based on such materials as vermiculite and resins, whereas until recently asbestos fibre was largely used. Although the latter has proved satisfactory when correctly applied, the present 'panic' against the use of asbestos fibre has made professional men reluctant to specify it.

The material selected should possess good thermal-insulating, sound-absorbing and fire-resisting properties. It must bond strongly to normal building materials and must not be affected by moisture. On the Continent special blocks of perforated glazed ceramic have been used very successfully for acoustic purposes.

When adhesives are used to fix any tiles or sheet material in or adjacent to a swimming pool hall, it is essential that the suppliers give a guarantee that the adhesive will be unaffected by damp; in other words, they must not be water-sensitive.

An excellent decorative material for the dry areas such as changing rooms, offices, café, etc., is 'Prodorglaze Textured Wall Surfacing'. This is basically a high-resin polyvinyl acetate (PVA) and is only supplied by the manufacturers to licensed applicators. It is made in a wide range of attractive colours and is hard-wearing.

While the prevention of condensation is probably one of the most important factors in the overall design of swimming pool halls and adjacent parts of the building containing 'wet' areas, solar heat gain must in some cases be given careful consideration. This may sound strange in a climate such as that in the United Kingdom, but it is nevertheless correct. Flat roofs are particularly vulnerable, also sloping roofs where there is no air space between the ceiling of the rooms below and the roof structure. The provision of thermal insulation on flat roofs is well known, but this can bring its own problems. In many cases a thermal insulating screed is laid on the structural slab. Until this is covered with a waterproof membrane, it is very vulnerable to saturation by rain. If this occurs, a high percentage of its insulating properties are lost. One solution is to use thermal insulation which is impermeable to water. The provision of a light-coloured surface to

FIG. 7.18.   Mastic asphalt roof finished with white Sandtex-Matt, to reduce solar heat gain
(Courtesy: Cement Marketing Co. Ltd).

the roof will reflect a significant amount of solar radiation and thus help to
keep the building cool in hot weather.

Figure 7.18 shows a roof waterproofed with mastic asphalt and finished
with Sandtex-Matt to reduce solar heat gain.

LIGHTING

The intensity of lighting is expressed in lumens (lm) per m^2 or lm/ft^2. The
figure can be readily checked on site by a small pocket-size light meter.

Both natural and artificial lighting should not cause glare or make it
difficult to see bathers in and under the water in the pool. It is most
important that the bottom of the pool should be clearly visible at all times.
Artificial lighting in the pool hall is usually in the form of strip lighting
running longitudinally rather than transversely. Recessed cold cathode
lighting is very effective and is for this reason often adopted. Figure 7.19
shows well-designed lighting in a public swimming pool in London, and
Fig. 7.20 shows the Commonwealth pool in Edinburgh. Well controlled
daylighting is shown in Fig. 7.21.

FIG. 7.19. Cold cathode ceiling lighting giving high level of illumination; all fittings readily accessible from ceiling void (Courtesy: Wingfield-Bowles and Partners, Consulting Engineers).

FIG. 7.20. View of Commonwealth pool, Edinburgh, showing non-glare ceiling lighting (Courtesy: *Swimming Pool Review*).

Fig. 7.21. Well-controlled daylighting in public pool (Courtesy: Walter Holme Ltd, Liverpool).

Levels of illumination vary from one part of the building to another, and from one type of building to another. For small pools 150–250 lm/m^2 (15–20 lm/ft^2) is quite usual and generally satisfactory. For large public pools the requirements are appreciably higher, up to 350 lm/m^2. Changing rooms often have 200–250 lm/m^2.

As with heating and ventilation, lighting is a specialised subject and is best dealt with by experienced consultants. Detailed information on this subject can be obtained from the relevant publications in the Bibliography at the end of this chapter.

BIBLIOGRAPHY

Anon., Investigations about the long term disinfection effect in the water in a swimming pool treated with ozone (not published). *Ozone Blatter*, Switzerland, p. 12.

Anon., Guideline: water treatment for swimming pool water, June 1972. *Archiv des Badewesens*, **29**, No. 4, (April 1976) 148–58; Construction and operation of swimming pool water treatment plants according to the 'Guideline'. *Archiv des Badewesens*, **29** (April 1976) 168–78 (both in German).

ANON., Solar heating. *Pool News*, July, 1974, pp. 17–24.

ANON., Product profile, simple chlorine dioxide production process. *Effluent Water Treatment J.*, **15**, No. 6 (June 1975) 1.

ANON., Solar collectors, AJ Information Library, *Architects J.*, 20 July 1977, pp. 123–36.

BARTON, J. J., *Electric Floor Warming*, George Newnes Ltd, London, 1967, p. 376.

BBR (Brunnenbau, Bau von Wasserwerken, Rohrleitungsbau), **26**, No. 5, (May 1975) 63–165 (in German).

BRAHAM, G. D., Conservation and management of energy. Paper presented at Annual Conference of Institute of Baths Management, 1975, p. 22.

CARTER, HON. MRS H., The use of solar energy for heating swimming pools. Paper presented at 2nd Annual Conference, Swimming Pools & Allied Trades Association, Brighton, 1973, p. 3.

CARTER, HON. MRS. H., Efficient and inefficient ways of heating pools by solar energy collectors. *Building Services Engineer*, **41** (Aug. 1973) 101–6.

CHARTERED INSTITUTE OF BUILDING SERVICES, IHVE Guide, booklet edition, in three sections and 35 booklets.

COURTNEY, R. G., *An Appraisal of Solar Water Heating in the UK*, Current Paper Cp. 7/76, Building Research Establishment, p. 8.

COURTNEY, R. G., *Solar Energy Utilisation in the UK: Current Research and Future Prospects*, Current Paper CP. 64/76, Building Research Establishment, p. 7.

COX, G. E. Water purification and heating equipment for domestic swimming pools. Paper presented at Symposium *Engineering in the Home*, Inst. Heating and Ventilating Engrs, London March 1969, p. 15.

DELAINE, J., Water conditioning without chemicals, the Vellos–Casanovas process. *Swimming Pool Review*, London, June 1967.

DEPARTMENT OF THE ENVIRONMENT, *The Purification of the Water of Swimming Pools* HMSO, London, 1976, p. 51.

DOE, L. N., GURA, J. H. and MARTIN, P. L., Building services for swimming pools. *J. Inst. Heating Ventilating Engrs*, **35** (Dec. 1967) 261–86.

EICHELSDORFER, D., SLOVAK, J., DIRNAGL, K. and SCHMID, K., Study of eye irritation caused by free and combined chlorine in swimming pool water. *Archiv des Badewesens*, **29**, No. 1 (Jan. 1976) 9–13 (in German).

ELPHICK, A., The treatment of swimming pool water with chlorine dioxide. *Baths Service*, July 1973, pp. 254–6.

ELPHICK, A., The use of ozone in swimming pool environment, *Baths Service*, Dec. 1969, pp. 179–94.

ELPHICK, A., *The Treatment of Swimming Pool Water with Sodium Hypochlorite*. Wallace and Tiernan, Tonbridge, 1978, p. 18.

EMMETT, J. R. and GRIFFITHS, B. K., Practical experience using various types of precoat filter media. *Proc. Soc. Water Treat. Exam.*, **16** (1967) 238–59.

FISCHER, L. J., Indoor swimming pools and public baths, Parts 1, 2, 3 and 4. *The Heating and Ventilating Engineer and Journal of Air Conditioning*, June, July, August and September, 1958, pp. 614–8; 22–7; 69–72; 140–7, respectively.

GARDEN, G. K., *Indoor Swimming Pools*, Canadian Building Digest, November 1966, CBD 83, p. 4.

GREATER LONDON COUNCIL, *Trial use of solar heating for a learner swimming pool.*
Bulletin No. 108 (2nd Series), Aug./Sept. 1977, pp. 7/1–7/5.
HENDRY, I. W. L., Design of roofs and walls to minimize condensation effects.
Paper presented at *Symposium on Aspects of Swimming Pool Design*, Building
Research Establishment, East Kilbride, June 1973, p. 5.
HEINTZ, A., Hygiene and disinfection in baths—requirements and practical
solutions. *Archiv des Badewesens*, **28**, No. 12 (Dec. 1975) 578–81 (in German).
HOATHER, R. C., The penetration of ultra-violet radiation and its effect on waters. *J.
Inst. Water Engrs*, **9**(2) (March 1955) 191–207.
ILLUMINATING ENGINEERS SOCIETY, *Lighting Guide for Sport*, London, 1974.
INSTITUTION OF ELECTRICAL ENGINEERS. *Regulations for the Electrical Equipment
of Buildings*, Latest edition, London, 1966, p. 236.
INSTITUTION OF WATER ENGINEERS, Symposium on the sterilisation of water. *J. Inst.
Water Engrs*, **IV**(7) (November 1950).
LANGLIER, W. F., The analytical control of anti-corrosion water treatment. *J.
American Water Works Assoc.*, **28**(10) (Oct. 1936) 1500–21.
MALPAS, J. F., *The Chemical and Bacteriological Purification of Swimming Bath
Water*, Technical Publication No. BRA-331, September 1967, Wallace and
Tiernan Ltd, England, p. 19.
MALPAS, J. F., The possibilities of bromination in swimming bath water. Paper
presented to the 33rd Annual Conference of the Institute of Baths Management,
1963.
MCVEIGH, J. C., Some experiments on heating swimming pools by solar energy. *J.
Inst. Heating Ventilating Engrs*, **39** (June 1971) 53–69.
MILBANK, N. O. *Energy Consumption in Swimming Pool Halls*, Current Paper
CP. 40/75, Building Research Establishment, p. 10.
MILBANK, N. O., Ventilation and humidity control. Paper presented at *Symposium
on Aspects of Swimming Pool Design*, Building Research Establishment, East
Kilbride, June 1973, p. 11.
NORDELL, E., *Water Treatment for Industrial and Other Uses*, 2nd edition, 1961,
Reinhold, New York and Chapman and Hall, London, p. 598.
PALIN, A. T., Methods for the determination in water of free and combined
available chlorine, chlorine dioxide, chlorite, bromine, iodine, and ozone using
diethyl-phenylene diamine. *J. Inst. Water Engrs*, **21**(6) (1967) 537–48.
QUIROUETTE, R. L., Solar heating—The state of the art. *Building Research Note*,
No. 102, Ottawa, Oct. 1975, p. 11.
SCOTTISH SPORTS COUNCIL, THE, *Ozone and Heat Recovery* (unpublished), March
1977, p. 18.
URQUHART, I. A., The use of ozone in swimming pools. *Baths Service*, **35**, No. 2, pp.
22–3.
WHITLOCK, E. A., The chlorination of water. *J. Inst. Public Health Engrs*, **53**(2)
(April 1954) 61–74.

CHAPTER 8

Maintenance and Repairs to Swimming Pools

THE MAINTENANCE OF SWIMMING POOLS AND SWIMMING POOL EQUIPMENT

GENERAL CONSIDERATIONS

This part of the chapter is intended more for the private pool owner and managers of hotel, club and school pools where full-time technical personnel are not usually available for supervision, maintenance and repair work. No hard and fast rules can be laid down for frequency of cleaning the pool, since this will depend on many factors, of which the following are the more important:

(*a*) Whether the pool is open or closed.

(*b*) If open, the type of surroundings, e.g. presence or otherwise of trees.

(*c*) The bathing load characteristics throughout the period the pool is in use, including type of user.

(*d*) The length of time the pool is in use each day.

(*e*) The efficiency of the water treatment plant.

(*f*) The type of finish given to the inside of the pool.

(*g*) Whether chemicals such as aluminium sulphate (alum) and sodium carbonate (soda ash) are used in the treatment process.

In these days of financial stress people are becoming more conscious of the cost of maintenance. Generally speaking, the lower the initial cost of the pool shell, finishes and equipment, the higher will be the cost of maintenance and operation, and the greater the risk of breakdowns. Prospective pool owners should realise that there is no such thing as a fully automatic pool. It is most advisable that the pool and equipment should be inspected every day the pool is in use. Most private pools in the United Kingdom are open-air and therefore the wear and tear on the pool itself is much more severe than with a covered pool.

All reputable pool contractors and suppliers of equipment provide fully detailed instructions for operation, servicing and maintenance, and these should be carefully followed. Generally, the maintenance schedule for a private pool can be divided into four sections. Sections (1) to (3) apply to both open-air and closed pools, while section (4) applies only to open-air pools.

(1) A visit should be paid every day to the plant room to check the equipment. Following this the pool water should be tested for 'free' chlorine and pH. A free-chlorine residual of 1·0 ppm and a pH in the range 7·2–7·8 will be satisfactory for most pool waters, and this should ensure a clear odour-free water. All pool owners should have a copy of the Wallace and Tiernan *Handbook of Pool Water Care*. The pool should be cleaned frequently. Leaves and ferrous objects will very quickly stain a Marbelite finish, and these stains are almost impossible to remove. A watch should be kept for algal growths both in the pool and on the surrounding paving. Methods for dealing with this problem are given later in this chapter.

(2) The checking and servicing of all equipment should be carried out as recommended by the suppliers. The details depend on the equipment installed, but will include cleaning the strainer on the pump inlet and back-washing the filter. Chemicals for water treatment and such items as fuse wire should not be allowed to go out of stock. Frequent blowing of a fuse indicates that something is wrong, and this should be attended to.

(3) The owner may wish to close the pool for a limited period; the procedure to be followed will depend largely on the expected duration of the shut-down. The pool should be cleaned and given a heavy dose of chlorine (or bromine if this is used for sterilisation), and the cover placed in position if it is an open-air pool. The main switch should be closed and the fuses removed. All containers holding chemicals should be carefully closed, and ventilation ensured for the plant room. Unless the shut-down is likely to be quite short, the recommended winterisation procedure for the water sterilisation equipment should be followed. Plant rooms are often cold and rather damp, and electrical equipment is vulnerable to moisture.

(4) The two important parts of winterisation are the closing down and the opening up. An excellent booklet on this subject is available from the Swimming Pool and Allied Trades Association (see Appendix 4). The most important points include the following:

(a) The pool should not be left empty during the winter. The pool should be thoroughly cleaned and given a heavy dose of algicide, and then covered; the water level should be just below the outlet. The provision of a perimeter 'buffer' consisting of thick timber or similar to reduce ice pressure on the walls is recommended. If the pool has a PVC lining, timber should not be used. It is important that the 'buffer' should extend below the water surface by at least 40 mm ($1\frac{1}{2}$ in), so that ice will not form below it.

(b) An alternative to (a) and one which will give better results is to keep the whole installation 'ticking over' during the winter, with the heater operating in periods of freezing weather. However, even in this case the winter period should be started with a clean pool.

(c) For a complete close-down, all pipework, the filter and the heater should be drained and the chlorinator disconnected and washed out. Unless the plant room is well ventilated and comparatively warm, it is better if the pump, motor, heater and chlorinator are removed to a dry warm store. All switches must be left in the off position and all fuses removed.

(d) Pool equipment should be properly stored, and it is advisable to remove the diving board. All ferrous fixtures should be cleaned and well greased.

(e) When starting the next season, the pool should be emptied and cleaned, grease removed from all fittings, and rust completely removed before repainting. If the pool is to be repainted, all old paint must be removed.

The whole installation should be given a trial run well in advance of the 'opening party'.

PREVENTION AND REMOVAL OF ALGAL GROWTHS

The situation may arise when, in spite of all normal precautions, a growth of algae occurs in the pool or on the surrounding paving. Apart from general objections, algal growth on paving where bathers walk with wet feet can be dangerous, since it may cause excessive slipperiness even though the paving was originally non-slip. If the water is filtered and continuously chlorinated so that a minimum free-chlorine residual of 1 mg/litre (1 ppm) is maintained in the pool, there will be little chance of algae breeding. However, if, despite all reasonable precautions, algae or similar growths do start to establish themselves, a powerful algicide must be used, and the sooner this is applied the better. If ultra-violet rays are used for sterilisation of the pool water, then special precautions will have to be taken to prevent algal growths.

There are a large number of proprietary compounds on the market, but the author recommends the use of proved basic chemicals (which are at least equally effective) at a much lower cost. One of the best is copper sulphate, since it is both safe to use and effective. The dosage required depends on the hardness and the temperature of the water. For a warm soft water, about 0·30 mg/litre (0·30 ppm) of copper is required. This is equivalent to 1·2 mg/litre of copper sulphate crystals ($CuSO_4 . 5H_2O$). For a cool hard water as much as 2·5 mg/litre of copper (10 mg/litre of copper sulphate crystals) may be needed. Copper sulphate can be obtained from such firms as ICI, British Drug Houses Limited and Monsanto Chemicals.

For dealing with algal growths above the water line and on paving, a thorough brushing with strong copper sulphate solution or calcium hypochlorite (bleaching powder) will be effective. Stronger algicides are based on highly poisonous compounds of mercury, arsenic and tin, and the author does not recommend their use unless the work is done under continuous and trained supervision. Careless use can lead to very serious consequences. When water for the pool is drawn direct from a river or lake, it may be advisable to treat it with chlorine or copper sulphate prior to filtration.

The following is a short explanation of proportions expressed as mg/litre and parts per million (ppm): mg/litre is milligrammes per litre, which means the same as parts per million (ppm); in other words, 1/1000 of a gramme in one litre of water. As a litre of water weighs one kilogramme (1000 grammes) this is the same as 1 gramme of the compound dissolved in 1 million grammes (1000 kilogrammes) of water. One cubic metre of water weighs 1000 kilogrammes, so that the quantity required can be calculated very easily if metric units are used. In Imperial units the calculation in this particular case is also simple because one gallon of water weighs approximately ten pounds; therefore a concentration of 1 ppm is 1 lb dissolved in 1 million pounds of water, which is equal to 100 000 gallons. Concentrations in liquids are always by weight.

SLIPPERY PAVING

Occasions sometimes arise when paving is found to be slippery; this may be due to a wrong selection of paving material in the first place or to excessive wear of a rather soft or poor-quality paving which was non-slip when it was first laid. The methods described here can be applied to natural stone and cementitious paving such as concrete (*in situ* and precast) and terrazzo. With other proprietary paving the manufacturers should be consulted. The methods are:

(*a*) Acid etching.
(*b*) Hacking, mechanical scabbling, grit blasting or high-velocity water jetting.
(*c*) Application of a new non-slip coating.

For natural stone paving only methods (*b*) and (*c*) should be used; all three can be used on concrete; for terrazzo, only (*c*).

Acid Etching

It is generally better to try this method first, as it is easier and cheaper than either (*b*) or (*c*), and even if the concrete is on the thin side, it is unlikely to do any basic damage to it. Dilute hydrochloric acid should be used: one part of commercial grade acid with 8–10 parts of water. Rubber gloves and an eye-shield should be worn and the work carried out with care. The dilute acid should be poured over a small area at a time and brushed in and allowed to remain for about 10 min before being washed off with plenty of water. The acid attacks the cement paste and exposes the aggregate, unless the aggregate itself is limestone, in which case that will also be attacked. If the exposure is insufficient to give the required degree of 'non-slip', then the process should be repeated, until the result is satisfactory. The concrete must be well washed down with water after each application of acid. Acid etching should not be used on terrazzo, as the aggregate is marble and will be attacked by the acid, and method (*c*) is recommended. With a normal limestone aggregate concrete, method (*b*) or (*c*) can be used.

Fig. 8.1.   Non-slip grooved surface to pool surround (open-air).

Hacking, Scabbling, Grit-blasting, and High-velocity Water Jets
Owing to the vibration set up, hacking and scabbling should only be used on good-quality concrete of adequate thickness. Recommended minimum thicknesses are:

Precast pressed paving slabs: 50 mm (2 in).
In situ paving: 75 mm (3 in).

It is not possible to give a thickness for natural stone slabs and ordinary hand-made concrete slabs, and the use of percussion tools on these is better avoided. The use of high-velocity water jets has been briefly described in Chapter 6; it is very efficient but is only justified when a large area is involved. This type of work should be carried out with care owing to possible damage to the paving. Figure 8.1 shows a non-slip grooved surface formed with special equipment.

Application of Non-slip Coating
A non-slip surface can be obtained by the application of a chlorinated rubber paint or epoxide resin, followed by a sprinkle of fine sand before the paint/resin has hardened.

REPAIRING LEAKS IN SWIMMING POOLS

It is hoped that if the advice previously given in this book is followed, there will be no leaks or other defects, but there are many structures built years ago which are in various ways defective and, of course, mistakes can always happen and careless work can occur on any site. It is intended to outline the various types of defects, discuss the tracing and location of leaks and give detailed recommendations for repair. Defects in pipework, installations and equipment are not dealt with, since this work can follow normal repair practice.

DESCRIPTION OF PRINCIPAL TYPES OF DEFECTS
The information which follows applies in a general way to new swimming pools and to existing ones. Leaks are usually due to cracks in the floor or walls which extend for the full thickness of the structure; there may also be leakage through areas of porous or honeycombed concrete. The leakage may be either outwards from the pool to the surrounding ground, or take the form of ingress of groundwater into the pool when the latter is partially or completely empty.

When the groundwater level is above the floor of the pool, equilibrium is sometimes reached; that is, the water level in the pool drops down until it is level with the water table outside and then remains steady. If the pool is

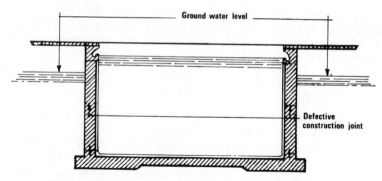

FIG. 8.2. Section through pool showing defective joints in walls.

emptied, then it would eventually fill up by seepage into the pool until the same level is reached. This is shown diagrammatically in Fig. 8.2. There are many reasons for leaks occurring, but the principal causes are as follows:

(*a*) Error in the structural design of the floor or walls (usually the latter) so that they are not strong enough to withstand the loads on them; these loads consist of pressure from the ground, and groundwater on the outside when the pool is empty, and water pressure on the inside when the pool is full. This is probably the most serious type of defect and is very expensive to remedy (can apply to both new and old pools).

(*b*) Settlement of the pool shell due to ground movement, resulting in cracking of the floor or walls or both; this is also expensive to remedy (generally applicable to older pools); shrinkage of clay during a long dry summer can cause severe cracking.

(*c*) Thermal and/or drying shrinkage stresses in the concrete exceeding the strength of the concrete in tension, resulting in cracking. Repairs are generally easy to carry out and not expensive, except where there is seepage into the pool from the surrounding ground (usually applies to new pools).

(*d*) Poor-quality concrete or careless work resulting in either:

(*i*) Weak and porous areas of concrete (honeycombing).
(*ii*) Inadequate preparation or sealing of the construction joints in walls and floor. Leaks at 'lift lines' in walls are one of the most common faults, and such defective areas are very vulnerable when there is a high water table, as the inside rendering is then of little help because it tends to be forced off the wall. (This generally applies to new pools.)

The cost of repairs will depend entirely on the extent of the defects and also whether there is leakage into the pool from the outside.

LOCATING AND DIAGNOSING LEAKS
Locating Leaks

Unfortunately, there is no simple and practical method of locating leaks in a pool in those cases where the water is escaping outwards into the ground and there are no visible defects on the inside of the pool. From time to time ingenious suggestions are put forward for using dyes, concentrations of salt or radioactive tracers. These may be useful in certain special cases such as where the water table is below the floor of the pool and the leak(s) is (are) large particularly if it is in the sump or a pressure relief valve. But to trace the dye, salt concentration or radioactive tracers necessitates taking out inspection pits at frequent intervals right round the pool down to the underside of the oversite concrete below the floor. Unfortunately, if the leak is towards the middle of the floor, the method does not work. Furthermore, it must be remembered that dyes will stain the surface of the walls and floor of the pool, which in most cases would be unacceptable. If the pool is new and the back-filling around the outside of the walls has not been carried out, then leaks in the walls are readily detected, but leaks through the floor are particularly difficult to trace.

The difficulty in tracing leaks is one of the principal reasons why the pool shell should be tested before any decorations or tiling is applied, and before placing the back-filling around the walls. While each case should be treated on its merits, and unless it is obvious where the leak is occurring, it is generally advisable to follow some basic procedure, as this will usually save time in the long run. Recommendations for this are:

(1) The pool should be filled to top water level and all inlet and outlet valves turned off.

(2) If the pool is emptied by gravity, the first manhole on the outlet drain should be checked for signs of seepage.

(3) The fall in water level should be measured over a period of not less than 24 h. The actual test period will depend on the severity of the leak, and by allowing a period of several days, even up to two weeks, useful information can be obtained. The drop in level should be measured at not more than 24 h intervals.

(4) A check should be made on the outlet pipelines.

For example, if the water table is below the floor level of the pool and over a period of a week the water level in the pool drops 1 ft, with the rate falling off towards the end of the week, this would indicate that the leak was about 1 ft below the top water level in the pool. A close inspection of the walls at this level is likely to reveal the defect. As previously mentioned, the most likely places for leaks are at construction joints, and these should always be carefully examined, particularly the one between the floor and wall, because it is here that stress is at a maximum.

Diagnosing the Leaks

Having located the leak, a decision must be taken as to which type it is before the method of repair can be decided on.

Repairs to leaks of type (*a*), caused by an error in design, are very difficult to deal with and advice should be obtained from a civil or structural engineer. This type of defect would be characterised by horizontal and/or diagonal cracking in the wall(s) or displacement from the vertical of one or more of the walls accompanied by serious cracking. Structural defects in the floor slab are less likely, but may occur if allowance has not been made for uplift in the middle of the slab in the case of a deep pool in ground with a high water table.

Defects of type (*b*) are due to settlement or expansion of the ground. In clay soil, expansion can cause intense pressure. Clays expand when they become wet and contract on drying. In certain clays pressure from the expansion of the soil on the walls and foundations may exceed $430 \, \text{KN/m}^2$ (4 ton/ft^2). There is no typical position or direction for cracks caused by ground movement.

Cracking due to thermal stresses and drying shrinkage (type (*c*)) is generally less serious than the two types previously mentioned, since the cracks are usually very fine—0·125–0·50 mm (0·005–0·02 in) wide. Both types are often self-sealing over a period of 1–2 weeks if the pool is kept full. In walls they are usually more or less vertical and occur within the middle third of the panel, starting near the base and running upward to about two-thirds of the height of the wall. In floors these cracks generally extend transversely across the bay(s). Cracks due to thermal stresses occur within the first few days after casting, and are often present when the formwork is removed, while those due to drying shrinkage may appear after several weeks.

While porous areas and honeycombing (type (*d*) defects) are usually clearly visible on the surface, they are sometimes covered by a thin skin of laitance which makes them difficult to detect. Leaks at horizontal construction joints (lift lines) in walls are generally easy to find because the water level falls to that level and then remains steady, but if the leak is in a vertical joint, this is more difficult to locate and careful examination may be needed. Fine cracks and porous areas tend to dry out slowly; by wetting the surface with a hose and then allowing it to dry, these defects will often stand out quite clearly. Tests with a Schmidt hammer can be useful.

Leaks through floors, except where there are visible cracks or obviously defective areas, are always difficult to trace. For pools constructed below groundwater level, under-drainage of the site is strongly recommended if the drains can discharge by gravity to a natural outfall. This has been discussed in Chapter 4. The presence of these under-drains can be a great help in locating a leak in the floor. The author had an opportunity of seeing how the exact location of a leak in the floor of a diving pool was determined by means of the under-drainage system. This system had been properly laid with necessary inspection chambers. During the water test, the diving pool lost water, and when it was emptied, the place of leakage could not be found. The contractor then decided to flood the under-drainage system, with the result that the water level in the inspection chambers was raised several feet, thus providing a head of water beneath the floor of the pool. Very soon water was observed seeping through the floor in one small area, and when this was cut out, it was found that a short length of reinforcing steel had inexplicably got completely out of position and was lying more or less vertically right through the floor slab. The concrete around the bar was slightly honeycombed and was sufficiently weak to permit leakage under pressure. These details are given to show how use can be made of facilities intended for quite a different purpose.

One way of locating honeycombed or weak porous areas is to use a Schmidt rebound hammer. This consists essentially of a spring-loaded plunger inside a cylinder. When the spring is released, the hammer (plunger) is propelled with considerable force against the concrete and the rebound of the hammer, which is shown on a graduated scale, is an indirect measure of the strength of the concrete. Good-quality concrete will give appreciably higher rebound numbers than weak concrete. A detailed description of this useful instrument is given in a paper by J. Kolek in the *Magazine of Concrete Research*, Vol. 10, No. 28, March 1958. Further information is given in Appendix 6.

REPAIRING LEAKS

A fundamental point about carrying out any repairs is that if groundwater is entering the pool, the inflow must be sealed off by plugging or other means before any surface repairs or coatings are applied. If extensive repairs are required it may be necessary to lower the water table below the level at which repair work has to be carried out.

Another matter of importance that applies to all repairs is that the existing concrete surface against which new concrete, mortar or any coating is to be placed must be thoroughly cleaned, i.e. all dirt, vegetable matter, old decorative materials and coatings must be removed.

The plugging of leaks against water pressure is easy in theory but not necessarily so in practice. On important jobs even large and experienced contracting firms often prefer to call in the services of a specialist subcontractor who will usually do the work under guarantee, but at his own price.

Quick-setting, in some cases almost instantaneous-setting, compositions are manufactured by well-known firms but require skilled application.

The three basic methods of dealing with the infiltration of groundwater are:

(a) To plug the leak(s) with an ultra-rapid-hardening cement or resin.
(b) To pressure grout the subsoil.
(c) To lower the groundwater level by well-point dewatering or pumping from sumps, and to carry out the repair work in the dry.

Of the three, method (a) is the one most frequently adopted, since it is usually quicker and cheaper because the contractor may guarantee the work and give a fixed price. With pressure grouting of the subsoil, a fixed price will not be given, nor will the work be guaranteed. Lowering the groundwater table is adopted only when extensive repairs have to be carried out.

Repairing Leaks Caused by Error in Structural Design or Settlement of Pool Shell

Before carrying out the repairs to the cracks caused by structural failure of the pool shell, consideration must be given to the strengthening of the pool; the services of an experienced engineer may be required if the pool is a large one. It is quite useless to spend money on patching up cracks of this type without remedying the basic structural defects; otherwise they are certain to open again. It is not practical to give detailed directions for such structural repairwork, since no two cases will be the same. However, some of the common methods adopted are:

(i) External piers or buttresses of reinforced concrete bonded into the walls.

(ii) An internal lining of reinforced gunite; or new walls and floor of in situ reinforced concrete constructed inside the existing pool shell. The new in situ concrete may or may not be bonded into the old concrete according to the structural design of the new work.

(iii) A combination of external piers or buttresses and internal gunite lining.

(iv) Providing a new independent inner pool shell of aluminium.

In any case the larger cracks should be cut out and repaired, and for these repairs gunite is very effective. All rust must be removed from the reinforcement by wire brushing or grit blasting and the cleaned reinforcement treated with a rust inhibitor. For the best results it is advisable to employ a contractor who has specialised in this type of work, since both care and experience are needed at all stages.

Gunite is a pneumatically applied mortar; the usual mix proportions are one part of ordinary or rapid-hardening Portland cement and three parts of specially graded concreting sand by weight. The water is added at the gun nozzle by the operator. If the repair consists of external piers or buttresses, then it is generally better if these are constructed first and the cracks repaired afterwards. A new lining to the whole of the inside of the pool is desirable if the cracking is at all extensive. Some detailed information on linings is given later in this chapter. From the above it can be seen that repairs of this nature are very expensive, and for small pools it is often quicker and cheaper to demolish the pool and build a new one.

Repairing Non-structural Cracks

As previously stated, cracks of this type are usually quite narrow and are in fact often self-sealing over a period of a few weeks if the pool is kept full. There are four basic methods of repair:

(*a*) By cutting out the crack in the pool shell to form a V and filling this with a high-quality mortar.

(*b*) Crack injection using polymer resins.

(*c*) Repair where flexibility is required.

(*d*) The application of a polymer resin (epoxide or polyurethane) by brush or spray, with or without glass-fibre mesh reinforcement; or the application of a proprietary 'bandage'.

While the method selected should be chosen on technical grounds, in practice the importance and cost of the job will influence the final decision.

The first point to consider is whether further movement across the crack is likely to occur; this will only apply to cracks which penetrate the full thickness of the wall or floor. With shallow cracks, the width and actual depth are important.

Method (*a*): This method is suitable when no further movement across the crack is anticipated, where the crack is at least 1 mm ($\frac{1}{25}$ in) wide, and where crack injection is not considered practical (possibly on grounds of cost). The concrete should be of reasonably good quality; otherwise cutting out the crack may cause considerable damage.

The crack is widened to about 12 mm ($\frac{1}{2}$ in) wide at the surface and to a depth of about 25–30 mm ($1–1\frac{1}{4}$ in), the cut being in the form of a V. All grit and dust must be removed and the surface wetted, preferably overnight. The cut-out section is then carefully filled with cement–sand mortar, gauged with a styrene butadiene latex emulsion. The mortar should be as stiff as practical and must be well pressed into the groove. The mix proportions are 1 part OPC to 3 parts clean building sand, with about 9 litres (2 gal) of latex to 50 kg of cement. If the concrete is of somewhat poor quality, a slightly leaner mix (1:3·5 or 1:4) should be used. To help improve bond between the mortar and the base concrete, the surface of the groove can be given a brush coat of grout made up with 2 parts OPC and 1 part latex, i.e. 25 litres (5·5 gal) of emulsion to a 50 kg bag of cement. The mortar must be applied within 15 min of the application of the grout. The mortar in the cracks should be covered with polyethylene sheets for 4 days, care being taken to prevent wind blowing underneath the sheets. As long as possible after the filling of the cracks (i.e. before the pool is refilled or decorated), two good brush coats of grout should be applied to the repaired areas extending well over onto the old concrete. The grout should be 2 parts OPC to 1 part SBR latex emulsion (50 kg OPC to 25 litres emulsion).

Method (*b*): Crack injection using polymer resins is particularly useful when it is desired to strengthen the wall or floor, as the resin will bond strongly to the concrete on both sides of the crack. This technique is highly specialised and is described in some detail in the author's book *Concrete Structures: Repair, Waterproofing and Protection*. When properly carried out by specialist firms, it can be very effective. Resins can be formulated

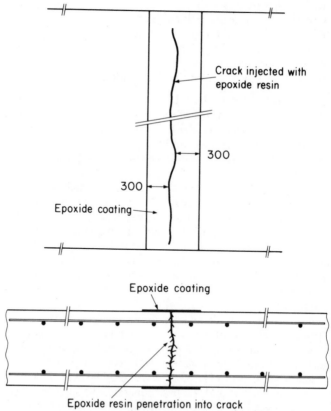

FIG. 8.3. Repair of crack in wall of pool by crack injection.

which possess some degree of flexibility as well as low viscosity. Figure 8.3 shows this method, with the addition of an epoxide coating on both faces of a wall to seal the concrete on each side of the crack. The coating should be applied after the concrete has been wire brushed, and should extend for about 300 mm on each side of the crack. If rendering has to be applied, then the surface of the resin can be sprinkled with coarse sand before it has set, to form a key.

Method (c): There are cases where it is anticipated that movement will take place across a crack during the normal operation of a swimming pool. An example is an elevated pool where the space around and below the pool shell is utilised as plant rooms, etc. It is therefore prudent to repair the crack in such a way that a certain amount of flexibility is maintained; this is particularly important when the pool is finished with tiles or mosaic. Figure 8.4 shows a method of repair using a patented channel section Neoprene gasket. If the pool is tiled, this can be fixed on the outside of the shell, and

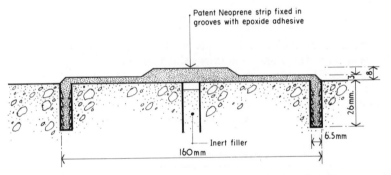

FIG. 8.4. Method of sealing defective joint in floor or wall of untiled swimming pool (Courtesy: Colebrand Ltd).

the inside of the pool can be dealt with as shown in Fig. 8.5, the channel section gasket replacing the epoxide resin coating. Figure 8.5 can be used for a crack in a floor or a wall where the outside is not accessible. It just means that the epoxide coating on the line of the crack is omitted.

Method (d): The surface of the concrete should be prepared by thorough wire brushing or light grit blasting to remove all dirt and weak laitance. The surface of the crack should be slightly opened by light tapping with a chisel. This should be followed by a brush coat of low-viscosity resin which will penetrate into the crack and the surrounding concrete. After this 'priming' coat, two good brush coats of resin should be applied, with the second coat at right angles to the first. A glass-fibre mesh, such as 'Tyglas' can be embedded in the first coat of resin after the primer. The glass-fibre mesh is

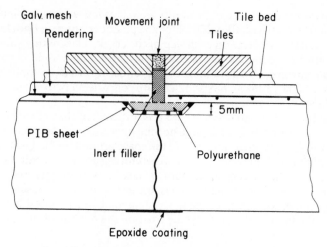

FIG. 8.5.   Method of sealing crack in wall of tiled pool.

not required for fine hair cracks, i.e. cracks not exceeding about 0·10 mm (0·004 in) in width. Figure 8.6 shows this method.

Since the first edition of this book was published, a new material has come onto the market under the trade name of 'ROK-RAP', developed by Evode Ltd. This consists of a woven cotton or alkali-resistant glass fabric impregnated with 'live' cement containing an admixture. The 'bandage'

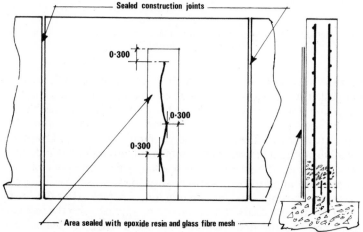

FIG. 8.6.   Repair of crack in wall of pool with epoxide resin and glass-fibre mesh.

comes in rolls, in widths from 75 mm to 200 mm (3 to 8 in). The surface of the concrete is prepared by thorough cleaning and removal of all weak laitance, dust and grit, etc. A primer is then applied and the impregnated fabric pressed down onto the concrete. The whole operation is simple and quick, and results so far have been generally good.

Repairs to Tiling and Mosaic
Unless large areas of tiling have to be removed and replaced, the work of repair can be carried out by the use of aqualung equipment and specially trained men. The new tiling/mosaic is fixed in position with resins which set rapidly under water.

Repairs to Defective Joints in the Swimming Pool Shell
There was detailed discussion on the design and detailing of joints in Chapter 4. It is general practice to provide water bars in joints in water-retaining structures, and, provided the conditions set out in Chapter 4 are complied with, the author is in favour of the use of water bars. Unfortunately, these sometimes get displaced during the placing and compaction of the concrete, and this can result in serious leakage through the joint. If it is established that water is passing through a joint which contains a water bar, then there is clearly something wrong with the water bar. Either it has been displaced or the concrete around the water bars is under-compacted (honeycombed), or both.

It is always advisable for joints (except the joint between the kicker and the wall) to be provided with a sealing groove and properly sealed. In theory, the sealant should ensure a watertight joint irrespective of the water bar, but in practice this is seldom the case, as it is difficult to ensure good bond between the sealant normally used and the concrete. When a full or partial movement joint is leaking, the following method of repair is suggested as one solution. There may well be other satisfactory methods of repair, and each case should be considered as a separate problem.

(a) The existing sealant should be removed.
(b) The groove should be widened and deepened, and both sides of the groove reformed with an epoxide mortar so as to give a straight line and even surface and true arrises.
(c) After the reformed groove has been carefully cleaned out a cellular Neoprene jointing strip should be inserted in the groove. Alternatively, the groove should be filled with a flexible resin compound.
(d) For a distance of 600 mm (2 ft) each side of the joint and for its full length, the surface of the concrete should be prepared by wire brushing or grit blasting to remove all weak laitance and lightly expose the coarse aggregate.

(e) On the prepared surface of the concrete a priming coat of low-viscosity resin should be applied, and then this should be followed by two heavy-build coats of resin. If the pool is to be tiled, then coarse sand should be sprinkled onto the last coat of resin while it is still tacky.

For joints which have been detailed and constructed to function monolithically, a rigid repair can be adopted. The repair can then be carried out as follows:

(a) The existing sealant (if any) should be removed.
(b) If there is a sealing groove, this should be widened and deepened. If there is no groove, then one should be formed by cutting the concrete with a saw, so as to provide a groove about 25 mm (1 in) wide and 15 mm ($\frac{5}{8}$ in) deep.
(c) The groove formed in (b) should be cleaned out and primed with a low-viscosity epoxide resin, and then filled with an epoxide mortar.
(e) The work should be completed by carrying out the procedure set out in (d) and (e) above for movement joints.

Repairs to Honeycombed Concrete
The first step is to ascertain the depth and extent of the honeycombing. If it is little more than a 'hungry' surface, then wire brushing, followed by two thick brush coats of grout consisting of 2 parts of OPC and 1 part latex emulsion (styrene butadiene), should be adequate. For more serious honeycombing, which penetrates down to the reinforcement or even deeper, the defective concrete should be cut out. Where it is found that the core of the wall is honeycombed, pressure grouting with specially formulated grouts is likely to be an effective remedy.

Where the defective concrete has to be cut out and replaced with new, the exact procedure, and whether to use mortar or concrete for the new work, will depend on circumstances. For relatively small repairs a cement–sand mortar is more practical, but for larger and deeper areas a concrete should be used. The honeycombed concrete should be cut out with pneumatic tools or high-velocity water jets. When the former are used, all grit and dust must be washed away before the mortar is filled into the void. The mix should be 1 part OPC or RHPC to 3 parts clean sharp building sand to Table 2 of BS 1198, with a styrene butadiene latex as a gauging liquid. The repaired area should be cured in the usual way, but if the latex emulsion is used, curing should be delayed for 12–24 h. Every effort should be made to compact the mortar into the void.

When concrete is used for the repair, a rather richer mix than that used for the original concrete should be employed. The water/cement ratio should be as low as possible consistent with workability, as full compaction

Section A-A

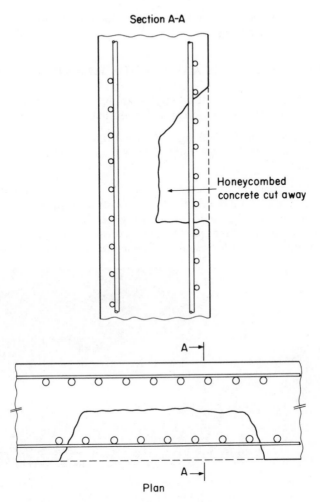

Honeycombed
concrete cut away

A→|

A→|

Plan

FIG. 8.7. Repair of honeycombed concrete in wall of pool.

of the concrete is essential. In difficult cases a super-plasticiser can prove
very useful; information on this type of admixture is given in Chapter 2.

Figure 8.7 shows suitable arrangements for the repair of honeycombed
concrete in the wall of a swimming pool.

With both concrete and mortar a fine hair crack is likely to form at the
junction of the old and the new work. This should be sealed by the
application of two brush coats of a latex grout (2 parts OPC to 1 part

emulsion). This should be well brushed in as long as possible after the completion of the new work.

COMPLETE COATINGS AND LININGS TO SWIMMING POOLS

It may be necessary to provide a complete lining to the inside of a swimming pool shell; the principal reasons for this are likely to be:

(a) The pool shell is leaking and structurally unsound.
(b) The pool shell is generally of poor quality from a watertightness point of view.

If condition (a) applies, the usual solution is to provide a new structural shell inside the existing one. This can be constructed in *in situ* reinforced concrete or reinforced gunite. The latter is generally the more economical, as little or no formwork is required and the construction time is appreciably less than that required for reinforced concrete. The new shell should be

FIG. 8.8.   Reconstruction of old deteriorated pool with new reinforced gunite lining
(Courtesy: Cement Gun Co. Ltd and Gunite Swimpools Ltd).

designed to be independent of the existing floor and walls, and in many cases a slip membrane is provided to separate the two. Figure 8.8 shows a pool being reconstructed with gunite.

Where the major defects consist of serious leakage in numerous parts of the pool shell, which is structurally sound, then a non-structural watertight lining is a practical solution. Such a lining can be:

(a) Cement–sand rendering to the walls and screed on the floor.
(b) Proprietary renderings based on cement and sand.

(*c*) Gunite.
(*d*) Epoxide or polyurethane coating.
(*e*) PVC sheeting as a waterproof membrane and decorative finish.
(*f*) Glass-fibre and polyester resin laminate.
(*g*) A butyl rubber or polyisobutylene sandwich membrane as shown in Fig. 8.9.

In a limited number of cases it may be possible to place a new pool shell of aluminium sheets or preformed laminated glass-fibre–polyester resin inside the existing shell. The space between the walls of the existing pool and those of the new shell should be carefully filled with sand or wet lean concrete. If the new shell is aluminium, then this must be protected against the highly alkaline cement paste by three good coats of bitumen. The 'wet lean' concrete should have mix proportions of about 1 part OPC and 20 parts of combined aggregate, maximum size 10 mm ($\frac{3}{8}$ in).

It is not possible to lay down precise recommendations as to when one type of lining or another should or should not be used. However, in all cases the first step is to seal off any inflow of water from the ground. Even in the

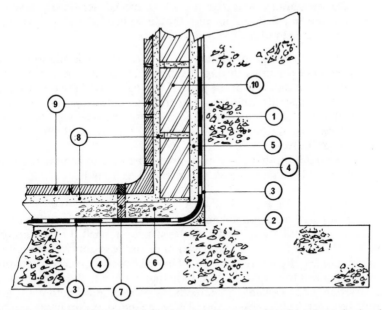

FIG. 8.9. Provision of new sandwich-type membrane to waterproof deteriorated swimming pool: 1, concrete shell of pool; 2, latex mortar cove; 3, adhesive for PIB sheeting; 4, PIB sheeting; 5, mortar backing for block wall; 6, concrete topping; 7, movement joint; 8, tile bed; 9, ceramic tiles or mosaic; 10, concrete blocks or bricks.

case of a new separate pool shell (mentioned above), all major infiltration points should be sealed off.

With regard to the sandwich-type membrane mentioned in (g) above, the following special precautions are desirable:

(1) The blockwork or brickwork inner skin should be tied back in some practical and effective way to the main wall of the pool.

(2) The mortar used for the backing to the blocks or bricks (5) in the sketch, for bedding blocks/bricks, and for any rendering which may be required to form a level bed for the tiles, should be gauged with a styrene butadiene latex emulsion (about 10 litres (2 gal) emulsion to 5 kg (1 bag) cement.

(3) If the wall tiles are bedded direct on the inner wall (as shown in the sketch), then the use of an epoxide resin-based adhesive is recommended, and an epoxide resin should be used to joint the tiles, irrespective of the method of bedding.

(4) The floor topping (item 6 in the sketch) should preferably be a fine concrete rather than a cement–sand mortar screed. Whichever is used, great care must be taken to ensure that no damage is done to the membrane, and the use of a special separating layer is recommended. The floor tiles should be bedded and jointed in an epoxide resin of a slightly flexible type.

The reasons for the recommendations in (1)–(4) are that it is important that water should not penetrate through to the surface of, and accumulate on, the membrane on the floor of the pool. If this happens, there is a risk that the whole floor may lift, causing severe cracking in the tiles. In a 'normal' pool the floor screed is fully bonded to the base concrete (see Chapter 6), and so, when the screed becomes saturated, there is negligible risk of debonding and lifting.

There is no doubt, that other methods can be used to achieve the same objective, and those given above are intended as a guide.

PREPARATION OF THE BASE CONCRETE

For fully bonded coatings and linings the first step is the preparation of the surface of the inside (water side) of the structural shell. In the author's opinion, the need for careful preparation of the base concrete cannot be overemphasised. Better results are obtained from a mediocre coating carefully applied to a well-prepared base than from a first-quality coating carelessly applied to a badly prepared base. As mentioned before, the aim should be to get the best possible bond between the coating or lining and the base concrete. This consists in a light exposure of the coarse aggregate, by grit blasting, pneumatic scabbling or high-velocity water jets. If for any reason it is decided not to expose the aggregate in this way, then, for cementitious linings, a thorough cleaning of the concrete, followed by an application of a cement grout containing a styrene butadiene-based artificial rubber latex can be adopted.

In Situ LININGS OF CEMENTITIOUS MATERIALS
These may be divided into two types:

(1) Gunite (pneumatically applied mortar).
(2) Hand-applied cement–sand rendering.

Gunite
The bonded gunite lining can be almost any thickness, but it is usually 50–100 mm (2–4 in). The surface of the concrete must be prepared as previously described and then the surface should be damped immediately before the gunite is applied. It is usual for gunite more than 50 mm (2 in) thick to be reinforced with a light high tensile mesh which is fixed by steel pins into the wall. Gunite work is described in Chapter 4, Part 2, and although it is the structural gunite shells of pools which is dealt with there, the same principles apply to the application of a gunite lining.

Hand-applied Cement–Sand Rendering
The concrete surface should be prepared as recommended and damped immediately before the rendering is applied. Full details of rendering are given in Chapter 6, Part 1.

In Situ LININGS OF OTHER MATERIALS
Coatings Applied by Brush or Spray (Epoxide Resins and Polyurethane Resins)
Epoxide resin coatings are about 0·25–1·5 mm (0·010–0·060 in) thick and are applied by brush or spray to the prepared and cleaned surface of the concrete. It is advisable to try to arrange for the supply and application of the coating to be the responsibility of one firm, since this will help to avoid arguments if there is some failure in the coating. When epoxide coatings are used, it is advisable for the surface preparation of the base concrete to be discussed and agreed with the firm supplying the resin (who should, if possible, also execute the work).

Grit blasting is usually advisable, but it should be very light, since it is only required to remove the comparatively weak skin of laitance; deep exposure of the aggregates is not necessary to secure bond, as is the case with gunite and hand-applied cement–sand rendering. The deeper the exposure of the aggregate, the more resin is required to cover it. With good-quality well-compacted concrete about 2 mm ($\frac{1}{12}$ in) is all that need be removed.

A minimum of two coats should be applied, but three are preferable, as it is impossible to completely eliminate 'holidays' (pin-holes); but it is most unlikely that these would coincide in two-coat work and certainly not in three. When applied by brush, each coat should be at right angles to the preceding one, because this helps to avoid pin-holes.

Epoxide and polyurethane resins are very durable and bond strongly to concrete when correctly formulated and properly applied. Some information on these materials is given in Chapter 2. The following is an outline of the procedure which should generally be followed, but special attention should be given to the detailed direction of the suppliers:

(a) Careful preparation of the base concrete by light grit blasting, followed by removal of dust and loose particles, is essential for obtaining the best results.

(b) If the surface of the concrete is deeply pitted, as sometimes happens, owing to large and deep blow-holes, it is advisable for these to be filled in with a fine cement–sand mortar mix 1 to 3 or 1 to 3·5. The addition of an artificial rubber latex of the styrene butadiene type, as previously recommended in this chapter for repairs and rendering, will help to improve bond and reduce shrinkage.

(c) Most epoxide resins require the concrete to be dry; drying is, of course, a difficult and time-consuming operation, and therefore the use of resins which will bond to damp concrete is advantageous.

(d) Another matter of importance is the ambient air temperature at the time of application; the permissible range varies with the formulation, and this must be ascertained when deciding on the type to be used.

(e) The resin should be applied in a minimum of two coats, with sufficient time between each for the preceding coat to harden. The hardening process may take 4–24 h; this should not be confused with 'curing' (or 'maturing', as it is sometimes called), which takes 7 days for most types of epoxide resins.

The best results will be obtained if the first coat of resin is of very low viscosity and penetrates into the concrete. It is better if the applicator is also the formulator of the resin, as this avoids divided responsibility.

PVC Sheeting
In the United Kingdom the usual method of using PVC as a lining to swimming pools is in the form of 'loose bag', which is really only fixed along the top of the walls under the coping. These 'loose bags' are purpose-made to suit the exact dimensions of the pool shell, and are brought to site and installed by special firms. In Germany it is more usual to bond the PVC to the pool shell and then the sheeting is cut to size and solvent-welded on site. In the opinion of the author this method is preferable, as damage to the

Fig. 8.10. View of open-air pool in Germany renovated and waterproofed with bonded PVC sheeting (Courtesy: Alkor Plastics (UK) Ltd, Borehamwood).

lining is much less likely to result in leakage. Figure 8.10 shows a pool lined in this way in Germany. It is essential that the PVC should be of high quality and of adequate thickness: not less than 0·75 mm (0·030 in) is the author's recommendation. The PVC sheeting forms a watertight membrane and a decorative finish; it can now be obtained in a range of attractive colours and patterns.

Sandwich-type Flexible Sheet Membranes
When a pool has numerous serious leaks but the walls and floor are structurally sound, and it is required to provide watertightness as well as a high-quality durable finish, a sandwich-type flexible sheet membrane can provide the answer. The author recommends a material which can be fully bonded to the base concrete, and for this polyisobutylene (PIB) is very suitable.

All infiltration of groundwater must first be sealed off and the surface of the concrete carefully prepared by removing all dirt, weak laitance, and high rough spots and areas. Holes and depressions in the surface of the base

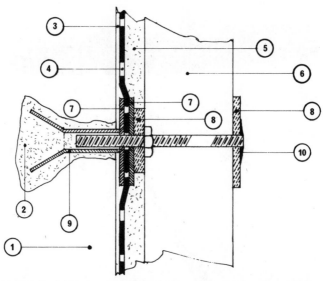

FIG. 8.11.   Details of tie for inner wall of pool where sandwich-type membrane has been used: 1, concrete shell of pool; 2, non-shrink grout; 3, adhesive for PIB sheeting; 4, PIB sheeting; 5, mortar backing for block wall; 6, concrete blocks or bricks; 7, fibre washer; 8, non-ferrous plate; 9, non-ferrous anchor with internal thread; 10, epoxide resin (Courtesy: Gunac Ltd, Wallington).

FIG. 8.12.   View of old deteriorated public pool before renovation.

Fig. 8.13.   View of pool in Fig. 8.12 after renovation and new 'Colmasyn' polyester
resin–glass-fibre laminate lining (Courtesy: Sika Contracts Ltd, Warrington).

concrete should be filled in and finished smooth and level. The filling-in
material should be a fine mortar gauged with a styrene butadiene emulsion.
All joints in the PIB should be solvent- or heat-welded, and it is essential
that the membrane be carried across any walkways around the pool and
finished off in such a way that water cannot penetrate down behind it.

Some general advice on the laying and securing of the inner block wall
and the precautions required to prevent accumulation of water on the
surface of the membrane has already been given. Figures 8.9 and 8.11 show
these recommendations in sketch form.

Polyisobutylene can be obtained in thicknesses of 0·75 mm, 1·0 mm and
1·5 mm ($\frac{30}{1000}$ in, $\frac{1}{25}$ in and $\frac{1}{16}$ in). The author recommends a thickness of
1·5 mm ($\frac{1}{16}$ in).

Glass-fibre and Polyester Resin Linings

The complete lining of new swimming pools with glass-fibre–polyester resin
laminate has been described in Chapter 6. This type of lining can in many
cases be useful in the renovation and waterproofing existing pools. Figures
8.12 and 8.13 show a fifty-year-old public swimming pool which was
satisfactorily renovated and waterproofed in this way.

REPAIR OF DEFECTIVE SCREEDS AND RENDERING IN
SWIMMING POOLS

The principal defect in screeds and rendering is loss of bond with the base concrete. This can be caused by a number of factors, of which the most usual are:

(a) Inadequate preparation of the base concrete (screeds and rendering).

(b) For screeds: the use of a semi-dry mix which makes it virtually impossible to compact the screed material which is then weak and permeable; the use of too much water in the mix, resulting in high drying shrinkage and a weak permeable screed.

(c) For rendering: the use of a weak mix for the first coat and a stronger mix for the second (instead of the other way round); the first and/or subsequent coats of rendering were too thick; the lower coat was not properly keyed to receive the subsequent coat; the use of too great a thickness of rendering without the incorporation of a galvanised (or better, a stainless steel) mesh, well pinned into the wall; insufficient effort used to compact the rendering when it was applied to the wall.

(d) For both screed and rendering, the use of too weak a mix.

(e) For both screed and rendering, inadequate protection and curing after application.

(f) Chemical attack from the pool water.

It has been mentioned in Chapter 6 that it is not advisable to tile over hollow-sounding areas of rendering or screed, as this indicates lack of proper bond with the base concrete. When large areas are found to be deficient in bond, then the best solution is to carefully remove the screed or rendering over these areas. Percussion tools should not be used. The best method is high-velocity water jets, as these cause no vibration. The next best thing is a concrete saw.

A real problem arises when the loss of bond is only in a few small scattered areas. It is then difficult to decide whether the screed or rendering should be cut out, or some other method adopted. There is no clear-cut solution to this problem. The author feels that if the hollow sound given out when the screed/rendering is tapped can be eliminated by resin injection, then this technique can be accepted. A contractor should be allowed to try it.

Unfortunately defects in bond can come to light after the pool has been tiled and commissioned, sometimes years later, and show themselves by cracking and lifting of the tiles. This is more prevalent in the floor than on the walls. The areas which have lifted are readily identified, but a careful check of the apparently sound areas often reveals lack of bond there also.

When the floor is tapped and emits a hollow note, it is impossible to tell whether the loss of bond is between tiles and screed or between screed and concrete. Tiles which have been laid by the notched trowel method may give out a slight hollow sound when tapped. However, this does not necessarily mean that there is sufficient loss of bond to constitute a 'failure'. It does indicate that the tiles were not sufficiently firmly pressed down when they were laid, and so 100 % bedding was not achieved. In spite of this, the tiles may still be strongly bonded to the screed. In such cases expert advice should be sought from either the tile manufacturer or the British Ceramic Tile Council (see Appendix 3).

Sometimes (very rarely) the screed is attacked by sulphates or acids in the pool water. When this happens, it is usually due to a combination of rather poor-quality screed and some maloperation of the water treatment plant. Nevertheless, if the attack is widespread, it may result in a failure requiring the removal and replacement of tiles, screed and rendering over the whole, or a substantial area, of the pool. Recommendations for the laying of screed, rendering and tiles have been given in Chapter 6, and Chapter 7 contains details of water treatment. However, the author wishes to emphasise the following points:

(1) The cement–sand mortar used for the jointing and bedding of tiles and for the screed and rendering is significantly more permeable than high-quality concrete; is therefore more vulnerable to sulphate attack and to attack by a water which is slightly acid, i.e. has a pH below the neutral point of 7·0.

(2) It is seldom found that regular samples of pool water have been taken for full chemical analysis, and therefore the levels of sulphate concentration during the whole period the pool has been in operation are not known. The actual amount of make-up water is generally not known, because the supply is not metered.

(3) The chemicals used in water treatment to secure good coagulation (aluminium and ferrous sulphates) are potentially aggressive to Portland cement mortar owing to their sulphate content and their acid reaction.

(4) Very few public baths have a pH meter, and the author has never seen one used in a private, club or hotel pool. The usual method of measuring the pH is by means of a comparator with phenol red indicator, but diphenol purple is sometimes used. Chlorine reacts with these two indicators to give a colour which corresponds to high pH values on the comparator disc, even when special tablets are used to eliminate the effect of the chlorine. From these facts it will be seen that recorded pH values may therefore be considerably higher than the correct values.

(5) The Langlier Index of the pool water should be positive.

BIBLIOGRAPHY

CEMENT AND CONCRETE ASSOCIATION, *Chemical Methods of Removing Stains from Concrete*, 45.015, 1968, p. 7.

FITZGERALD, G. P. AND DER VARTANIAN, M. E., Algicide effect of chlorine studied at Wisconsin. *Swimming Pool Weekly and Swimming Pool Age*, June 22, 1970, pp. 24–8.

KEEN, R., *Controlling Algae and Other Growths on Concrete*, Cement and Concrete Association, London, 45.020, 1971, p. 6.

MALPAS, J. F., *The Chemical and Bacteriological Purification of Swimming Bath Water*, Publication BRA.331, Wallace and Tiernan Ltd, Sept. 1967, p. 20.

NATIONAL SWIMMING POOL INSTITUTE, *Pool Care Guide*, Washington D.C., p. 9.

NORDELL, E., *Water Treatment for Industrial and Other Uses*, 2nd edition, 1961, Reinhold, New York, and Chapman and Hall, London. p. 598.

PERKINS, P. H., *Concrete Structures: Repair, Waterproofing and Protection*, Applied Science Publishers, London 1977, p. 302.

STERN, R. M., The American approach to water chemistry and its relationship to swimming pool maintenance. Paper presented at the 42nd Annual Conference of Institute of Baths Management, Sept. 1972, Aberdeen.

SWIMMING POOLS AND ALLIED TRADES ASSOCIATION, *Winterization Guide for Swimming Pools*, p. 8.

WALLACE AND TIERNAN LTD, *Handbook of Pool Water Care*, Tonbridge, p. 62.

APPENDIX 1

National Standards

UK STANDARDS AND CODES OF PRACTICE

Cements and Admixture

Portland cement, ordinary and rapid hardening	BS 12
Portland cement, white and coloured	BS 12
Portland cement, sulphate-resisting	BS 4027
Portland cement, ultra-high early strength	None (Agrément Certificate 73/170)
Portland—blastfurnace cement	BS 146
Portland blastfurnace cement, low heat	BS 4246
Portland cement, low heat	BS 1370
High alumina cement	BS 915
Supersulphated cement	BS 4284
Masonry cement	BS 5224
Pigments for cement and concrete	BS 1014
Pulverised-fuel ash (PFA) for use in concrete	BS 3892
Cement Standards of the World published by Cembureau, Paris, 1968	
Mortar plasticisers	BS 4887
Concrete admixtures	BS 5075

Aggregates

Aggregates from natural sources for concrete (including granolithic)	BS 882 and 1201
Building sands from natural sources	BS 1198–1200

Testing Concrete

Methods of testing concrete	BS 1881
Methods for sampling and testing of mineral aggregates, sands and fillers	BS 812

Methods of sampling and testing lightweight   BS 3681
  aggregates for concrete
Tests for water for making concrete   BS 3148
Test sieves   BS 410
Ready-mixed concrete   BS 1926
Methods of specifying concrete   BS 5328
Recommendations for non-destructive methods   BS 4408
  of test for concrete

Steel Reinforcement
Expanded metal (steel) for general purposes   BS 405
Hard drawn mild steel wire for the   BS 4482
  reinforcement of concrete
Hot rolled steel bars for the reinforcement of BS 4449
  concrete
Cold worked steel bars for the reinforcement of BS 4461
  concrete
Steel fabric for the reinforcement of concrete BS 4483
Steel wire for prestressed concrete   BS 2691
Stress relieved-wire steel strand for prestressed BS 3617
  concrete
Galvanised steel reinforcement   None
Structural steel sections   BS 4
Galvanised iron and steel wire for telegraph and BS 182–4
  telephone purposes
Galvanised wire netting   BS 1485
The use of structural steel in building   BS 449
Wrought steels—blooms, billetts, bars and   BS 970
  forgings
(stainless, heat-resisting and valve steels)   BS 970, Part 4
Steel plate, sheet and strip   BS 1449
(stainless heat-resisting plate, sheet and strip) BS 1449, Part 4
Hot-dip galvanised coatings for iron and steel BS 729
Cold worked high tensile alloy bars   BS 4486
Bending dimensions and schedules of bars for   BS 4466
  reinforced concrete

Precast and Preformed Materials
Precast concrete flags   BS 368
Precast concrete blocks   BS 2028

Joint Sealants, Water Proofing Materials and Flooring
Cold poured joint sealants for concrete   BS 5212
  pavements

Hot applied joint sealing compounds for concrete pavements	BS 2499
Corrugated copper jointing strip for expansion joints for use in general building construction	BS 1878
Two-part polysulphide-based sealing compounds for the building industry	BS 4254
One-part gun-grade polysulphide-based sealants	BS 5215
Preformed neoprene joint sealants	None
Mastic asphalt for tanking and damp-proof courses	BS 1097 and 1418
Mastic asphalt for roofing	BS 988 and 1162
Water bars, rubber	None
Water bars, PVC	None
Mastic asphalt for flooring	BS 1076, 1410 and 1451
Low and medium density polyethylene sheet for general purposes	BS 3012
Materials for damp-proof courses	BS 743
Roofing felts	BS 747
Glossary of terms applicable to roof coverings	BS 2717
Black pitch mastic flooring	BS 1450 and 3672

General

Conversion factors and tables	BS 350
Asbestos cement decking	BS 3717
Guide to the selection and use of control systems for heating, ventilation and air conditioning	BS 5384
Methods of test for building sealants	BS 3712
Glossary of terms for concrete and reinforced concrete	BS 2787
Glossary of general building terms	BS 3589
Fire tests on building materials and structures	BS 476
Building drawing practice	BS 1192
Schedule of weights of building materials	BS 648
Surface finish of blast-cleaned steel for painting	BS 4232
External rendered finishes (previously CP 221)	BS 5262
Calorifiers	BS 853
Cast iron boilers	BS 779
Sprayed asbestos insulation	BS 3590
Timber grades for structural use	BS 4978
Methods for specifying concrete	BS 5328

The structural use of concrete for retaining aqueous liquids (previously CP 2007)	BS 5337
Basic data for the design of buildings: the control of condensation in dwellings	BS 5250
Methods of test for resistance to air and water penetration	BS 4315
Code of basic data for the design of buildings, Chapters I–X	CP 3
Demolition	CP 94
Metal scaffolding	CP 97
Access for the disabled to buildings	CP 96
Preservative treatments for constructional timber	CP 98
Recommendations for the co-ordination of dimensions in building	BS 4011
Accuracy in building	PD 6440
Boilers of more than 150 000 Btu	CP 332, Part 3
Foundations and sub-structures for non-industrial buildings of not more than four storeys	CP 101
Protection of buildings against water from the ground	CP 102
Structural recommendations for load bearing walls	CP 111
The structural use of timber	CP 112
The structural use of concrete	CP 110
The structural use of reinforced concrete in buildings	CP 114
The structural use of prestressed concrete in buildings	CP 115
The structural use of precast concrete	CP 116
Composite construction in structural steel and concrete	CP 117
Walling	CP 121
Walls and partitions of blocks and slabs	CP 122
Suspended ceilings and linings	CP 290
Precast concrete cladding	CP 297
Natural stone cladding	CP 298
The protection of structures against lightning	CP 326
Sprayed asbestos insulation	CP 299
The design and construction of ducts for services	CP 413

Electric fire alarms	CP 1019
Fire fighting installations and equipment (now superseded by BS 5306)	CP 402
Cathodic protection	CP 1021
Site investigations	CP 2001
Foundations	CP 2004
Protection of iron and steel structures from corrosion	BS 5493
Painting of buildings	CP 231
Sewerage	CP 2005
Pipelines	CP 2010
Thermal insulation of pipework and equipment in temperature range $-73\,°C$ to $+816\,°C$	CP 3005
Cleaning and preparation of metal surfaces	CP 3012
Oil firing	CP 3002
Earthworks	CP 2003
Electric floor-warming systems	CP 1018
Electric lifts	CP 407
Mechanical ventilation and air conditioning in buildings	CP 352
Installation of pipes and meters for town gas	CP 331
Water supply	CP 310
Building drainage	CP 301
Sanitary pipework above ground	CP 304
Sanitary appliances	CP 305
Wall tiling	CP 212
Internal plastering	BS 5492
Slating and tiling	CP 142
Sheet roof and wall coverings (only Part 6 still valid) (see BS 5247)	CP 143
Roof coverings	CP 144
Glazing systems	CP 145
Doors and windows including frames and linings	CP 151
Glazing and fixing of glass for buildings	CP 152
Windows and rooflights	CP 153
Roof deckings	CP 199
Timber flooring	CP 201
Tile flooring and slab flooring	CP 202
Sheet and tile flooring	CP 203
In situ floor finishes	CP 204
Care and maintenance of floor surfaces	CP 209
Code of Practice for sheet roof and wall, in 14 parts (this supersedes most of CP 143)	BS 5247

Methods of testing windows	BS 5368
Code of Practice for fire extinguishing installations on premises (this supersedes CP 402)	BS 5306
Fire hose reels for fixed installations	BS 5274
Sampling and testing mastic asphalt and pitch mastic used in building	BS 5284
Coated macadam for roads and other paved areas	BS 4987
Methods of test for structural fixings in concrete	BS 5080
Drawing practice for engineering diagrams	BS 5070
Fire hydrant systems and equipment	BS 5041

SELECTED LIST OF RELEVANT ASTM STANDARDS (UNITED STATES OF AMERICA) RELATING TO CONCRETE

Cements

Spec. for Portland cement	C 150–68
Spec. for air entraining Portland cement	C 175–68
Spec. for blended hydraulic cement	C 595–68
Chemical analysis of Portland cement	C 114–67
Test for fineness of Portland cement by the turbidimeter	C 115–67
Test for fineness of Portland cement by air permeability apparatus	C 204–55 (1967)
Test for specific gravity of hydraulic cement	C 188–44 (1967)
Test for heat of hydration of Portland cement	C 186–68
Test for normal consistency of hydraulic cement	C 187–68
Test for time of setting of hydraulic cement by Vicat needles	C 191–65
Test for time of setting of hydraulic cement by Gillmore needles	C 266–65
Test for compressive strength of hydraulic cement mortars	C 109–64
Test for autoclave expansion of Portland cement	C 151–66
Test for chemical resistance of mortars	C 267–65
Test for potential expansion of Portland cement mortars exposed to sulfate	C 452–68
Fly-ash and raw or calcined natural pozzolans for use in Portland cement concrete	C 618–68

Spec. for sieves for testing purposes (wire cloth sieves, round-hole and square-hole plate screens or sieves) ⎱ E 11–61 / E 323–67

Aggregates

Spec. for concrete aggregates	C 33–67
Descriptive nomenclature of constituents of natural mineral aggregates	C 294–67
Rec. practice for petrographic examination of aggregates for concrete	C 295–65
Spec. for lightweight aggregates for structural concrete	C 330–68
Spec. for lightweight aggregates for concrete masonry units	C 331–64T†
Spec. for lightweight aggregates for insulating concrete	C 332–66
Test for sieve or screen analysis of fine and coarse aggregates	C 136–67
Test for materials finer than No. 200 sieve in mineral aggregates by washing	C 117–67
Test for specific gravity and absorption of coarse aggregate	C 127–68
Test for specific gravity and absorption of fine aggregate	C 128–68
Test for unit weight of aggregate	C 29–68
Test for voids in aggregate for concrete	C 30–37 (1964)
Test for surface moisture in fine aggregate	C 70–66
Test for organic impurities in sands for concrete	C 40–66
Test for clay lumps in natural aggregates	C 142–67
Test for lightweight pieces in aggregate	C 123–66
Test for soundness of aggregates by use of sodium sulphate or magnesium sulphate	C 88–63
Test for resistance to abrasion of small size coarse aggregate by use of the Los Angeles machine	C 131–66
Test for abrasion of rock by use of the Deval machine	D 2–33 (1968)
Test for abrasion of graded coarse aggregate by use of the Deval machine	D 289–63
Test for potential reactivity of aggregates (chemical method)	C 289–66

† T denotes Tentative Standard.

Test for potential alkali reactivity of   C 227–67
cement–aggregate combinations (mortar bar
method)
Test for potential volume change of cement   C 342–67
aggregate combinations

Concrete
Test for flow of Portland cement concrete by   C 124–39 (1966)
use of the flow table
Test for slump of Portland cement concrete   C 143–66
Test for ball penetration in fresh Portland   C 360–63
cement concrete
Test for time of setting of concrete mixtures by C 403–68
penetration resistance
Test for bleeding of concrete   C 232–58 (1966)
Test for weight per cubic foot, yield, and air   C 138–63
content (gravimetric) of concrete
Test for air content of freshly mixed concrete   C 173–68
by the volumetric method
Test for air content of freshly mixed concrete   C 231–68
by the pressure method
Test for single-use molds for forming 6 in by   C 470–67T
12 in concrete compression test cylinders
Test for compressive strength of molded   C 39–68
concrete cylinders
Making and curing concrete compression and   C 31–66
flexure test specimens in the field
Test for compressive strength of concrete using   C 116–68
portions of beams broken in flexure (modified
cube method)
Making and curing concrete compression and   C 192–68
flexure test specimens in the laboratory
Test for flexural strength of concrete (using   C 78–64
simple beam with third-point loading)
Text for flexural strength of concrete (using   C 293–68
simple beam with centre-point loading)
Obtaining and testing drilled cores and sawed   C 42–68
beams of concrete
Test for static Young's modulus of elasticity   C 469–65
and Poisson's ratio in compression of
cylindrical concrete specimens
Test for fundamental transverse, longitudinal,   C 215–60
and torsional frequencies of concrete specimens

Test for abrasion resistance of concrete	C 418–68
Test for length change of cement mortar and concrete	C 157–66T
Test for cement content of hardened Portland cement concrete	C 85–66
Spec. for air entraining admixture for concrete	C 260–66T
Rec. practice for microscopical determination of air-void content, specific surface, and spacing factor of the air-void system in hardened concrete	C 457–67T
Test for resistance of concrete specimens to rapid freezing and thawing in water	C 290–67
Test for resistance of concrete specimens to rapid freezing in air and thawing in water	C 291–67
Spec. for ready-mixed concrete	C 94–68

CODES OF PRACTICE RELATING TO CONCRETE IN USE IN THE UNITED STATES OF AMERICA

American Concrete Institute

†Spec. for structural concrete for buildings	(ACI 302.66)
†Building code requirements for reinforced concrete	(ACI 318–71)
Commentary on building code requirements for reinforced concrete	
Structural plain concrete	(322.1–322.9)
Tentative recommendations for design of concrete beams and girders for buildings	(333.1–20)
Concrete shell structures. Practice and commentary	(334.1–18)
Suggested design procedures for combined footings and mats	(336.1–16)
Recommended practice for shotcrete	(ACI 506–66)

CANADA

CSA A23.1	Concrete, materials and methods of construction
A23.2	Methods of test for concrete

† Approved by USA Standards Institute as a USA standard.

CSA A 5   Portland cement
CSA A 8   Masonry cement
19 GP–3b   Sealing compounds—two-part polysulphide chemi-
                   cal curing
19 GP–5b   Sealing compounds—one-component silicone
                   based chemical curing
19 GP–13b   Sealing compounds—polysulphide one-
                   component, chemical curing
CG SB 19GP–23   Standard for guide to selection of sealants on a use
                   basis

NATIONAL STANDARDS AND CODES: AUSTRALIA

For complete list of Publications and Subject Index of Australian Standards, 1976, reference should be made to the Standards Association of Australia, Standards House, 80–86 Arther Street, North Sydney, N.S.W.
   The following are some of the principal standards relating to cement and concrete:

A S 2   Portland cement
A S 1316   Masonry cement
A S 1317   Blended cement
A S 100 *et seq.* Methods of testing concrete
A S 1480   Concrete structures code
A S 1481   Prestressed concrete code
A S MP 27   Manual of physical testing of Portland cement
Admixtures: A173,CA.58, MP.20, 1478–9
Aggregates for concrete: 1465 to 1467
Tests on aggregates: 1141
Readymixed concrete: A64 1379
Reinforcement for concrete, bars, wire and rods: A81–84,A92,A97, 1302–1304.

NEW ZEALAND STANDARDS RELATING TO CEMENT AND CONCRETE

Aggregates
NZ3111: 1974 Methods of test for water and aggregates for concrete
NZS3121: 1974 Water and aggregate for concrete
NZS1958: 1965 Lightweight aggregate for structural concrete
NZS1959: 1965 Lightweight aggregate for concrete masonry units
NZS1960: 1965 Lightweight aggregates for insulating concrete

Cements
NZS3122: 1974 Portland cement (ordinary, rapid hardening, and modified)
NZS3123: 1974 Portland pozzolan cement

Concrete Construction
NZS3101P: 1970 Reinforced and plain concrete construction

Concrete Mixers
NZS3105: 1975 Concrete mixers

Concrete Testing
NZS3112: 1974 Methods of test for concrete

Fire Resistance
NZ MP9   Reports on fire resistance ratings of elements of building structure
NZ MP911: 1962 Fire resistance ratings of walls and partitions: structures of concrete masonry blocks
NZ MP9/2: 1962 Fire resistance ratings of walls and partitions: structural concrete
NZ MP9/5: 1972 Fire resistance of prestressed concrete
NZ MP9/6: 1966 Fire resistance of beams and columns, excluding timber
NZ MP9/7: 1966 Fire resistance ratings of floor/ceiling combinations

Foundations
NZ MP420400: 1973 Metric handbook to NZS4204P: 1973 Code of practice for foundations for buildings not requiring specific design
NZ MP420500: 1973 Metric handbook to NZS4205P: 1973 Code of practice for design of foundations for buildings
NZS4204P: 1973 Foundations
NZS4205P: 1973 Foundations

Lightweight Concrete (see also *Aggregates*)
NZ3152: 1974 Manufacture and use of structural and insulating lightweight concrete
NZS3141P: 1970 Precast lightweight concrete panels and slabs

Masonry (see also 1900 *below*)
NZS3102P: 1974 Concrete Masonry units

Pavements
BS5215: 1975 Cold poured joint sealant for concrete pavements (endorsed by NZ)

Precast Concrete
NZ3151: 1974 Precast lightweight concrete panels and slabs

Prestressed Concrete
NZSR 3R32: 1968 Prestressed concrete Amdt no. 1: 1970
NZ1417: 1971 Steel wire for prestressed concrete (amended to suit NZ conditions from BS 2691: 1969)
NZMP32x000: 1974 Metric handbook to NZSR32: 1968 Prestressed Concrete

Ready Mixed Concrete
NZS2086: 1974 Ready mixed concrete production
MP208600: 1975 Metric handbook to NZS2086: 1968 Ready mixed concrete

Reinforced Concrete
NZ3101P: 1970 Code of practice for reinforced concrete—design
NZ MP310100: 1973 Metric handbook to NZS3101P: 1970 Code of Practice for reinforced concrete design

Reinforcement
NZS3402P: 1973 Hot rolled steel bars for concrete reinforcement
NZS3403 Hot-dip galvanised corrugated or profiled steel sheet
NZS3421: 1975 Hard drawn mild steel wire for concrete reinforcement
NZS3441 Hot-dip galvanised plain steel sheet and strip
NZS3422: 1975 Welded fabric of drawn steel wire for concrete reinforcement

Sands
NZ2129 Sands for mortars, plasters and external renderings Amdt. no. 1, 1971

Shells
NZ1826: 1964 The design and construction of shell roofs

Swimming Pools
NZS4441: 1972 Code of Practice for swimming pools

1900 (*Model Building Bylaw*)
Ch 6.2: 1964 Masonry Amdt. No. 1, 1973
Ch 9.2: 1964 Design and construction Amdt No. 1, 1965, No. 2, 1973 (to be reconstituted incorporating NZS2086)
Ch 9.3A: 1970 Concrete—general requirements and materials and workmanship No. 11970 n2 1971, No. 3, 1973 (to be reconstituted incorporating NZS2086)
Ch. 11. Special structures
    11.1: 1964 Concrete Structures for the storage of liquids Amdts No. 1, 1964, No. 2, 1973
MP 190093A: Metric handbook to NZS1900 Chapter 93A: 1970 Concrete design and construction general requirements

INDIA

I S 476 Code of Practice for plain and reinforced concrete
I S 269 Portland cement, ordinary rapid hardening and low heat
I S 455 Portland blastfurnace cement
I S 1489 Pozzolanic cement
I S 516 Methods of test for strength of concrete
I S 3466 Masonry cement
I S 6452 High alumina cement for structural use

SABS STANDARDS AND CODES OF PRACTICE

Standards (Metric units, unless otherwise indicated)

28–1972	Metal ties for cavity walls
82–1976	Bending dimensions of bars for concrete reinforcement
197–1971	Test sieves
248–1973	Bituminous damp-proof courses
471–1971	Portland cement and rapid-hardening Portland cement
523–1972	Limes for use in building
527–1972	Concrete building blocks
541–1971	Precast concrete paving slabs
626–1971	Portland blastfurnace cement
794–1973	Aggregates of low density
831–1971	Portland cement 15 and rapid-hardening cement 15
878–1970	Ready mixed concrete
920–1969	Steel bars for concrete reinforcement
927–1969	Precast concrete kerbs and channels (not metric)
973–1970	Standard form of specification for concrete work

975–1970	Prestressed concrete pipes
986–1970	Precast reinforced concrete culverts
987–1970	Cement bricks
993–1972	Modular co-ordination in building
1024–1974	Welded steel fabric for concrete reinforcement
1083–1976	Aggregates from natural sources

Standard Building Regulations
Note: The Standard Building Regulations cover all aspects of building construction in areas controlled by local authorities, although not all cities and towns in South Africa have adopted them. The main chapter headings cover definitions, administration in the four provinces of South Africa, loads and forces, foundations, plain and reinforced concrete, structural steelwork, structural timber, masonry and walling, miscellaneous materials and construction, water supply, lighting, drainage and sewerage, ventilation, fire protection, public safety, urban aesthetics and advertising.

Codes of Practice

03A–1969	The protection of dwelling houses against lightning
021–1973	Waterproofing of buildings
043–1965	The laying of wood floors
058–1955	Sewer and drain jointing (not metric)
062–1956	Fixing of concrete roofing tiles (not metric)
073–1974	Safe application of masonry-type facings to buildings
088–1972	Pile foundations
0102–1968	The structural design and installation of precast concrete pipelines
0109–1969	Floor finishes on concrete

DEPARTMENT OF INDUSTRIES

No. R.1830.]   [23rd October, 1970.

STANDARDS ACT, 1962

STANDARD BUILDING REGULATIONS

In terms of section 14*bis* (1) of the Standards Act, 1962 (Act No. 33 of 1962) the Council of the South African Bureau of Standards, with the approval of the Minister of Economic Affairs, hereby publishes standard building regulations under the chapter headings listed in this notice.

LIST OF CHAPTERS

WEST GERMAN STANDARDS (DINs)

Concrete and reinforced concrete structures; design and construction	DIN 1045
Reinforcing steel; definitions, properties, markings	DIN 488
Testing methods for concrete	DIN 1048
Steel in structural engineering; design and construction	DIN 1050
Masonry; design and construction	DIN 1053
Design loads for buildings	DIN 1055
Highway bridges; design loads	DIN 1072
Steel highway bridges; design principles	DIN 1073
Composite girder highway bridges; code of practice for design and analysis	DIN 1078
Symbols for structural design calculations in civil and structural engineering	DIN 1080
Quality control in concrete and reinforced concrete construction	DIN 1084
Portland cement 'Eisen' portland cement, 'Hochofen' cement and trass cement; definitions, constituents, requirements, delivery	DIN 1164
Reinforced lightweight concrete slabs	DIN 4028
Assessment of waters, soils and gases aggressive to concrete	DIN 4030
Water pressure retaining bituminous seals for structures: code of practice for design and construction	DIN 4031
Welding of reinforcing steel; requirements and tests	DIN 4099
Fire behaviour of materials and components of structures; definitions, requirements and tests for components	DIN 4102
Light partitions; code of practice for construction	DIN 4103
Thermal insulation in building construction	DIN 4108
Sealing of structures against ground moisture; code of practice for construction	DIN 4117
Intermediate components of concrete for reinforced and prestressed concrete floors	DIN 4158
Floor blocks and blocks for wall panels, structurally co-operating	DIN 4159
Contract procedure for building work, Part C, technical specification for grouting work	DIN 18 309
Contract procedure for building work, general technical specification for concrete and reinforced concrete work	331

Portland Cements

OCI	Portlandzement	Z 375 I	⎫
OCII		Z 375 (f)	⎪
HSC I		Z 450 I	⎬ DIN 1164 1969
HSC II		Z 450 f	⎪
HSC III		Z 530	⎭

(NOTE: The figures '375–450', etc., refer to 28 day compressive cube strength expressed in kg/cm^2.)

AUSTRIA

A 2050	Building contracts, placing contracts
ONORM B 2110	Building construction, general conditions for building contracts
ONORM B 2211	Concrete and reinforced concrete construction
ONORM B 3303	Testing concrete
ONORM B 3305	Water, soils and gases aggressive to concrete-evaluation and chemical analysis
ONORM B 4200	Concrete structures, design and construction
ONORM B 4250	Prestressed concrete structures
ONORM B 3310	Portland cements, Types OCI, OCII, HSC, and blastfurnace cements
ONORM B 4200	Part 7 Steel reinforcement for concrete

NETHERLANDS

NEN 3861–3867	Concrete Code of Practice in 7 Parts
NEN 6008	Steel reinforcement for concrete
N 481	Portland cement
N 483 and 484	Portland blastfurnace cements
N 618	Pozzolanic cement
NEN 3868	Prestressing steel
NEN 3869	Anchorages for post-tensioned concrete structures

ITALY

UNI 595	Portland cement, blastfurnace cement and pozzolanic cements
UNI 6132 and 6135	Testing of concrete

BELGIUM

NBN 15 Concrete construction
NBN 15 201–205, 211–214, 216, 218, 220, 227 and 250 Concrete tests
NBN A24.301–303 Steel reinforcement for concrete
NBN 460.01–03 Wind loads on structures
NBN 48 Portland cement
NBN 130, 131 and 198 Portland blastfurnace cement

FRANCE

CC BA 68 Reinforced concrete Code
CM 66 Structural steelwork Code
NV 65 Snow and wind loading
P O 3–011 Standard contracts for private building work, general clauses
NFP 15–302 Portland cement
   303, 304, 305 and 311 Portland blastfurnace cement
NFP 18–102, 404, 405, 406 Tests for concrete
NF A.35.015 and 016. Steel reinforcement for concrete
DTU 32.1. Steel construction in building; structural steelwork
NF A 03-151 Iron and steel—tensile testing of steel.

GENERAL NOTE

For English translations of National Standards and Codes of Practice from overseas countries, reference should be made to:

Technical Help to Exporters
British Standards Institution
Maylands Avenue
Hemel Hempstead
Herts. (Tel.: 0442-3111).

APPENDIX 2

Conversion Factors and Coefficients

$1\,m^2$ $= 10 \cdot 7\,ft^2$
$1\,ft^2$ $= 0 \cdot 093\,m^2$
$1\,kg$ $= 2 \cdot 26\,lb$
$1\,lb$ $= 0 \cdot 45\,kg$
$1\,m$ $= 3 \cdot 28\,ft$
$1\,ft$ $= 0 \cdot 31\,m$
$1\,lb/ft^2$ $= 4 \cdot 85\,kg/m^2$
$1\,m^3$ $= 1 \cdot 31\,yd^3$
$1\,m^3$ $= 220\,gal\,(Imp)$
$1\,gal\,(Imp) = 4 \cdot 5\,litres$
$1\,litre$ $= 0 \cdot 22\,gal\,(Imp)$
$1\,US\,gal$ $= 0 \cdot 852\,Imp\,gal$
$1\,inch$ $= 25 \cdot 4\,mm$
$1\,m$ $= 1 \cdot 1\,yd$

Conversion from Imperial to Metric
D_i = Density in lb/ft^3
D_m = Density in kg/m^3

$$D_m = \frac{D_i}{62 \cdot 4} \times \frac{1000}{1} = 16\,D_i\,(approx.)$$

Density of Structural Concrete, Made with Aggregates from Natural Sources
$148\,lb/ft^3 = 4000\,lb/yd^3 = 2385\,kg/m^3 = 2400\,kg/m^3$
(approx.)

Bulk Densities of Concreting Materials
   Cement $1400\,kg/m^3 = 88\,lb/ft^3$

Sand $\qquad$ 1600 kg/m^3 = 100 lb/ft^3
Coarse aggregate $\qquad$ 1450 kg/m^3 = 91 lb/ft^3
These figures are very approximate.

Modulus of Elasticity of Concrete: $E = 4\cdot5 \times 10^6$
$\qquad\qquad\qquad$ Range: $E = 2\cdot5\text{–}6 \times 10^6$

Specific Gravity
Water	1·0
Cement, Portland	3·12
Cement, high-alumina	3·20
Pit sand	2·65
Flint gravel	2·55
Limestone	2·80
Granite	2·75
Basalt (whinstone)	2·90
Concrete structural	2·38

Specific Heat
	Imp	Metric
Concrete	0·25 Btu	0·063 k/cal
Mild steel	0·12 Btu	0·031 k/cal

Latent Heat
Fusion of ice $\qquad\qquad$ 144 Btu/lb $\quad$ 37 k/cal/g
Evaporation of water $\quad$ 970 Btu/lb $\quad$ 250 k/cal/g
1 Btu/lb = 2326 J/kg

Force
1 lbf $\qquad$ = 4·45 N
1000 lbf/in^2 = 7 N/mm^2 (approximately)
143 lbf/in^2 = 1 N/mm^2 (approximately)
$\qquad\qquad$ 1 kN/mm^2 = 1000 N/mm^2
$\qquad\qquad$ 1 MN/m^2 = 10^6 N/m^2 = 1 N/mm^2

Thermal Transmittance (U) Value

$$\text{Btu ft}^2\,\text{h}^{-1}\,\text{F} = \frac{\text{W/m}^2\,{}^\circ\text{C}}{5\cdot678}$$

$$= 0\cdot176\,(\text{W/m}^2\,{}^\circ\text{C})$$
$$\text{W m}^{-2}\,\text{deg C}^{-1} = 5\cdot678\,(\text{Btu ft}^{-2}\,\text{h}^{-1}\,\text{F})$$

Thermal Conductivity, Coefficient of Heat Transfer
   1 Btu ft/ft² hour °F = 1·731 W/m °C

Coefficient of Thermal Expansion of Concrete
   Imperial: Range: $3·5 \times 10^{-6}$–$6·5 \times 10^{-6}$ °F
   Metric: Range: $6·3 \times 10^{-6}$–$11·7 \times 10^{-6}$ °C

Heat Flow
   1 Btu/h   = 0·293 W
   100 000 Btu = 1 therm
   1 therm   = 29·3 kWh
   1 Btu   = 1055 J
   1 calorie   = 4·18 J

To convert lb/yd³ of compacted concrete to kg/m³ multiply by 0·6.

To convert kg/m³ of compacted concrete to lb/yd³ multiply by 1·67.

Concrete strengths are designated in newtons per square millimetre (N/mm²). Sometimes meganewtons per square metre (MN/m²) are used. The two units are equal numerically.

$1 \, \mu m = 10^{-6} \, m$

Power
   1 Watt = 1 J/s

APPENDIX 3

Construction Associations and Research Organisations

UNITED KINGDOM

The Cement and Concrete Association
52 Grosvenor Gardens
LONDON SW1W 0AQ
Telephone: 01-235 6661

The Building Research Establishment
Garston
WATFORD, Herts
Telephone: Garston (092 73) 76612 and 01-477 4040
and at East Kilbride Tel: 035-52 33941

The British Standard Institution
2 Park Street
LONDON W1A 2BS
Telephone: 01-629 9000

The British Concrete Pumping Association
c/o Kitsons Taylor and Co
52 Lincoln's Inn Fields
LONDON WC2
Telephone: 01-405 9292

British Precast Concrete Federation
60 Charles Street
LEICESTER LE1 1FB
Telephone: Leicester (0533) 28627

The Electricity Council
Energy Sales Division
30 Millbank
LONDON SW1
Telephone: 01-834 2333

British Ready-mixed Concrete Association
Shepperton House, Green Lane
SHEPPERTON, Middlesex
Telephone: Walton-on-Thames 43232

The Aluminium Federation
60 Calthorpe Road
Fiveways
BIRMINGHAM 15
Telephone: 021-454 3805

The Construction Industry Research and Information Association
6 Storey's Gate
LONDON SW1
Telephone: 01-839 6881

The British Constructional Steel Association (CONSTRADO)
12 Addiscombe Road
CROYDON CR9 3JH
Telephone: 01-686 0366

The Mastic Asphalte Council
24 Grosvenor Gardens
LONDON SW1W 0DH
Telephone: 01-730 7175

Reinforcement Manufacturers Association
16 Tooks Court
LONDON EC4
Telephone: 01-242 4259

Special Steels User Advisory Service
B.S.C. Swinden Laboratories
Moorgate
ROTHERHAM S60 3AR
Telephone: 0709 73661

Copper Development Assoc.
Orchard House
Mutton Lane
POTTERS BAR EN6 3AP, Herts
Telephone: Potters Bar 50711

The Corrosion Advice Bureau
Corporate Engineering Laboratory
British Steel Corporation
140, Battersea Park Road
LONDON SW11 4LZ
Telephone: 01-622 5511

The British Ceramic Tile Council
Federation House
STOKE-ON-TRENT, Staffs
Telephone: Stoke-on-Trent (0782) 45147

The Brick Development Association
19 Grafton Street
LONDON W1X 3LE
Telephone: 01-409 1021

WEST GERMANY

Bundesverband der Deutschen
   Zementindustrie e.V.
Riehlerstrasse 8
(Postfach 140105)
5 KÖLN 1
T 73 00 76   C Zementverband
Tx 08881603

(Cement industry
and technical
advisory services)

Forschungsinstuit der Zementindustrie
Tannenstrasse 2
4 DUSSELDORF-NORD
T 43 44 51   C Zementforschung
Tx 08584876

(Research institute
of the cement
industry)

Verein Deutscher Zementwerke e.V.
Tannenstrasse 2
4 DUSSELDORF-NORD
T 43 44 51   C Zementforschung
Tx 08584876

(Technical association
of the cement industry)

Deutscher Beton-Verein e.V.   (Concrete)
Bahnofstr 61
62 WIESBADEN

UNITED STATES OF AMERICA

Portland Cement Association   (Research, information
Old Orchard Road   and technical advisory
SKOKIE, Illinois   services)
T (312) 9666200

American Concrete Institute   (Technical and
P.O. Box 4754   Educational Committee
Redford Station   activities and
DETROIT, Michigan 48219   publications for
                                               manufacturers and users
                                               of concrete)

Architectural Precast Association (APA)   (Precast concrete)
2201 East 46th Street
INDIANAPOLIS, Indiana 46205
T (317) 2511214

National Concrete Masonry Association   (Precast concrete)
   (NCMA)
Pompino East Building–1800 Kent Street
P.O. Box 9185 Rosslyn Station
ARLINGTON, Virginia 22209
T (703) 5240815

National Precast Concrete Association   (Precast concrete)
   (NPCA)
2201 East 46th Street
INDIANAPOLIS, Indiana 46205
T (317) 2530486

Prestressed Concrete Institute (PCI)   (Prestressed concrete)
20 North Wacker Drive
CHICAGO, Illinois 60606
T (312) 3464071

American Concrete Pipe Association   (Concrete pipes)
  (ACPA)
1501 Wilson Boulevard
ARLINGTON, Virginia 22209
T (703) 5243939

American Concrete Pressure Pipe   (Concrete pipes)
  Association (ACPPA)
1501 Wilson Boulevard
ARLINGTON, Virginia 22209
T (703) 5243939

Concrete Reinforcing Steel Institute   (Concrete reinforcing
  (CRSI)   steel)
228 North LaSalle Street
CHICAGO, Illinois 60601
T (312) 3725059

National Ready Mixed Concrete   (Ready-mixed
  Association (NRMCA)   concrete)
900 Spring Street
SILVER SPRING, Maryland 20910
T (310) 5871400

Expanded Shale, Clay and Slate Institute   (Structural lightweight
1041 National Press Building   concrete)
WASHINGTON, D.C. 20004

International Ozone Institute
Merrill Lane
Skytop Complex
SYRACUSE NY 13210

CANADA

Portland Cement Association   (Research, information
116 Albert Street   and technical advisory
OTTAWA   services)
T 236 9471

Canadian Prestressed Concrete   (Prestressed Concrete)
   Institute (CPCI)
120 Eglington Avenue, East
Toronto 12
ONTARIO
T (416) 4895616

National Concrete Producers'   (Concrete industry)
   Association (NCPA)
3500 Dufferin Street
Suite 101
Downsview 460
ONTARIO
T (416) 6301204

AUSTRALIA

Cement and Concrete Association of
   Australia
147–152 Walker Street
NORTH SYDNEY, N.S.W. 2060

Concrete Institute of Australia   (Concrete research)
147 Walker Street
NORTH SYDNEY, N.S.W. 2060
T 92 0316

Concrete Masonry Association of   (Concrete masonry)
   Australia
147 Walker Street
NORTH SYDNEY, N.S.W. 2060
T 92 0316

National Ready Mixed Concrete   (Ready-mixed
   Association   concrete)
332 Albert Street
MELBOURNE, Victoria 3001
T 419 1313

Precast Concrete Manufacturers   (Precast concrete)
   Association
12 O'Connell Street
SYDNEY, 2001
T 250 5401

C.S.I.R.O. Division of Building Research
P.O. Box 56
HIGHETT, Victoria 3190

Department of Construction, Experimental
   Building Station
P.O. Box 30
CHATSWOOD, N.S.W. 2067

It should be noted that most universities carry out research on concrete.

NEW ZEALAND

N.Z. Portland Cement Association   (Information and
Box 2792   technical advisory
WELLINGTON   services)

N.Z. Concrete Masonry Association   (Concrete masonry)
Box 9130
WELLINGTON

N.Z. Concrete Products Association   (Concrete products)
Box 9130
WELLINGTON

N.Z. Prestressed Concrete Institute   (Prestressed concrete)
11th floor Securities House
126 The Terrace
P.O. Box 969
WELLINGTON C.1.

N.Z. Ready Mixed Concrete Association   (Ready mixed
Box 12013   concrete)
WELLINGTON

NZ Concrete Research and Information Organisations: Associations and Related Bodies
Building Research Association of New Zealand
42 Vivian Street
P.O. Box 9375 (Postal)
WELLINGTON, N.Z.

Department of Scientific and Industrial Research
Chemistry Division
Gracefield Road
LOWER HUTT
Private Bag (Postal),
PETONE, N.Z.

Department of Scientific and Industrial Research
Physics and Engineering Laboratory
Gracefield Road
LOWER HUTT
Private Bag (Postal),
LOWER HUTT, PETONE, N.Z.

Ministry of Works and Development
Vogel Building
Aitken Street
P.O. Box 12-041 (Postal),
WELLINGTON 1, N.Z.

N.Z. Concrete Research Association
13 Wall Place
TAWA
P.O. Box 50-156 (Postal)
PORIRUA N.Z.

N.Z. Institute of Architects
Maritime Building
2–10 Customhouse Quay
P.O. Box 438 (Postal)
WELLINGTON 1, N.Z.

N.Z. Institution of Engineers
Molesworth House
101 Molesworth Street
P.O. Box 12-241 (Postal)
WELLINGTON 1, N.Z.

University of Auckland
School of Engineering
24 Symonds Street
Private Bag (Postal)
AUCKLAND, N.Z.

University of Canterbury
School of Engineering
Creyke Road
Ilam,
CHRISTCHURCH 4,
Private Bag (Postal)
CHRISTCHURCH, N.Z.

REPUBLIC OF SOUTH AFRICA

Portland Cement Institute
Head Office: 18 Kew Road
                                Richmond
                                JOHANNESBURG
                                2092

Natal Regional Office: P.O. Box 90
                                WESTVILLE
                                Natal
                                3630

Western Cape Regional Office: Molteno Street
                                GOODWOOD
                                Cape Province
                                7460

Eastern Cape Regional Office: P.O. Box 1540
                                PORT ELIZABETH
                                Cape Province
                                6000

South African Council for Scientific and Industrial Research
                                P.O. Box 395
                                PRETORIA
                                Transvaal
                                0001
National Building Research Institute
National Institute for Transport and Road Research

Research (only) Organisations
South African Railways Research Laboratories

Leyds Street
JOHANNESBURG
2001

Universities
The Department of Civil Engineering at the following Universities:

University of the Witwatersrand   (This university also
1 Jan Smuts Avenue   has a department of
JOHANNESBURG   Building Science)
2001

University of Cape Town
Private Bag
RONDEBOSCH
Cape Province
7700

University of Natal
King George V Avenue
DURBAN
4001

Randse Afrikaanse Universiteit
Posbus 524
JOHANNESBURG
2000

University of Pretoria
Brooklyn
PRETORIA
0181

University of Stellenbosch
STELLENBOSCH
Cape Province
7600

APPENDIX 4

National and International Organisations Concerned with Swimming and Swimming Pools

UNITED KINGDOM

Amateur Swimming Association

Harold Fern House
Derby Square
LOUGHBOROUGH LE11 0AL
Telephone: 050 93 30431

Sports Council and Technical
  Unit for Sport

70 Brompton Road
LONDON SW3
Telephone: 01 589 3411

Royal Society for Prevention
  of Accidents (Water
  Safety Committee)

Royal Oak Centre
Brighton Road
PURLEY CR2 2UR
Telephone: 01668 4272

Institute of Baths Management

Giffard House
36/38 Sherrard St.
MELTON MOWBRAY LE13
1XJ
Telephone: 0664 5531

Swimming Pool and Allied
  Trades Association

87 London Road
CROYDON CR0 2RS
Telephone: 01 688 3681

375

International Aquatics Board (IAB)   UK Representative:
L. G. Fischer Dip.Ing.,
MIMechE, FIHVE
57a Thicket Road
SUTTON, Surrey
Telephone 01 642 8358

Swimming Pool Review   Armour House
Bridge Street
GUILDFORD, Surrey
Telephone 0483 76333

OVERSEAS

International Working Group for Construction of Sports and Leisure Facilities
Kolner Strasse 68
5000 Koln 40 (Lovenich)
GERMANY

SportfondsenNederland NV
Singel 40–42
Amsterdam
HOLLAND

Parks and Recreation Department (South Africa)
P.O. Box 2824
Johannesburg 2000
SOUTH AFRICA

The International Ozone Institute
Suit 206-Warren Building
14805 Detroit Avenue
Lakewood, Ohio
USA

Internationale Akademie für Bader, Sport und Freizeitbauten EV
c/o Vice-president Dr D. Fabian
Markplatz 27,
D 8740 Bad Neustadt
GERMANY

Academie Internationale de l'Equipment des Piscines, des Sports et des
Loisirs
   c/o Prof. P. Jost
   Rue Klein 17
   Diekirch
   LUXEMBURG

The National Swimming Pool Institute,
   200 K Street NW
   Washington D.C. 20006
   USA

The American Public Health Association
   1790 Broadway,
   New York 19
   USA

Piscines	9 Rue Condorcet 94800 Villejuif FRANCE
Sport Bader Freizeit Bauten	Postfach 1680 874 Bad Neustadt/Saale GERMANY
Schwimmbad und Sauna	Fachschriften-Verlag GmbH and Co. KG Hohenstrasse 17 Postfach 1329 7012 Fellbach bei Stuttgart GERMANY
Pool News	Leisure Publications 3923 West South Street Los Angeles California 9005 USA

APPENDIX 5

Suggested Tolerances in *In Situ* Reinforced Concrete for the Construction of Water-Retaining Structures, Swimming Pools and Ancillary Buildings

INTRODUCTION

The recommendations apply only to the *in situ* concrete itself and not to any added finishes such as rendering, screeds, etc. The tolerances are those which should be achieved by experienced contractors exercising reasonable care and attention. If a contractor is required to produce *in situ* concrete with certain tolerances of line, level and dimension, then these tolerances should be written into the specification and reference made to them on the drawings.

There will be cases when the engineer or architect may demand work finished within closer tolerances than those suggested here, and in such circumstances it must be realised that the finer the tolerance the more expensive the work, and this applies both to the formwork and the placing, compacting and finishing of the concrete. It is therefore considered that tolerances finer than those recommended should only be asked for when there is a sound reason for such a requirement.

WALLS

    (a) Deviation from the vertical or specified inclination:

      Height not exceeding 6·0 m (20 ft) ± 10 mm ($\frac{3}{8}$ in)

      Height not exceeding 15·0 m (50 ft) ± 15 mm ($\frac{5}{8}$ in)

    (b) Irregularity in surface finish in any direction under 3·0 m (10 ft) straight edge $\pm$ 5 mm ($\frac{1}{5}$ in)

    (c) Difference in level across joints, i.e. the 'lip' not to exceed $\pm$ 5 mm ($\frac{1}{5}$ in)

(d) Deviation in level of top wall:

    (i) Irregularity in surface finish under 3·0 m
       (10 ft) straight edge $\pm$ 5 mm ($\frac{1}{5}$ in)

    (ii) Deviation in top level from the horizontal or prescribed inclination along the length of the wall between specified level points $\pm$ 5 mm (0·02 ft)

(e) Deviation in prescribed overall length of the wall between movement joints:

Length not exceeding 15·0 m (50 ft) $\pm$ 15 mm ($\frac{5}{8}$ in)
Length not exceeding 30·0 m (100 ft) $\pm$ 20 mm ($\frac{3}{4}$ in)
Length not exceeding 60·0 m (200 ft) $\pm$ 25 mm (1 in)

(f) Deviation from prescribed thickness:

Thickness not exceeding 300 mm (12 in) $\pm$ 10 mm ($\frac{3}{8}$ in)
Thickness exceeding 300 mm (12 in) $\pm$ 15 mm ($\frac{5}{8}$ in)

COLUMNS

(a) Deviation from the vertical:

Height not exceeding   6·0 m (20 ft)   10 mm ($\frac{3}{8}$ in)
Height not exceeding 15·0 m (50 ft)   15 mm ($\frac{5}{8}$ in)

(b) Deviation in cross sectional dimensions:

For dimensions not exceeding 500 mm (20 in) $\pm$ 5 mm ($\frac{1}{5}$ in)
For dimensions exceeding 500 mm (20 in) $\pm$ 15 mm ($\frac{5}{8}$ in)

FLOORS

(a) Deviation from prescribed level for distance between prescribed levelling points $\pm$ 5 mm (0·02 ft)

(b) Surface finish

    (i) Irregularities in bays not to exceed under 3·0 m (10 ft) straight edge in any direction $\pm$ 5 mm ($\frac{1}{5}$ in)

    (ii) Difference in level across joints, i.e. the 'lip' not to exceed $\pm$ 5 mm ($\frac{1}{5}$ in)

(c) Overall internal dimensions of the floor slab on plan between movement joints
Deviation from prescribed dimensions:

Dimensions not exceeding 15·0 m (50 ft) $\pm$ 15 mm ($\frac{5}{8}$ in)
Dimensions not exceeding 30·0 m (100 ft) $\pm$ 20 mm ($\frac{3}{4}$ in)
Dimensions not exceeding 60·0 m (200 ft) $\pm$ 25 mm (1 in)

(d) Smoothness of surface, or absence of roughness
Where site conditions permit, the use of a scraping straight edge, followed at the correct time by a power float and then a final finish by a steel or wood float, may be called for

BIBLIOGRAPHY

ANON. Are your tolerances really necessary? *Concrete, London*, July 1971, p. 235.

BRITISH STANDARDS INSTITUTION, *The Structural Use of Concrete*, CP. 110, Sect. 9; Cl. 9.4.

BRITISH STANDARDS INSTITUTION, *The Structural Use of Precast Concrete*, CP. 116, Cl. 407.

BRITISH STANDARDS INSTITUTION, *Accuracy in Building*, PD. 6440, 1969.

BRITISH STANDARDS INSTITUTION, *Recommendations for Co-ordination of Dimensions in Building*, Pd. 6444, 1969.

BRITISH STANDARDS INSTITUTION, *Guidance on Dimensional Co-ordination in Building*, 1977, DD. 51.

BUILDING RESEARCH ADVISORY BOARD, FEDERAL CONSTRUCTION COUNCIL, *Dimensional Tolerances for Cast-in-place Concrete*, Tech. Report No. 49 (NAS–NRC, Publication No. 1227), USA, 1964, p. 22.

FIORATO, A. E., Geometric variations in precast concrete structures. *Nordisk Beton*, No. 6, 1976, pp. 27–29.

FISHER, A. E., Tolerances involving reinforcing bars. *J. American Concrete Institute*, Feb. 1977 pp. 61–70.

STEVENS, A., How accurate is building? Building Research Establishment, *BRE News*, No. 36, Summer 1976, pp. 11–13.

VANDERWAL, M. L. and WALKER, H. C. Tolerances on precast concrete structures. *J. Prestressed Concrete Institute USA*, July/August 1976, pp. 44–57.

APPENDIX 6

Notes on the Testing of Concrete in Structures

There are three principal methods of testing the strength of concrete in a structure:

(1) Non-destructive testing
   (a) The Schmidt rebound hammer
   (b) Gamma radiography
   (c) Ultrasonic pulse velocity
   To the above can be added the use of an electromagnetic cover meter for determining whether there is in fact steel reinforcement in the concrete, and, if so, its depth below the surface from which the instrument is used.

(2) Core taking and testing
   This is only partly non-destructive as the core holes have to be made good, and in a water-retaining or water-excluding structure this is not easy.

(3) Load testing on individual members or groups of members.

Each of the three methods given above is a subject in its own right, and readers who wish to obtain detailed information should refer to the Bibliography at the end of this appendix, as only a few general notes will be given here.

Methods in (1) are covered by a British Standard, BS 4408: Recommendations for Non-Destructive Methods of Test for Concrete. Method (2) is covered by BS 1881: Methods of Testing Concrete, and Method (3) is dealt with in Code of Practice CP110: The Structural Use of Concrete, as well as the three 'parallel' Codes, CP 114, CP 115 and CP 116.

NON-DESTRUCTIVE TESTING

THE SCHMIDT REBOUND HAMMER
This is a useful and practical instrument for site work, but the results must be interpreted with caution, taking into account its limitations.

The instrument measures the surface hardness of the concrete, but experience based on tests has shown that this (the rebound number) can be related empirically to the compressive strength, provided certain precautions are taken. These are:

(i) The instrument should be calibrated on the type of concrete being tested; 150 mm cubes are better than 100 mm.
(ii) A minimum of 15 readings should be taken on each structural unit.
(iii) The instrument should be recalibrated when used on concrete made with cements other than Portland, e.g. HAC.
(iv) The highest and the lowest reading should be eliminated and the average taken of the remainder. The average rebound number is then referred to the calibration chart and the strength read off. Alternatively, each of the readings, except those rejected, can be converted to compressive strength, and then these strengths are averaged.

It is useful to compare the readings on concrete which has been accepted as satisfactory with those on similar concrete in similar structural unit(s) which has given cause for concern. The usual reason for this 'concern' is that the cube results were below the specified minimum. If the readings on the suspect unit(s) are significantly lower, then this would support the view that the concrete was in fact of lower compressive strength. However, the results are only indicative, and if it is decided to continue with the investigation, the next step would be to take cores. It is, of course, assumed that the sampling and testing procedure for the cubes has been checked and found to be in order.

BS 4408: Part 4 gives recommendations for surface hardness methods of non-destructive tests for concrete.

GAMMA RADIOGRAPHY

This method of inspection of hardened concrete is suitable for thicknesses up to about 450 mm. It should be noted that gamma radiography comes within the scope of the Factories Acts and the Ionising Radiations (Sealed Sources) Regulations 1961. It is used for checking the efficiency of the grouting in cable ducts in post-tensioned prestressed concrete, to detect voids (honeycombing) in concrete, and to determine accurately the position and size of reinforcement.

Recommendations for this method of non-destructive testing are given in BS 4408: Part 3. The work is expensive and requires specialist operators as well as experience in the interpretation of the photographs; also, it must be possible to have access to both sides of the structural unit under investigation.

ULTRASONIC PULSE VELOCITY TESTING
The author wishes to record that the information which follows is largely based on discussions which he has had with Mr H. S. Tomsett of the Cement and Concrete Association, and a reference to a paper by Mr Tomsett is given in the Bibliography at the end of this Appendix.

The basic principle of ultrasonic testing of concrete in the structure is that concrete is an elastic material and will transmit longitudinal, compression and shear waves. The velocity with which these waves travel through the concrete is determined by the properties of the concrete which control the elastic modulus. These properties are in turn related to the strength of the concrete. The apparatus used generates a pulse in the concrete by the application of a mechanical impulse; it collects the impulse at some point at a measured distance from the point of generation, and contains a timing mechanism which accurately measures the time taken for the leading edge of the pulse to pass from the transmitter to the receiver.

A number of advisory engineers in the Cement and Concrete Association have over the past few years used this ultrasonic pulse velocity equipment on numerous sites in various parts of the country. In this way they have gathered considerable experience of the use of the equipment and, perhaps more important, the practical interpretation of the results, so that the quality of the concrete as based on strength can be reasonably assessed. The apparatus used is that developed by Elvery at University College London and produced by C.N.S. Instruments Ltd. It has the trade name of Pundit (Portable Ultrasonic Non-destructive Digital Indicating Tester). The apparatus is small and readily portable, as it weighs only about 3 kg.

There are three basic ways in which the pulse can be transmitted and recorded. There is direct transmission, which is most satisfactory; in this case the time measured is that for the longitudinal compression wave to pass between the transmitter and the receiver; the transmitter and receiver are on opposite sides of the structural unit concerned. The next method, which is not so satisfactory as the previous one, is semidirect, and is used for such units as thick floor slabs, where access can be obtained to the top surface of the unit and to the side, but not to the underside. The third method, which is the least satisfactory, is indirect, where transmission and receiving has to be carried out from one side only, as in ground floor slabs and basement walls after back-filling has been carried out.

There is a British Standard, BS 4408: Recommendations for Non-destructive Methods of Test for Concrete, of which Part 5: The Measurement of the Velocity of Ultrasonic Pulses in Concrete, was published in 1974.

In this book it is not possible to go into the details of ultrasonic pulse velocity testing, but those who consider using it, and there is no doubt it is an extremely useful method of testing concrete in the structure, should bear in mind the factors which affect the pulse velocity through concrete: these are:

Aggregate type.
Aggregate grading.
Cement type.
Cement content.
W/c ratio.
Degree of compaction of the concrete.
Curing temperature.

The presence of reinforcement will affect the velocity obtained, and it is therefore advisable to make every effort to transmit the pulses in the concrete structure between the reinforcing bars as far as this is practicable.

When used by an experienced engineer, the pundit can in most cases satisfactorily determine the depth of cracks and the location and extent of undercompacted poor-quality concrete.

The author feels that the ultrasonic pulse velocity method of non-destructive testing is particularly applicable to water-retaining structures, because the taking of cores in such structures below the water line is something which should be avoided whenever possible.

COVER METER SURVEYS BY ELECTROMAGNETIC COVER MEASURING DEVICES
This is a comparatively simple piece of equipment. The cover to reinforcement is shown on a graduated scale, and, on a construction site, the accuracy of a good commercial instrument is about ±5 mm.

It is normal to calibrate it for mild steel and for use with Portland cement concrete, but it can be used satisfactorily with other types of cement and high-tensile steel, provided it is specially calibrated for the purpose. Some types of stainless steel are non-magnetic and so this type of instrument will not detect the metal; in such cases the alternative is gamma radiography.

Change in bar diameter from, say, 10 mm to 32 mm will not appreciably affect the cover shown, but for small-diameter bars of, say, 5 mm, there will be a considerable difference between the indicated cover and the true cover; the cover shown on the scale is likely to be greater than the actual cover.

The relevant British Standard is BS 4408: Part 1.

CORE TESTING

Core testing of the concrete in a structure is generally the last but one resort when cube results are significantly below the specification and the concrete is seriously suspected of being below the required strength. It is expensive and time-consuming, and the results may not be as clear-cut as one would wish. In 1977, taking 100 mm cores through a 250 mm thick roof slab cost about £75 per core.

The taking of cores in a liquid-retaining structure should not be lightly undertaken, as it means boring holes 100 mm or 150 mm diameter through the structure and is not easy to ensure a watertight joint afterwards when these are reinstated.

The cores should be taken and tested in accordance with BS 1881: Methods of Testing Concrete. The standard gives detailed recommendations for the preparation, testing and examination of cores, but the interpretation of results requires considerable experience.

If the coring, testing and examination is carefully carried out it will give a considerable amount of information about the quality of the concrete in the structure. On the basis of the core results, a decision can be taken as to whether the concrete is satisfactory or whether the section in question may have to be demolished, and this is a very serious matter. When the results are still not entirely clear, a load test may be ordered.

In some cases attempts are made to establish a correlation between the core strengths and the cube strengths. While it may be possible to establish a reasonable relationship under strictly controlled conditions, the author does not consider that this can be done satisfactorily on normal construction sites. The cubes are usually taken at the point of delivery of the concrete from the ready-mixed concrete lorry, or near the site batching plant. The cubes are then made, cured and tested in accordance with BS 1881.

The history of the two lots of concrete (cubes and that in the formwork) is quite different. The cubes are dealt with in a detailed and meticulous way, while the bulk of the concrete is transported by skip or pump, dropped into formwork containing reinforcement, compacted by poker vibrators by men working perhaps in strong winds and driving rain.

Apart from what has been said above, the following factors also introduce variables between cube and core strength:

The presence of reinforcement in the core.

The difference in age; cores are usually taken later than 28 days after casting the concrete; see also remarks below.

Depending on the position in the structure, the core may have dried out a little more on one side than on the other; a curing membrane would influence the drying-out process.

There may be a noticeable difference in compaction between one end of a core and the other, particularly in floor slabs; in cores taken at the bottom of a lift and near the top, as in walls and columns; the strength of the former may be 20% higher than that of the latter.

In view of the above, the author considers it unrealistic to try and assess the quality of the concrete as it was delivered to site (or as it left the batching plant), on the basis of core test results. A core will only indicate the type and quality of the concrete in the structure.

A further complication is the rate of gain of strength with age between the concrete in the structure and the test cubes. Codes of Practice, standards and specifications normally assume that the rate of gain of strength for both concretes (cubes and structure) is the same. As far as the author is aware, this vital assumption has only recently been queried. Work and investigations by W. Murphy of the Cement and Concrete Association has raised serious doubts about the validity of this age–strength relationship in structures. Conclusions to date suggest that in fact there may be little increase in strength in the concrete in what may be termed a normal building structure after about 28 days from casting. There is no doubt, however, that test cubes dealt with as prescribed in BS 1881 do gain in strength after the first 28 days. As a guide only, the strength of concrete in a structure can be taken as about 70 % of the average cube strength.

LOAD TESTING

Load tests are only likely to arise for suspended slabs and beams, including supporting columns, when all other methods of non-destructive testing which are practical to the circumstances of the case have failed to resolve satisfactorily the question as to whether or not the part of the structure in question is structurally sound.

This type of testing is covered by Section 9 of British Standard Code of Practice, CP 110: The Structural Use of Concrete. For readers who prefer to keep to the original Codes (CP 114, 115, and 116), the relevant clauses are: CP 114: Clause 605; CP 115: Clause 602; CP 116: Clauses 504 and 505.

A useful paper on the load testing of *in situ* reinforced concrete structures in accordance with CP 114 was presented by G. F. Blackledge at the Symposium on Concrete Quality, held in London in November 1964. In this paper the author drew attention to the considerable differences in the requirements of the British Code and the American Concrete Institute Standard 318–63 and the Australian Code for Concrete in Buildings As-CA2-1963. Doubts as to the structural soundness of a structure or part of a structure can arise from a number of reasons, of which the following are the most usual:

Failure of test cubes, followed by failure to resolve this by core testing and/or other non-destructive tests.
An acknowledged error in design.

An acknowledged or suspected error in construction.
Cracking and/or excessive deflexion.
An increase in operating load conditions not anticipated during design and construction.

Load testing is a tedious business and should only be resorted to when all else has failed and the responsible engineer is faced with a decision to either order the demolition of the structure (or part) or accept a structure of which he has doubts about its strength.

BIBLIOGRAPHY

ELVERY, R. H. AND FORRESTER, J. A., *Progress in Construction Science Technology*, Medical and Technical Publishing, Aylesbury, 1971, Chapter 6, pp. 175–216.

FORRESTER, J. A., Gamma radiography of concrete. Paper presented at *Symposium on Non-Destructive Testing*, London, June 1969, Cement and Concrete Association, p. 19.

JONES, R., *Non-Destructive Testing of Concrete*, Cambridge University Press, 1962, p. 102.

KOLEK, J., An appreciation of the Schmidt rebound hammer, *Mag. Conc. Res.*, 1958, **10**(28), 27–36.

LEVITT, M., 'The ISAT—a non-destructive test for the durability of concrete', *Brit. J. Non-destructive Testing*, **13**(4) (July 1971) 106–11.

MURDOCK, L. J. AND BLACKLEDGE, G. F., *Concrete Materials and Practice*. Edward Arnold, 4th edition, London, 1968, p. 398.

SHACKLOCK, B. W., *Concrete Constituents and Mix Proportions*, Cement and Concrete Association, London, 1974, p. 102.

TOMSETT, H. N., Ultra-sonic testing for large pours. Paper presented at the Concrete Society *Symposium on Large Pours*, Birmingham, Sept. 1973, p. 4.

TOMSETT, H. N., The non-destructive testing of floor slabs, *Concrete*, (March 1974) 41, 42.

TOMSETT, H. N., Site testing of concrete. *Brit. J. Non-Destructive Testing*, May 1976.

APPENDIX 7

Notes on the Use of the Rapid Analysis Machine for the Determination of the Cement Content of Fresh Concrete

Until the introduction by the Cement and Concrete Association of their patented equipment for determining the cement content of fresh concrete, determinations of cement content had to be made by a chemical analysis of the hardened concrete. This meant that there could be no check on site at the time the ready-mixed concrete was delivered, or when concrete came from the batching machine on one of the most important aspects of a concrete mix—namely, the quantity of cement in it. The reasons for the need for an adequate cement content and a low w/c ratio in concrete in order that it should be durable and protect embedded reinforcement has been discussed at length in this book. For many years there has been a pressing need for the development of a quick and reliable method of estimating the cement content of fresh concrete.

The principle of this machine, which is known as a Rapid Analysis Machine (RAM), is that of separating material in the mix which has the same particle size as cement. This means that if there is other material in the mix which has the same or very similar particle size (for example, PFA), then the Rapid Analysis Machine as normally used would not be able to distinguish between the cement and the PFA. However, it is normal practice for the specifications to include a requirement that no admixtures are permitted in a concrete mix without special approval being obtained from the professional firm which is responsible for the design and supervision of the project. It is reasonable to assume that reputable contractors and suppliers of ready-mixed concrete would not deliberately include in a concrete mix material having the same particle size as cement without informing the client and obtaining his approval first. If this were done, then the firm responsible might find themselves in the position of being held responsible for the removal of a large part of a structure and its rebuilding, and this would certainly not be worthwhile. Some sands contain silt, but an allowance for this can be readily made by a sieve analysis of a sample of the sand.

It would be reasonable to assume that the machine can estimate the cement content with a degree of accuracy of about ± 20 kg/m^3 of concrete.

Index